# Getting Started with Game Maker

Jerry Lee Ford, Jr.

**Course Technology PTR**
*A part of Cengage Learning*

Australia • Brazil • Japan • Korea • Mexico • Singapore • Spain • United Kingdom • United States

**Getting Started with Game Maker**
**Jerry Lee Ford, Jr.**

**Publisher and General Manager, Course Technology PTR:** Stacy L. Hiquet

**Associate Director of Marketing:** Sarah Panella

**Manager of Editorial Services:** Heather Talbot

**Marketing Manager:** Jordan Casey

**Senior Acquisitions Editor:** Emi Smith

**Project Editor:** Jenny Davidson

**Technical Reviewer:** Parker Hiquet

**PTR Editorial Services Coordinator:** Jen Blaney

**Interior Layout Tech:** Macmillan Publishing Solutions

**Cover Designer:** Mike Tanamachi

**Indexer:** Sharon Shock

**Proofreader:** Sara Gullion



Library of Congress Control Number: 2008940719

ISBN-13: 978-1-59863-882-0

ISBN-10: 1-59863-882-3

**Course Technology, a part of Cengage Learning**
20 Channel Center Street
Boston, MA 02210
USA

Cengage Learning is a leading provider of customized learning solutions with office locations around the globe, including Singapore, the United Kingdom, Australia, Mexico, Brazil, and Japan. Locate your local office at: **international.cengage.com/region**

Cengage Learning products are represented in Canada by Nelson Education, Ltd.

For your lifelong learning solutions, visit **courseptr.com**

Visit our corporate website at **cengage.com**

Printed in Canada
1 2 3 4 5 6 7 11 10 09

*To my mother and father for always being there, and to my wonderful children, Alexander, William, and Molly, and my beautiful wife, Mary.*

# Acknowledgments

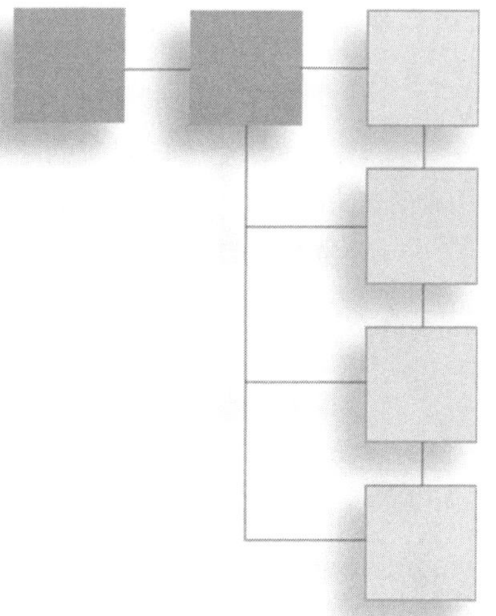

Special thanks go to Mitzi Koontz, for helping to make this book a reality and for her efforts as acquisitions editor. I also need to thank this book's project editor, Jenny Davidson, for working hard to make sure that in the end all of the different parts of this book came together like they were supposed to. I also need to thank this book's technical editor, Parker Hiquet, for providing invaluable insight and advice. Last but not least, I would like to thank everyone else at Course Technology PTR for all their contributions and hard work.

# About the Author

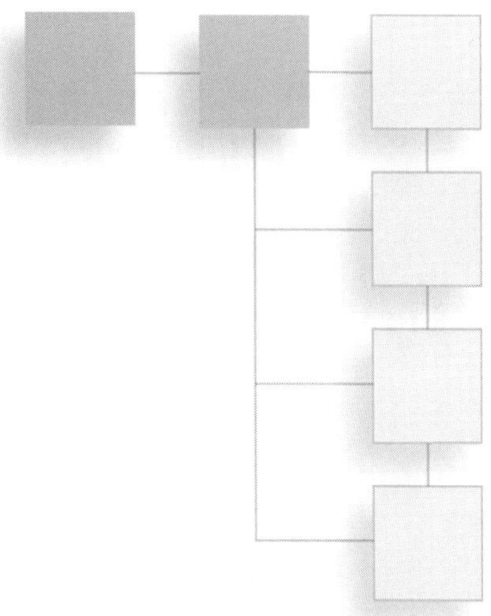

**Jerry Lee Ford, Jr.** is an author, educator, and an IT professional with over 20 years of experience in information technology, including roles as an automation analyst, technical manager, technical support analyst, automation engineer, and security analyst. He is the author of 32 books and co-author of two additional books. His published works include *DarkBASIC Programming for the Absolute Beginner*, *Scratch Programming for Teens*, *Microsoft Visual Basic 2008 Express Programming for the Absolute Beginner*, and *Phrogram Programming for the Absolute Beginner*. Jerry has a master's degree in business administration from Virginia Commonwealth University in Richmond, Virginia, and he has over five years of experience as an adjunct instructor teaching networking courses in information technology.

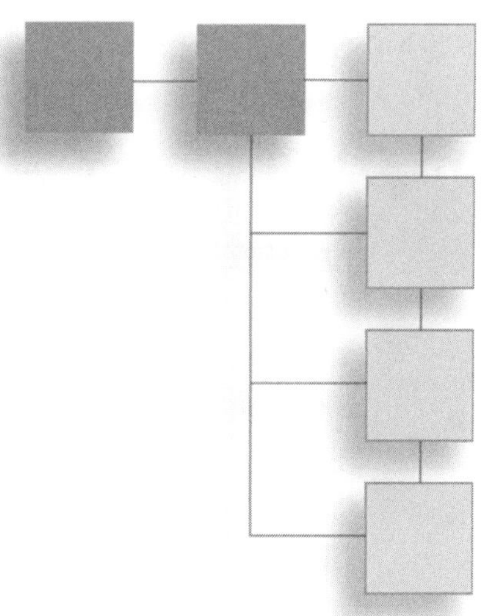

# Contents

## BONUS WEBSITE MATERIAL:



found on www.courseptr.com/downloads

# Introduction

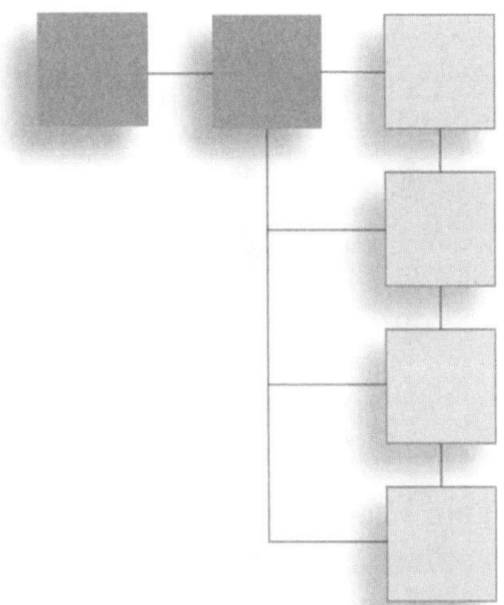

Welcome to *Getting Started with Game Maker*! Game Maker is a computer programming language created with one purpose in mind: to support the development of computer games. Game Maker provides everything you need to create professional-quality computer games of all types, without requiring you to first learn how to use a complicated programming language or get a degree in computer science.

This book will teach you how to work with Game Maker and will show you how to create all kinds of games, complete with graphics, sound effects, and music. It will provide you with step-by-step instruction and demonstrate how to create a number of different computer games. Although Game Maker can be used to create just about any type of computer game imaginable, this book's emphasis will be on the development of classic-style arcade games, resembling games like *Pong*, *Tanks*, *Pac-Man*, *Breakout*, and *Space Invaders*. Game Maker makes short work of the development of these types of games, which makes them perfect candidates for demonstrating the basic principles of game development.

Game Maker comes in two forms: Lite and Pro. Both versions let you create computer games. Game Maker Lite is free but displays messages and banners prompting you to purchase Game Maker Pro. Game Maker Pro provides additional features and functionality needed to create advanced games. Both versions of Game Maker offer everything needed to create professional-quality computer games, which you can share with your friends or even sell royalty free.

Game Maker supports both 2D and 3D game development. It lets beginner developers create new games using a drag-and-drop development approach, while also allowing advanced game developers to use its built-in scripting language to create more complex games, supplying easy access to a large collection of pre-built functions. So, whether you are just starting out or are interested in creating and selling the next great 2D or 3D computer game, Game Maker will suit your needs well.

## Why Game Maker?

Game Maker provides an intuitive development environment that supports the creation of computer games using a collection of different icons representing events and actions that control the movement and interaction of different objects. What this really means is that Game Maker lets you create computer games without having to know how to program. This allows you to focus instead on the design of your game without having to first learn the ins and outs of computer programming.

As you learn more about good game design and begin to push the limits of Game Maker's drag-and-drop application development methodology, you can begin learning how to work with Game Maker's built-in Game Maker Language (GML), which provides you with the ability to develop highly advanced computer games and applications.

**Hint**

At the time this book was written, a beta version of Game Maker for Mac OS X was being tested. Once officially released, this will allow you to develop games on either Microsoft Windows or Mac OS X! For more information on the Mac OS X version of Game Maker, visit the Game Maker Community forums located at http://gmc.yoyogames.com/.

Game Maker provides everything you need to create, test, debug, and run computer games on a Windows computer. Because it lets you create computer games without knowing how to program, it's perfect for beginners. For advanced game developers, its built-in scripting language is easier to learn than most other programming languages like Microsoft Visual Basic .NET. By supplying you with access to a huge collection of pre-written functions, Game Maker greatly simplifies application development, allowing you to develop professional-quality computer games, which you can then distribute and even sell royalty free.

Game Maker supports both 2D and 3D graphics. The different types of games that you can create with Game Maker include:

- Classic arcade games like *Space Invaders*
- First-person shooter games like *Doom* and *Call of Duty*
- Maze games like *Pac-Man* and *Ms. Pac-Man*
- Third-person shooter games like Atari's original *Tank* game and *Berzerk*
- Multiple-player games like *Monopoly* or *Warcraft*
- Strategy games like *Command & Conquer* and the *Age of Empires*
- Network games that can be played on home network or over the internet like *Star Wars Galaxies* or *Command & Conquer*
- Sports games like the classic Atari *Pole Position* racing game or perhaps a wrestling or baseball game

Of course, Game Maker does not limit you to the development of the types of games listed above. It can be used to create just about any type of game or simulation and can even be used to create regular Windows applications.

## Who Should Read This Book?

*Getting Started with Game Maker* is designed to meet the needs of anyone who loves to play computer games and wants to take things to the next level by learning how to design and create their own games. As this book will demonstrate, while playing computer games is fun, making them yourself is even more fun. This book will teach you how to create all sorts of different types of games and you will be surprised how quickly and easily you will be able to develop them. All you need is a copy of Game Maker and this book.

Game Maker is designed to serve the needs of both beginning and advanced game developers. Beginner developers only need a good understanding of how to work with a computer—no special expertise is required. As long as you can operate a computer and are comfortable working with the mouse, you will be able to use Game Maker's drag-and-drop approach to game development to create all kinds of computer games, all without having to write a lick of program code. Advanced game developers, on the other hand, will find that Game Maker's built-in programming language provides all of the programming power needed to build the most complex games.

This book will cover the fundamental steps involved in creating games using Game Maker. Although previous programming experience is helpful, it is not required. No assumptions are made regarding your computer background other than that you have a good understanding of how to work with Microsoft Windows. Once you have mastered the basics, the book will cover advanced development concepts and will wrap up by teaching you how to work with the Game Maker Language (GML), allowing you to take your development skills to the next level.

So, whether you are an experienced programmer interested in learning Game Maker or you are just starting out, this book will provide everything you need to get started. In no time at all, you will be developing all kinds of games and impressing all your friends.

## What You Need to Begin

Many of the examples presented in this book can be developed using Game Maker Lite. At the time this book was written, Game Maker Pro was available for $20. It is well worth every penny, and you will need to purchase it to be able to work with some of the more advanced examples covered in this book. If you have not already done so, you can download a trial copy of Game Maker at http://www.yoyogames.com/gamemaker/try. Once downloaded and installed, you will be prompted to upgrade Game Maker to the Pro version each time you start it.

All of the figures and examples that are presented in this book are shown using Game Maker Pro, running on a computer using Microsoft Vista. If your computer is running a different version of Windows, you may notice small differences in the way things look. However, all of the basic features and functionality will work exactly the same way.

In addition to downloading a copy of Game Maker, you will need a computer running one of the following versions of Microsoft Windows.

- Windows 2000
- Windows XP
- Windows Vista

**Table I.1** Game Maker Requirements

| Requirement | Minimum |
|---|---|
| Processor | Pentium or equivalent |
| Memory | 128 MB |
| DirectX | Version 8 or later |
| DirectX Graphics Card | 32 MB memory |
| Sound Card | DirectX compatible |

You also need to make sure that your computer meets the minimum hardware requirements, listed in the table above, to run and develop Game Maker applications.

DirectX is a Microsoft technology that facilitates the development and execution of high-performance graphics and audio applications. Game Maker requires DirectX 8.0 or higher. In addition, any computer on which your games will execute also requires DirectX 8.0 or higher. Odds are that unless you are working with a very old computer, you already have an appropriate version of DirectX installed. If this is not the case, you can download and install it by visiting http://www.microsoft.com/windows/directx.

As long as your computer meets the requirements outlined in Table I.1, all you need to get started creating your own computer games is a copy of Game Maker. This book provides all of the instruction and guidance that you will need to get started.

## Conventions Used in This Book

This book uses a number of conventions to make it easier for you to read and work with the information that is provided. These conventions are as follows.

**Hint**

Tips for doing things differently and things that you can do to become a more proficient Game Maker programmer.

**Trap**

Areas where problems are likely to occur and advice on how to stay away from or deal with those problems, hopefully saving you the pain of learning about them on your own the hard way.

## Trick

Programming shortcuts designed to help make you a better and more efficient programmer.

## Challenges

Each chapter in this book ends with a series of challenges intended to provide ideas that you can apply to improve chapter game projects and further your programming skills.

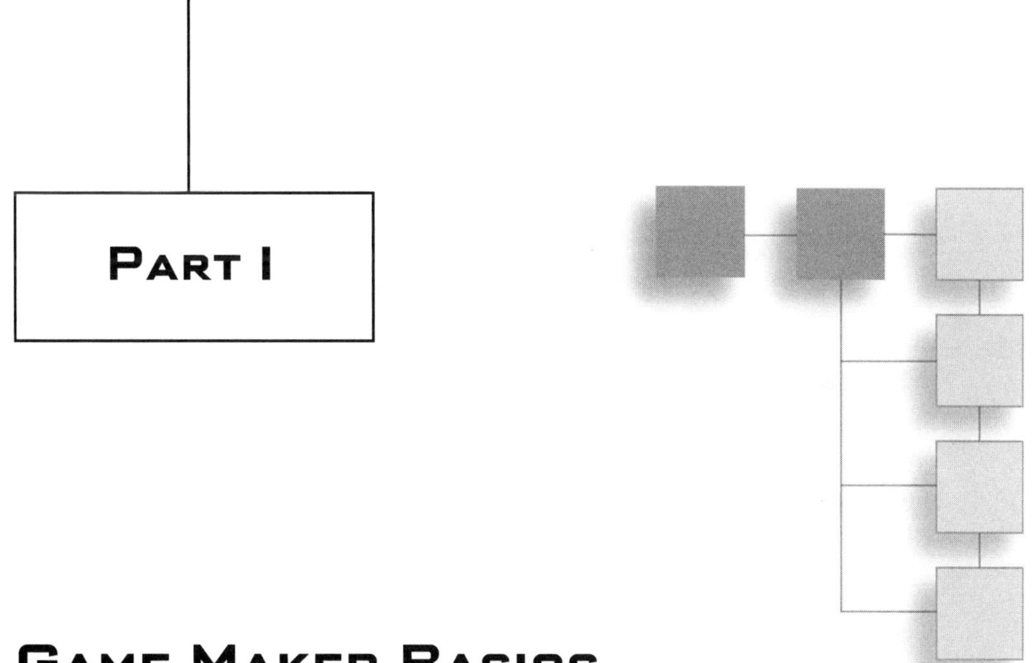

# Part I

# Game Maker Basics

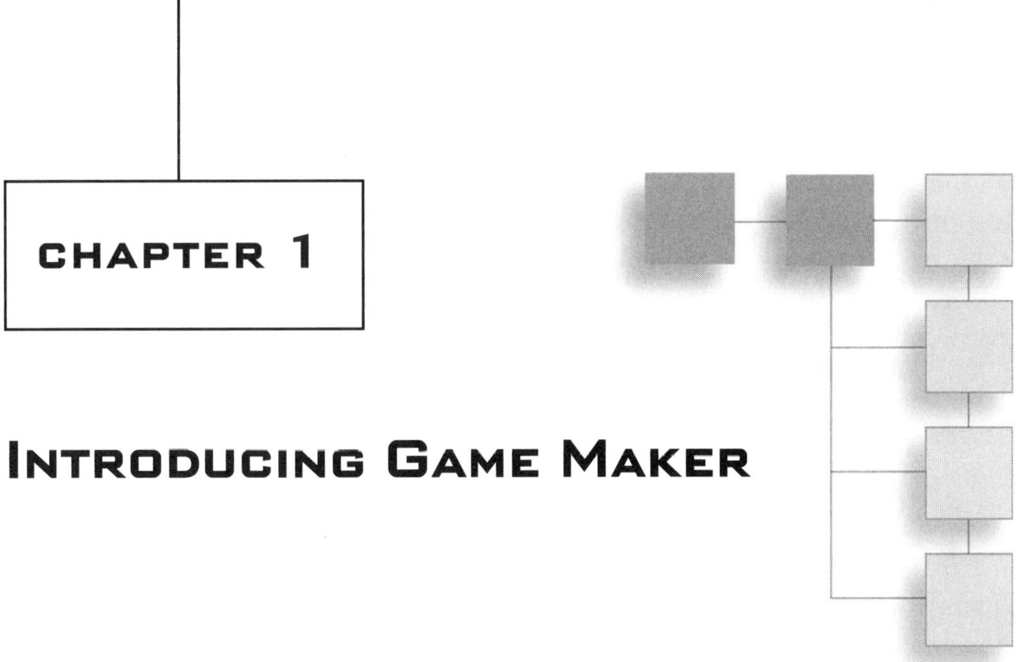


# Introducing Game Maker

A computer game is video game played on a personal computer. In computer games, one or more players interact and compete in a make-believe world. Game Maker is a software development tool that provides a robust development environment designed to support the creation of computer games. It uses icons that represent events and actions that control the movement and interaction of objects within games. Using these resources, Game Maker assists you in creating computer games without requiring that you know how to program. At the same time, it provides a scripting language that experienced developers can use to create advanced games. In this chapter, you will learn more about Game Maker and how it works.

An overview of the major topics covered in this chapter includes:

- A review of Game Maker's key components and supporting technologies
- Instruction on how to install Game Maker
- An introduction to the Game Maker community and how to participate in it
- A demonstration of how to load and execute Game Maker applications

## Computer Game Development Is Serious Business

From its origin in the early 1970s with games like *Pong*, *Space Invaders*, *Breakout*, and *Asteroids*, to the latest generation of games like *World of Warcraft*, *Call of Duty*, and *Guitar Hero*, computer game development has always been serious business. Over the years, game play has evolved from single-player arcade games to games involving thousands of players from around the world played on the Internet. Games and the platforms they are played on also have evolved and changed over the years and now include home computers, PDAs, cell phones, game consoles, etc.

The video game industry generates more than $10 billion in revenues every year. Individuals with game development skills are in high demand and can demand lucrative salaries. To meet this demand, colleges and universities like the University of Southern California, ITT Technical Institute, and DeVry are creating degree programs in video game design.

If you are someone who is interested in breaking into this exciting field, there is no better place to begin than right here, right now, learning the basics of game design and development using Game Maker. On the other hand, if your aspirations are not so lofty and all you want to do is have a lot of fun learning how to create computer games that demonstrate your own personal sense of style and fun, then you'll be pleased to know that Game Maker will suit your needs well. In fact, you may even find that the process of creating and developing computer games is actually a lot more fun than the playing of games.

**Hint**

It is important to know that most modern computer games sold today were developed by large teams of people, including programmers, graphic artists, audio technicians, and project managers, and probably took months or years to create with budgets of millions of dollars. Together, these people make sure their games have a good design and vision, backed up by exciting sound effects and stunning graphics, all of which is tied together using program code. The purpose of this book is not to try to teach you how to become a graphics designer or a sound technician, disciplines that can take years to learn and master. Still, you have to start somewhere. Using simple graphics and sound files included with Game Maker, along with the vast number of graphics and audio files available on the Internet, you will be able to produce some pretty fancy games all by yourself.

## Getting to Know Game Maker

Most people think of computer game development and computer programming as a complex and mysterious process, requiring years of training and advanced technical education. This was once true but not any more. In recent years, a new generation of software development tools has appeared, specifically geared towards simplifying the process of developing computer games. One of the very best is Game Maker.

Game Maker was created for the sole purpose of facilitating computer game development. Game Maker was created by Mark Overmars, who initially released it as a graphics tool under the name of Animo on November 15, 1999. Since then it has evolved into a full-featured game development tool. Today, Game Maker is developed and supported by YoYo Games (http://www.yoyogames.com), which was established for the purpose of supporting the continued development of Game Maker.

Game Maker provides a great environment within which to learn how to develop computer games. Game Maker provides everything you need to create 2D and 3D computer games of all types. It lets you use a simple drag-and-drop approach to game development that allows you to get started without spending a lot of time learning how to program. This significantly reduces the complexity involved in game development, allowing you to focus on good game design instead of being bogged down in the details of computer programming.

**Hint**

Game Maker and the applications you make with it run on all versions of Microsoft Windows starting with Windows 2000 and later. At the time this book was written, the most current version of Game Maker was 7.0, which is the version used in all of the examples presented in this book.

## Game Maker Uncovered

Game Maker provides a framework that supports the development of computer games. This framework consists of a number of components, including:

- The Game Maker IDE
- The Game Maker game engine
- DirectX
- The Game Maker language

### *Game Maker's Integrated Development Environment*

Game Maker's *integrated development environment* or *IDE* provides a software development environment equipped with all the tools needed to develop new games and applications. Using its menus, toolbar, and a collection of built-in windows and editors, you can create a host of different types of games. A notable feature of Game Maker is its icon-based drag-and-drop approach to game

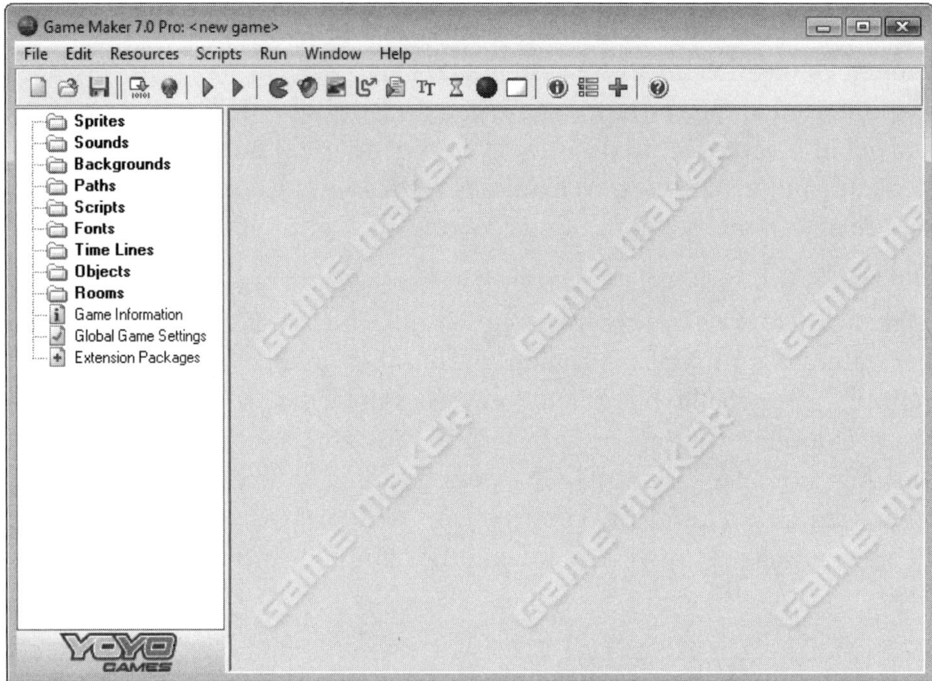


**Figure 1.1**
The Game Maker IDE provides a work environment within which you can create and test Game Maker applications.

development, which allows you to develop computer games without having to write a single line of program code.

As shown in Figure 1.1, the Game Maker IDE looks in many ways like a typical Windows application, with menus and a toolbar running along the top, and a list of folders containing application resources displayed on the left-hand side of the IDE. To the right of the folder listing is the main work area, where you will see and work on your games as you build them.

As you will learn in Chapter 2, "Getting Comfortable with the Game Maker Development Environment," the Game Maker IDE also consists of a large collection of Windows and editors that enable you to create and edit graphics, work with sound files, design backgrounds, and outline the logic used to control the execution of your games.

### *Game Maker's Game Engine*

A *game engine* is a software system that facilitates the development of computer games. It provides all of the core functionality required to render

2D or 3D graphics and to manage all aspects of computer games, including things like:

- Managing the playback of sound effects and background music
- Managing graphic animation and special effects
- Managing the game's use of computer memory
- Executing program logic, including scripts (when included as part of games)
- Determining when objects collide and how they should respond

The basic idea behind the development of game engines is that since all computer games share a common set of functionality, their development can be simplified through the use of a common framework that is responsible for managing common core components, allowing game developers to focus on the design and development of unique features that make their games operate. Without a game engine, game developers would be forced to create games from scratch, reinventing core game functionality common to every computer game, thus significantly increasing the amount of time and effort that goes into game development.

Game Maker's game engine consists of a large collection of pre-written program code, referred to as functions, that you can add to your computer games. Each of these functions is designed to perform a specific type of task. By incorporating these functions into your applications, you save yourself the time and trouble of having to reinvent the wheel. These functions provide everything you need to display graphics, manage interaction with players, control game execution, and manage the playback of sound effects and background music. The functions are designed to work with a Microsoft technology called DirectX, which you will learn about in the next section.

### *DirectX*

*DirectX* is a Microsoft technology that enables the execution of commands that control and manage the high-end graphics and audio. DirectX manages the interaction required for games to access resources provided by your computer's hardware. DirectX provides hardware-independent access to the computer's input devices like the mouse, keyboard and, if present, joysticks, as well as the sound and video cards. Learning how to work with DirectX is no simple matter.

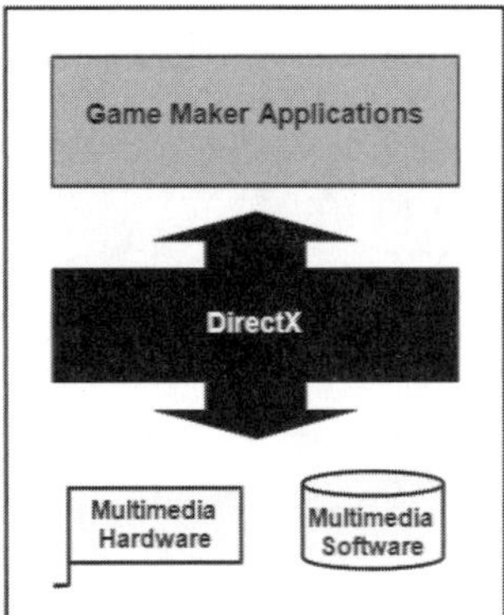


**Figure 1.2**
Understanding the role DirectX plays in supporting the development of Game Maker games.

Thanks to the game engines, DirectX is no longer a barrier to game development that can only be overcome by advanced programmers.

By calling on reusable functions that make up Game Maker's game engine, you can create realistic games that leverage all of the multimedia capabilities provided by DirectX. This alleviates you from having to learn or even worry about how DirectX works and allows you to focus on what you are trying to create.

As depicted in Figure 1.2, the Game Maker game engine serves as an interface between your Game Maker applications and DirectX. Thanks to the Game Maker game engine, you can spend your time working on the fun part of developing computer games, ensuring a good design, and leave the rest to Game Maker, all without worrying about the inner workings of DirectX.

**Hint**

Microsoft initially released DirectX in 1995. DirectX has been updated many times since then. The current version of DirectX is DirectX 10. DirectX 10 ships with Microsoft Vista. Any computer you use to work with Game Maker and any computer the player uses to play your game on must run DirectX version 8 or higher. DirectX 8 was initially released in November 2000, so it has been around for a long time. As a result, unless you are working on a really old Windows computer, DirectX 8 or higher is almost certainly already installed, which means you do not have to worry much about whether other people will have the hardware needed to play your games.

### *The Game Maker Language (GML)*

Game Maker's unique icon-based approach to game development allows you to create all kinds of professional-looking games without having to know a thing about computer programming. This frees you from having to learn and master the ins and outs of a new computer programming language and instead lets you focus all your attention on good game design. However, there are limitations to this approach, and after a while, you may find yourself wanting to push the envelope of Game Maker's icon-based capabilities. Game Maker also has its own full-featured scripting language known as the *Game Maker Language* or *GML*, which allows you to create more advanced games.

Game Maker provides an *object-oriented* programming environment in which you define objects representing different characters and objects that make up computer games. GML lets you exercise great precision over the ways these objects interact with one another and various events that occur during game play. GML is an interpreted programming language that is syntactically similar to programming languages like C, C++, and Pascal. As an interpreted language, GML statements are converted into an executable format every time programs are executed. This differs from compiled programs created by other programming languages in which program code is pre-compiled into an executable format, allowing programs to start executing the moment they are loaded. Game Maker automatically includes its interpreter, the program responsible for converting code statements into an executable format, as part of every executable game. As a result, interpreted programming languages like GML execute a little slower. However, given the power of modern computers, GML's interpreted execution tends not to pose much of a restriction on game development.

GML supports all of the programming features found in any modern programming language, including things like variables, arrays, conditional logic, loops, etc. As such, learning GML provides excellent preparation for other languages like C++ and Java, which are programming languages used by the gaming industry to develop some of the world's most popular games. You will learn about GML and how to use it to support the development of different kinds of games in Chapters 8 through 11.

## Game Maker's Unique Drag-and-Drop Approach

Game Maker supports a drag-and-drop approach to game development that aids beginning game developers. It allows developers to drag-and-drop different icons representing different actions that can be taken, assigning them to different events belonging to the objects that make up the game. As demonstrated in Figure 1.3, you can develop the logic needed to create your games by arranging

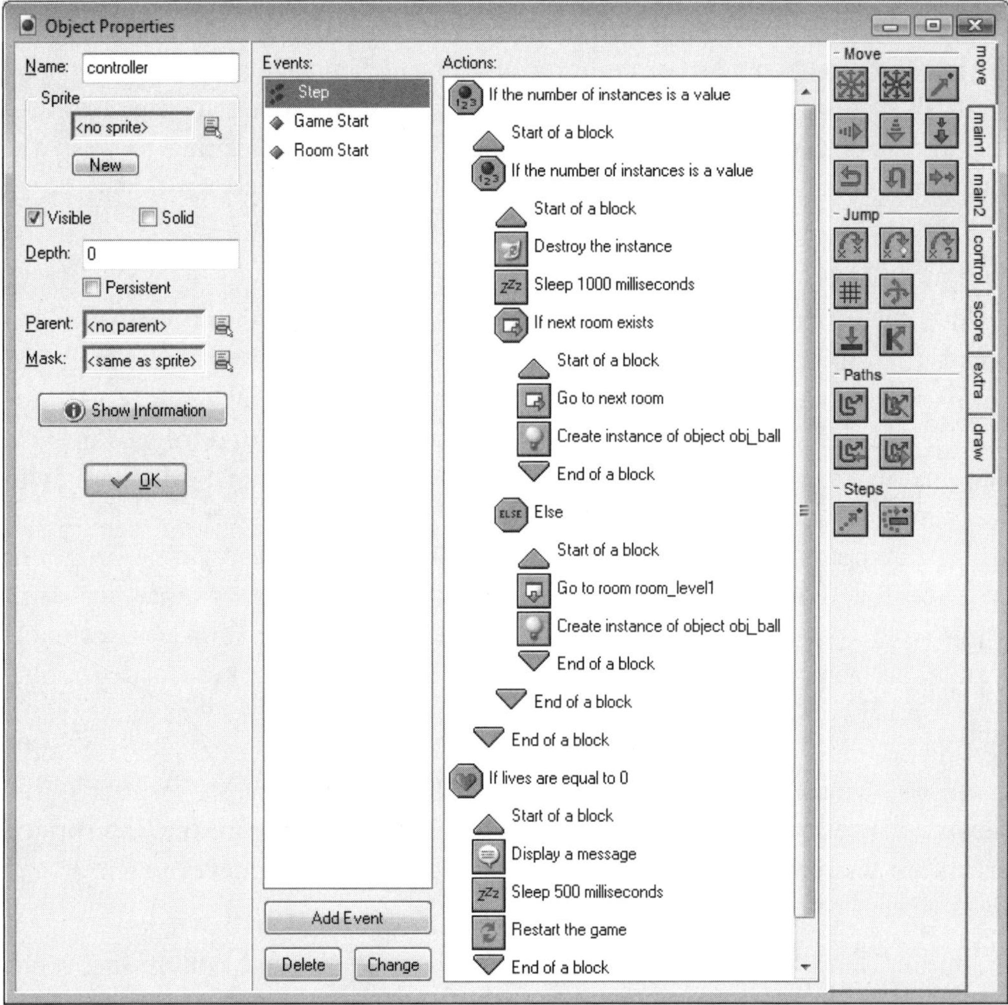


**Figure 1.3**
An example of how event and action icons are used to outline an object's programming logic.

event and action icons into logical collections, instructing Game Maker how you want the objects to behave.

Through the arrangement of different event and action icons, Game Maker is able to support the same basic types of programming techniques and constructs used in computer programming languages. Game Maker supports the use of variables, iterative and conditional logic, as well as event-driven programming. It also supports the manipulation of graphics and the integration of sound effects and music. It can even play video files.

## Two-Dimensional Versus Three-Dimensional Game Development

Game Maker specializes in the development of 2D computer games. This means that you can use it to create games like *Pac-Man*, *Asteroids*, and a host of related arcade-style games. However, there is no end to the different types of 2D games that you can create. Although 3D games represent the current state of the art in computer game programming, new 2D games are being released all the time, including such titles as *Odin's Sphere*, *Super Street Fighter Turbo*, and the *Command & Conquer* series.

Taking advantage of Direct3D, a component of DirectX, Game Maker Pro edition also provides limited support for 3D graphics, supporting 3D particle effects like clouds, rain, explosions, and snow. Though not designed to create 3D worlds, you can incorporate 3D graphics in 2D games, generating games that look and feel like 3D games, and 2D games are a lot easier to create.

# Getting Started with Game Maker

Before starting Game Maker's install process, make sure that your computer's software is up to date, which you can do by clicking on Start > All Programs > Windows Update and then running the Windows Update process.

As I mentioned previously, Game Maker depends on DirectX to support various graphic and audio operations and requires that DirectX version 8.0 or above is installed on your computer and on any computer that runs the games you create with Game Maker. The good news is that DirectX has been around for some time and any computer that meets Game Maker's minimum hardware requirements will most likely have DirectX installed.

**Hint**

However, if necessary, you can download DirectX from Microsoft's DirectX web page located at http://www.gamesforwindows.com/en-US/AboutGFW/Pages/DirectX10.aspx.

## Downloading Game Maker

Game Maker's installation package is available as a free download at http://www.yoyogames.com/gamemaker/try. To start the download process, click on the DOWNLOAD GAMEMAKER 7 HERE button located at the bottom of the page. Click on Save when prompted for permission to continue the download and then specify the location on your computer where you want to save Game

Maker's installation package and click on Save. The download will begin and should only take a few moments if you are using a high-speed Internet connection. Once completed, click on Close to complete the process. Go to the location you specified as the destination location for the download and you should see a file named gmaker.exe.

## Installing Game Maker

Game Maker installs on Microsoft Windows like any other Windows application. The following procedure outlines the steps involved in completing Game Maker's install process.

1. Double-click on the gmaker.exe file.
2. If a security message is displayed, clicked on Allow to give permission for the installation process to continue.
3. The Game Maker 7.0 Install Program Welcome window will then appear as demonstrated in Figure 1.4. Click on Next to continue the installation process.
4. Information about Game Maker, its requirements, and how to upgrade to the Pro edition is displayed. Click on Next to continue.

**Figure 1.4**
Installing Game Maker on Microsoft Windows.

5. Game Maker's license agreement is displayed. Read the agreement, select the I agree with the above terms and conditions radio button, and click on Next to continue.

6. The next screen shows the default location where Game Maker will be installed (C:\Program Files\Game_Maker7). Unless you have a reason to change this location, leave it as is and click on Next to continue.

7. A popup window will appear stating that the specified destination directory does not exist. Click on Yes to create it.

8. The install program now has all the information needed to install Game Maker. Click on Start to install Game Maker.

9. Once the install process has finished copying Game Maker's program files to your computer, its closing installation screen prompts you to view Game Maker's Readme file. When you are done, click on Exit to close the install program.

Game Maker will automatically start when its installation process is complete. The first time Game Maker starts, it will prompt you to run it in either Simple or Advanced mode. When prompted, click on `Yes` to run Game Maker in Advanced mode. You will then see the Upgrade to the Pro Edition window shown in Figure 1.5.

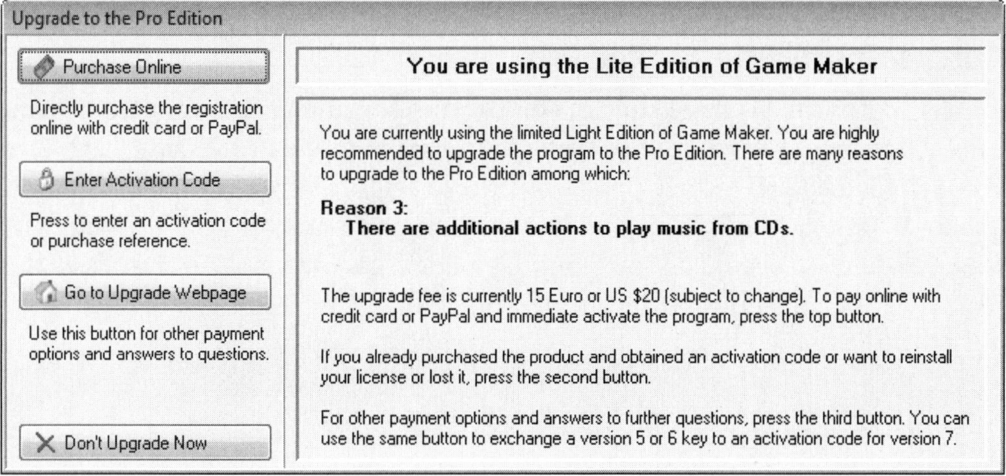


**Figure 1.5**
Unless you upgrade to Game Maker Pro edition, you will see this window every time you start Game Maker.

In addition to starting Game Maker, the installation process also adds a shortcut for Game Maker to the Windows desktop. You will also find a new menu entry for Game Maker on the Windows Start menu (Start > All Programs > Game Maker 7 > Game Maker).

## Simple Versus Advanced Mode

Game Maker supports two modes of operation: Simple and Advanced. Simple mode displays fewer features, reducing, for example, the number of toolbar buttons and menu commands, leaving only those buttons and commands that are required to create basic applications. In Advanced mode, all of Game Maker's features are made available to you.

Beginners may find that running Game Maker in Simple mode helps to make things easier to manage. However, the differences between these two modes are not that significant. So, for the sake of simplicity, all of the figures and examples that you will see in this book assume that you are working in Advanced mode.

The first time Game Maker starts, it will prompt you to enable Advanced mode. Click on Yes when prompted. Otherwise, click on No to run Game Maker in Simple mode. If you change your mind later, you can switch from Simple mode to Advanced mode by clicking on File > Advanced mode. Likewise, you can switch from Advanced mode to Simple mode by clicking on File > Simple mode.

Figures 1.6 and 1.7 demonstrate the differences in the way the IDE looks when run in Simple and Advanced modes.

## Purchasing Game Maker Pro

To take advantage of all of Game Maker's features, you must upgrade from Game Maker Lite to Game Maker Pro. Until you upgrade to the Pro version, each time you start Game Maker, the Upgrade to the Pro Edition window will be displayed, as shown in Figure 1.5. You can close this window and continue working with Game Maker by clicking on the Don't Upgrade Now button. You can access this window any time you want by clicking on Help > Upgrade.

Upgrading to Game Maker Pro provides you with numerous features, including:

- The Game Maker logo will no longer appear in your games.
- You can extend Game Maker's capabilities using extension packages.
- You can create multi-player network games.

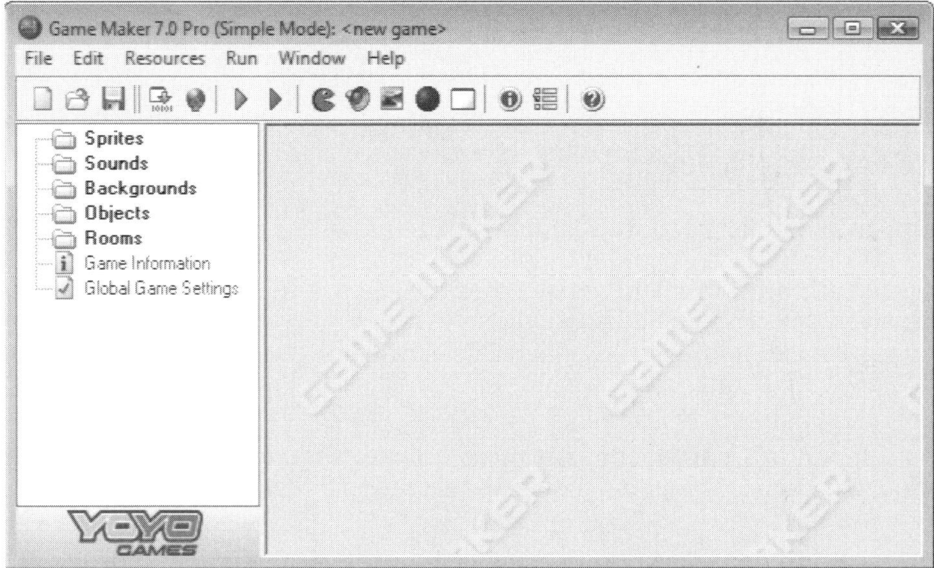


**Figure 1.6**
In Simple mode, Game Maker games consist of sprites, sounds, backgrounds, and rooms.

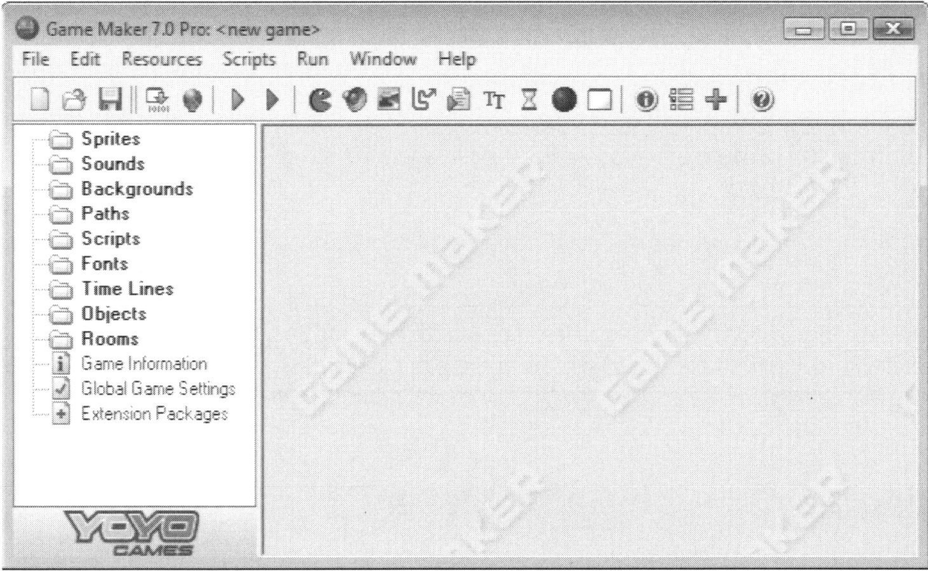


**Figure 1.7**
In Advanced mode, Game Maker adds the ability to include paths, scripts, fonts, and time lines to your games.

- You can add special sound effects and create particles like rain, snow, and explosions.
- You can add custom splash screens, including images, text, and even movie clips to your applications.
- You can access new actions for playing CD music.
- You can add transitions to your games for when it moves between rooms.
- You can include additional files needed to run your games within your game executable (.exe) files.
- You can perform a number of advanced drawing functions like textured and colorized shapes.
- You get access to a collection of advanced drawing functions supporting 3D game development.
- The Upgrade to the Pro Edition window will disappear.

To upgrade from Game Maker Lite to Game Maker Pro, click on the Purchase Online button located on the Upgrade to the Pro Edition window. When you do, your default web browser is used to connect to a web page at the YoYo Games website where you can use your credit card or PayPal to pay for the upgrade. Once you have completed the transaction, your copy of Game Maker is automatically upgraded to the Pro version. In addition, you will receive an e-mail with your registration code, which you will want to save, just in case you ever need to reinstall Game Maker.

**Hint**

Game Maker Pro edition provides considerably more functionality than the Lite edition. Given the Pro edition's modest $20 cost, it is well worth the cost to upgrade from Lite to Pro.

## Creating Games with Game Maker

As listed next, Game Maker games are made up of collections of different resources. You will learn how to work with all of these resources as you make your way through this book.

- **Sprites.** Two-dimensional bitmap images drawn on a transparent background that are used to represent objects during game play. For example, in a *Pac-Man* game, sprites would be used to represent Pac-Man and the ghosts that chase him. Sprites can consist of any number of images that are used to generate animation.
- **Objects.** A logical representation of an item in a computer game. Objects provide the basis for creating things like ships, tanks, monsters, etc.
- **Instances.** The representation of an object within a computer application. One or more instances can be created for each object in a game. Instances are generally, though not always, represented by sprites.
- **Scripts.** Collections of code statements that outline the programming logic that controls the operation of object instances within games.
- **Rooms.** An area within a game where sprites interact with one another as the game is played.
- **Backgrounds.** A graphic image used to decorate a room and provide it with appropriate background scenery. Backgrounds can be tiled or stretched as necessary to fill a room.
- **Sounds.** Audio files (wave and midi files) played when events occur during game play or played as background music in order to provide the game with appropriate atmosphere.

All Game Maker games are made up of two-dimensional rooms. A game can be played within a single room or may consist of multiple rooms. When multiple rooms are used, each room may serve as a different area in the game world where game play can occur. Rooms can also be used to provide different levels in which players advance to the next level after completing the current level.

Objects represent the heart of every game. Objects are used to define game resources like characters, vehicles, and all of the other things in games that interact with one another. In order to populate a game world, you must add instances of objects to the game's rooms. Most of the objects you add to your games will be represented by sprites, making them visible to players. You can create sprites using Game Maker's built-in sprite editor. Alternatively, you can use another paint program or you can download sprites from the internet.

During game play, objects interact with one another. Players can interact with and control objects during game play in one of several different ways, including:

- Pressing keys on the keyboard
- Moving the mouse and clicking on its buttons
- Using one or more joysticks attached to the computer

Objects can also interact and respond to one another. During game play, all kinds of different events are constantly occurring. When you define objects, you specify the different types of events that the objects respond to. In addition, you can specify the different types of actions that objects should take when specific types of events occur.

You can populate game worlds with as many instances of different objects as you want, each of which act and behave in the manner you defined. In addition to populating the game world with different objects, you can add different backgrounds to rooms and add sound effects and music to your games.

## Joining Game Maker's Global Community

Game Maker is supported by a large community of game developers from around the world. YoYo Games facilitates sharing and communications among these individuals by sponsoring a collection of forums on its website (http://gmc.yoyogames.com), as shown in Figure 1.8.

The forums available on the YoYo Games website are organized into four categories, as shown here.

- **General.** These forums are used to post announcements, introduce Game Maker websites, discuss community topics, and to solicit help with projects.
- **Working with Game Maker.** These forums support communication about tutorials, 3D game development, and how to extend Game Maker's capabilities. They also facilitate discussions between novice and intermediate users and between advanced users.
- **Games.** These forums provide a place to talk about individual game projects, work in progress, new game ideas, as well as how to distribute your games.

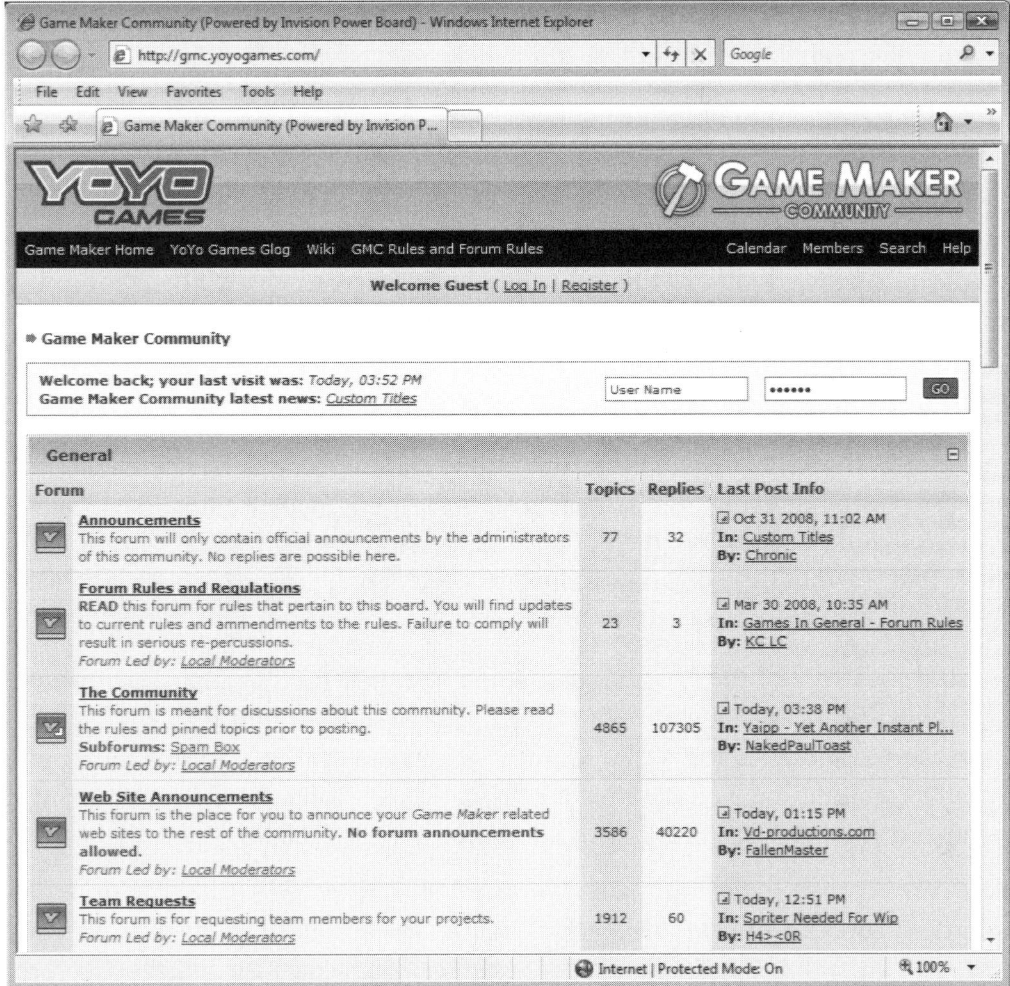


**Figure 1.8**
The YoYo Games website provides a central location where members of the Game Maker community come to learn from one another.

- **Resources.** These forums sponsor communications about where to find graphics, sound, and music for your games.

As of the writing of this book, the Game Maker community consisted of over 78,000 active users who had made more than 1.7 million postings. You should take advantage of these forums to interact with other Game Maker developers and to keep an eye on the latest developments and happenings. You can learn a lot about game development in general and Game Maker specifically through these forums. You can also post questions and ask for help when you run into problems that you are unable to solve yourself.

In addition to sponsoring numerous forums, the YoYo Games website also provides access to all kinds of useful resources designed to assist game developers. This includes providing access to Game Maker documents and tutorials. It also provides access to collections of sprites, backgrounds, tiles, sounds, music, scripts, and other resources that you can use when creating your own computer games.

## Sharing Your Games with the World

Creating new computer games is fun, but sharing what you have created with others can provide even more satisfaction. Let's face it, people really like to share. How else could you explain the massive popularity of websites like youtube.com that allow people to upload and share their video creations? The result is an exchange of ideas and creativity on a global scale.

Sharing is also an important part of the Game Maker game development experience. Game Maker games can be run on Windows computers, and they can be executed online at the YoYo Games website, provided you download and install a free plug-in. You can make your games available for download. If you want, you can even make your game's source code available.

You can read and add comments to any games posted to the YoYo Games websites. You can use the feedback provided by others to help improve your games, by incorporating their suggestions and eliminating or improving features that nobody seems to like. Figure 1.9 provides an example of how games appear when on the YoYo Games website.

**Note**

You will learn how to share your Game Maker games when you get to Chapter 13, "Sharing Your Game Maker Projects Over the Internet."

## Signing Up with the Game Maker Website

In order to join the Game Maker community, you first need to register with the YoYo Games website by signing up for a free account. Once you do this, you can begin participating in forum discussions and start sharing your games.

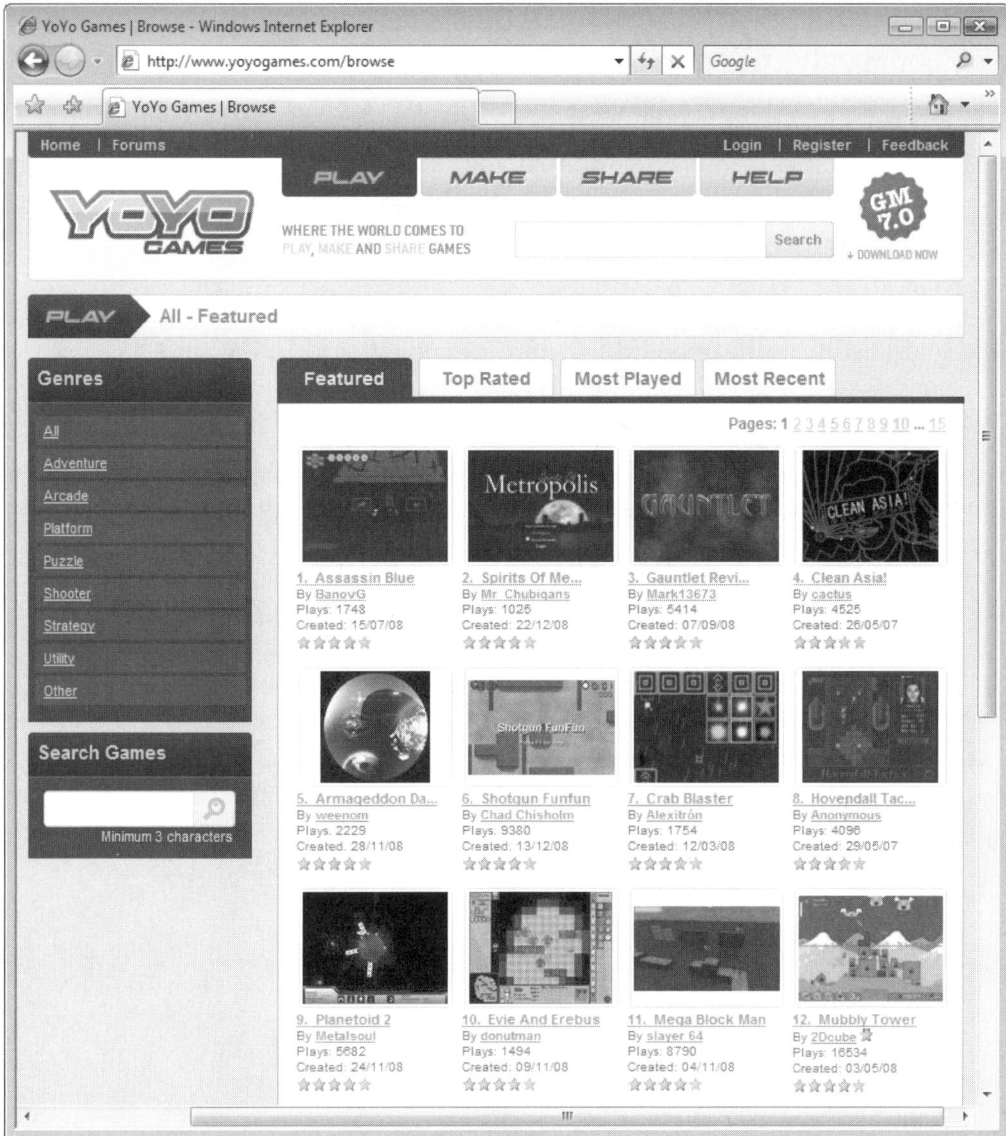


**Figure 1.9**
The YoYo Games website helps promote community member's games by providing a global audience.

Registering for a new account only takes a couple of minutes. The steps you need to follow are outlined here:

1. Go to http://www.yoyogames.com.
2. Click on the Register link located in the upper-right corner of the web page.

3. Fill in the required form and click on the Register button located at the bottom of the web page.

4. Within a few minutes you will receive an email welcoming you to YoYo Games. In it you will see a link that you must click in order to confirm your registration. As soon as you click on the link, your new account will become active.

As soon as you complete this procedure, you can return to http://www.yoyogames.com/user/login and log in, as demonstrated in Figure 1.10.

## Loading and Running a Sample Game

A number of sample games are loaded on your computer as part of Game Maker's installation. As your first foray into working with Game Maker, let's learn how to start it and then use it to run one of these games. Start Game Maker

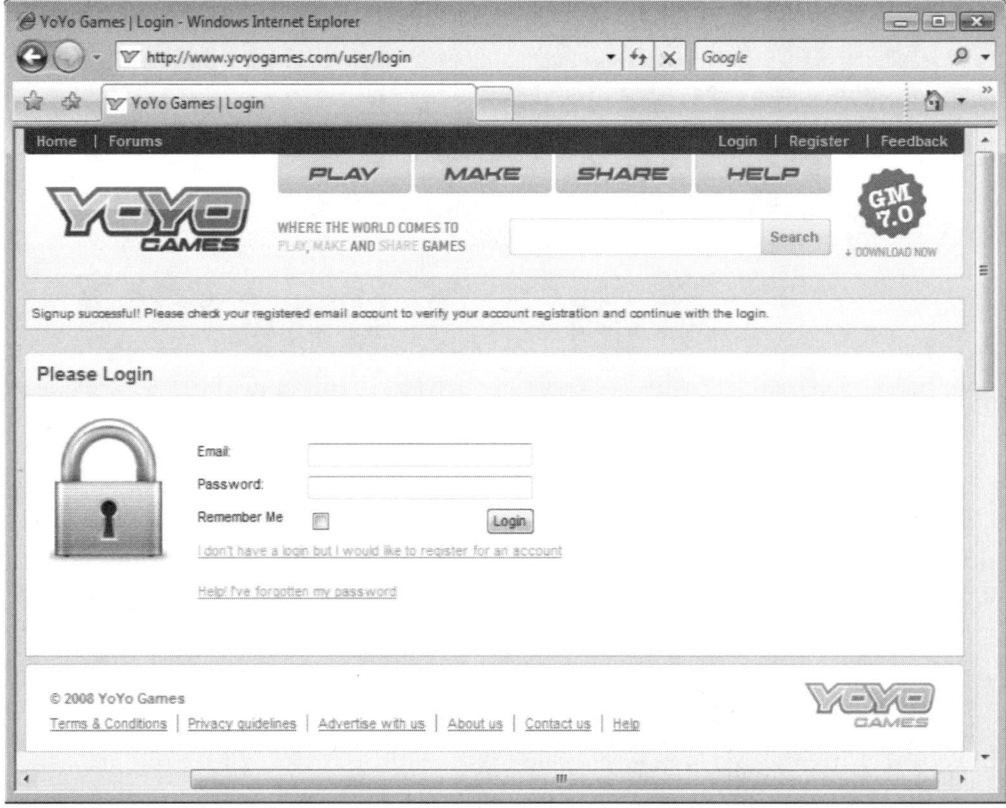


**Figure 1.10**
Registering and logging into the YoYo Games website is the first step in joining the Game Maker community.

by clicking on Start > All Programs > Game Maker 7 > Game Maker. Game Maker's integrated development environment (IDE) will appear.

Once started, you can load and run any of Game Maker's sample games by executing the following procedure, which demonstrates how to run a game named Treasure.

1. Click on File > Open. The Load a Game dialog window appears.

2. By default, a list of sample game projects provided with Game Maker is displayed. Locate and select the file named treasure.gmk and click on the Open button.

**Hint**

Games created using Game Maker 7 are assigned a three-character file extension of .gmk.

3. The game project is loaded into Game Maker, allowing it to be edited and executed. To run it, click on Run > Run Normally or click on the green Run the Game button located at the top of the IDE on Game Maker's toolbar.

4. Within a few moments you'll see Game Maker's default splash screen appear, as demonstrated in Figure 1.11.

5. A moment later the splash screen will close and the game will begin executing, as demonstrated in Figure 1.12.

To play, you must use the keyboard's arrow keys to move a treasure hunter around the game, collecting treasure and evading or killing poisonous scorpions. You can display instructions for playing the game at any time by pressing the F1 key, and you can stop game play whenever you want by pressing the Escape key.

If you look closely, you'll notice that the game automatically keeps track of the number of points scored and the number of lives you have left. By default, you begin with three lives. At the end of the game, which occurs when you have run

**Figure 1.11**
You can replace this splash screen with a customized splash screen of your own.

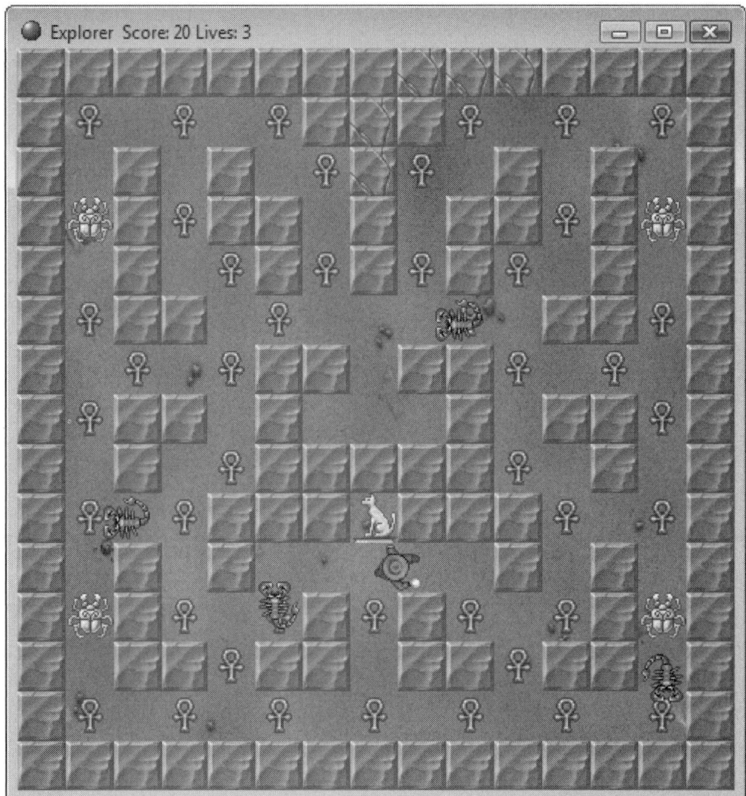


**Figure 1.12**
Treasure is a multi-level *Pac-Man* styled maze game.

out of lives, a high score window is displayed. If all this seems pretty cool, it is. If you want to learn how to create games like this yourself, keep reading.

Once you are done playing, close the game. To do this, press the Escape key or click on the Close icon located at the top-right corner of the game window. The Game Maker IDE should reappear. If you are done working with it, you can close it by clicking on File > Exit (or on the IDE's Close button).

## Summary

This chapter provided a broad understanding of Game Maker and its capabilities. This included a review of its major features and capabilities. You learned how to install it and use it to open, compile, and execute a game. You were also introduced to the YoYo Games website and its support for the Game Maker community. You also learned how to sign up for a free user account and the importance of becoming a participating member of the Game Maker community.

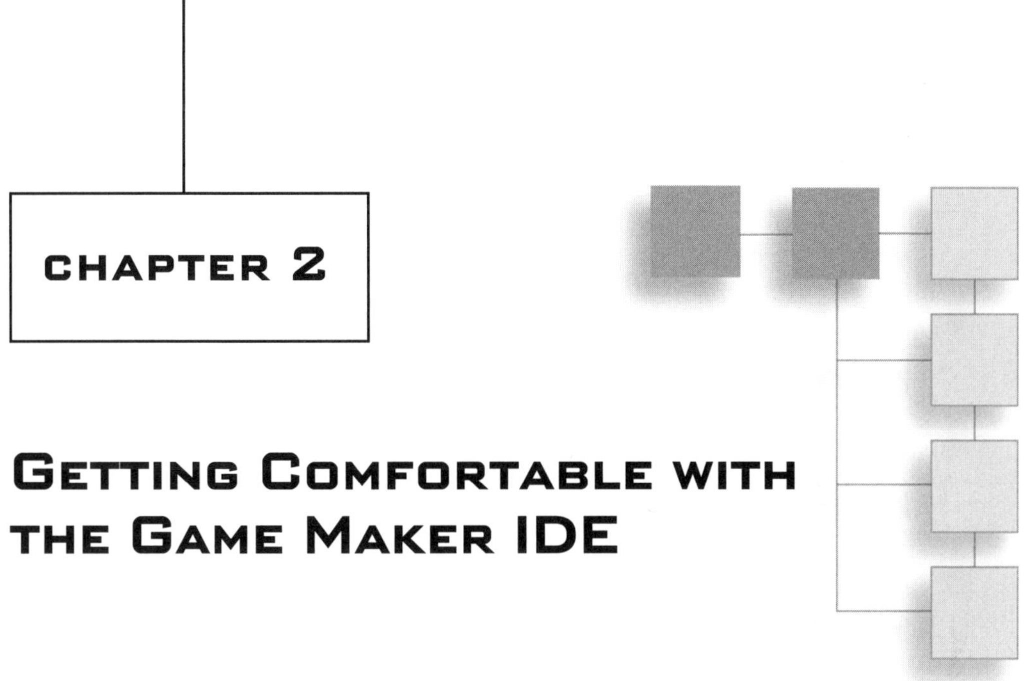

# Chapter 2

# Getting Comfortable with the Game Maker IDE

This chapter introduces most of the menus, toolbar buttons, and windows that make up the Game Maker integrated development environment or IDE. You will learn how to create all of the basic types of resources that make up Game Maker games, including things like objects, sprites, sounds, and backgrounds. In addition to an overview of the different components that make up the IDE, this review will include an examination of Game Maker's configuration settings.

Specifically, you will learn:

- About the different parts of the Game Maker IDE
- How to work with menu and toolbar commands
- How to work with the windows responsible for creating different game resources
- How to configure different IDE preferences and settings
- How to access Game Maker help files

## Exploring the Game Maker IDE

The Game Maker IDE provides access to all of the tools you need to create computer games. It is your primary interface for creating, testing, and compiling games. Figure 2.1 shows how Game Maker Pro's IDE looks when run in Advanced mode.

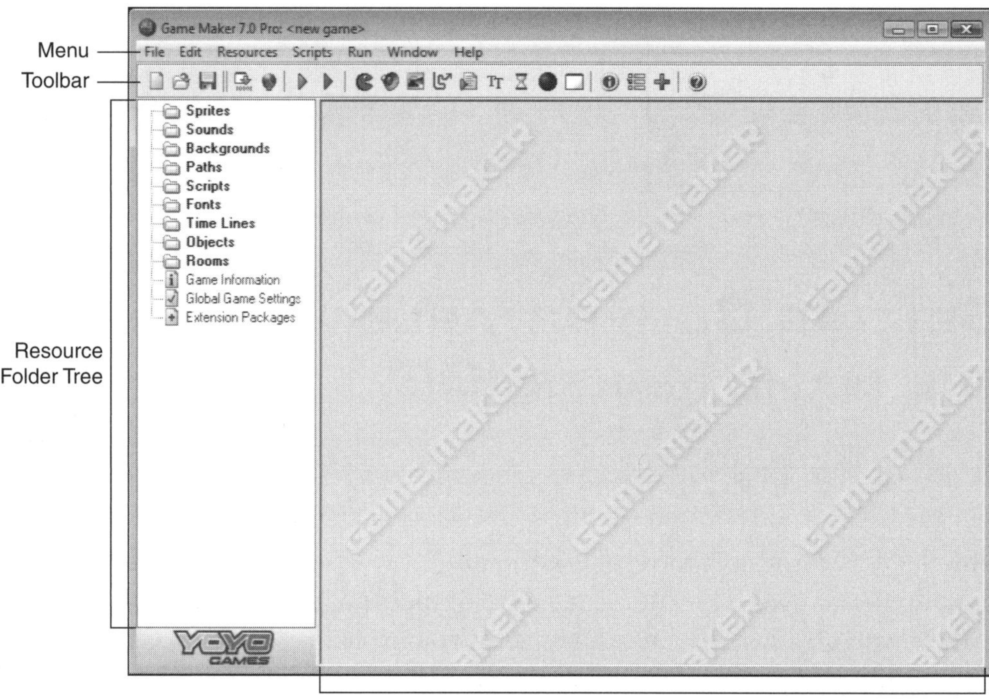


**Figure 2.1**
The Game Maker IDE provides all the tools needed to develop computer games.

As you can see, Game Maker's IDE is organized into a number of different parts. Like most Windows applications, there is a menu and toolbar located along the top of the IDE. On the left-hand side of the IDE, you will find the resource folder tree, which is where all of the resources that you add to your Game Maker games are listed and organized. The rest of the IDE serves as the IDE's main working area, providing you with space in which to work with other Game Maker windows (when you open them).

**Hint**

> If you do not see all of the menus, toolbar buttons, and resources listed in the resource folder tree area, then you must be running Game Maker in Simple mode. To switch to advanced mode, click on File > Advanced.

Game Maker's IDE includes all of the editing commands that you have come to expect from Windows applications, including copy, cut, and paste. In addition, it provides specialized commands designed to create, test, compile, and execute Game Maker games. Game Maker's IDE is set up as the default application for any Game Maker files (e.g., files with a .gmk file extension). So, if you double-click on a Game Maker file, Windows will automatically start Game Maker and load that file into its IDE, allowing you to edit and make changes to it.

## Access Menu Commands

Game Maker Pro provides access to numerous commands through menus located at the top of the IDE. The File menu offers commands that let you create new games, open existing ones, save, and close projects. You will also find commands that permit you to create a standalone executable version of your games, allowing them to run outside of Game Maker, like other Windows applications.

The Edit menu offers commands that allow you to copy, create, delete, and rename resources. The Edit menu also lets you open the properties window for any selected resource, display information about objects, and search for resources in your games. The Resources menu contains commands that create all of the different resources that make up Game Maker games. The Scripts menu holds commands that you need to work with when developing GML scripts in advanced games.

The Run menu contains two commands that allow you to run your games within the IDE normally or in a special debug mode. The Window menu contains commands that let you cascade the display of windows in the IDE and arrange IDE icons. The Help menu provides access to Game Maker's help file, information about extension packages, online help, and access to the YoYo Games website and forums.

## Working with Game Maker's Toolbar

As is the case with its menus, the number of buttons available on Game Maker's toolbar varies depending on whether you are working in Simple or Advanced mode. Each button provides access to a commonly used Game Maker command, all of which can also be found in Game Maker's menus. Figures 2.2 and 2.3 show how the IDE's toolbar looks when run in Simple and Advanced modes, respectively.

The toolbar provides access to the most commonly used Game Maker commands. Using the toolbar, you can create, open, and save games, run them, create new game resources and access game information, global game settings, and

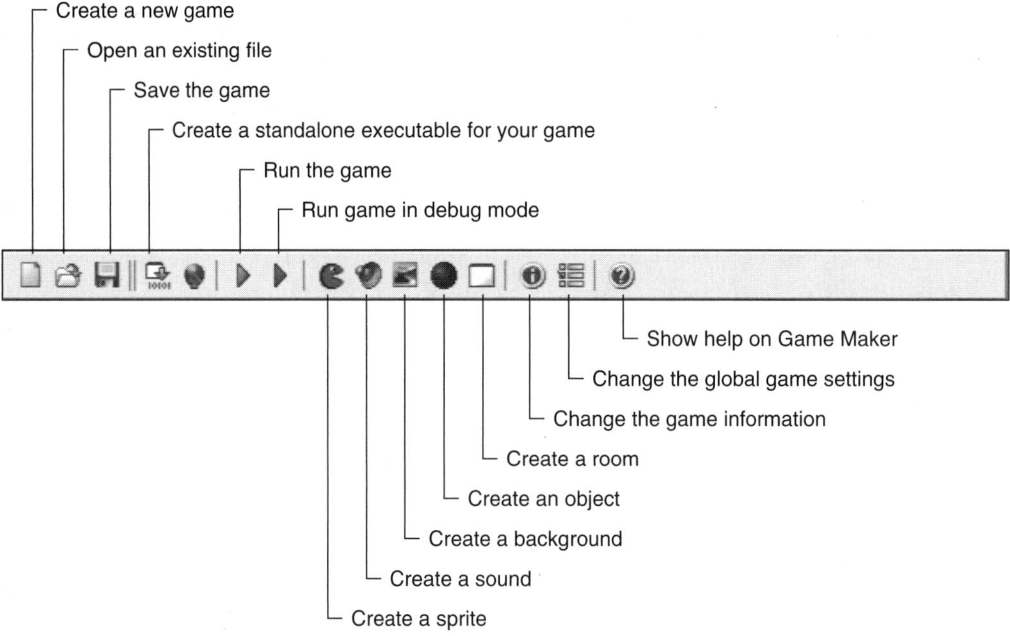


**Figure 2.2**
The Game Maker IDE toolbar when running in Simple mode.

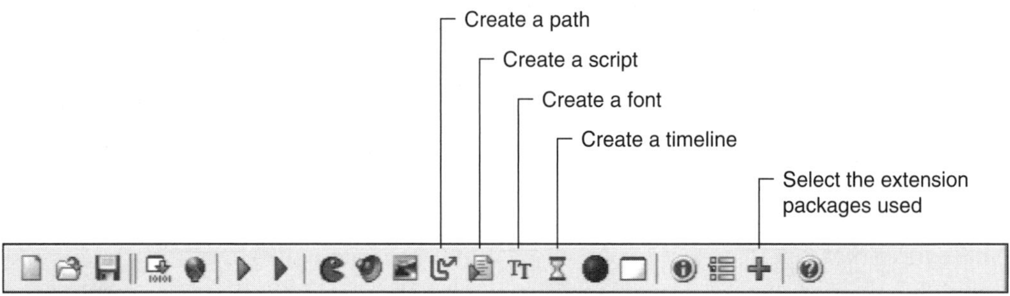


**Figure 2.3**
The Game Maker IDE toolbar when running in Advanced mode.

extensions. You can also access Game Maker's help files. The IDE's toolbar is static, which means you cannot add or remove toolbar icons.

## Keeping an Eye on Project Resources

As already pointed out, the resource folder tree resides on the left-hand side of the Game Maker IDE. It displays a tree-like view of all of the resources that make up your games. As you work with the IDE and add resources to your games, you will see an instance of the resources represented in the appropriate folder on the resource folder tree. Any folder with a + sign in front of it contains resources. You can drill into these folders and display their contents by clicking on the + sign or by double-clicking on the folder name.

Once visible, you can double-click on a resource to open its respective editor or window and work with it. You can right-click on these folders to display a context menu that provides access to commands that allow you to create new resources or subfolders. Likewise, you can right-click on any resource made visible in the resource folder tree to access a context menu that will allow you to copy, delete, rename, and access the resource's properties window.

In addition to displaying and allowing you to access and work with the resources that make up games, the resource folder tree also provides access to the following resources.

- **Game Information.** Allows you to type in information that the player can display by pressing the F1 key when playing the game. Typically, this is where you enter information on how to play the game.
- **Global Game Settings.** These settings control the way Game Maker displays your game, loads images, manages player interaction, and allows you to specify any external files needed by your game.
- **Extension Packages.** Allows you to install extension packages that add new capabilities and features to Game Maker, letting you create more advanced games.

More information and how to work with all three of the above listed resources is provided later in this chapter.

## The Main Work Area

Game Maker's main work area is the part of the IDE where most of the windows that you will work with are opened. For example, when you add or edit a sprite in your game, the Sprite Properties window is displayed in the work area. Likewise, when you add a sound file to a game, the Sound Properties window is opened in the main work area. Although most of Game Maker's windows are open and confined to the main work area, some windows, such as the Game Information window and Game Maker's Help window, open outside of the Game Maker IDE, allowing you to move them anywhere you want on your computer screen.

## Working with Project Resources

Within Game Maker, games are created by adding different types of resources to them. Games created when working in Game Maker's Simple mode consist of five types of resources, as listed here:

- **Sprites.** Graphic representations of objects that make up a computer game.
- **Sounds.** Sound files that provide sound effects and background music in games.
- **Background.** Graphic images used to provide interesting backdrops in games.
- **Objects.** Resources in games that you control and interact with while playing (e.g., plans, bullets, monsters, etc.).
- **Rooms.** Locations in the game world where objects interact.

Games created in Advanced mode can include any of the following additional resources.

- **Paths.** A predetermined direction and course along which games are played.
- **Scripts.** Programming logic outlined within GML that provides greater control over the operation of games than is possible using drag-and drop events and predefined actions.
- **Fonts.** Definitions that specify the type, size, and other attributes of the fonts used to display text in games.
- **Time Lines.** Timers that execute predefined actions at predetermined intervals during game play.

Much of the rest of this chapter is dedicated to explaining how to work with the menus, toolbar commands, and windows used to create all of these different types of resources. Once you are familiar with these resources, Chapter 3, "A Review of the Basic Components of Game Maker," offers a more detailed explanation of how these resources are defined and used to create computer games.

## Creating Sprites

One of the first steps in creating a computer game is to design the graphics that will be used to represent various objects that make up the game. The graphics will represent different things in your games, including such things as monsters, cars, planes, and aliens. You can create these graphics yourself using third-party graphic applications or you can get them from other places like the internet. Optionally, you can create them yourself using Game Maker's built-in graphics editor.

Most of the graphics that you will create will be used to represent different objects in your games. These graphics, when added to Game Maker, will be used to create sprites. A *sprite* is a 2D bitmap image representing an object such as a tank or other game character. To add a new sprite to your game, you must click on Resources > Create Sprite or click on the Create a Sprite button located on the toolbar. In response, the Sprite Properties window is displayed, as demonstrated in Figure 2.4.

**Trick**

> You can also add a sprite to your game by right-clicking on the Sprites folder located in the resource folder tree and selecting the Create Sprite option.

Using the Sprite Properties window, you can assign a name to the sprite and then click on the Load Sprite button to locate and load an existing graphics file, or you can click on the Edit Sprite button to open Game Maker's Sprite Editor window, allowing you to create a new sprite from scratch. Game Maker provides its own

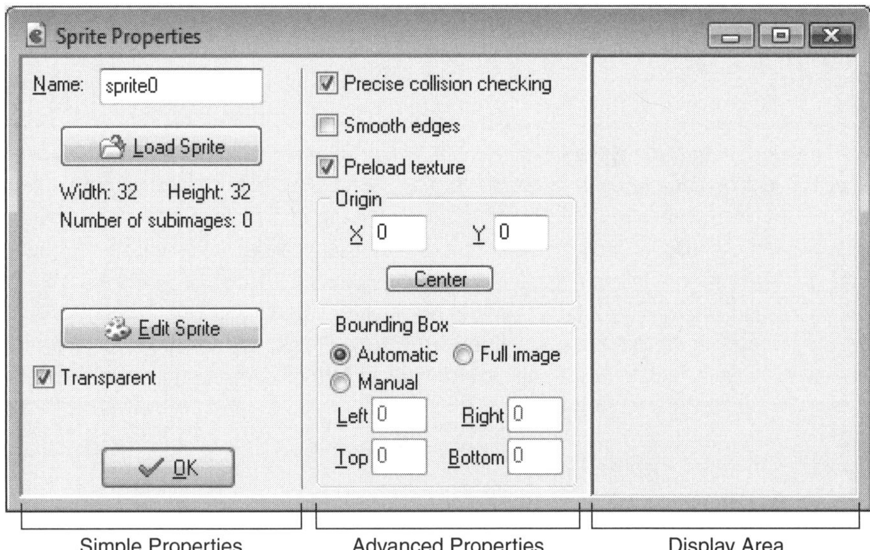


**Figure 2.4**
Sprites provide a visual reference to objects that make up your games.

sprite editor, which you will learn about in later chapters. You can use it to create and edit all of the sprites that make up your games. Using this editor, you can draw lines, rectangles, different freeform shapes, as well as draw filled in shapes using solid colors or gradient colors.

**Hint**

You can also create graphics for your sprites using any third-party graphics application and then import them into Game Maker. However, creating graphics from scratch is a labor-intensive task. You may find that you are better off looking for sprites on the internet where you will find no shortage of professional graphic artists eager to sell you collections of graphics at affordable prices.

## Creating Sounds

Computer games can be enhanced significantly through the clever application of sound effects and mood setting background music. Before you can add actions to objects to play background music and sound effects, you must first add sounds to your games, after which you can assign the audio files you want to play in your games. To add a Sound to your game, click on Resources > Create Sound. In response, the Sound Properties window appears, as shown in Figure 2.5.

When assigning a name to the sound, it is a good idea to supply a name that describes the sound and its purpose. To assign an audio file to a sound, click on the Load Sound button and specify the name and location of the audio file in the window that appears.

**Hint**

Game Maker can work with three types of sound files. Wave files are compressed audio files used to store small sound files and are used in games to play sound effects. Midi files do not contain any actual audio, just instructions that tell your computer's built-in midi player what notes must be played to play a particular sound. Midi files are typically used to provide games with background music and are not well suited to other purposes like providing sound effects. MP3 files are used to store digital music and provide an alternative way to supply a game with background music. However, MP3 files must be decompressed before they can be played and this takes time, which usually make them poor candidates as a source of sound effects or background music.

## Creating Paths

When creating games in Advanced mode, you can specify a path along which a game should follow. You can then add an action to the objects in your game to make them follow that path. Paths are created by drawing them. To do so, click

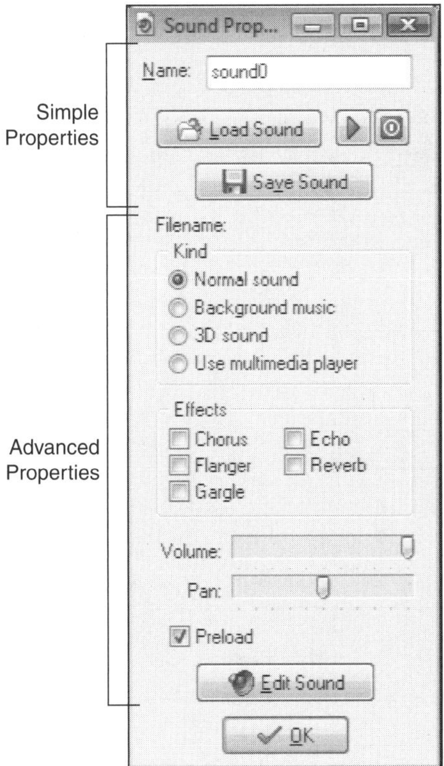


**Figure 2.5**
Sounds can be used to make games more exciting and interesting.

on Resources > Create Path. In response, the Path Properties window appears, allowing you to specify a name for the path and to begin defining the points that outline the path, as demonstrated in Figure 2.6.

To add a point, click on the Add button. A copy of the current position is made, which you can then move to a specified point by clicking on the desired location in the grid area. To insert a point before the current point, click on the Insert button, and to delete the current point just click on the Delete button. The coordinates of the points that make up the path are displayed in the properties pane and the resulting path is outlined on the right-hand side of the window in the grid area. A red dot identifies the currently selected point on the path. A green square identifies the starting part of the path. Blue dots identify all of the other points that make up the path.

You can modify the shape of the path at any time by clicking and dragging a portion of the path to another location. Using property settings located at the

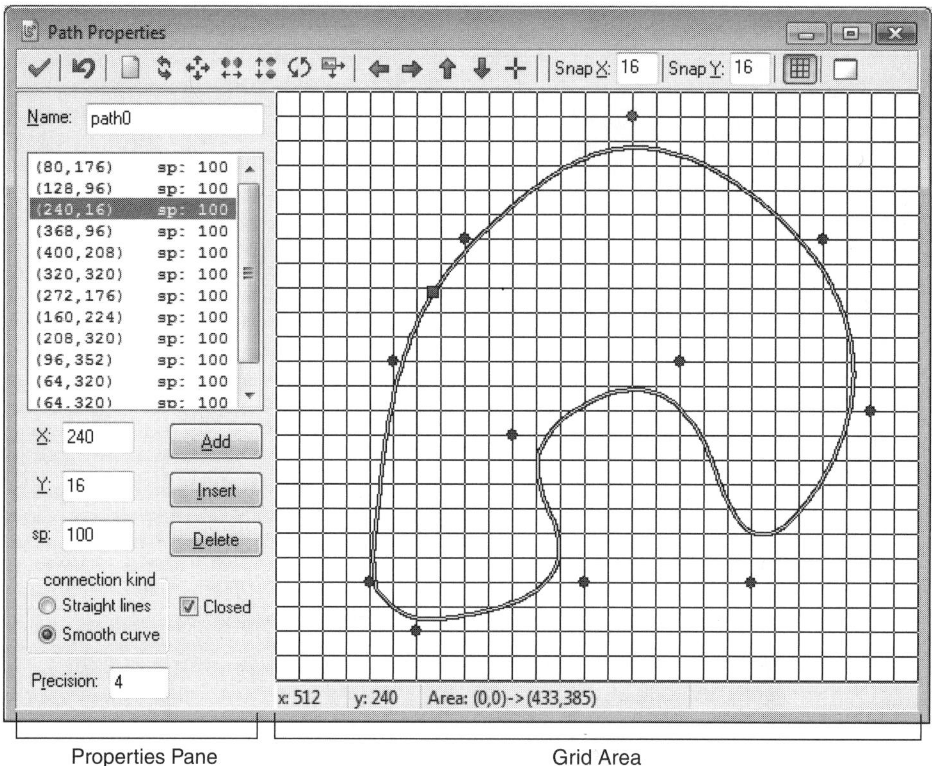


**Figure 2.6**
You can determine the precise path that you want players to take during game play.

bottom-left side of the Path Properties window, you can specify whether a path should be made up of straight lines or curved lines and whether the path should be closed.

## Creating Fonts

By default, Game Maker displays any text that is drawn and displayed during game play using a font type of Arial with a point size of 12. However, when creating games in Game Maker's Advanced mode, you can display text using different fonts and assign them different point sizes and other attributes by adding fonts resources to your games. To add a new font, click on Resources > Create Font. In response, the Font Properties window appears, as shown in Figure 2.7.

Once added, you can assign a unique name to the font and then specify its properties. You can determine which font resource should be used at any point in time by selecting different fonts using different action icons.

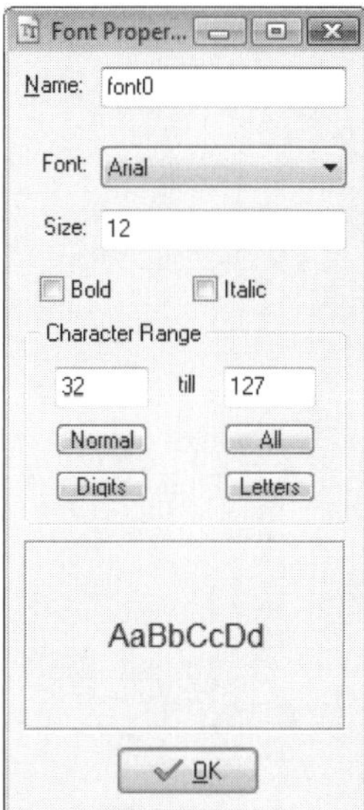


**Figure 2.7**
You can specify the type, size, and different attributes of the fonts used to displayed text in your games.

## Creating Timelines

Another resource available to you when working in Advanced mode is timelines. A *timeline* is a resource that lets you set up a schedule that controls the execution of actions at predetermined intervals, measured in steps. A *step* is a measurement of time. In Game Maker, 30 steps equal one second. By creating a timeline and assigning it to an object, you can use it to control the performance of specified actions during game play. For example, you might create a timeline that generates waves of alien spaceships at specified intervals in a space shootout game.

To create a timeline, click on Resources > Create Time Line. In response, the Time Line Properties window appears, as shown in Figure 2.8.

You begin building a timeline by assigning it a unique name and then clicking on the Add button to add a new moment to the timeline. For example, to set up a moment that occurs 20 seconds after its associated object is created, click on the Add button and enter **600** as the moment value when prompted by the Adding a Moment window. To add a second moment that occurs one minute later, click on the Add button and enter **1800** as the moment. Once you have added all of the moments to the timeline, you can select each moment and then drag and drop any actions you want to be executed to the actions area.

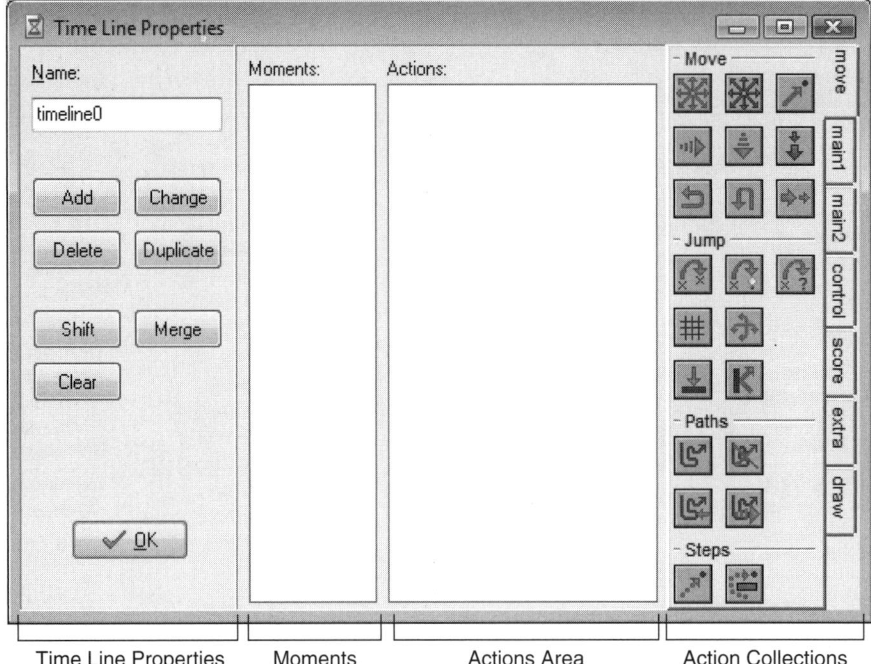


**Figure 2.8**
You can control when different actions occur using timelines.

In addition to adding new timeline moments, you can modify them by selecting a specific moment from the Moments list and then clicking on the Change button. You can delete and copy moments by clicking on the Delete and Duplicate buttons. Deleting a moment deletes any actions that you have assigned to it and duplicating a moment also duplicates all of that moment's assigned actions.

Using the Shift button you can shift some or all moments forward or backward a specified number or steps in time. The Merge button lets you merge all or some of the moments that make up the timeline into a single moment. Clicking on the Clear button clears out all moments as well as any actions that have been assigned so that you can start creating the timeline all over again from scratch.

## Creating Objects

Objects represent the components within games that move about and interact with one another and the player(s). In most cases, you will want to make objects visible so that the player can see them. You do this by assigning sprites to your

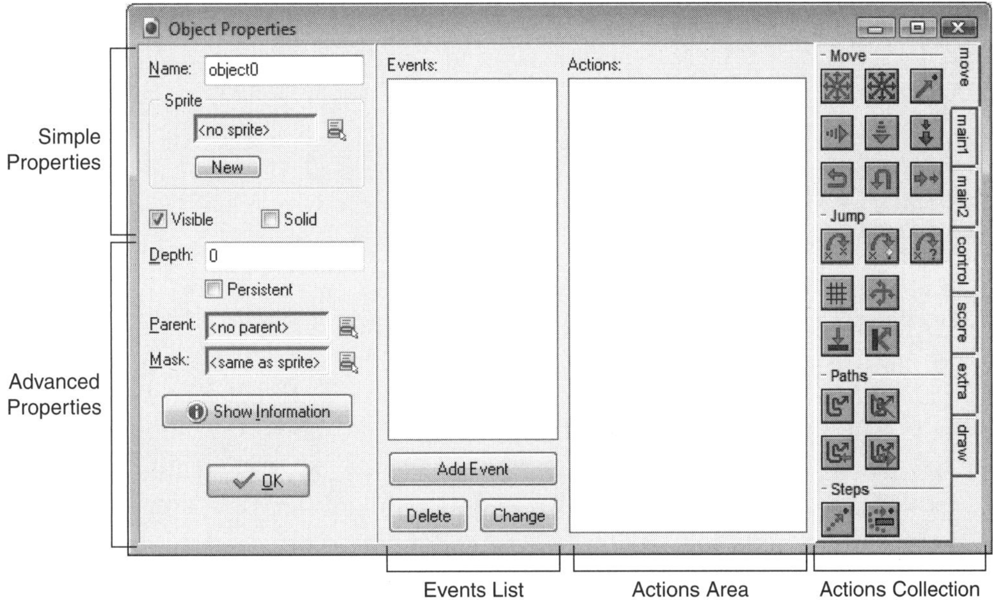


**Figure 2.9**
Computer games consist of different objects that interact with one another.

objects. To do so, click on Resources > Create Object. In response, the Object Properties window is displayed, as demonstrated in Figure 2.9.

All objects require a name. If they are to be visible, they also need you to assign them a sprite. To do so, click on the icon located at the end of the Sprite field. This will display a context menu listing all of the sprites that you have added to your game. To assign a sprite to an object, all you have to do is select it from this list.

**Trap**

> When naming objects, make sure you give them names that are unique. Otherwise, errors will occur. Consider developing and applying a naming convention for all of your game's resources. For example, you will notice that in every sample game created in this book, the names of sprites begin with the characters spr_ whereas all objects begin with the characters obj_. This not only helps to explicitly identify different types of resources but ensures that you do not accidently assign duplicate names to different types of resources.

Objects are controlled by different events and actions that occur during game play. You specify the different types of events you want an object to respond to by clicking on the Add Event button located at the bottom of the event lists area. In response, the Event Selector window shown in Figure 2.10 is displayed.

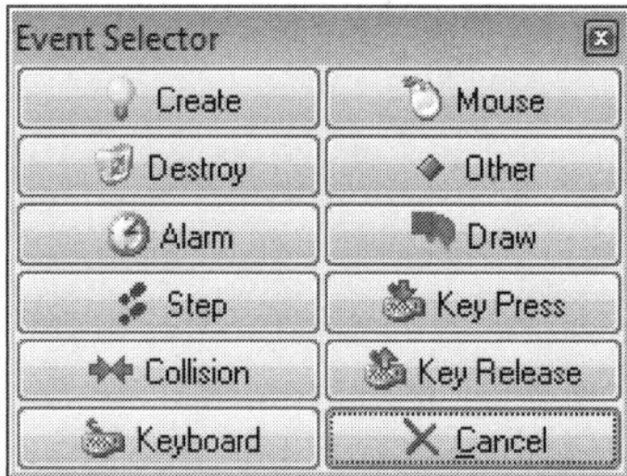


**Figure 2.10**
Objects can respond to a host of different types of events.

Events occur for various reasons. For example, events occur when the player moves the mouse, presses a keyboard key, and when objects collide with one another. Once you add an event to an object's events list, you assign the actions you want the object to take by dragging and dropping different action icons from the actions collections located on the right-hand side of the window onto the actions area. You can add as many different events as you want to an object. Each event that is assigned can have any number of actions. Actions are executed in the order that you add them to the actions area.

Game Maker supplies you with access to over 100 different actions, each of which performs a specific task. These actions are organized into groups that you can access by clicking on tabs located on the right-hand side of the Object Properties window. There are, for example, actions that create and destroy objects, modify the player's score, and alter object movement when objects collide with one another. Game Maker supports a drag-and-drop approach to game development, which aids beginning game developers in getting started. This allows them to drag and drop different icons, representing actions that can be taken, onto different events belonging to the objects that make up computer games.

Once defined, you can add instances of objects to your games. You may add as many instances as you want, and the behavior of each of these objects will be governed by the events and actions that you assigned to its object definition. You will learn a lot more about objects and their associated events and actions throughout the remainder of this book.

## Creating Rooms

In games created with Game Maker, game play occurs inside rooms. Your games may consist of one or more rooms. For example, a game like *Pong* is played

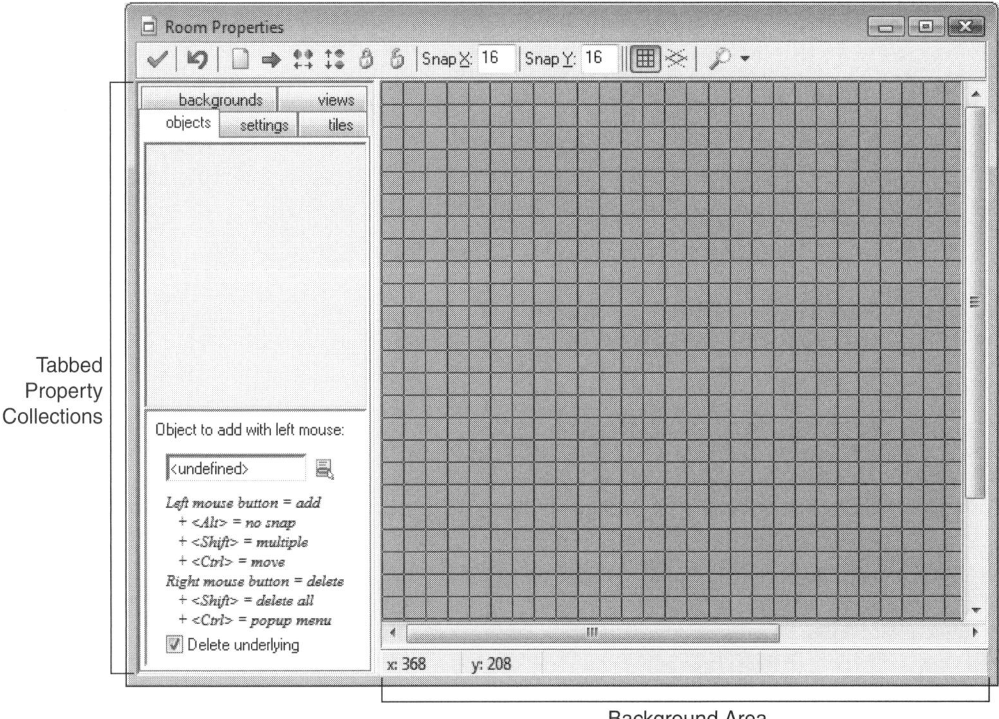


**Figure 2.11**
Games are played in a game world that consists of one or more rooms.

within a single room, whereas a game like *Pac-man* is played in different rooms, each of which would represent a different level in the game. Every Game Maker game must have at least one room to run. To add a room to a game, click on Resources > Create Room. In response, the Room Properties window is displayed, as shown in Figure 2.11.

Like all resources, rooms need a name and should be assigned a caption, representing text that will be displayed at the top of the game window in the titlebar. You specify this by selecting the Settings tab located on the left-hand side of the Room Properties window. Technically, all of the other resource types (sprites, objects, sounds, etc.) are optional, although without them your game would consist of empty rooms. To demonstrate, create a new game by clicking on File > New and then add a new room to it by clicking on Resources > Create Room. Now click on Run > Run Normally or the Run the Game button to run your new game. In response, Game Maker will compile your application and then run it, displaying an empty window.

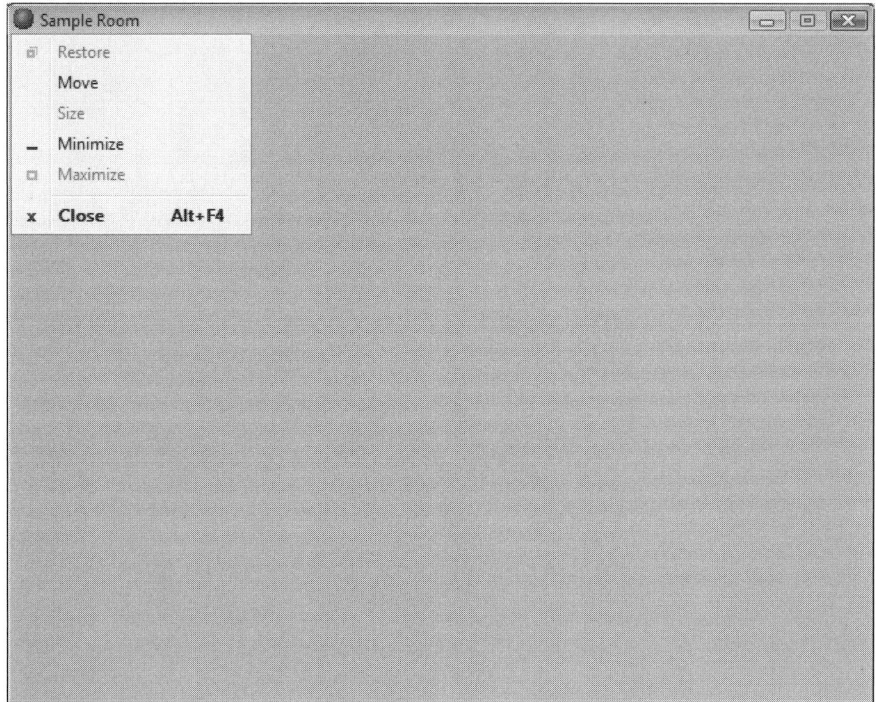


**Figure 2.12**
An example of a game consisting only of an empty room.

As demonstrated in Figure 2.12, you can click on the Game Maker icon located in the upper-left corner of the window to access a context menu with commands that you can use to control the size of the window and to close your application. Alternatively, you can click on the minimize, maximize, and close buttons located in the upper-right corner of the window. You can also move the window around by clicking and dragging on its toolbar. You can close the application by pressing the Escape key. All of the functionality is provided automatically, without you having to do anything to your application other than adding a room to it. Pretty cool, don't you think?

Of course, in order for your application to do something, you will need to add objects to it, assigning them different events and actions. You will also want to add different sprites, sounds, backgrounds, etc.

**Hint**

If you want, you can save your new application by clicking on File > Save. In response, the Save the Game window is displayed, allowing you to assign a name to your game and specify where you want it saved. Note that all Game Maker games are saved with a .gmk file extension.

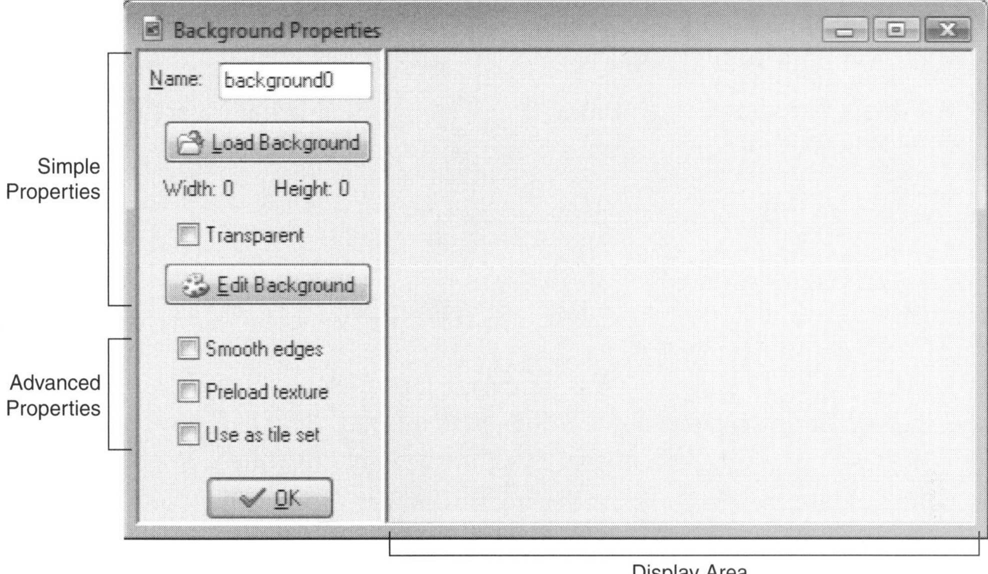


**Figure 2.13**
Backgrounds are used to enhance the visual appearance of your games.

## Creating Backgrounds

In order to make the rooms for your games more interesting, you can add graphical backgrounds to them. For example, if your game is one involving a spaceship shootout in outer space, you can make the game more interesting by adding a background of planets and stars. To add a background to your game, click on Resources > Create Background. In response, the Background properties window is displayed, as shown in Figure 2.13.

Using the Background Properties window, you can assign a name to the background and then click on the Load Background button to locate and load an existing graphics file, or you can click on the Edit Background button to open Game Maker's Sprite Editor window, allowing you to create a new background from scratch.

## Creating Scripts

You can create entire computer games using all of the previously described resources. However, there are limits as to how far you can go using only Game Maker's drag-and-drop icon based approach to game development. To create really advanced games, you need to learn how to program using Game Maker's built-in Game Maker Language (GML) scripting language. You work with GML in several ways, including:

- Adding scripts to your games and executing them using an action, or by calling upon them from within other scripts.
- Executing GML code statements as actions.
- Adding GML code to a room that will execute when the room is initially created.

For example, to add a script to your game, click on Resources > Create Script. In response, the Script properties window is displayed. This window services as Game Maker's script editor. You assign a unique name to your script by filling in the name field located in the script editor's toolbar. You can then add whatever code statements are required to accomplish your intended task, as demonstrated in Figure 2.14.

The script editor provides a number of handy features that help you when creating scripts. It has a toolbar that provides single-click access to various commands like copy and paste. It supports both undo and redo operations as

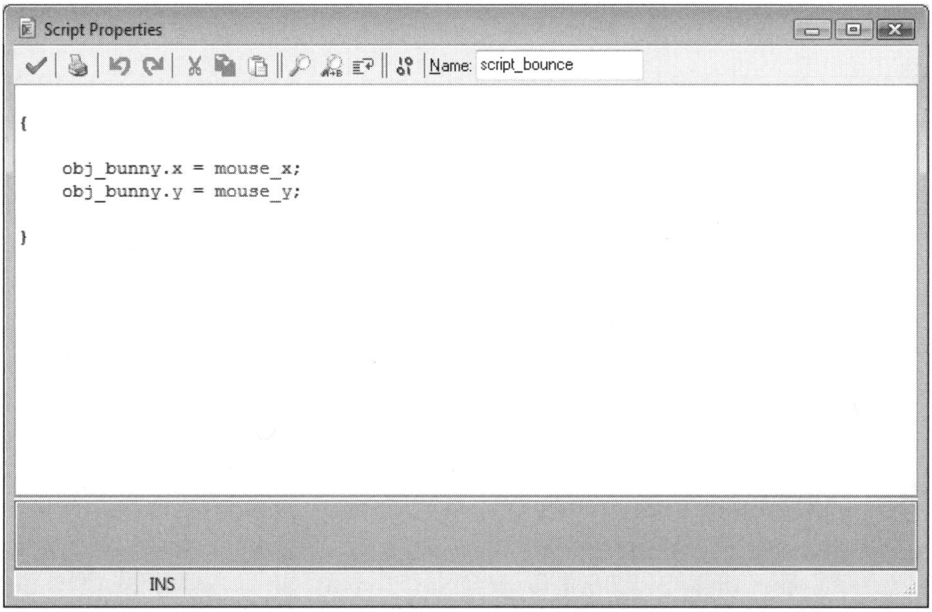

**Figure 2.14**
You can exercise greater control over the execution of your games using scripts.

well as search and replace. It automatically color codes all statements that you type and supports auto indenting of statements and intelligent tabbing. In addition to the toolbar commands, you can access editor commands from a context menu from within the windows by right-clicking in the code editing area and then selecting the appropriate command.

You will learn all about Game Maker's scripting capabilities and the Game Maker Language in Chapters 9 through 11.

## Outlining Game Information

An important feature for any game is the ability to display information about the game. This information may include instructions on how to play, as well as information about its creator and your website. To add this information to your game, double-click on the Game Information entry in the resource folder tree. In response, the Game Information window is displayed. This window looks and works just like a simple word processor, allowing you to enter text, specify different font types and sizes, and to specify various other attributes like bold, italics, underline, and color. Text can also be left or right justified or centered. Figure 2.15 shows an example of how you might use this window to provide the player with information about a game.

The player can access this information at any time during game play by pressing the F1 key. By default, when the F1 key is pressed, game play freezes and the game

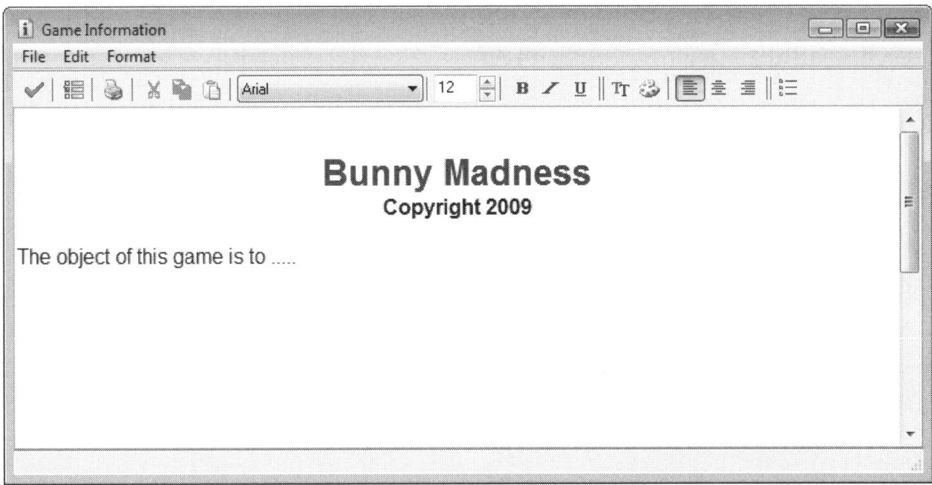


**Figure 2.15**
Enter game instructions and other text you want your users to see when they press the F1 key.

**Figure 2.16**
Configuring your game to display game information in a separate window.

information is displayed in the game window. If you want, you can instruct Game Maker to display game information in a separate window by opening the Game Information window and then clicking on File > Options. In response, the Game Information Options window is displayed, as shown in Figure 2.16.

To display game information in its own window, select the Show Help in a Separate Window option. You can specify a text string that will be displayed in the titlebar of the Game Information window. You can also specify the width and height of this window and various options that determine how the window is displayed.

## Specifying Global Game Settings

The Global Game Settings entry in the resource folder tree provides access to settings that control the configuration of various aspects of game operation, including things like whether the game loads in full screen mode or in a window and the resolution settings used to run the game. As shown in Figure 2.17, these settings are organized into a series of tabs located on the Global Game Settings window.

The following list provides a high level overview of the settings found on each of the tabs in the Global Games Settings window.

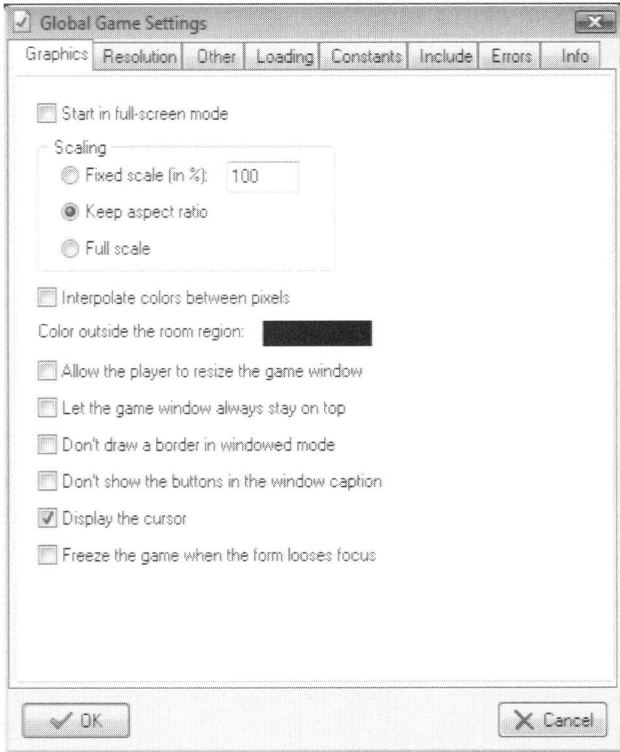


**Figure 2.17**
Game Maker allows you to configure a host of different settings that affect the operation of your games.

- **Graphics.** Contains options that govern whether the game is played within a window or in full screen mode as well as how games played in a window behave and whether or not the cursor should remain visible.
- **Resolution.** Allows you to determine whether the game changes the player's screen resolution. If this option is selected, screen resolution is returned to its previous state once the game is closed.
- **Other.** This tab allows you to prevent the Escape key from ending the game, prevent the F1 key from displaying the Game Information window, and disable operations associated with other function keys.
- **Loading.** This tab lets you replace Game Maker's default splash screen with an image of your own and lets you replace or suppress the progress bar and substitute the default game icon with one of your own choosing.

- **Constants.** Allows you to define global constant values that you can then reference from within scripts and actions.
- **Include.** Allows you to specify external files needed by your computer game to execute. These files will be included as part of your game's execution file, which will automatically export them when run. (Available only in the Pro version of Game Maker.)
- **Errors.** The configuration settings located on this tab determine whether error messages are displayed, whether they are recorded in the game_errors.log file, and whether your game terminates when non-fatal errors occur.
- **Info.** This tab allows you to enter your name, a version number for the game, as well as any other additional information you feel is important to maintain. Although not accessible to players, it helps to document your application and may prove useful to other game developers if you share the game's source code with them.

## Enhancing Game Maker's Capabilities

Game Maker is a highly extensible software development tool. One way of extending its capabilities is through the installation and addition of extension packages. Extension packages can add new actions, functions, and constants to Game Maker. Game Maker 7.0 comes with three extension packages. You can view these extension packages by double-clicking on the Extension Packages entry in the resource folder tree, as demonstrated in Figure 2.18.

If you select one of these extension packages, information about the package is displayed at the bottom of the window. If you want to use one of these extension packages in your game, select the package. In response, a button will be displayed between the used packages and the available packages lists. Click on this button to move the package to the used packages list.

Additional extension packages are available on the YoYo Games website by clicking on the Extensions link located on the http://www.yoyogames.com/resources page. To download one of these packages, click on its Download link and specify the location where you want to store the download. Depending on the download, you may get a file with a .gex file extension or a zip file with multiple files in it, including a .gex file. Once downloaded, you can install the

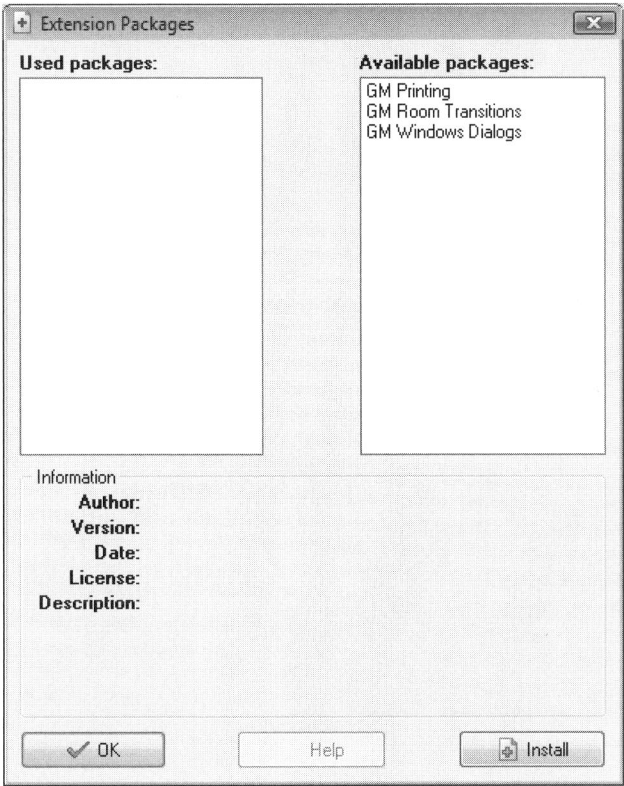


**Figure 2.18**
You can extend Game Maker's capabilities by installing additional extension packages.

extension package by opening the Extension Packages window and then clicking on the Install button. In response, the Installing Extension Packages window appears. Click on its Install button and then locate and select the .gex extension package's .gex file and click on Open.

**Hint**

> If you want to try your hand at creating extension packages, visit http://www.yoyogames.com/extensions and click on the Extension Maker link. This will initiate the download of a zip file containing a program that you can use to create new extension packages.

## Accessing Game Maker's Help Files

Another useful IDE resource that you will want to get familiar with is the Game Maker Help window, which you can access by clicking on Help > Contents. As demonstrated in Figure 2.19, you can access Game Maker's official document by

**Figure 2.19**
Game Maker's help file gives you easy access to technical information.

opening this window. Using the window's Index and Search options, you can quickly look up information on different topics, including all of Game Maker's events, actions, and functions.

## Configuring Game Maker Preferences

Game Maker is highly configurable. You make configuration changes to Game Maker by modifying its preferences, which you can access by clicking on File > Preferences. This displays the Preferences window, which is organized into a series of six tabbed screens. By default, Game Maker automatically displays the preferences belonging to the General tab as shown in Figure 2.20.

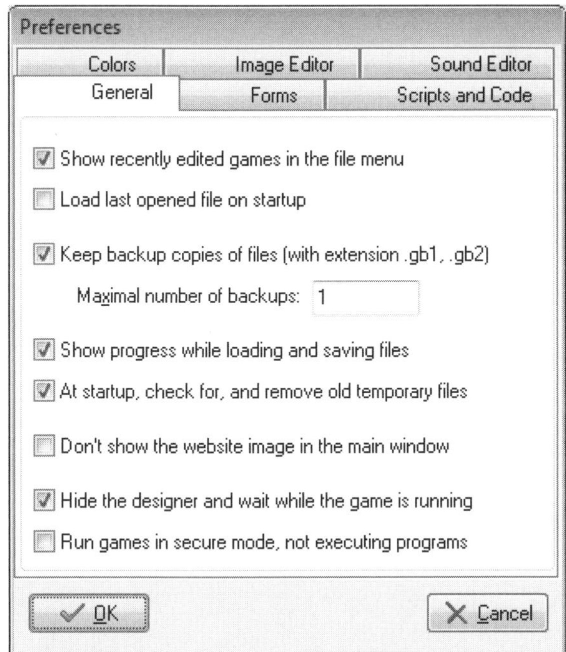


**Figure 2.20**
General preferences control what happens when Game Maker is initially started.

By modifying these preference settings you can configure the way Game Maker manages the display of recently edited games in the File menu and determine whether Game Maker automatically makes backups of your game files. From here you can also specify whether you want to see Game Maker's progress bar when it loads and saves your game files.

As shown in Figure 2.21, the Forms tab provides access to preference settings that affect the appearance and operations of the Sprite window, the Object window, and the Room window. By default, most of these settings are enabled. However, as you become more experienced with Game Maker, you may want to disable some of them.

Once you begin working on more advanced games, you will need to learn how to work with Game Maker's scripting language. The setting located on the Scripts and Code tab, shown in Figure 2.22, gives you control over a number of the editor controls provided by Game Maker's built-in Script Editor window.

Note that the last setting on the Script and Code tab allows you to stipulate an external code editor. If selected, Game Maker will load this editor in place of its

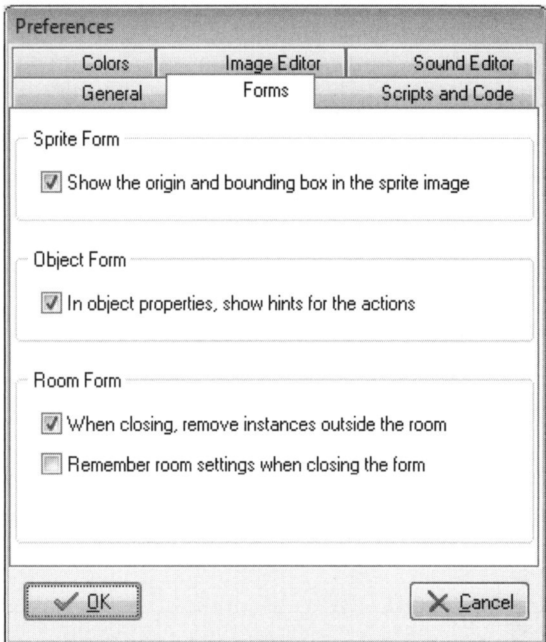


**Figure 2.21**
Form preferences affect the operation of different application form windows.

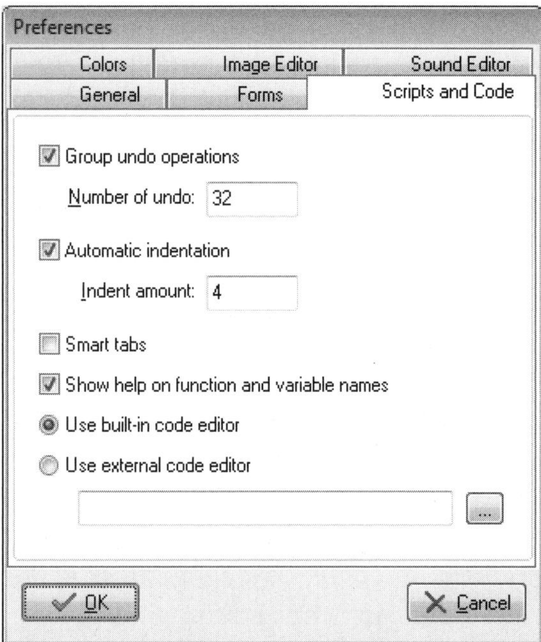


**Figure 2.22**
Scripts and Code preferences control the operation of Game Maker's built-in script editor.

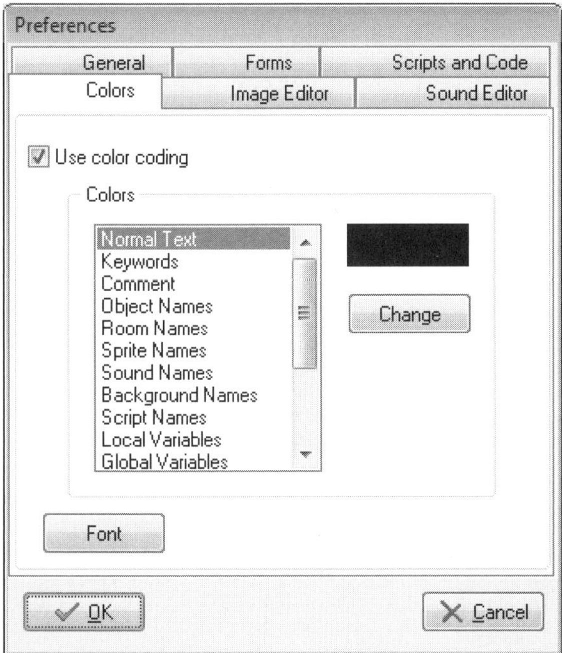


**Figure 2.23**
Color preferences specify the colors used by Game Maker to display text.

built-in editor, allowing you to work with a third-party script editor you are already familiar with.

By default, Game Maker's built-in script editor color-codes the words that make up script statements. This allows you to visually identify language keywords, comments, resource names, and so on and results in more readable code statements. You can turn off this feature by clicking on the Preferences window's Colors tab, shown in Figure 2.23.

Note that you can change the color scheme that Game Maker uses when displaying different parts of code statements. In addition, you can also modify the font and various font attributes to suit your own liking.

If you have a third-party graphics application that you would like to work with in place of Game Maker's built-in image editor, you can configure Game Maker to do so from the Image Editor tab, as shown in Figure 2.24. You may want to change image editors given that Game Maker's built-in editor only provides basic graphics manipulation and editing functionality.

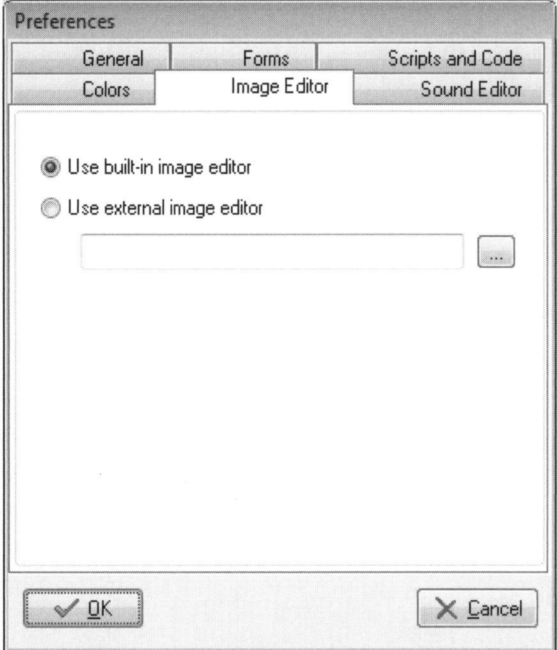


**Figure 2.24**
Image editor preferences allow you to specify an optional external image editor to be used when creating and editing sprites and backgrounds.

Lastly, one feature that is completely lacking in Game Maker is a sound editor. You will have to use a third-party sound editor if you need to create or modify your sound files. While Game Maker lets you import any wave or midi file, it cannot assist you in creating them. However, to make things more convenient, it allows you to configure Game Maker so that it can automatically load a third-party sound editor of your choice. To set this up, click on the Sound Editor tab, as shown in Figure 2.25.

**Trick**

Microsoft Windows comes equipped with a basic sound editor that you can configure Game Maker to use to edit wave files. On Windows Vista, this program is named SoundRecorder.exe and by default is located in C:\Windows\Systems32. On Windows XP this program is named Sndrec32.exe.

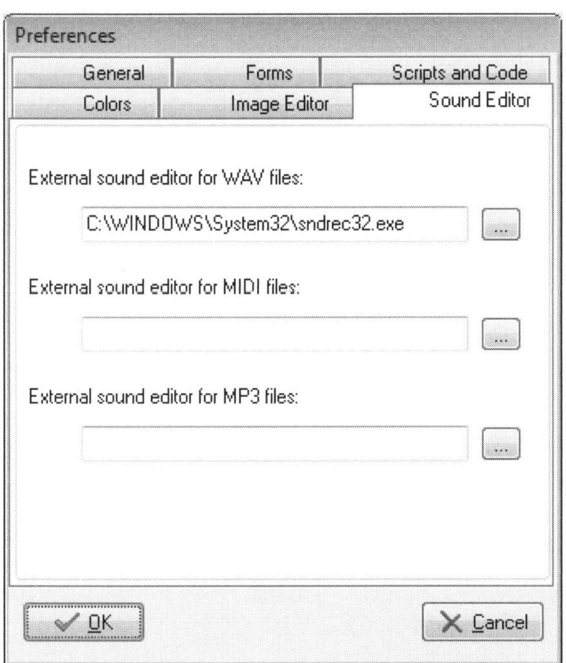


**Figure 2.25**
Sound Editor preferences allow you to specify a third-party application to be used when editing different types of sound files.

## Summary

This chapter introduced you to Game Maker's integrated development environment. You learned about all of the major parts of the IDE. This included learning how to work with menu and toolbar commands and to work with windows responsible for creating different types of game resources. You also learned how to configure various IDE preferences and settings as well as how to access Game Maker's help files.

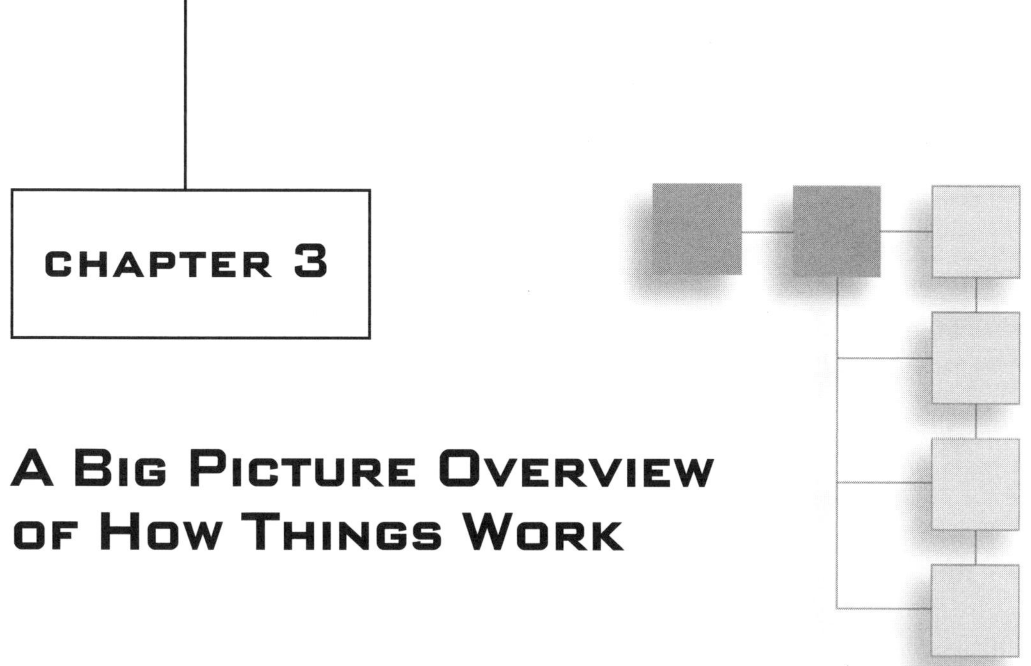

# Chapter 3

# A Big Picture Overview of How Things Work

Game Maker games consist of many different types of resources. At a minimum, every game must consist of at least one room. However, to really do anything, you must add different types of objects to your games and configure their appearance and behavior. Objects are the core components of every game, so a good understanding of them is essential. This chapter provides you with an overall view of how things work in Game Maker and then focuses in on objects, explaining how they are created and how to make them respond to events and perform actions. To help tie everything together, the chapter ends by walking you through the creation of a demo application, giving you the opportunity to make use of your new understanding of the objects and the Game Maker IDE.

An overview of the major topics covered in this chapter includes:

- How objects, sprites, rooms, sounds, and backgrounds come together to create games
- How to create objects and configure their properties
- How to configure objects to respond to different types of events
- How to use action icons to specify object behavior

## Big Picture Time

As you learned in Chapter 2, every Game Maker game consists at an absolute minimum of at least one room, although games can consist of as many rooms as necessary. These *rooms* can serve as different locations or parts of a larger game world. Alternatively, in a game made up of different levels, you can use rooms as the basis for each new level. To bring your games to life, you need to add different objects to these rooms. These *objects* are things like planes, cars, tanks, and monsters as well as missiles, bullets, bouncing balls, and obstacles like walls.

Objects are the key elements upon which games are based. In order to be able to see them, objects must be assigned *sprites*. Sometimes objects are represented by more than one sprite to allow for the animation of that object. For example, the sprite shown in Figure 3.1, which consists of two subimages, might be used to animate the movement of a bug. If you look closely at both images, you will notice that the bug's limbs are at different locations. By switching between the two images when the sprite moves, you can create the illusion that the sprite is walking.

Most objects are visible to the user during game play, but they don't have to be. While some objects, such as walls, don't do anything, most of the objects in games move around and interact with one another in some form. Objects can move on their own or under the control of the player. As objects move, they may collide within one another, such as when a player hits a ball with a bat in a baseball game or when a missile hits a spaceship in an outer space shootout game.

Players control certain objects in games. For example, in an adventure game the player may move the main character around the game world in search of treasure and adventure. In a *Pac-man*-style game, the player moves the Pac-man character around a maze. In addition, other things occur during game play that the player has little if any control over. For example, in *Pac-man*, ghosts move around the maze and sometimes chase the Pac-man.

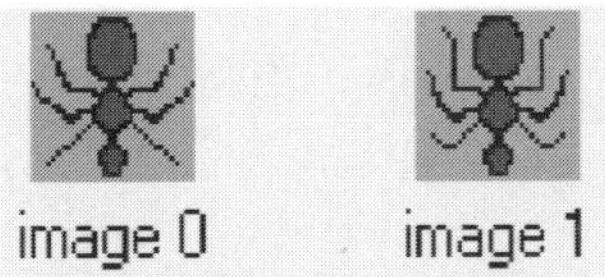


**Figure 3.1**
Using a sprite with multiple subimages, you can animate sprite movement.

The different things that occur during game play are referred to as *events*. Events occur for all sorts of reasons. For example, events automatically occur when a game is first started or when a room is first displayed. Using these events, your game can set certain things into motion, such as the movement of ghosts in *Pac-man* or the launching of missiles at enemy space ships in a space shootout game. Events also occur when the player does something. For example, events occur when the player presses keyboard keys or moves the mouse around. Events also occur when objects run into one another, creating *collision* events. Game Maker support dozens of different types of events.

A big part of game development is deciding to what events you want the objects to react. You specify the actions that objects make in response to events by assigning different action icons to events belonging to objects. For example, if a missile object collides with a spaceship object, you might specify a series of actions that might include:

- Destroying the missile object
- Destroying the spaceship object
- Creating and displaying an explosion object
- Playing a sound
- Subtracting one from the number of player lives
- Restarting the current room (level)

The actions outlined above represent only a small subset of the number of actions that Game Maker supports. As of the writing of this book, Game Maker 7.0 Pro supports 125 different action icons.

To make the rooms in your games more interesting, you will want to decorate them by either assigning them a background color or by using one or more graphic background images to create a suitable playing field or backdrop. In addition to using colorful and well-designed graphics for sprites and backgrounds to make your games visually appealing, you will also want to add sounds to your games to make them more realistic and fun. Use of sound usually involves the addition of sound effects that are played to identify when events occur, such as when a ball slams into a wall or when a missile hits a plane and blows it up. In addition to sound effects, most games include background music that helps to establish a mood and to convey a sense of urgency, suspense, excitement, etc.

To summarize, to create a game using Game Maker you must:

- Create at least one room
- Populate the room(s) with its objects (which are represented by sprites)
- Specify the different types of events that the objects should respond to
- Assign actions to objects that tell them what actions to perform when events occur.

**Hint**

The key components to any Game Maker game are objects, rooms, sprites, sounds, and backgrounds. In addition to these components, more advanced games may consist of other types of components, including paths, scripts, fonts, and timelines. This chapter's primary focus is on objects. You'll dig deeper into sprites, sounds, backgrounds, and rooms in Chapter 4. In addition, other game resources will be demonstrated in some of the book's later chapters.

## Understanding Objects

A critical component in any game is the objects that you define. These objects represent everything that the player sees and interacts with in the game, except for backgrounds. In addition, many games make use of invisible objects, which although unseen by the player, are used to control key activities within the game. A good understanding of objects, their relationship to one another, and their interactions with each other and the player is essential to any Game Maker developer.

Objects represent things like cars, ships, planes, monsters, bullets, missiles, and so on in games. Most, though not all, objects are represented by a graphical sprite. Objects are designed to react to events that occur during computer games, such as when the player presses a keyboard key or moves the mouse or when two objects collide with one another, such as when a missile hits a tank in a tank battle game. Objects are created by clicking on Resources > Create Object. This displays the Object Properties window as shown in Figure 3.2.

Objects are really just blueprints or templates that define all attributes of an entity in your game as well as the events that the entities respond to and the actions the entities take in response to those events. Once defined, you can add instances of objects to your game. Each instance that you add is a mirror copy of the object.

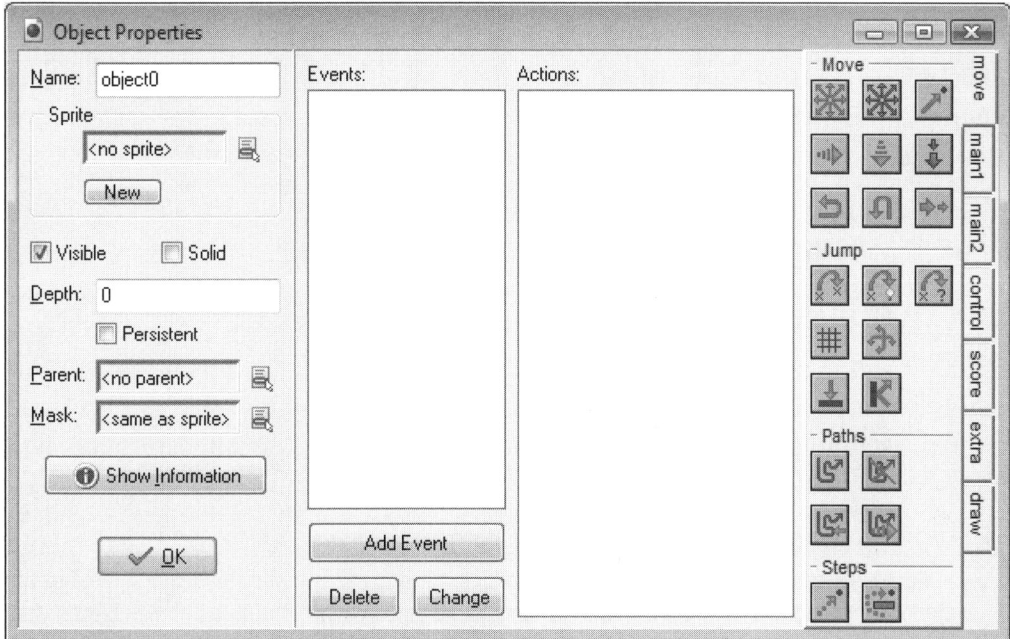


**Figure 3.2**
Adding a new object to a Game Maker game.

You can add as many instances of an object as you want to a game. As such, you can define an object representing an enemy fighter plane and then use it as the basis for instantiating any number of enemy aircraft in a computer game.

## Setting Object Properties

Objects are complex entities that consist of a number of properties. Objects have a name, which must be unique within an application. By assigning an object a sprite, you make it possible for the game to display it. In addition, by displaying an object's `Visible` property, you can control whether its sprite is visible or not. By enabling or disabling an object's `Solid` property, you can determine whether an object can create a collision when it makes contact with other solid objects.

Objects also have a `Depth` property that determines whether they are drawn on top of or under other objects when they overlap one another. Objects with a higher depth value are drawn first. Objects with a lower value are drawn last (on top). You can even assign a negative value to an object to ensure that it is always drawn on top of other objects. Objects assigned the same depth are drawn in the order in which they are created.

By default, objects are deleted when they leave rooms. However, by enabling an object's `Persistent` property, you can keep it alive for as long as you want, thus making it possible to move objects between rooms. An object's `Mask` property is used when working with 3D objects to help determine when collisions occur.

Objects can also have child/parent relationships with one another. Objects in Game Maker support a mechanism known as inheritance, which provides you with a powerful means of managing and configuring common object properties and actions. Every object can be assigned a parent. Property changes made to a parent object are automatically reflected in its child objects. Thus if you create a game that uses an army of robots, you can create a parent robot object and configure it, and then, by assigning it as the parent object for other robot objects, automatically configure all of the child objects. That's a real time-saver.

**Hint**

As already stated, parent objects can also have parent objects, but you need to make sure that you do not create any cyclical relations. In other words, you cannot assign a parent object's child object as its parent object.

If necessary, you can further configure child objects. Any changes made to the child object that conflict with those specified in the parent object automatically override the parent's settings. Objects inherit both the properties and actions of their parents. You can create as many levels of parent/child relationships as you need, in effect defining child, parent, and grandparent objects and so on. One common development technique that Game Maker developers often use is to create a *master* object and use that object to outline default properties and actions for other objects. This way, if you ever need to modify object behavior, all you need to do is to modify the master object. This can save you tons of time in creating and modifying your games and sure beats having to create objects from scratch or even creating new objects by copying existing ones.

**Hint**

If you elect to use the master object as an active character within a game, any collisions that occur with this object also apply to all of its child objects. So you'll need to be careful if you use this approach. Note, however, that if a child object has a collision, the collision has no effect on the child's parent object.

## Configuring Objects to React to Events

In order for objects to do anything, you must configure them to respond to different types of events that occur during game play. Events are a type of message that Game Maker generates during game play, informing objects when things occur. Using Game Maker's event-driven approach, you can specify different types of actions you want the object to take when different types of events occur. Table 3.1 provides a high-level overview of the different types of events to which all objects can be configured to respond.

**Table 3.1** Game Maker Events

| Event | Icon | Description |
|---|---|---|
| Create | Create | Occurs when an instance is created |
| Destroy | Destroy | Occurs when an instance is destroyed or deleted |
| Alarm | Alarm | Occurs after a specified number of steps elapse (every instance supports up to 12 alarm events) |
| Step | Step | Occurs continuously throughout application execution providing you with the ability to repeatedly execute actions during game play |
| Collision | Collision | Occurs when two instances collide (touch) one another during game play |
| Keyboard | Keyboard | Occurs when the player presses a keyboard key, allowing your application to repeatedly execute one or more actions for as long as a keyboard key is being pressed |
| Mouse | Mouse | Occurs when the player moves the mouse or clicks on one of its buttons, allowing your application to respond to user input |
| Other | Other | A collection of events that do not fit into other categories that can be used to initiate actions in response to events that occur, for example, when a game or room is started or ended, when a player runs out of lives or health, or when an object moves outside of a room |
| Draw | Draw | Allows you to take control of game activity when a sprite drawing event occurs, allowing you to draw a different sprite or to execute any number of alternative actions |
| Key Press | Key Press | Occurs when the player presses down on a keyboard key allowing your application to respond when a keyboard key is initially pressed |
| Key Release | Key Release | Occurs when the player releases a keyboard key, allowing your application to respond whenever a pressed key is released |
| Cancel | Cancel | Closes the Event Selector window (not an event) |

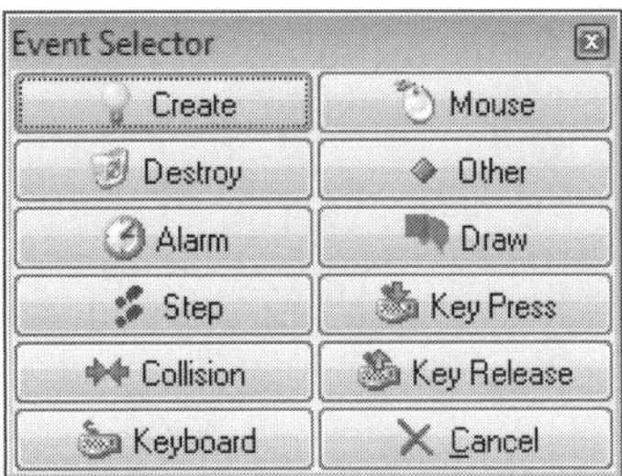


**Figure 3.3**
Click on a button to specify the type of event you want an object to work with.

As you can see, Game Maker supports a considerable number of events. To specify the events you want to assign to an object, you click on the Object Properties window's Add Event button located below the events list. This displays the Event Selector window shown in Figure 3.3.

Once added, events are displayed in the events list column of the Object Properties window.

**Trick**

> You can drag and drop a copy of an event between objects. Doing so copies any actions associated with the event.

## Adding Actions to Objects

Adding events to objects is only half of the story. In order to enable objects to respond to events, you must assign and configure specific types of actions to those events. Game Maker comes equipped with all kinds of predefined actions that it makes accessible on seven sets of tabs located on the right-hand side of the Object Properties window, shown in Figure 3.4 and as listed here:

- **Move.** The actions that control the movement of objects.
- **Main1.** These actions create, modify, and destroy instances of objects; change the sprites assigned to objects; control sound playback; and control movement between different rooms.
- **Main2.** These actions control timing within a game, allow a scene to be paused for a specified period of time, display text messages and game information, and provide the ability to restart, terminate, save, and load games.
- **Control.** These actions perform the conditional execution of actions, execute GML code and scripts, and create and access variable data.

**Figure 3.4**
Game Maker provides easy access to 125 different actions.

- **Score.** These actions assist you in keeping track of player score, health, and lives.
- **Extra.** These actions work with Game Maker's particle system, enabling you to add various special effects to your games, including rain, snow, smoke, and explosions.
- **Draw.** These actions facilitate the drawing of sprites within rooms, allowing you to take control of and manage Game Maker's drawing operations.

To assign one or more actions to an event, you must select the event and then drag and drop actions onto the actions area. Each action is identified by a description icon that identifies what the action does. In addition, if you move the mouse pointer over an action, Game Maker will display a brief description of the action in a popup window.

Depending on the action selected, Game Maker may display a configuration window when you drop the action on the actions area, allowing you to specify how the action should execute. While configuration options may vary, two common parameters appear on most actions. These options include the Applies to and Relative options. For example, Figure 3.5 shows the window that appears when the Moved Fixed action is added to an event.

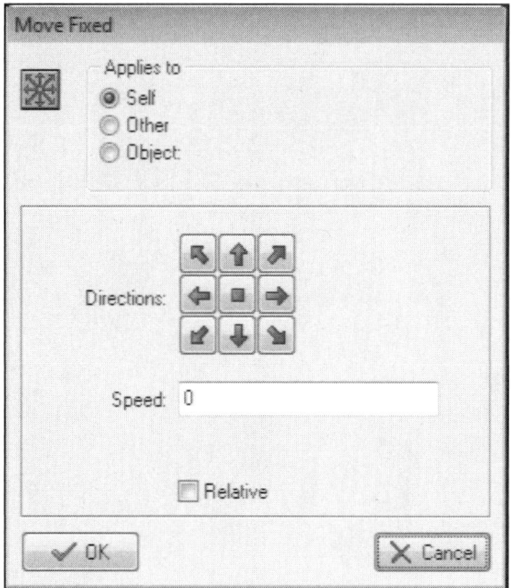


**Figure 3.5**
Most actions include the Applies to and Relative options located at the top and bottom of the Action Configuration window.

The `Applies to` option allows you to select one of three choices. `Self` sets the object to which the action belongs as the target for the action. When working with collision, the `Other` option lets you apply the action to the other object involved in the collision. Lastly, the `Object` option lets you specify the name of any object you want as the target of the action. By default, when assigning a numeric value of an object, Game Maker replaces its value with the value specified on the configuration window. However, by selecting the `Relative` option, you can instruct Game Maker to increment the value by the amount specified.

A quick review of all of the actions provided through the Game Maker IDE is provided in the sections that follow. This is followed by how to create a demo application, with specific focus on the definition of objects, events, and actions.

**Hint**

> The sheer number of available actions can be a little difficult to take in all at once. I suggest you glance through the tables shown in the following sections and that you bookmark these pages so that you can come back to them later when you need to locate a specific type of action.

### *Controlling Object Movement*

Game Maker provides a large number of actions that control the movement of objects. The actions, located on the Move tab, are outlined in Table 3.2.

**Table 3.2** Game Maker's Move Actions

| Subcategory | Icon | Action | Edition | Description |
|---|---|---|---|---|
| Move |  | Move Fixed | Lite/Pro | Moves an instance in one of a number of predefined directions |
| |  | Move Free | Lite/Pro | Moves an instance in a specified direction (between 0 and 360 degrees) |
| |  | Move Towards | Lite/Pro | Specifies a position and speed an instance should move toward |
| |  | Speed Horizontal | Lite/Pro | Sets the speed of an instance as it moves horizontally |
| |  | Speed Vertical | Lite/Pro | Sets the speed of an instance as it moves vertically |
| |  | Set Gravity | Lite/Pro | Specifies the direction and speed at which gravity affects an instance |
| |  | Reverse Horizontal | Lite/Pro | Reverses the horizontal direction of an instance |
| |  | Reverse Vertical | Lite/Pro | Reverses the vertical direction of an instance |
| |  | Set Friction | Lite/Pro | Applies friction to an instance as it moves |
| Jump |  | Jump to Position | Lite/Pro | Jumps an instance to a specific location |
| |  | Jump to Start | Lite/Pro | Jumps an instance to the location where it was created |
| |  | Jump to Random | Lite/Pro | Jumps an instance to a random location within a room |
| |  | Align to Grid | Lite/Pro | Ensures that an instance's location is kept in alignment with the room's grid |
| |  | Wrap Screen | Lite/Pro | Moves an instance exiting one side of a room to the other side of the room |
| |  | Move to Contact | Lite/Pro | Moves an instance until it collides with another instance |
| |  | Bounce | Lite/Pro | Bounces an instance away from another instance when a collision occurs |
| Paths |  | Set Path | Lite/Pro | Instructs an instance to follow a specific path |
| |  | End Path | Lite/Pro | Instructs an instance to stop on its specified path |
| |  | Path Position | Lite/Pro | Changes an instance's position on a path |
| |  | Path Speed | Lite/Pro | Modifies the speed at which an instance moves along a path |
| Steps |  | Step Towards | Lite/Pro | Instructs an instance to move toward a position on a path |
| |  | Step Avoiding | Lite/Pro | Moves an instance along a path while attempting to avoid any obstacles that may be in the way |

### *Actions that Affect Objects, Sprites, Sounds, and Rooms*

Game Maker has a large number of actions that can do things like create instances of objects, change sprites, play sounds, and move between the different rooms that make up your games. These actions, outlined in Table 3.3, are located on the Main1 tab.

**Table 3.3** Game Maker's Main1 Actions

| Subcategory | Icon | Action | Edition | Description |
|---|---|---|---|---|
| Objects | | Create Instance | Lite/Pro | Creates a new instance of a specified object |
| | | Create Moving | Lite/Pro | Creates a new object, assigning it a speed and direction |
| | | Create Random | Lite/Pro | Creates an instance using a pool of 1 to 4 objects at a specified location |
| | | Change Instance | Lite/Pro | Changes the current instance of an object into an instance of another object |
| | | Destroy Instance | List/Pro | Destroys an instance of an object |
| | | Destroy at Position | Lite/Pro | Destroys any instances within a specified area |
| Sprite | | Change Sprite | Lite/Pro | Changes the sprite or subimage used to represent an instance |
| | | Transform Sprite | Pro | Changes the size and orientation of an instance's sprite |
| | | Color Sprite | Pro | Changes a sprite's color by blending its colors with a specified color |
| Sounds | | Play Sound | Lite/Pro | Plays a specified Sound resource |
| | | Stop Sound | Lite/Pro | Stops playback of a specified Sound resource |
| | | Check Sound | Lite/Pro | Checks to see if a specified Sound resource is being played |
| Rooms | | Previous Room | Lite/Pro | Moves to the game's previous room |
| | | Next Room | Lite/Pro | Moves to the game's next room |
| | | Restart Room | Lite/Pro | Restarts a room back to its initial state |
| | | Different Room | Lite/Pro | Moves to a specified room |
| | | Check Previous | Lite/Pro | Checks to see if a previous room exists |
| | | Check Next | Lite/Pro | Checks to see if the next room exists |

### *Controlling Game Timing, Restarts, and Resources*

Game Maker also provides access to actions that you can use to control timing within a game, allow a scene to be paused for a specified period of time, and display text messages and game information. In addition, there are actions that provide you with the ability to restart, terminate, save, and load games. These actions, located on the Main2 tab, are outlined in Table 3.4.

### *Adding Actions that Control Object Execution*

Actions located on the Control tab, listed in Table 3.5, control when other types of actions are performed. These actions involve some sort of analysis in which a

**Table 3.4** Game Maker's Main2 Actions

| Subcategory | Icon | Action | Edition | Description |
|---|---|---|---|---|
| Timing | | Set Alarm | Lite/Pro | Sets one of twelve alarm clocks for an instance |
| | | Sleep | Lite/Pro | Pauses a scene for a specified amount of time |
| | | Set Time Line | Lite/Pro | Assigns a timeline to an instance |
| | | Time Line Position | Lite/Pro | Sets or modifies the position within a timeline |
| Info | | Display Message | Lite/Pro | Displays a text string in a dialog window |
| | | Show Info | Lite/Pro | Displays game information in a window |
| | | Show Video | Pro | Plays a video |
| Game | | Restart Game | Lite/Pro | Restarts a game |
| | | End Game | Lite/Pro | Terminates a game |
| | | Save Game | Lite/Pro | Saves the current status of a game |
| | | Load Game | Lite/Pro | Loads game status for a previously saved game |
| Resources | | Replace Sprite | Pro | Replaces a sprite with an image from a graphic file |
| | | Replace Sound | Pro | Replaces a sound with a sound loaded from an audio file |
| | | Replace Background | Pro | Replaces a background with an image loaded from a graphic file |

**Table 3.5** Game Maker's Control Actions

| Subcategory | Icon | Action | Edition | Description |
|---|---|---|---|---|
| Questions | | Check Empty | Lite/Pro | Determines if an instance would generate a collision if placed in a specified location (e.g., to determine if it is safe to move the instance) |
| | | Check Collision | Lite/Pro | Determines if a collision has occurred |
| | | Check Object | Lite/Pro | Determines if an instance has come into contact with another specified instance |
| | | Test Instance Count | Lite/Pro | Counts the total number of instances for a specified object |
| | | Test Chance | Lite/Pro | Generates a random value by rolling a virtual die |
| | | Check Question | Lite/Pro | Interacts with the player by displaying a text string and prompts the player to click on a Yes or No button |
| | | Test Expression | Lite/Pro | Evaluates an expression and executes the next action if the expression evaluates as being true |
| | | Check Mouse | Lite/Pro | Determines whether a mouse button is being pressed |
| | | Check Grid | Lite/Pro | Determines whether an object is evenly aligned with the grid |
| Other | | Start Block | Lite/Pro | Specifies the beginning of a block of actions |
| | ELSE | Else | Lite/Pro | Executes the next action when the results of the previous evaluation proves false |
| | | Exit Event | Lite/Pro | Stops the execution of actions for the current event |
| | | End Block | Lite/Pro | Specifies the end of a block of actions |
| | | Repeat | Lite/Pro | Repeats the execution of one or more blocks a specified number of times |
| | CALL EVENT | Call Parent Event | Lite/Pro | Calls an event within a parent object |
| Code | | Execute Code | Lite/Pro | Executes GML code typed into the action form |
| | | Execute Script | Lite/Pro | Executes GML code stored as a script |
| | | Comment | Lite/Pro | Adds a comment line to the actions lists, displays text in italic |
| Variables | VAR | Set Variable | Lite/Pro | Creates a variable and assigns a value to it |
| | VAR | Test Variable | Lite/Pro | Evaluates the value assigned to a variable |
| | VAR | Draw Variable | Lite/Pro | Draws (displays) the value assigned to a variable |

condition is examined. If the condition proves true, one or more additional actions are performed; otherwise, they are skipped. Other actions let you specify actions to be performed in the event an analysis proves false. Using Start blocks and End blocks you can even group collections of actions together, allowing you to conditionally control the execution of all the actions embedded within the block, in very much the same manner that programmers control the conditional statement execution when writing program code.

### *Keeping Score and Managing Player Lives and Health*

Game Maker maintains a built-in score feature that makes it easy for you to keep track of the player's score. Game Maker also facilitates the tracking of player lives, which you can interact with and control using various actions. Lastly, Game Maker maintains a mechanism for assigning and tracking a player's health that, like score and lives, can be managed using various actions. All of these actions, outlined below in Table 3.6, are available on the Score tab.

### *Creating Special Effects and Playing Music CDs*

The actions located on the Extra tab, outlined in Table 3.7, are designed to work with Game Maker's particle system, which can add a variety of special effects to your games. These special effects include things like fireworks, rain, and snow, and are made possible through Game Maker's built-in particle system.

**Hint**

> You can exercise even more detailed control over Game Maker's particle system using functions made available to scripts written in GML. You will learn about programming using GML later in this book, in Chapters 9 through 11.

*Particles* are small, consisting of individual pixels or small sprites. A subset of Game Maker's particle system can be accessed through different particle actions. Particles have a shape, size, and color. They exist for a limited amount of time and move in a specified speed and direction and are affected through the application of gravity. Particles are created using particle emitters and can be created in bursts or a constant stream. Game Maker allows you to work with up to eight particle emitters at a time. Also included on the Extra tab are actions that allow you to play and control the playback of CDs.

### *Drawing Shapes, Sprites, and Text*

The default behavior in Game Maker is for games to manage the drawing of sprites within rooms. However, using various actions made available on the

**Table 3.6** Game Maker's Score Actions

| Subcategory | Icon | Action | Edition | Description |
|---|---|---|---|---|
| Score | | Set Score | Lite/Pro | Sets or changes the player's score |
| | | Test Score | Lite/Pro | Evaluates the value of the player's score |
| | | Draw Score | Lite/Pro | Draws (displays) the value assigned to the player's score |
| | | Show Highscore | Lite/Pro | Displays the top ten scores for the game in a highscore list table |
| | | Clear Highscore | Lite/Pro | Clears out the values stored in the highscore list table |
| Lives | | Set Lives | Lite/Pro | Sets or changes the number of lives the player has left in the game |
| | | Test Lives | Lite/Pro | Evaluates the value of lives the player has left in the game |
| | | Draw Lives | Lite/Pro | Draws (displays) the number of lives that the player has left in the game |
| | | Draw Life Images | Lite/Pro | Substitutes graphic images representing player lives in place of text when displaying the number of lives remaining |
| Health | | Set Health | Lite/Pro | Sets or changes the player's health |
| | | Test Health | Lite/Pro | Evaluates the value of the player's health |
| | | Draw Health | Lite/Pro | Draws (displays) the value assigned to the player's health |
| | | Score Caption | Lite/Pro | Allows you to specify whether Game Maker should display the player's score, lives, and health in the game window's titlebar |

Draw tab, outlined in Table 3.8, you can modify this behavior and dictate how drawing operations are handled.

## Putting Everything Together

Okay, now that we have reviewed the overall big picture of game development using Game Maker and spent some time focusing on the importance of objects and their support for events and actions, let's work on a demo program named BouncingBall that will help tie everything together. To begin, start Game Maker,

**Table 3.7** Game Maker's Extra Actions

| Subcategory | Icon | Action | Edition | Description |
|---|---|---|---|---|
| Particles | | Create Part System | Pro | Creates a particle system |
| | | Destroy Part System | Pro | Destroys a particle system |
| | | Clear Part System | Pro | Clears out any currently displayed particles |
| | | Create Particle | Pro | Creates a specified particle type |
| | | Particle Color | Pro | Sets the color used when drawing a particle |
| | | Particle Life | Pro | Specifies how long a particle is to remain visible |
| | | Particle Speed | Pro | Assigns the speed and direction used when particles move |
| | | Particle Gravity | Pro | Allows you to affect the movement of particles by applying gravity to them |
| | | Particle Secondary | Pro | Allows you to create new particles from existing ones |
| | | Create Emitter | Pro | Creates up to eight particle emitters, which are required to generate particles |
| | | Destroy Emitter | Pro | Destroys a specified particle emitter |
| | | Burst from Emitter | Pro | Instructs a particle emitter to begin generating particles |
| | | Stream from Emitter | Pro | Instructs Game Maker to begin streaming a specified number of particles |
| CD | | Play CD | Pro | Plays tracks located on a CD |
| | | Stop CD | Pro | Stops CD playback |
| | | Pause CD | Pro | Pauses CD playback |
| | | Resume CD | Pro | Resumes CD playback |
| | | Check CD | Pro | Checks to see if there is a CD in the computer's default CD drive |
| | | Check CD Playing | Pro | Checks to see if the computer's default CD contains a CD |
| Other | | Set Cursor | Pro | Replaces the mouse pointer with a sprite |
| | | Open Webpage | Pro | Opens a specified web page using the player's default web browser |

**Table 3.8** Game Maker's Draw Actions

| Subcategory | Icon | Action | Edition | Description |
|---|---|---|---|---|
| Drawing |  | Draw Sprite | Lite/Pro | Draws a sprite and subimage at a specified position |
| |  | Draw Background | Lite/Pro | Draws a background at a specified position |
| |  | Draw Text | Lite/Pro | Draws text at a specified position |
| |  | Draw Scaled Text | Pro | Draws text using a specified horizontal and vertical scaling at a specified position |
| |  | Draw Rectangle | Lite/Pro | Draws a rectangle shape based on specified attributes |
| |  | Horizontal Gradient | Pro | Draws a rectangle using a horizontally drawn gradient color |
| |  | Vertical Gradient | Pro | Draws a rectangle using a vertically drawn gradient color |
| |  | Draw Ellipse | Lite/Pro | Draws an ellipse using specified attributes |
| | 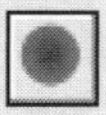 | Gradient Ellipse | Pro | Draws an ellipse using gradient color |
| |  | Draw Line | Lite/Pro | Draws a line between two specified sets of coordinates |
| |  | Draw Arrow | Lite/Pro | Draws an arrow between two specified sets of coordinates |
| Settings |  | Set Color | Lite/Pro | Specifies the color to be used when performing a drawing operation |
| |  | Set Font | Lite/Pro | Specifies the font type and attribute data used when drawing text |
| |  | Set Full Screen | Lite/Pro | Changes screen display mode to either full screen or a window |
| Other |  | Take Snapshot | Pro | Captures a screen shot of the game, storing it as a bitmap (.bmp) file |
| |  | Create Effect | Pro | Creates various effects like rain, snow, smoke, and explosions |

or if Game Maker is already running, click on File > New to create a new application. In response, the Game Maker IDE appears as shown in Figure 3.6.

Once complete, the demo will display a window that shows a purple ball bouncing around the screen. The demo will execute within a single window. Each time the ball moves across the screen, it eventually makes contact (collides) with a wall that surrounds the window. After hitting the wall, the ball will bounce off,

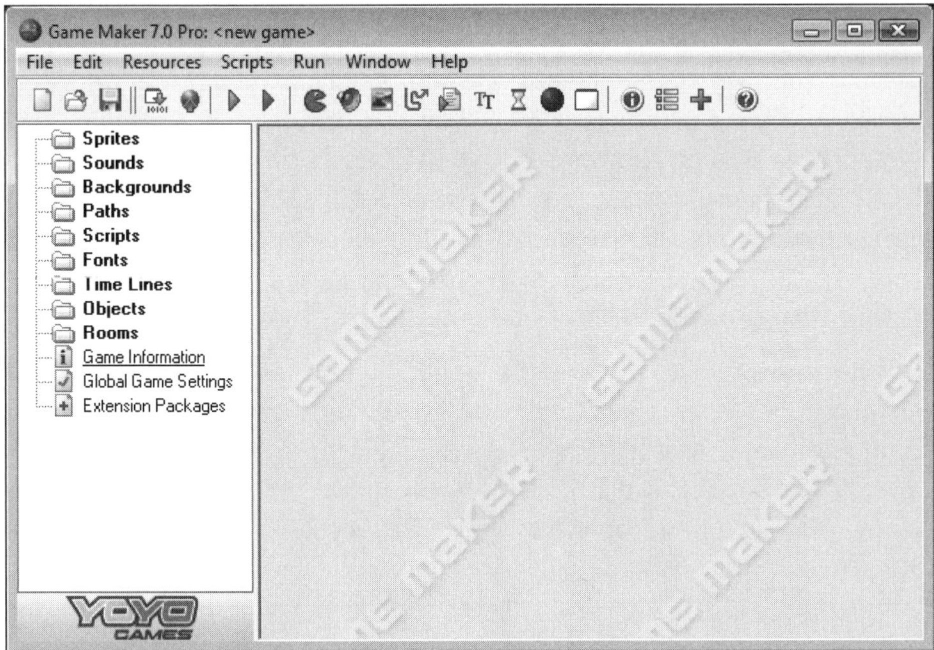


**Figure 3.6**
Beginning the development of a New Game Maker application.

heading in a different direction. In addition, each time the ball collides with one of the game's four walls a sound is played.

In order to create this game, you will need to perform a number of steps, as outlined here:

1. Define two sprites, one to represent the purple ball, and one to represent the wall.
2. Define the sound that will be use to generate the game's sound effect.
3. Configure the game's background.
4. Define two objects, one representing the ball and another representing the wall object.
5. Add a room to the game; populate the room with instances of both objects and configure various room properties.
6. Configure the ball object to respond to various events and perform specific actions.

Once you have completed these steps, you will be able to save and run the demo.

## Step 1—Defining Sprites Used by the Demo

The first step in creating the BouncingBall demo is to create the sprites it will use to represent objects during game play. While you can certainly use Game Maker's built-in graphic editor to create your sprites from scratch, this editor only provides basic editing capabilities. Most game developers elect instead to either create their sprites using a more powerful third-party tool or to acquire their sprites from other sources, such as purchasing them from professional graphic artists or myriad of sprite packages that can be purchased and downloaded from the Internet.

For this demo, you will use two sprites supplied by Game Maker (as part of the collection of sprites that it stores by default in a collection of folders located at C:\Program Files\Game Maker7\Sprites). Let's begin by creating a sprite for the game's ball. To do so, click on Resources > Create Sprite. This will add a new sprite to the application and open the Sprite Properties window, as shown in Figure 3.7.

Type **spr_ball** in the Name file and then click on the Load Sprite button. Using the Open dialog window that appears, drill down into the Sprites\Various folder, select the Ball2.ico file, and then click on the Open button. A picture of the purple ball should be visible when you are returned to the Sprite Properties window. Click on OK to close the Sprite Properties window.

Repeating the steps outlined above, create a second sprite, this time naming it spr_wall and loading Square.ico file, also located in the Sprites\Various folder. These two sprites are the only sprites that you will need to define to create the BouncingBall demo program.

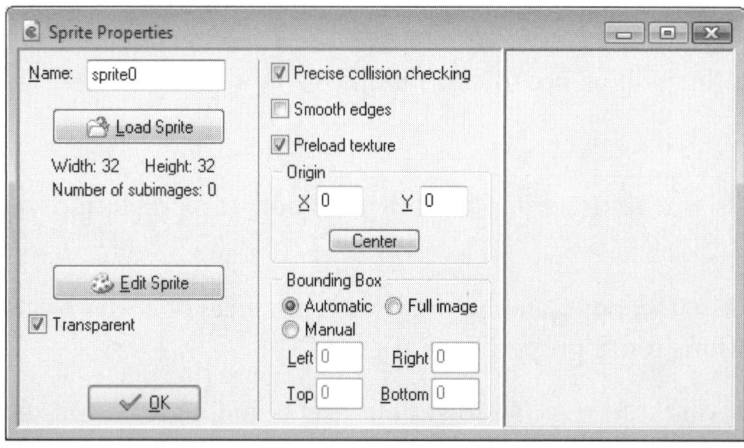


**Figure 3.7**
Adding a new sprite to the Demo application.

## Step 2—Defining the Game's Sound Effect

The next step in the development of the demo program is to define and generate a sound effect that will be played whenever the ball collides with and bounces off one of the game's walls. To do so, click on Resources > Create Sound. This will open the Sound Properties window as shown in Figure 3.8. Assign a name of **snd_collision** to the sound. To import the sound file used as the basis for defining this sound resource, click on the Load Sound button and drill down into the C:\Program Files\Game Maker7\Sounds folder, select the beep2.wav file, and click on the Open button. When done, the Sound Properties window should look like the example shown in Figure 3.8.

### Hint

As you can see in Figure 3.8, Game Maker allows you to configure numerous properties that affect the playback of sounds. You will learn about these properties in Chapter 4.

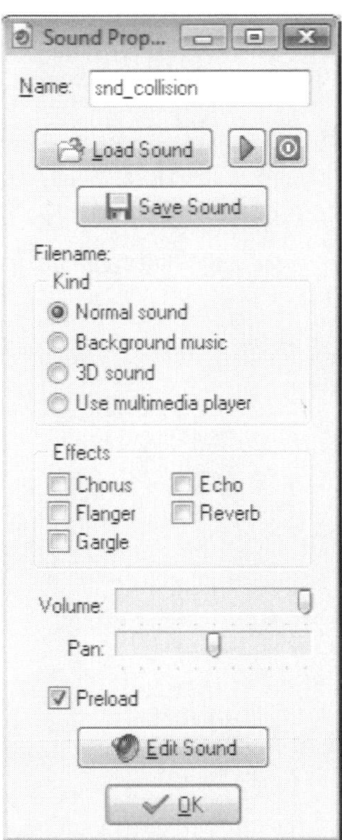


**Figure 3.8**
Adding a new sound to the demo application.

## Step 3—Configuring the Game's Background

With the demo's sprites and sound resources now defined, the next step is to define the application's background. To do so, click on Resources > Create Background. In response, Game Maker displays the Background properties window. Once displayed, enter **bck_field** into the Name file and then click on the Load Background button and drill down into the C:\program Files\Game Maker7\Backgrounds folder, select the gray2.wav file, and click on the Open button. When done, the Background Properties window should look like the example shown in Figure 3.9.

**Hint**

As you can see in Figure 3.9, Game Maker lets you specify a number of different properties that affect the appearance of backgrounds. You will learn about these properties in Chapter 4.

## Step 4—Defining Ball and Wall Objects

As previously stated, the core components of any Game Maker application are the objects that interact with one another and the player. To create the BouncingBall demo, you need to define two objects, a ball object and a wall object. To create the ball object, click on Resources > Create Object. In response, the Object Properties window is displayed. Next, type **obj_ball** in the Name field and then click on the context menu icon located at the end of the Sprite text field. In response, a context menu is displayed that lists all of the sprites that have been defined in the application. Select the `spr_ball` object by clicking on its name in

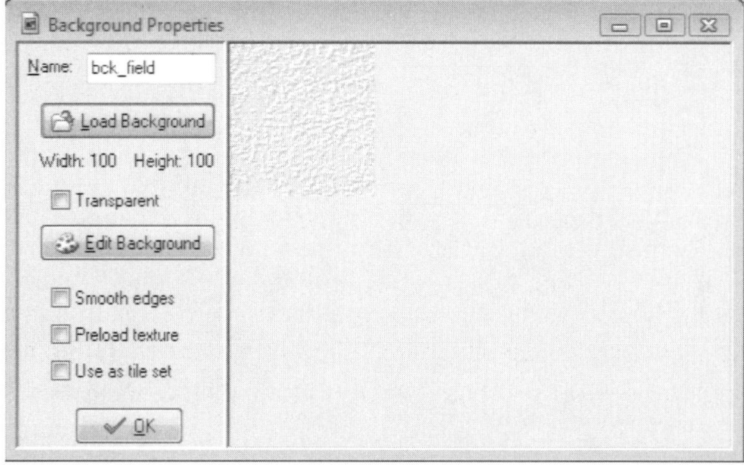


**Figure 3.9**
Adding a background to the demo application.

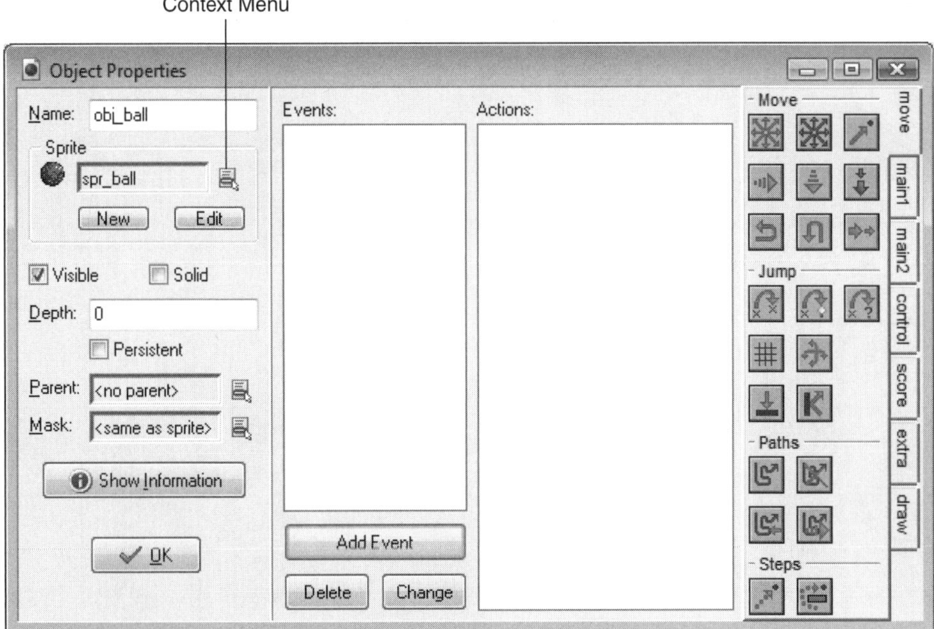


**Figure 3.10**
Defining an object to represent a bouncing ball.

the context list. At this point, the Object Properties screen should look like the example shown in Figure 3.10.

Click on the OK button to close the Object Properties window. Now, repeating the steps outlined above, create a new object named `obj_wall` and assign it the `spr_wall` sprite, as demonstrated in Figure 3.11.

Before closing the Object properties window for the `obj_wall` object, enable the `Solid` property. This is necessary to ensure that a collision event occurs when the `obj_ball` object comes into contact with it.

## Step 5—Adding a Room to the Game and Configuring Room Properties

Now that the application's objects have been created, you need to create a room within which the objects can be placed and interact with one another. To do so, click on Resources > Create Room. In response, the Room Properties window appears as shown in Figure 3.12.

Once created, you need to add instances of the objects that make up the demo application to the room. Let's begin by adding as many instances of the `obj_wall`

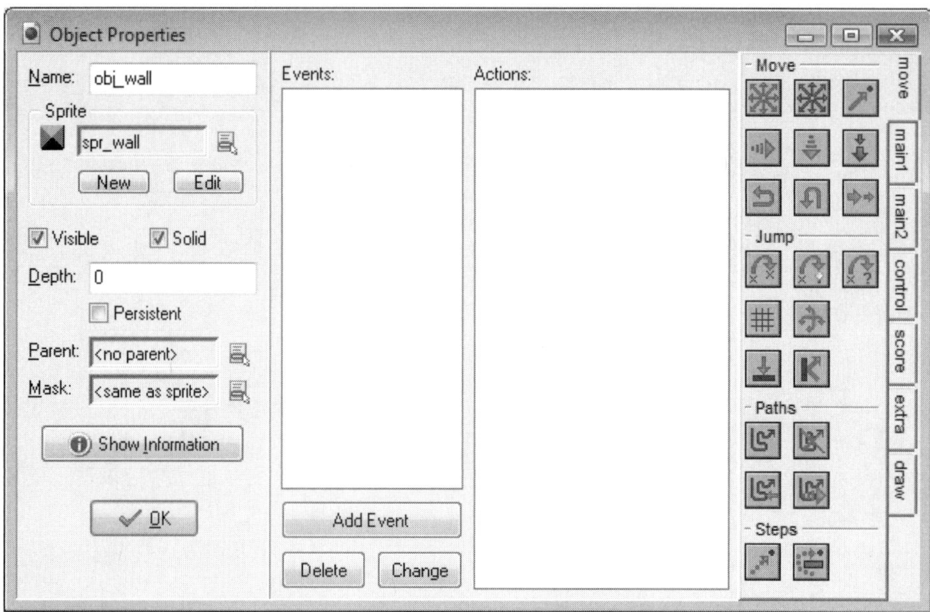


**Figure 3.11**
Defining an object to represent a solid wall.

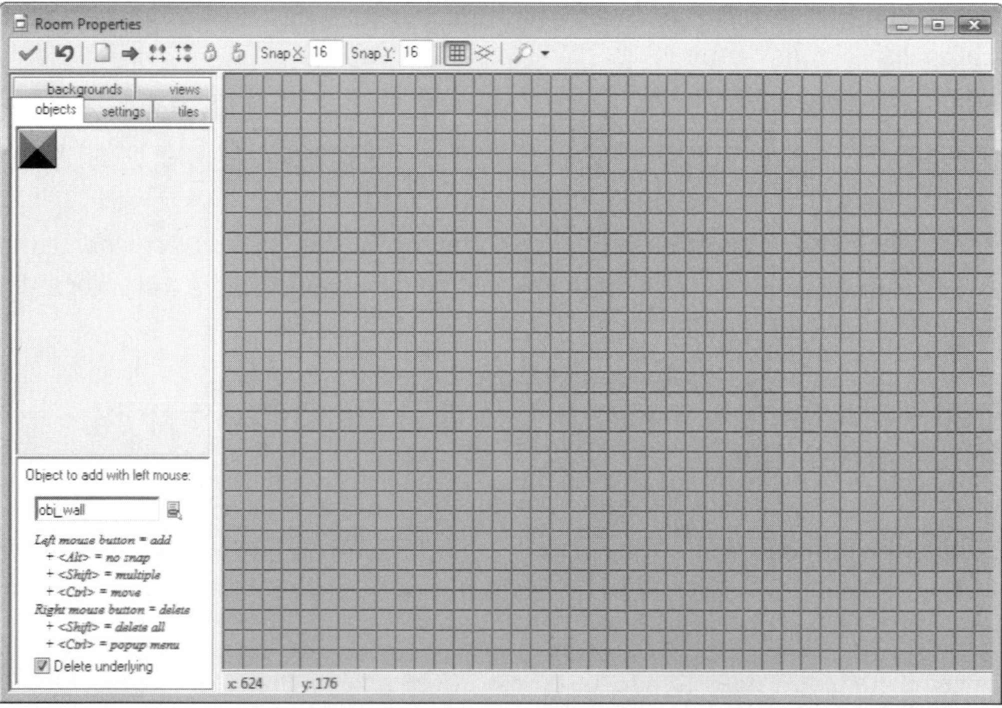


**Figure 3.12**
Defining a room within which the objects that make up the application will interact.

object as are needed to completely close in the entire room. To do so, click on the context menu icon located at the end of the object name file located on the middle of the Objects tab and then select the `obj_wall` object. You should now see the object's sprite displayed at the top of the Objects tab. Now, using the mouse pointer, left-click on the upper-left grid square. When you do, an instance of the `obj_wall` object is displayed in that location in the room. Left-click on the upper-left square just to the right of the instance that you just added to add another object. Repeating this process, add as many instances of the `obj_wall` object as needed to wall in the entire outer perimeter of the room.

**Trick**

If you need to add entire rows or columns of the same object, you can quickly do so by moving the mouse pointer to the location where you want to place the first instance of the object and then press and hold the Shift key while also pressing and holding down the left mouse button as you move the mouse. In response, Game Maker will automatically add repeated instances of the object to the window for you.

Once you have completed the above task, you need to add an instance of the `obj_ball` object to the center of the room. To do so, click on the context-menu icon next to the object name field and select the `obj_ball` object. Next, left-click just once in the middle of the room. At this point, the room should look like the example shown in Figure 3.13.

**Hint**

If you want to delete an object instance from a room, all you have to do is right-click on it.

Before closing the Room Properties window, let's assign the room a name and specify a text string to be displayed in the application window's titlebar area. To do so, click on the Settings tab and then enter **Level1** in the Name field and then type **Bouncing Ball Demo** in the Caption for the room field, as demonstrated in Figure 3.14. When you are done, click on the green checkmark button located on the Room Properties window's toolbar to close the Room Properties window.

**Hint**

As you can see in Figures 3.13 and 3.14, Game Maker lets you specify a number of different properties that affect the appearance and operation of rooms. You will learn about these properties in Chapter 4.

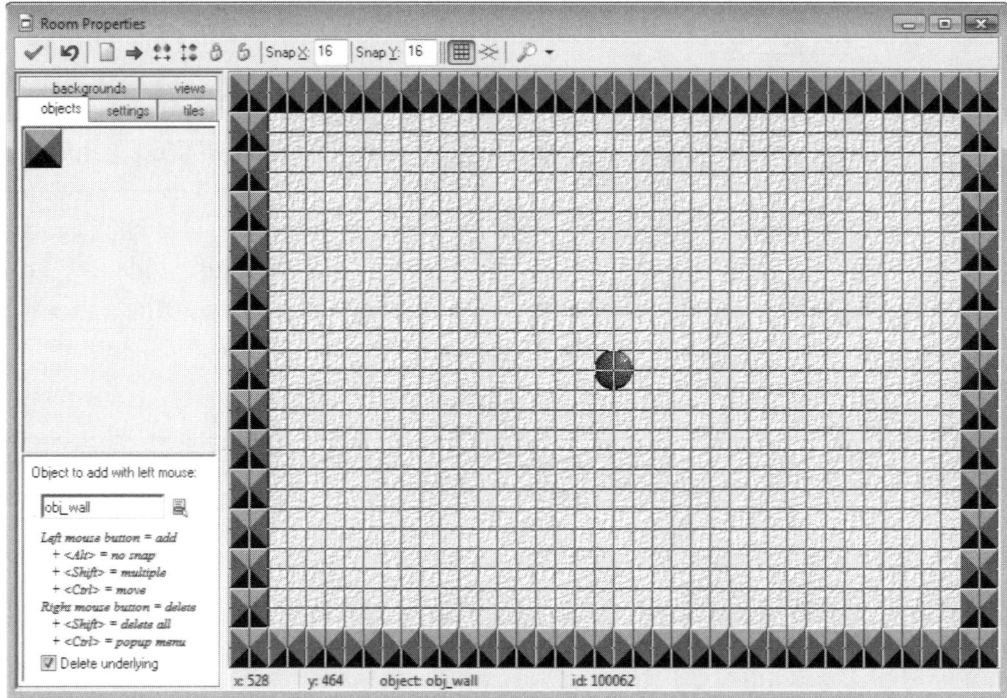


**Figure 3.13**
Designing the layout of the game's room.

## Step 6—Developing Program Logic for the Ball Object

At this point, you have added and configured all of the different resources needed by the demo application. If you want, you can run the application by clicking on the Green arrow button located on the Game Maker toolbar. In response, Game Maker will load the application and you will see the purple ball and the surrounding walls. However, because you have not yet added any program logic to the game, nothing will happen.

There are two objects in this application. The `obj_wall` object does not do anything, meaning that it does not respond to any events or execute any actions. The `obj_ball` object, on the other hand, is supposed to move around the room and bounce off the walls. To set this up, you need to drill down into the Object folder located in the resource folder tree and then double-click on the `obj_ball` object to re-open its properties window.

In order to get things started, you need to provide instructions to the `obj_ball` object that will make it move. To accomplish this, you need to first add the Create

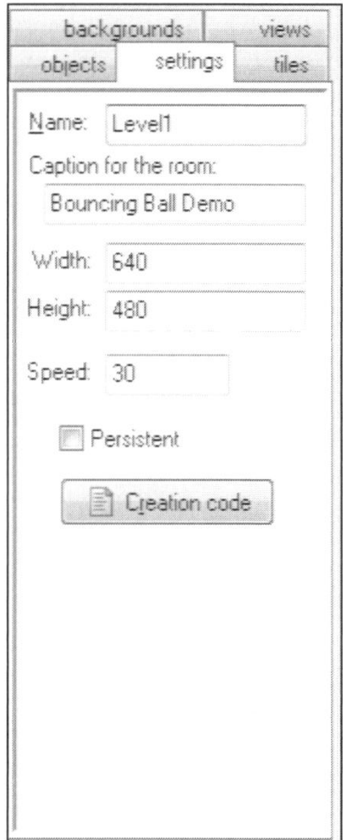


**Figure 3.14**
You can display any text you want in the application's window when the room is loaded.

event to the `obj_ball` object and then add the Moved Fixed actions to it. To add the Create event, click on the Add Event button located at the bottom of the events list area. In response, the Event Selector window is displayed. Click on the Create button to add the Create event to the object's events list. Now, select the Create event in the events list and click on the Move tab located on the right-hand side of the Object Properties window. Next, drag and drop an instance of the Moved Fixed icon onto the actions area. When you do, the Move Fixed window appears as shown in Figure 3.15, allowing you to configure the operation of this action.

For this demo, the ball will begin moving in one of four randomly selected directions. To set this up, click on each of the four diagonally oriented arrows. As you click on each arrow, it will turn from blue to red, indicating its selection. Next, in order to get the ball moving, specify a value of 8 in the Speed text field. This setting instructs Game Maker to begin moving the ball at a speed of 8 pixels per step. In Game Maker, activity is measured in steps. By default, Game Maker takes 30 steps every second.

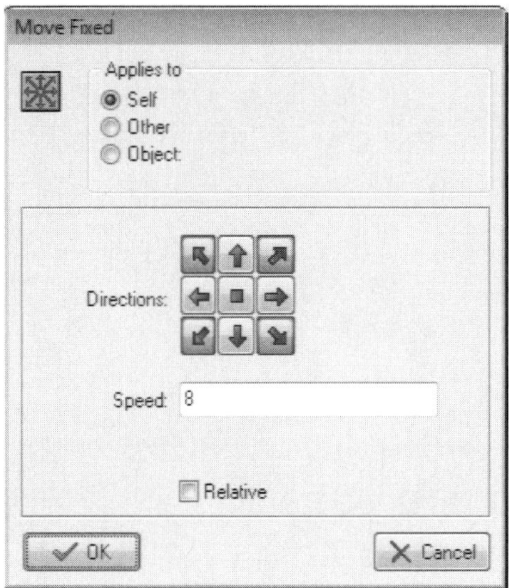


**Figure 3.15**
Using the Move Fixed action, you can instruct Game Maker to move an object in any of up to eight randomly selected directions at any speed you specify.

### Hint

A *step* is a period of time in which Game Maker performs operations, such as moving sprites around in a room. By default, Game Maker executes 30 steps every second. However, as will be explained in Chapter 4, you can override this behavior by modifying the Speed setting located on the Room Properties Settings tab. A *pixel* (picture element) is the smallest addressable area that can be drawn on the screen or window.

Click on the OK button to save the changes outlined above. Game Maker will respond by closing the Move Fixed window, leaving the Object Properties window visible. At this point, the Object Properties window for the `obj_ball` object should look like the example shown in Figure 3.16.

If you try running the demo at this point, you will see that when initially started, the ball will randomly move in one of four possible directions. However, instead of bouncing off the walls that make up the perimeter of the game window, the ball keeps moving and disappears. Obviously, this is not how things should work. To correct the situation, you need to add a Collision event to the `obj_ball` object and then add an action that instructs the ball to bounce away from walls when it comes into contact with them. To accomplish this, click on the Add Event button and then click on the Collision button when the Event Selector window appears. In response, Game Maker will display a context menu, listing all of the

**Figure 3.16**
Configuring this instance of the `obj_ball` object's direction and speed.

objects defined in the application. Click on the `obj_wall` object. This tells Game Maker that you want to do something whenever the ball collides with a wall.

Now that you have configured the required collision event, select it and then drag and drop the Bounce action (located on the Move tab) to the actions area. When you do, the Bounce window appears. You do not need to make any changes on this window, so click on its OK button to close it. To make the demo more interesting, let's add an action that plays a sound effect whenever a collision occurs with the ball and a wall. To set this up, click on the Main1 tab and then drag and drop the Play Sound icon onto the actions area. In response, Game Maker will display the Play Sound window. To tell Game Maker what sound you want it to play, click on the context menu icon located at the end of the sound field. Game Maker will then display a context list showing all of the Sounds added to the application. Click on the entry for the `snd_collision` sound, which you previously added to the application. At this point, the Object Properties window for the `obj_ball` object should look like the example shown in Figure 3.17.

## Running the Demo Program

Assuming that you followed along carefully with the instructions provided in the previous sections, your copy of the BouncingBall demo should be ready for

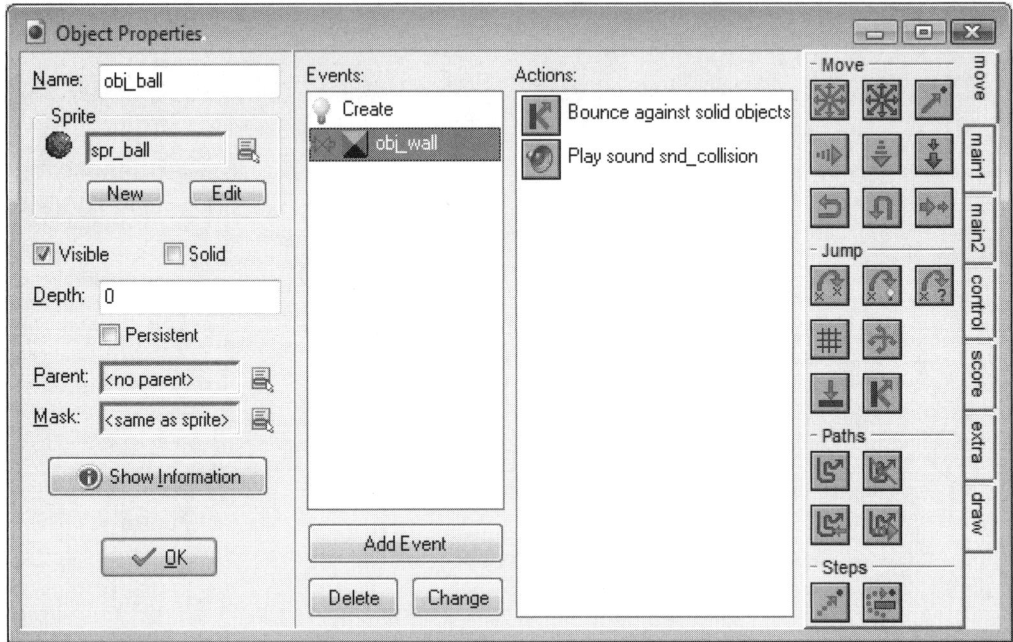


**Figure 3.17**
All of the program logic required to automate the movement of the balls has now been defined.

execution. To test it, click on Run > Run normally or click on the Run the game button located on the IDE's toolbar. In response, the Game Maker IDE will disappear and within a few moments the demo will load and execute, as demonstrated in Figure 3.18.

As you observe the execution of the demo, note the smooth movement of the ball as it glides across the screen, bouncing off each wall in different directions. Also note that every time the ball collides with a wall, the game's sound effect is played. Further, take note that the text "Bouncing Ball Demo" is visible in the application window's titlebar. Although it is not a very complex application, the development of this demo application has shown you the basic steps that you need to follow when creating Game Maker games and has demonstrated how Game Maker's drag-and-drop icon-based approach to program development works.

Once you are done watching the bouncing ball, close the demo application. The Game Maker IDE will reappear. At this point, you may want to save the demo application. To do so, click on File > Save and specify a filename of BouncingBall

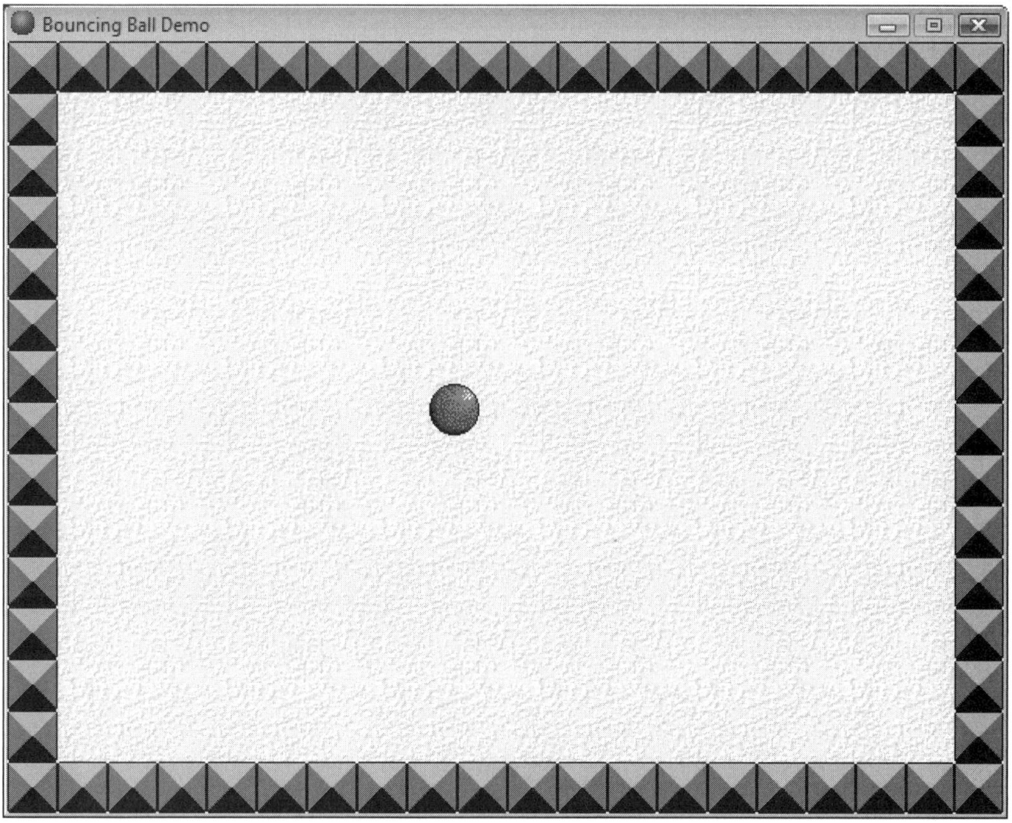

**Figure 3.18**
The purple ball will bounce around the window until you decide to close the application.

**Figure 3.19**
Game Maker assigns a file extension of .gmk to your application.

when prompted to name your application. Game Maker will then save your game in whatever location you specified. You can later reopen the application by clicking on File > Open or by double-clicking on its file icon, as shown in Figure 3.19.

## Summary

This chapter provided you with a big picture overview of how objects, sprites, backgrounds, sounds, and rooms are used in the creation of Game Maker games. Since the formulation of objects is the most important part of the game development process, the chapter focused on providing you with a solid understanding of how objects are defined and an outline of all of the different events and action icons that are available to you through the Game Maker IDE. To help tie everything together, the chapter concluded with a demo project that showed you the basic steps involved in application creation.

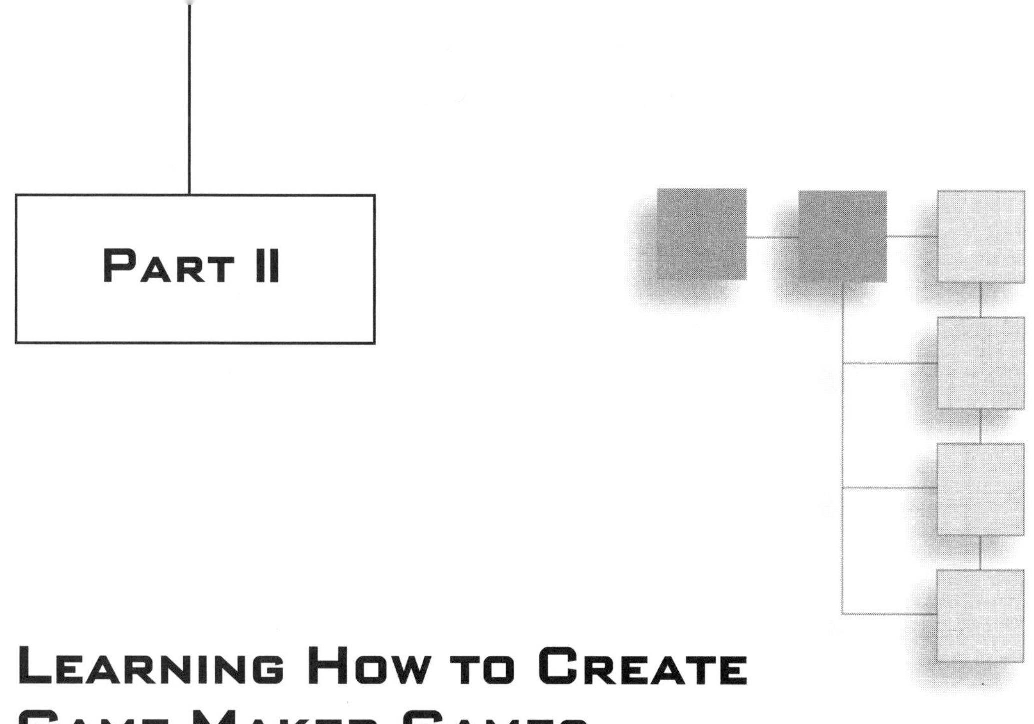

# Part II

# Learning How to Create Game Maker Games

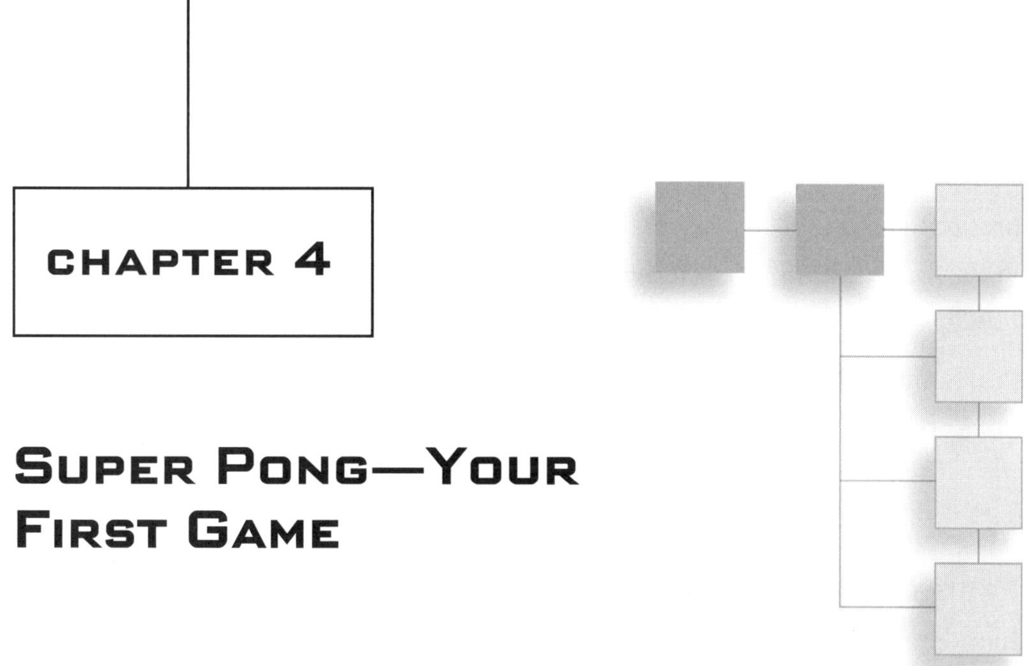

# Chapter 4

# Super Pong—Your First Game

Games developed using Game Maker consist of many different types of resources in addition to objects. These resources include sprites, sounds, backgrounds, and rooms. You've already learned a little about these resources. This chapter will take a much deeper delve, providing you with an in-depth understanding of these resources and their use. By the time you reach the end of the chapter, you will have a good understanding of all of the basic components that make up Game Maker computer games. To wrap things up, the chapter concludes by guiding you through the development of the Super Pong game.

An overview of the major topics covered in this chapter includes:

- An examination of sprites and their properties and usage
- The use of sounds as a means of adding special effects and background music to games
- An examination of backgrounds and their configuration
- A detailed review of rooms, their role in games, and their property settings

## Essential Game Resources

In Chapter 3 you learned all about objects, including how to create them, modify their property settings, and to add them to rooms. You also learned how to bring them to life through the specification of events and the addition and configuration of actions. Objects are but one resource that is essential to game development; other essential resources include:

- Sprites
- Sounds
- Backgrounds
- Rooms

## Representing Objects with Sprites

In order for objects to be seen during game play, you must assign sprites to them. A *sprite* is a graphic image or a collection of graphic images used to animate the movement of an object. You can create sprites yourself using Game Maker's built-in graphics editor or a third-party graphic editor or you can purchase and download them from various sources on the internet. You can also find various collections of sprites on the YoYo Games website.

Sprites are created in Game Maker by clicking on Resources > Create Sprite. This opens the Sprite Properties window and begins a new sprite definition. To finish the process of adding a sprite to a game, you should assign the sprite a descriptive name. Of course, you also need to assign a graphic to represent the sprite, as demonstrated in Figure 4.1. Game Maker supports many different types of graphics, including .png, .gif, .pic, .pcx, .tif, .jpg, .bmp, .wmf, and .ico.

**Trick**

Although it is not a hard and fast requirement, the Game Maker documentation recommends that you limit resource names to letters, numbers, and the underscore character and that you begin all names with a letter.

**Trap**

Be sure to follow a consistent naming policy in assigning names to different game resources and that you do not assign the same name to more than one resource; otherwise, an error will occur.

### *Loading an External Sprite File*

To use an existing graphic file as the basis for defining the sprite, click on the Load Sprite button. This displays a standard Open dialog window, allowing you to specify the name and location of the graphic file you want to use. Once

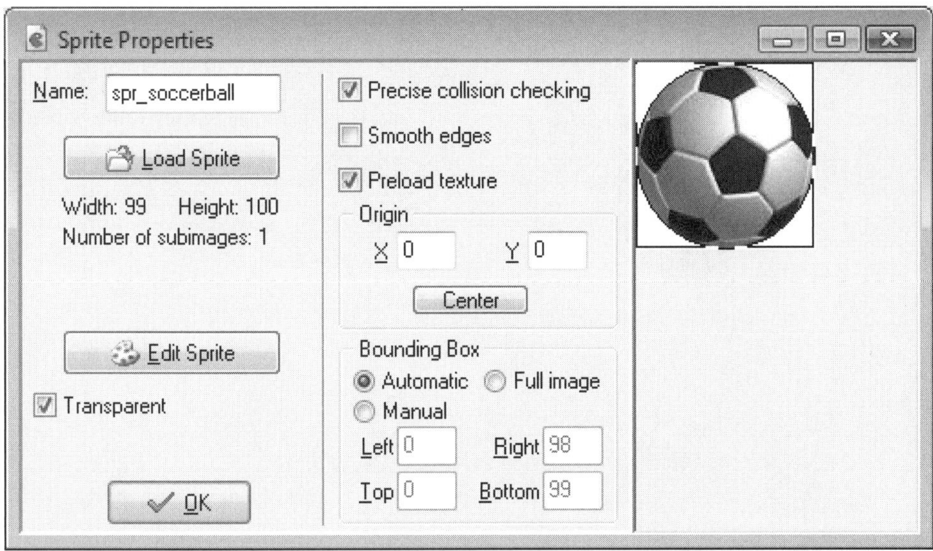


**Figure 4.1**
Adding and configuring a sprite in a Game Maker game.

selected, the Open dialog window is closed and the sprite's graphic image should be visible in the Sprite Properties window. Note that Game Maker displays three pieces of information about the image just under the Load Sprite button, indicating the image's width and height as well as a count of the number of subimages that image consists of (if the file is an animated .gif file).

By default, all sprites are defined as transparent, which means that only the sprite and not the rectangular background in which the sprite resides is displayed. However, if you want, you can clear the Transparent checkbox to display the entire contents of the graphic image.

**Trick**

> Game Maker determines the transparent area of a sprite by checking the lower-left corner of a graphic image. So, to make sure that only the actual image is displayed when transparency is used, you need to ensure that the lower-left pixel is assigned the same color as the sprite's transparent background. If necessary, you can enlarge the rectangular background that encloses a sprite.

### *Creating and Modifying Graphic Images*

If you need to, you can edit a sprite once it has been loaded or you can create a new sprite from scratch by clicking on the Edit Sprite button. When you do this, the Sprite Editor window is opened showing the sprite's image, as demonstrated in Figure 4.2.

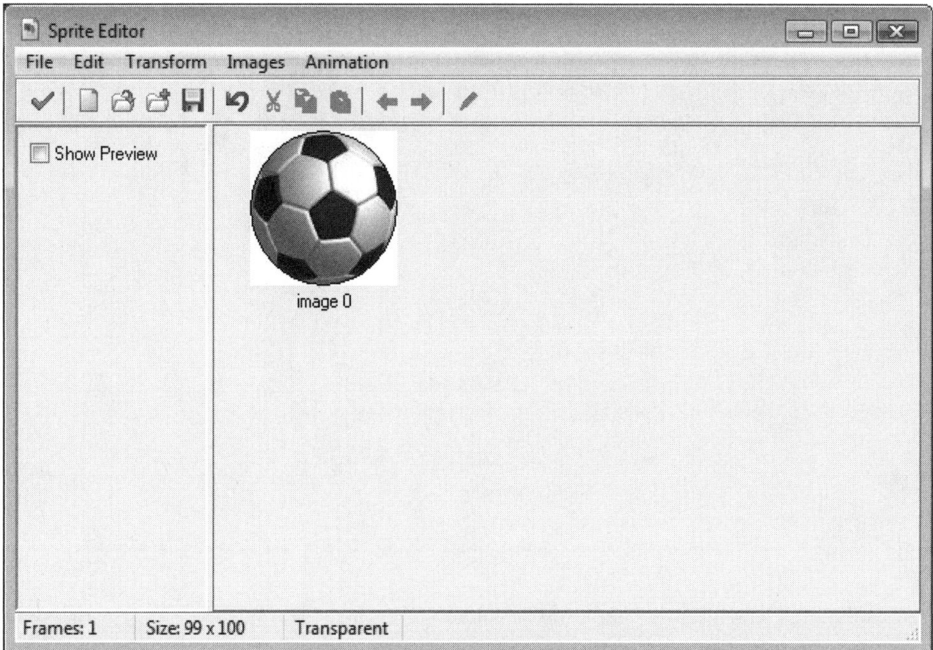


**Figure 4.2**
Examining the graphic image that makes up a sprite.

If a sprite consists of multiple subimages, all of the subimages will be displayed. By default, the Show Preview option is disabled; however, by selecting this checkbox, you can see a preview of the resulting animation for the sprite on the left-hand side of the window. When working with subimages, it is essential that they all have the same width and height dimensions; otherwise, the animation sequence will not work correctly.

You can test the animation at various speeds by overtyping the value displayed in the Speed text field. Note, however, that this setting does not control the speed of the animation in the game. This is determined by the speed assignment configured for the room in which the sprite's object is placed. If you want, you can also change the background color for the sprite by clicking on the Background Color button and selecting a different color from the Color dialog window that appears.

**Trick**

> You can remove a subimage from a sprite with multiple subimages by selecting a subimage and clicking on Edit > Delete. You can create a copy of one of the subimages by selecting it and then clicking on Edit > Copy followed by Edit > Paste. Other commands on the Edit menu change the order in which subimages are listed by letting you move them left and right, clear out or erase a

subimage, and add new blank images. Commands on the Transform menu let you flip, rotate, resize, stretch, and scale images. The Images menu contains commands that let you modify an image's color and apply different effects to it like blur and fade. The Animation menu contains commands that let you do things like flatten, grow, and shrink images.

### *Creating Sprites from Strips*

Another way of animating sprites in your games, in addition to adding animated gif files, is to work with strips. A *strip* is a graphic file that contains all of the graphic images needed to generate an animated sequence. An example of a small graphic strip is provided in Figure 4.3.

As you can see, graphics are drawn on strings in rows and columns. To use them, you must load them into Game Maker and then provide Game Maker with a little information about how the graphics are organized. To do so, open the Sprite Editor window and click on File > Create from Strip. This will open a standard Open dialog window, which you can use to specify the name and location of the graphic file containing the strip. Once this is done, the window shown in Figure 4.4 opens.

**Hint**

If you want to perform any of these examples covered in this section yourself, you will need to download the graphic files that are used from this book's companion website located at www.courseptr.com/downloads.

In order to work with the strip, you have to provide Game Maker with a little information. In the case of the example shown in Figure 4.4, the strip consists of eight images stored in a single row. Each image is 64 pixels wide and 64 pixels tall. So, to set things up, type **8** in the Number of images field, **8** in the Images per row field, and **64** in both the Image width and Image height fields. Once you have made these changes, you will be able to visually verify that Game Maker has correctly mapped out the strip into separate subimages, as demonstrated in Figure 4.5.

**Figure 4.3**
A strip made up of eight images stored in two rows of four.

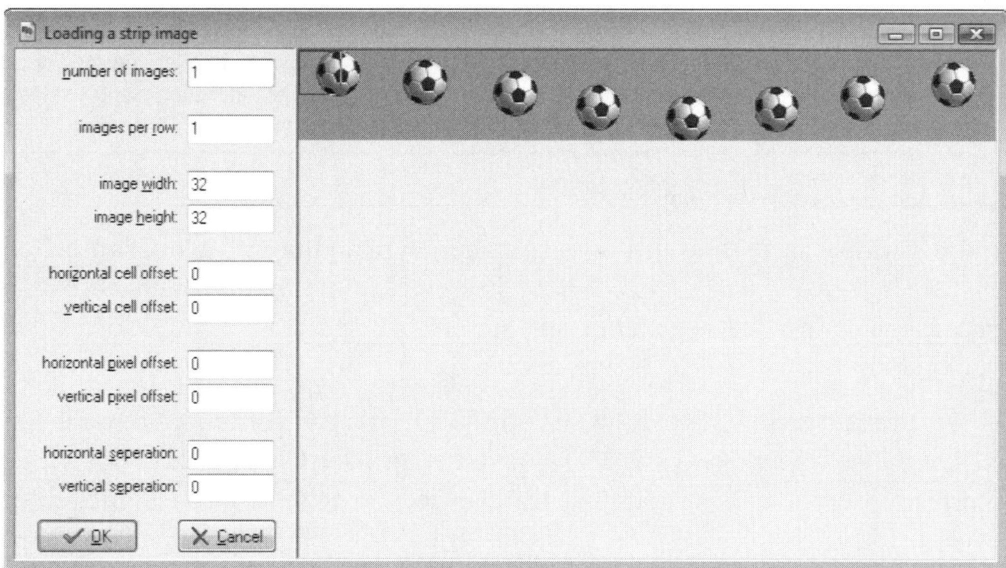


**Figure 4.4**
An example of a graphic strip made up of eight images organized into a single row.

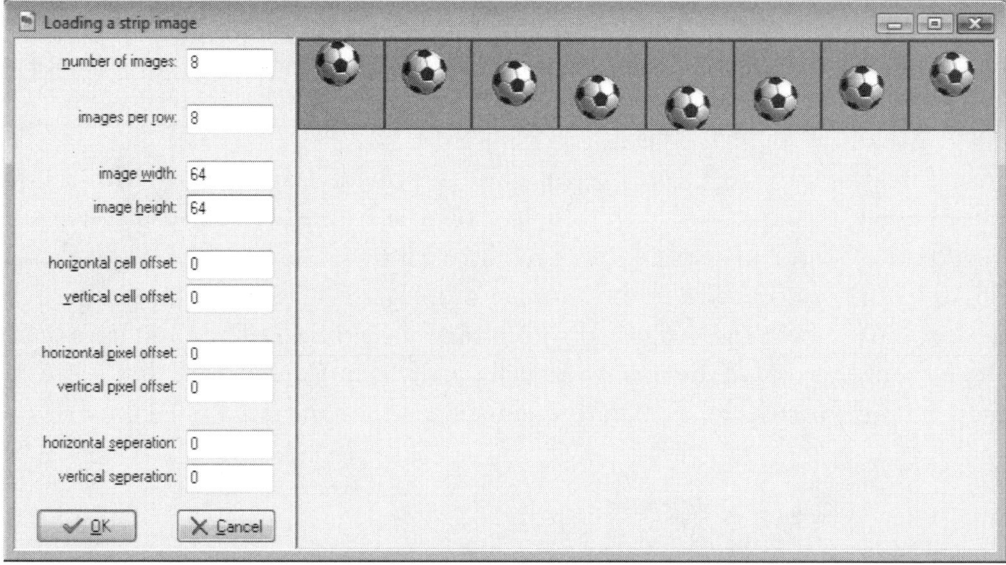


**Figure 4.5**
Game Maker now has the information needed to generate subimages from the strip.

Once the strip has been mapped out, you can click on the OK button to close the Loading a strip image window. You will then see each of the separate subimages that Game Maker has created in the Sprite Editor window, as demonstrated in Figure 4.6.

**Figure 4.6**
Click on the Show Preview checkbox to preview the animation that Game Maker will generate for the sprite.

### *Editing Graphic Images*

You can use Gamer Maker's built-in image editor to modify any graphic image or subimage. To do so, double-click on the image or subimage in the Sprite Editor window. When you do, the image editor application starts and the image or subimage is automatically loaded into it, as demonstrated in Figure 4.7.

This image editor works very much like the Microsoft Windows Paint program. Coverage of how to work with this program or any other paint program is outside the scope of this book. Once you have used the image editor to modify the graphic image, close the Image Editor window and click on Yes when prompted to save the changes you have made. The results of your changes should be immediately evident when you are returned to the Sprite Editor window.

### *Setting Sprite Properties*

Sprites have a number of properties that you can modify from the Sprite Properties window. The first of these properties is precise collision checking.

**Figure 4.7**
Using Game Maker's image editor to modify a graphic image.

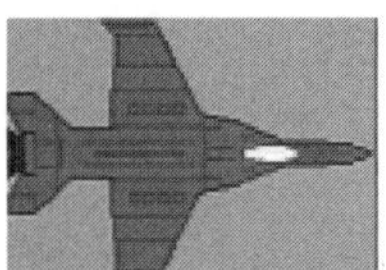

**Figure 4.8**
An example of a typical sprite inside its transparent bounded box.

*Collisions* occur when two objects touch one another. Collision detection is a key aspect of most computer games. Game Maker supports two types of collision detection: bounded rectangle collision detection and precise collision detection.

As demonstrated in Figure 4.8, sprites are images displayed within transparent bounded rectangles in which the sprite is completely enclosed. Here, a jet fighter plane is depicted on a transparent background.

With bounded rectangle collection detection, a collision occurs when two bounded sprites come into contact with one another. Figure 4.9 demonstrates how bounded collisions occur. Here two bullet sprites have both collided with the bounded portion of the sprite.

**Figure 4.9**
A bounded collision occurs when the bounded boxes within which sprites exist come into contact with each other.

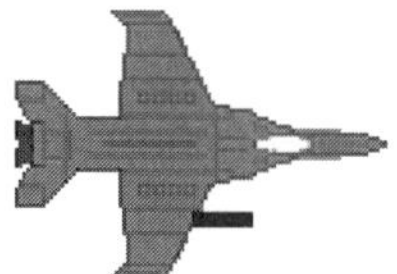

**Figure 4.10**
With Precise collision checking the pixels that make up sprites must come into contact with one another.

Bounded collisions occur when both sprites' bounding rectangles make contact. As a result, each rectangle is made up of just four sets of coordinates, making it easy to detect collisions and consume fewer resources in games where large numbers of objects are moving about, colliding with one another. However, the disadvantage of bounded collisions is that they lack precision. Therefore, bounded collisions sometimes occur in situations where two sprites are not actually on a true collision course with one another (e.g., near misses).

If your games require greater precision, you can enable the Precise collision checking option. When enabled, collisions occur only when the pixels that make up the sprites come into contact with each other, as demonstrated in Figure 4.10.

The advantage of precise collision detection is that it removes all ambiguity from your games when collisions and near misses occur. The disadvantage of precise collision detection is that it consumes more resources and may slow down game play on resource-constrained computers.

Another sprite property, disabled by default, is the smooth edges option. When enabled, this option makes the outer edge of the sprite transparent, which can sometimes make sprites look less blocky. All sprites are converted to textures that must be moved into memory before they can be used by games. By default, Game Maker loads sprites only when they are needed. However, by enabling the preload texture, you instruct Game Maker to automatically load the sprite when the game loads. This will eliminate any delay during game play. However, if your game consists of lots of sprites, particularly large complex sprites, enabling this option for every sprite can use up a lot of memory and make things run unnecessarily slow.

All sprites have a point of origin, which identifies how the sprite aligns by default with the grid that makes up rooms. By default, every sprite's point of origin is its upper-left corner. However, you can change this using the mouse to point and click on the location on the sprite where you want to set its origin. In response, coordinates representing the sprite's point of origin are updated on the Sprite Properties window. A common point of origin for sprites is the center, which you can specify by clicking on the Center button.

By default, the size of a sprite's bounding rectangle is determined when you add it. However, if you want, you can modify its size using the settings made available in the Bounding Box section of the Sprite Properties window. In most situations, it's best to let Game Maker set up a sprite's bounding rectangle itself.

## Getting Creative with Sound

An important component of any game is the clever use of sound, including both sound effects and background music. Game Maker supports the playback of two types of audio files, wave and midi. Wave files are generally used for sound effects because, even though they use of a lot of memory, they can be played instantly. Midi files are usually used to add the playback of background music to games. They have lower memory requirements because they only support instrumental playback. In order to add a sound to a game you must click on Resources > Create Sound, opening the window shown in Figure 4.11.

You can create your own sounds using any third-party audio application you want or you may purchase and download sound files from the internet. Once you have your audio files ready, you can add them to your games. To do so, click on the Sound Properties window's Load Sound button and then specify the name and location of your audio file. Once loaded, you can click on the green Play the Sound button to hear what the audio file will sound like when played. The sound will play continuously. To stop its playback, click on the red Stop the Sound button. Immediately beneath these buttons is a button labeled Save Sound. This button allows you to save a copy of the sound file on your computer but otherwise is of little use.

**Trap**

When downloading a sound file from the internet, be careful to follow any copyright restrictions its creator may set.

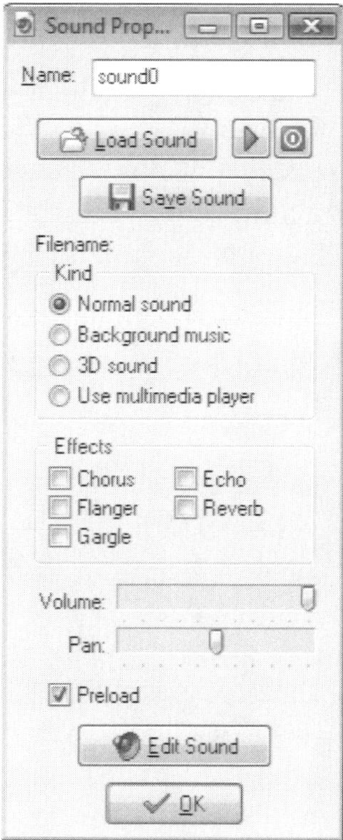


**Figure 4.11**
Adding a sound to a game and configuring its type, effects, and volume.

You can specify what kind of file you have loaded by selecting from one of the following four options in the file name section.

- **Normal sound.** Sounds (wave files) used to generate special sound effects.
- **Background music.** Sounds similar to normal sound files but which can only be played one at a time.
- **3D sound.** Sounds to which 3D effects can be programmatically applied.
- **Use multimedia player.** MP3 audio files that Game Maker plays using the computer's default media player.

If you load a wave file, Game Maker will automatically configure it as a normal sound. If you add a midi file, Game Maker configures it as background music. If you load an MP3 file, Game Maker automatically configures it to use the multimedia player option. The advantage of using normal sounds is that games can simultaneously play multiple normal sounds. Background sounds can only be played one at a time. Game Maker supplies a number of built-in functions that you can programmatically apply when playing sounds configured as 3D sounds. MP3 files are played using the computer's media player instead of DirectX. Unlike other sounds, you cannot control the volume or specify any effects when playing MP3 files. In addition, because MP3 files are highly compressed files, they take extra time to load and play, which can result in delays and pauses during game play.

You can apply any of the following combination of five sound effects to normal, background, and 3D sounds.

- Chorus
- Flanger
- Gargle
- Echo
- Reverb

Using the two scrollbars located at the bottom of the Sound Properties window, you can specify the volume level at which the sound is played as well as control how sound is panned between the computer's left and right speakers. Lastly, you can specify whether a sound is preloaded into memory. Preloaded sounds are loaded when games first start and are thus ready for immediate playback. However, preloading files consumes more memory up front and can needlessly consume unnecessary resources. When not preloaded, sound files are loaded only when needed. Game Maker does not have a built-in sound editor. So unless you configure it to use one, as described in Chapter 2, "Getting Comfortable with the Game Maker IDE," the Edit Sound button does not do anything.

## Setting the Mood with Backgrounds

An important component of most computer games is the use of creative and colorful backgrounds that help to add an important element of realism or establish an element of excitement. These backgrounds can then be added to the rooms you add to your games. Backgrounds are added by clicking on Resources > Create Background. This opens the Background Properties window.

To use the contents of an existing graphic file as the basis for creating a background, click on the Load Background button and specify the name and path of

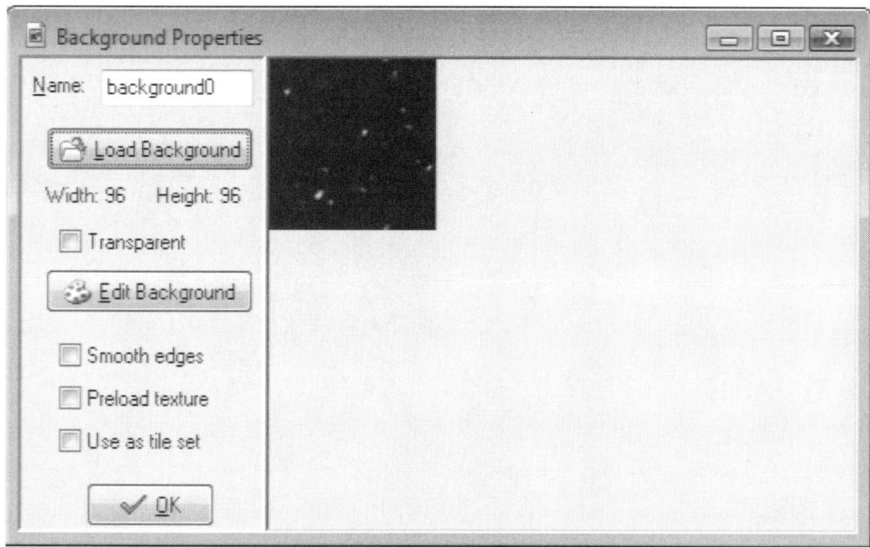


**Figure 4.12**
Adding and configuring a background to a game.

the file. Once loaded the width and height of the image are displayed (in pixels), just under the Load Background button, as demonstrated in Figure 4.12.

You can create a background image from scratch or modify a loaded background by clicking on the Edit Background button. This opens Game Maker's Image Editor window. This is the same editor that you use to edit sprites.

By default, Game Maker displays backgrounds as solid images. However, by clicking on the Transparent option, you can make backgrounds transparent. Game Maker provides three additional options that you can enable. The first of the options is Smooth Edges, which when enabled helps to alleviate any choppiness of the edges of backgrounds by drawing the outer pixels as partially transparent. The second option is Preload Texture, which when enabled instructs Game Maker to load the texture, which it creates to represent the background, into video memory when the game initially loads. The last option is Use as Tile Set. When enabled, this option allows you to create a tile set from a background file. A *tile set* is a background made up of a collection of smaller graphic images that can be added to rooms.

To work with a tile set, create a new Background and then enable the Use as Tile Set option. As demonstrated in Figure 4.13, a new set of properties is displayed in the middle of the Background Properties window. The `Tile width` and `Tile height` properties let you tell Game Maker how to map out and identify the different pieces of the tile set. The `Horizontal offset` and `Vertical offset`

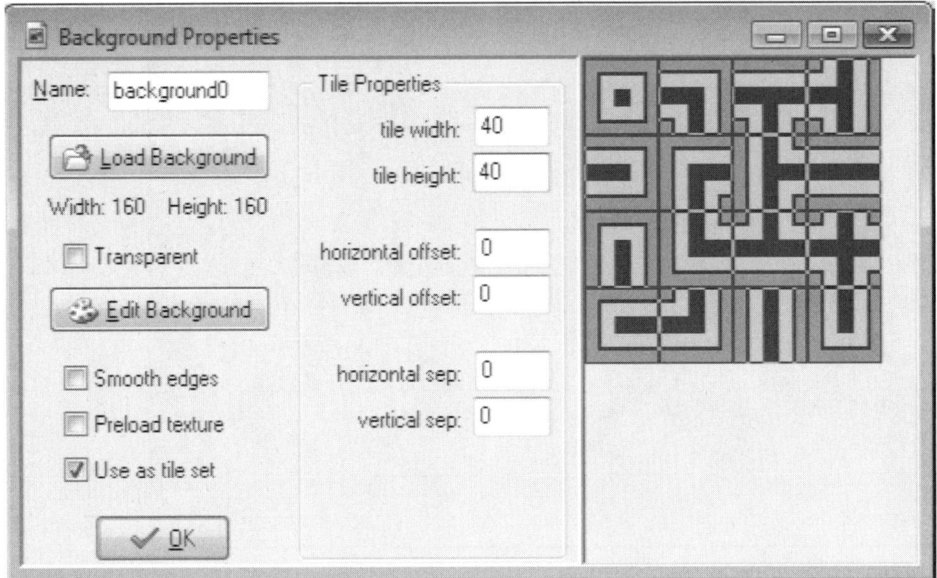


**Figure 4.13**
You can use the different graphics that make up a tile set to decorate rooms and create exciting looking levels.

properties let you specify where the top-left tile starts on the tile set (in pixels), and the `Horizontal sep` and `Vertical sep` properties let you specify whether there is any separation (in pixels) between tiles.

## Creating Levels and Game Worlds Using Rooms

As has already been stated, every Game Maker game has to have at least one room. However, you can add as many rooms as needed to your games, using them to create different parts or levels in your games. To add a room to your game, you must click on Resources > Create Room. This adds a new room and opens the Room Properties window shown in Figure 4.14 so that you can configure the room and begin adding instances of objects to it.

The Room Properties window has its own toolbar along the top of the window, as shown in Figure 4.15.

If you add a large number of object instances to a room, it is sometimes useful to click on the Lock All Instances toolbar button. This will prevent you from accidentally moving instances around the room. If you want to move something, you can always click on the Unlock All Instances button, make the changes, and then lock things back down again. By default, Game Maker organizes rooms using a grid

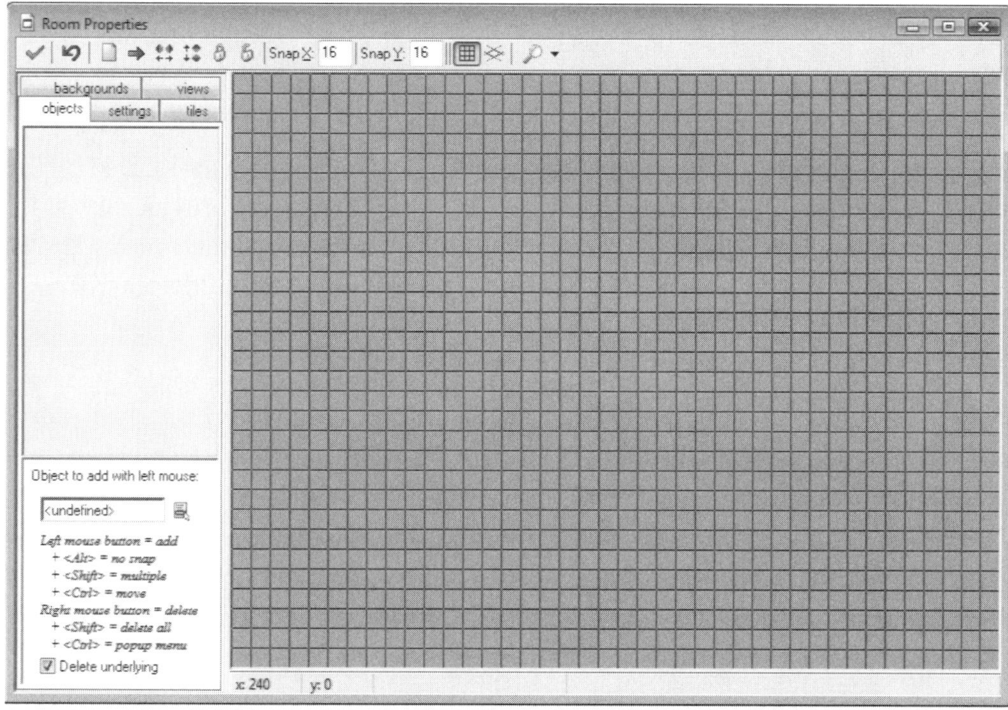


**Figure 4.14**
Tabs located on the left-hand side of the Room Properties window provide everything you need to configure rooms.

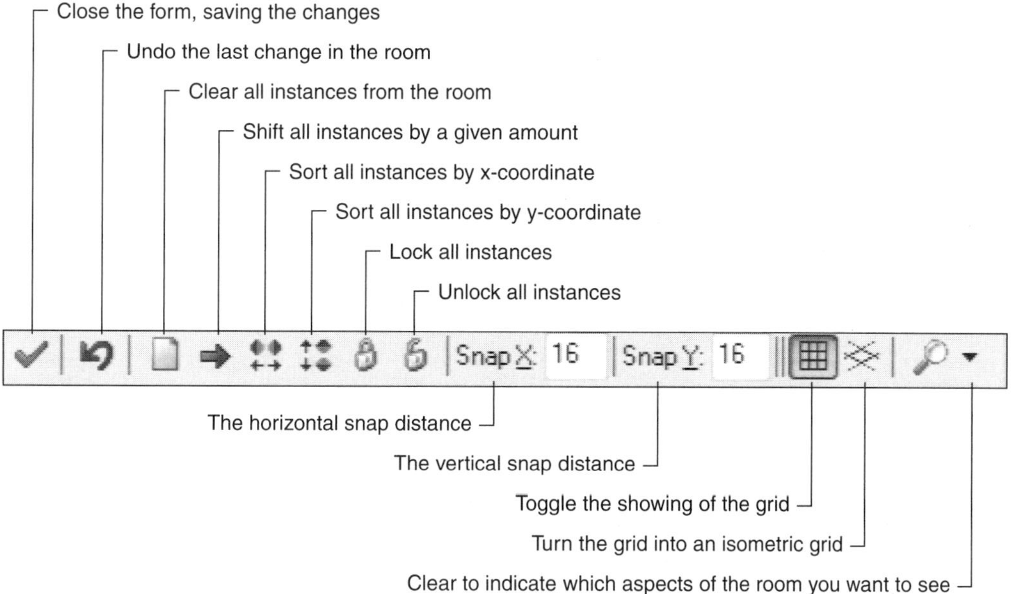


**Figure 4.15**
The Room Properties window's toolbar.

made up of squares that are 16 pixels wide by 16 pixels high. Depending on the type of game you are creating, you may need to modify these settings. For example, when creating maze games, you will probably want to set grid size to at least 32 × 32.

In order to work with rooms, you need to click on any of the six tabs located on the left-hand side of the Room Properties window. These tabs provide access to commands and settings that let you add object instances, configure room settings, work with tile sets, add and configure backgrounds and set up different views.

### *Adding Objects to Rooms*

By default, Game Maker always displays the contents of the Objects tab whenever you create a new room. As shown in Figure 4.16, this is the tab that you must select in order to add instances of objects to rooms. This is accomplished by clicking on the context menu icon located at the end of the Object to Add with Left Mouse text field and then selecting the sprite representing the object you want to work with from the list that is displayed. Once selected, the object's sprite is displayed in a graphic pane

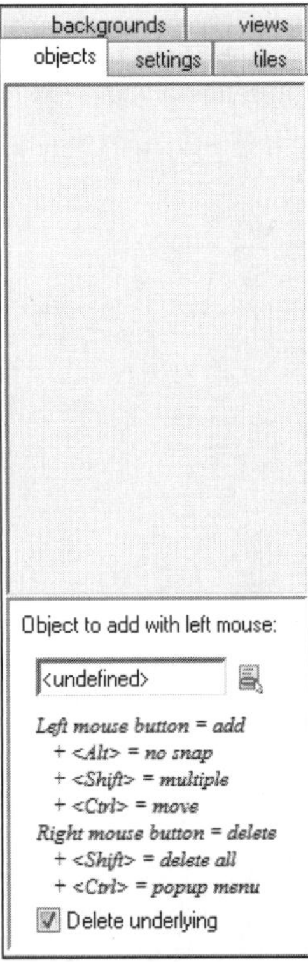


**Figure 4.16**
Select the Objects tab to add instances of objects to your games.

loaded at the top of the Objects tab. You can then add instances of the object to the room by left-clicking on the appropriate location in the room. Instances automatically align with the room's grid based on how you set the origin of its sprite.

**Trick**

> You can exercise more precise control over a sprite's location by pressing and holding the Alt key when adding sprites to the room. This allows you to place the instance on the room without it automatically aligning to the grid. You can add instances of objects one at a time or you can add repeated instances by pressing and holding the Shift key when holding down and moving the mouse button. You can delete instances by right-clicking on them and selecting the Delete option.

By default, if you place one instance on top of another, Game Maker will remove the underlying instance. However, if you disable the Delete Underlying option, you can turn off this behavior.

### *Configuring Room Settings*

Game Maker applies a number of configuration settings to every room that you add to your games. These settings are displayed on the Room Properties window's Settings tab, shown in Figure 4.17.

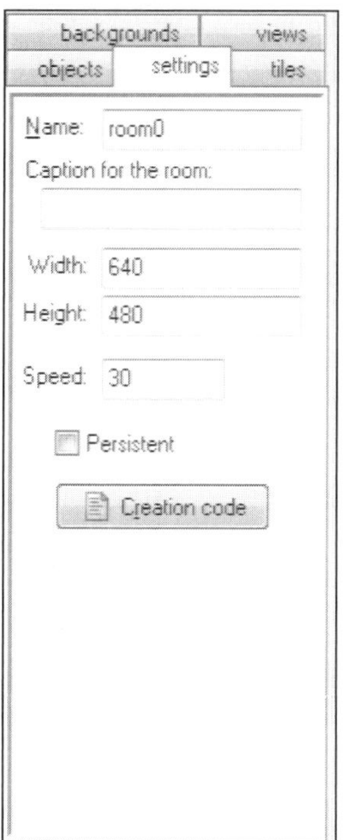


**Figure 4.17**
Configuring a room's property settings.

Every room needs a name and can be assigned a text string that will be used to display a caption message that will appear in the game window's titlebar when the room is loaded. By modifying the Width and Height settings, you can specify the height and width (in pixels) of the room. Every room has a `Speed` property that determines the speed at which object instances move in the room. By default, all rooms are assigned a speed of 30.

Every room also has a Persistent setting, which is disabled by default. As a result, when you leave a room in a game and return back to it later in the game, the room is returned to its initial status. By enabling the Persistent option, you instruct Game Maker to maintain the state of the room so that when returned to it, things are restored to the state that they were when you left the room. Lastly, there is a Creation code button located at the bottom of the Settings tab that when clicked opens a code editor window, into which you can add a GML script that will automatically be run whenever the room is opened.

### *Working with Tile Sets*

If you have added a tile set background to your game, you can work with that tile set by clicking on the Room Properties window's Tiles tab as shown in Figure 4.18.

**Figure 4.18**
Using a tile set in the development of a maze game.

Tiles are often used in the creation of maze games as a means of spicing up their appearance. This works better than using large numbers of differently drawn wall objects, which if used will consume large amounts of system resources. To work with a tile set you first need to modify the grid size of the room to match the dimension of the tiles in the tile set. Once you have modified the room's grid size and have added a background to your application and configured it as a tile set, all you have to do is click on the Tiles tab and then click on the context menu icon in the middle of the tab pane in order to select the tile set. Once added, you can select the different pieces of the tile set and begin adding them to the room, using them to outline the shape of the walls you want to create, as demonstrated in Figure 4.19.

With the outline of the wall now laid out using decorative tiles, all you need to do is create a square-shaped sprite with the same dimensions as the tiles in the tile set and then create an object, assigning it the sprite. Once this new wall object has been created, use it to outline the wall, placing as many instances of the object as it takes to cover all of the tiles. Once this task has been completed, open the wall object and make it invisible.

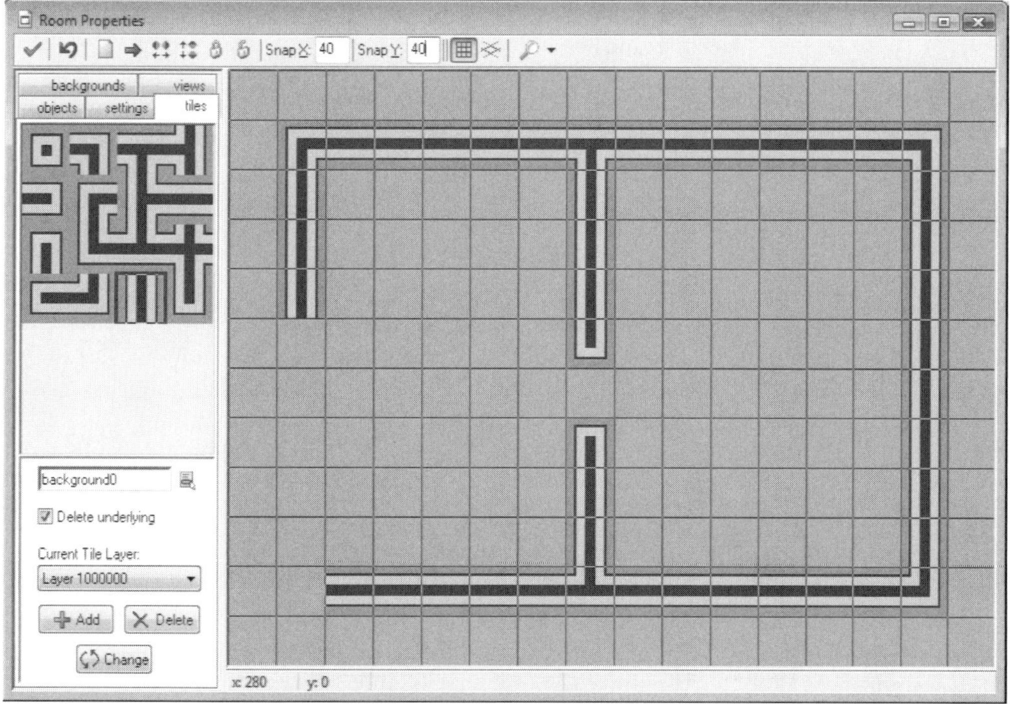


**Figure 4.19**
An example of a partially drawn wall created using a tile set.

This leaves the wall invisible but still in place. The player will not be able to see the wall even though it is still there. Instead, the decorative tiled outline of the wall is all that is visible. This approach reduces the overall number of resources required to create and manage the game by allowing you to work with a single object instead of having to create a dozen or more different objects that would have otherwise been required to create the wall.

### *Adding a Background*

Most rooms in games include either a background color or one or more backgrounds. To assign a solid color background to a room, click on the Backgrounds tab as shown in Figure 4.20 and select the Draw Background Color checkbox. If you plan on assigning a background image to be used as the room's background, you should instead clear the Draw Background Color option.

You can assign a single graphic image to be used as the background for the entire room or you can assign two or more graphic images to fill in the room's background. Game Maker allows you to assign as many as eight backgrounds to a

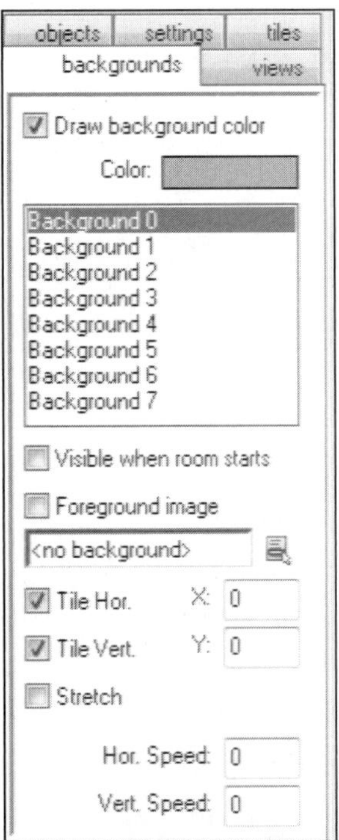


**Figure 4.20**
Adding a background to a room.

room, although at most you only usually need 1 or 2. To assign a single background image to the room, select the `Background 0` entry (selected by default) and then click on the context menu icon located in the middle of the Backgrounds tab and select the background from the list that appears. Next, select the Visible When Room Starts option so that the background will be made visible when the room loads.

The next configuration setting on the Backgrounds tab is the Foreground Image option, which when enabled turns the background image into a foreground image, drawing it on top of everything in the room. To be useful, you need to make the background transparent when you add it to the game. The Backgrounds tab has three options that you can use to tell it what to do when the size of the background is smaller than the size of the room to which it has been assigned.

- Tile Hor.
- Tile Vert.
- Stretch

The last two settings located at the bottom of the Backgrounds tab allows you to set the room up as a horizontal or vertical scrolling background by specifying the speed at which the background should be moved within the room. To create a horizontal scrolling game, assign a speed to Hor. Speed and leave Vert. Speed set to zero. To create a vertical scrolling game, do the opposite. By creating scrolling room, you can create the illusion that game characters are moving through a larger virtual world, which is a key technique used in the development of scrolling shooter games. You learn how to create one such game in Chapter 7.

### *Specifying Different Views*

The last of the tabs on the Room Properties window is the Views tab. The settings on this tab allow you to draw different parts of a room at different locations on the screen. Views let you limit how much of a room is visible at any one time. Views can also be used to create a split-screen view within a room, so that two players can view the game from their own slightly different perspectives. Views are also instrumental in creating rooms with a status panel, where the panel remains fixed while the rest of the room scrolls.

As shown in Figure 4.21, you must select the Enable the Use of Views option in order to use views with a room.

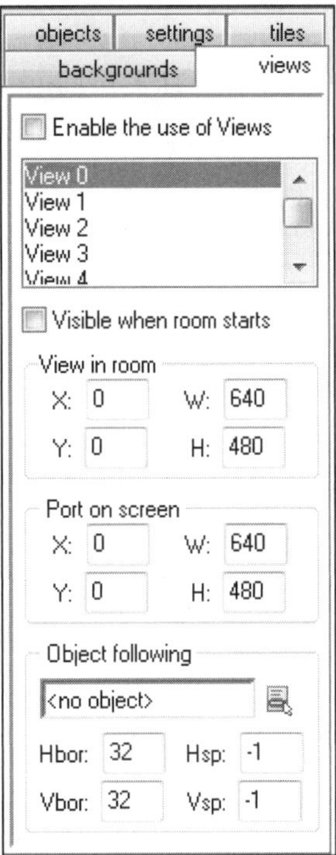


**Figure 4.21**
You can define as many as eight views per room.

Settings that you can use to configure each view are shown below the views list. For starters, you can specify whether a view should be enabled when the room is started. Each view that you define lets you view the area within a rectangular portion of the room to be seen. You must define two things for each view, the actual area within the room that is visible within the view and the area on the screen where the view is to be placed.

**Hint**

Game Maker maps out the coordinates of the area in which game play occurs using a coordinates system depicted in Figure 4.22.

As shown in Figure 4.22, the upper-left corner of the game play area is located at coordinates (0, 0). The game area has both an X-axis and a Y-axis.

You define the coordinates for this area by first specifying the upper-left corner of the view and then the width and height of the view. You then repeat these steps by specifying the location on the screen where the view is to be displayed. You will often want to configure a view to follow the movement of an object, typically the object controlled by the player during game play. To set this up, click on the

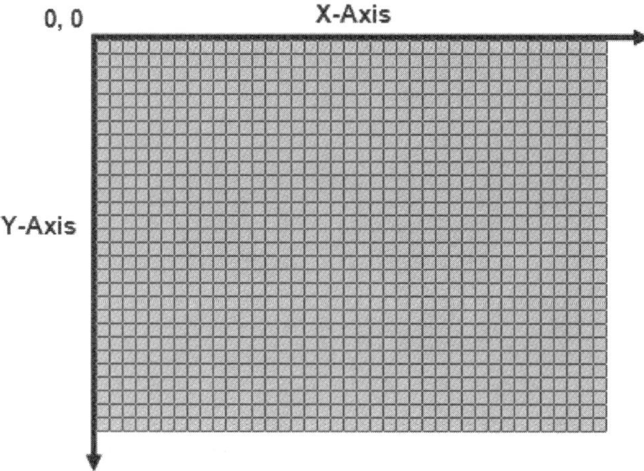


**Figure 4.22**
Game Maker's coordinate system provides a pixel-based representation of the game area.

context menu icon located at the end of the Object Following field and then select the object for which the view should follow.

Rather than have the view constantly move every time the object it tracks moves, you typically want to allow the object to move around within the view without constantly adjusting it, moving it only when the object reaches a predefined boundary within the view. To set this up, you specify the number of horizontal (`Hbor`) and vertical (`Vbor`) pixels from the outer edge of the view at which this boundary resides. You can also configure the speed at which views change by specifying a horizontal (`Hsp`) and vertical (`Vsp`) speed. A value of −1 forces an immediate change. A higher value may result in a better transition but may also result in a small delay in the updating of the view when the object being tracked moves out of sight.

## Creating the Super Pong Game

All right, let's change focus a bit and get to work on developing Super Pong, your first real computer game. As its name implies, Super Pong is based on the original Atari *Pong* game, which pits two players against one another in a video game version of ping-pong. Each player is assigned a paddle that is moved by pressing on keyboard keys. The goal is to keep each other from scoring points by deflecting a bouncing ball past the other player's side of the screen. Game play ends when one of the players scores 11 points. Figure 4.23 shows an example of the game in action.

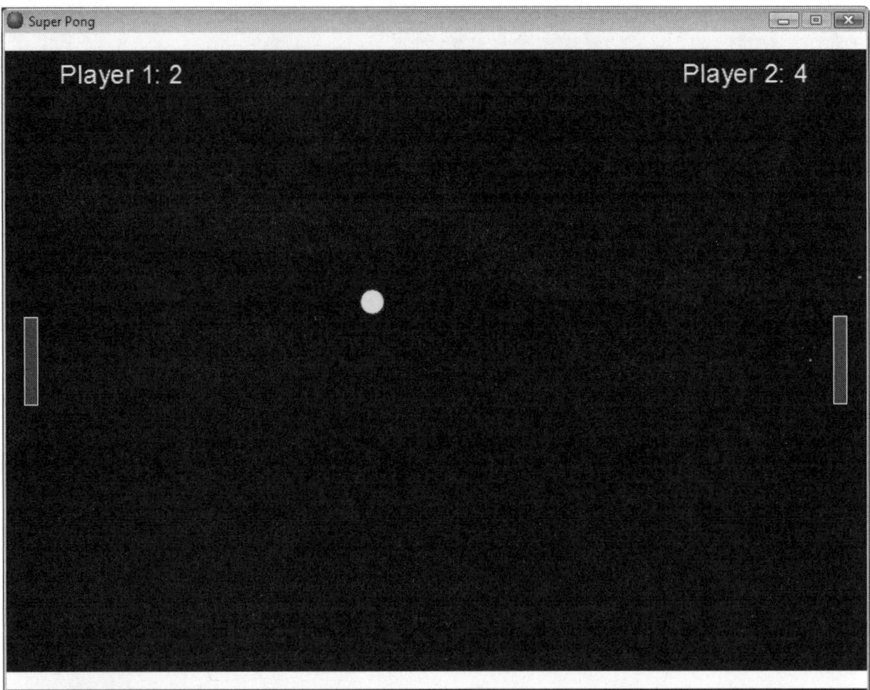


**Figure 4.23**
An example of Super Pong in action.

In order to create this game, you will need to perform a number of steps, as outlined here:

1. Define the sprites representing the game ball, paddle, goal, and wall.
2. Define sounds that will be played when the ball collides with a wall or player paddle and when a player scores.
3. Configure the game's background.
4. Add and configure a font.
5. Define objects representing the game ball, player paddles, game walls, invisible left and right goals, and a special controller object.
6. Configure the ball object to respond to various events and perform specific actions.
7. Add a room to the game and populate it with the ball, player paddles, walls, invisible goals, and the controller object.

## Step 1—Creating the Game's Sprites

To create this game you will need to add four sprites to it, representing a ball, paddle, goal, and wall. The ball sprite will be used later to create a ball object that will bounce around the screen. The players will attempt to keep the ball in play, using a paddle object represented by the paddle sprite. As the ball moves across the screen, it may bounce off the game's upper and lower walls, represented by repeated instances of the wall sprite. Lastly, an invisible goal object will be placed along the left and right sides of the screen. Players will score points when they hit the ball past their opponent's paddle into the invisible goal.

If you have not already done so, begin by starting Game Maker, or if Game Maker is already running, click on File > New to create a new application and then use the following steps to add the game's first sprite.

1. Next, click on Resources > Create Sprite and then type **`spr_ball`** as the name for the game's first sprite.

2. The graphic files you will need to create each of the game's sprites are available for download on this book's companion web page located at www.courseptr.com/downloads. Once downloaded, click on the Load Sprite button to navigate to the location where you saved the files and select the ball.gif file and then click on Open.

3. Click on OK to close the Sprite Properties window.

Using the process outlined above, create a new sprite named `spr_paddle`, assigning it the paddle.gif file; a sprite named `spr_goal`, assigning it the goal.gif file; and a sprite named `spr_wall`, assigning it the wall.gif file. Unlike all of the other sprites, the `wall.gif` file does not have a transparent background, so disable the `spr_wall` sprite's Transparent setting.

**Hint**

If you have not already done so, go ahead and save your game by clicking on File > Save and then assigning it a name of SuperPong. Saving your game early and often is a good habit to get into, as it can prevent the loss of work should Game Maker crash or a power failure occur.

## Step 2—Creating Sounds

The second step in the development of the Super Pong game is to define the sounds that will be used to play the game's sound effects. You will need to create two sounds, one for when the ball collides with the wall or a paddle and one for when a player scores. Game Maker comes equipped with a nice collection of audio files that are perfect for generating sound effects. By default, these audio files are stored in the C:\Program Files\Game Maker7\Sounds folder. Two of these files will be used as the basis for creating the game's sounds.

The following procedure outlines the steps required to create the first sound.

1. Click on Resources > Create Sound. This will open the Sound Properties window.
2. Assign a name of `snd_collision` to the sound.
3. Click on the Load Sound button and navigate to the C:\Program Files\Game Maker7\Sounds folder and select the Beep1.wav file and then click on Open.
4. Click on OK to close the Sprite Properties window.

Using the process outlined above, create a new sound named `snd_score`, assigning it the zap.wav file.

## Step 3—Adding a Background

Now that the game's sprites and sounds have been defined, it is time to define a background for the game. The steps required to add the game's background are outlined here:

1. Click on Resources > Create Background. Game Maker will respond by displaying the Background Properties window.
2. Enter **`bck_black`** into the Name file.
3. The graphic file you will need to create the background is available for download on this book's companion web page located at www.courseptr.-com/downloads. Once downloaded, click on the Load Background button and navigate to the location where you saved the file and select the black.bmp file and then click on Open.
4. Click on OK to close the Background Properties window.

## Step 4—Adding a Font

In this game, player scores are going to be displayed, well actually drawn, at the top of the screen. By default, Game Maker draws all text using a font type of Arial

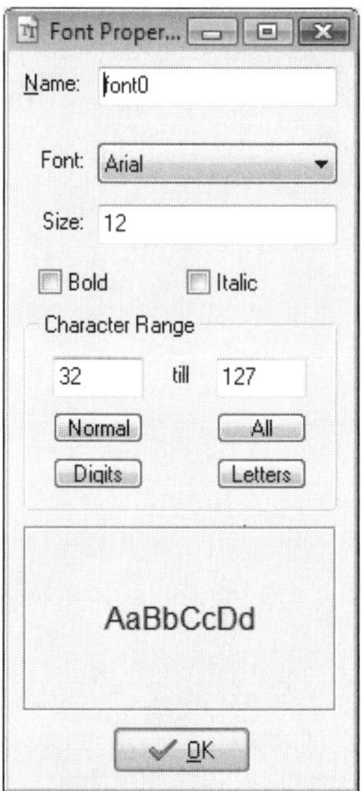


**Figure 4.24**
Adding and then configuring a new font for your game.

at a font size of 12 points. This is too small to suit the game's needs. To make player's scores stand out, the game needs a larger-sized font. To set this up, you need to add a font to your game. The steps that you need to follow are outlined here:

1. Click on Resources > Create Font. Game Maker will respond by displaying the Font Properties window as shown in Figure 4.24.

2. Enter `font_text` into the Name file.

3. Leaving the Font type set to Arial, enter **18** as the size of the font, and then click on OK.

Now that a new font has been added, you will be able to tell Game Maker to use it later in the development of the game to display player scores.

## Step 5—Defining the Game's Objects

Super Pong consists of a number of objects, some of which players can see and some of which they cannot. The visible objects include the ball, paddles, and walls. The invisible objects include the left and right goals and a special controller object. A *controller* object is an object that is usually not visible and its purpose is to perform actions that help initiate, manage, and terminate game play. In this game, the controller object will be used to do the following:

- Initialize special values used to keep track of player scores
- Display a caption in the game window
- Create the first instance of the ball, thus starting game play
- Specify the font to be used when drawing player scores
- Specify the color to be used when drawing
- To draw both player's starting scores (0)

None of the actions listed above are directly associated with any of the ball, paddle, or wall objects, so it makes sense that they be performed by a different special-purpose object (e.g., the controller object).

Let's begin by defining all of the objects that will be visible to the players, starting with the ball object and then moving on to the paddle objects followed by the wall object.

#### Creating the ball object

1. Click on Resources > Create Object. Game Maker responds by displaying the Object Properties window.
2. Type **`obj_ball`** in the Name field.
3. Click on the context menu icon located at the end of the Sprite text field. A list of all the sprites defined in the application appears.
4. Select the `spr_ball` object.
5. Click on the OK button to close the Object Properties window.

#### Creating the right paddle object

1. Click on Resources > Create Object. Game Maker responds by displaying the Object Properties window.
2. Type **`obj_rightpaddle`** in the Name field.
3. Click on the context menu icon located at the end of the Sprite text field. A list of all the sprites defined in the application appears.

4. Select the `spr_paddle` object.

5. Click on the OK button to close the Object Properties window.

### Creating the left paddle object

1. Click on Resources > Create Object. Game Maker responds by displaying the Object Properties window.

2. Type **`obj_leftpaddle`** in the Name field.

3. Click on the context menu icon located at the end of the Sprite text field. A list of all the sprites defined in the application appears.

4. Select the `spr_paddle` object.

5. Click on the OK button to close the Object Properties window.

### Creating the wall object

1. Click on Resources > Create Object. Game Maker responds by displaying the Object Properties window.

2. Type **`obj_wall`** in the Name field.

3. Click on the context menu icon located at the end of the Sprite text field. A list of all the sprites defined in the application appears.

4. Select the `spr_wall` object.

5. In order to facilitate collision with the ball object, enable the object's `Solid` property.

6. Click on the OK button to close the Object Properties window.

Now that all of the visible objects have been accounted for, let's create the object that the players cannot see.

### Creating the right goal object

1. Click on Resources > Create Object. Game Maker responds by displaying the Object Properties window.

2. Type **`obj_rightgoal`** in the Name field.

3. Click on the context menu icon located at the end of the Sprite text field. A list of all the sprites defined in the application appears.

4. Select the `spr_goal` object.
5. This object is not to be seen by the player, so clear its `Visible` property.
6. Click on the OK button to close the Object Properties window.

**Creating the left goal object**

1. Click on Resources > Create Object. Game Maker responds by displaying the Object Properties window.
2. Type `obj_leftgoal` in the Name field.
3. Click on the context menu icon located at the end of the Sprite text field. A list of all the sprites defined in the application appears.
4. Select the `spr_goal` object.
5. This object is not to be seen by the player, so clear its `Visible` property.
6. Click on the OK button to close the Object Properties window.

**Creating the controller object**

1. Click on Resources > Create Object. Game Maker responds by displaying the Object Properties window.
2. Type **`obj_controller`** in the Name field. This object will not be visible to the player and therefore will not be assigned a sprite. Note that although this object will not be seen, it will be assigned an action that draws player's scores on the screen and therefore its `Visible` property must remain enabled.
3. Click on the OK button to close the Object Properties window.

## Step 6—Developing Object Program Logic

Now that you have added all of the objects that are needed to play the game, it is time to go back and add the program logic to those objects to bring them to life. This of course means assigning events to objects and then the actions those events will trigger. Some objects, specifically the `obj_wall`, `obj_rightgoal`, and `obj_leftgoal` objects, do not do anything during game play other than simply exist. Therefore, you will not have to assign any program logic to these objects, only to the special controller object and the objects that move about the screen.

When initially created, an instance of the `obj_ball` object becomes visible. It should pause briefly and then begin moving randomly in one direction. The `obj_ball` object must be programmed to respond to collisions with the wall, player paddles, and the left and right goals.

### Adding programming logic to the `obj_ball` object

1. Begin by expanding the Objects folder located in the resource folder tree and then double-click on the `obj_ball` object and the Add Event button and then click on the Create Event button to add the Create event to the object.

2. Click on the main2 tab and drag and drop an instance of the Sleep action onto the actions area. A window will appear prompting you to specify how long the object should pause before resuming its execution. Enter **2000** to pause the object for two seconds.

3. Click on the Move tab and drag and drop an instance of the Move Fixed action onto the actions area. Click on all three of the arrows located in the first and last columns, instructing Game Maker to move the object in one of six random directions. Then enter **10** in the Speed field to get the object moving 10 pixels per step in the randomly selected direction, as shown in Figure 4.25.

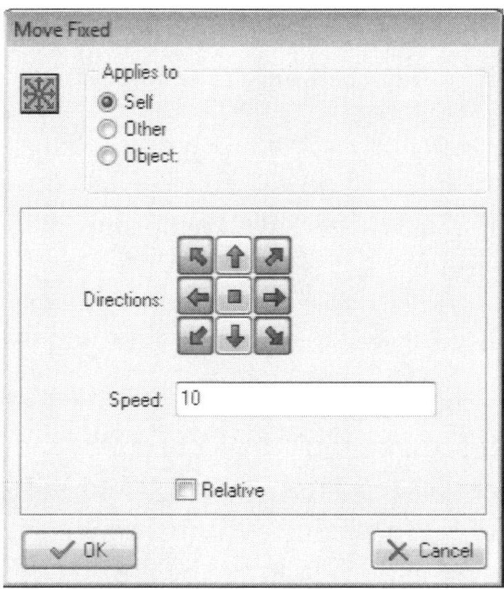


**Figure 4.25**
Configuring the speed and random direction of the ball.

4. Click on the Add Event button and then click on the Collision Event button. Game Maker will display a list of objects in the application. Select the `obj_rightpaddle` object, click on the Move tab, and drag and drop an instance of the Move Fixed action onto the actions area. Click on all three of the arrows located in the first column, and then enter **10** into the Speed field.

5. Click on the main1 tab and drag and drop an instance of the Play Sound action onto the actions area. Click on the context menu icon located at the end of the Sound field and select the `snd_collision` sound.

6. Click on the Add Event button and then click on the Collision Event button. Select the `obj_leftpaddle` object. Drag and drop an instance of the Move Fixed action onto the actions area. Click on all three of the arrows located in the last column, and then enter **10** into the Speed field. Drag and drop an instance of the Play Sound action onto the actions area and assign it the `snd_collision` sound.

7. Add a new collision event to the object and set it to the `obj_wall` object. Click on the Move tab and drag and drop an instance of the Bounce action into the actions area. No changes are required for this action so click on OK to close its configuration window. Add the Play Sound action to the actions area and configure it to use the `snd_collision` sound.

8. Add a new collision event to the object and set it to the `obj_leftgoal` object. Click on the Score tab and drag and drop an instance of the Set Score action to the actions area. Type **1** in the New Score field and enable the Relative option. This will increase Player 1's score by one point when he scores a point.

9. Select the main1 tab and add an instance of the Destroy Instance action. Leave the default setting of Self selected and click on OK to close its configuration window when it is displayed. This will remove the current instance of the `obj_ball` object from the room.

10. Drag and drop the Play Sound action onto the actions area and set it to play the `snd_score` sound.

11. Now it is time to do a little conditional programming logic. Begin by selecting the Score tab and adding the Test Score action. Enter **11** into the Value field and leave the Operation field set to a value of "equal to." Next, click on the Control tab and add the Start of a Block followed by the End of a Block actions to the actions area. Any actions placed inside the two blocks will execute when the value of score is equal to 11.

12. Select the main2 tab and drag and drop an instance of the Sleep action in between the Start of a Block action and the End of a Block action and enter **500** (a half second) in the Milliseconds field. Add an instance of the Display Message action to the actions area, immediately following the Sleep action and enter "**Game over. Click on OK to play again.**" in its message field. Lastly, add an instance of the Restart Game action to the Actions area immediately following the Display Message action.

13. Next, select the Control tab and add an instance of the Else action to the bottom of the actions area followed by a Start of a Block and an End of a Block action. Any actions you embed inside the Start of a Block and End of a Block actions will only be executed when the value of score is not equal to 11.

14. Select the main1 tab and drag and drop an instance of the Create Instance action in between the Start of a Block and an End of a Block actions, selecting `obj_ball` and entering **384** and **284** as the value to the objects starting X and Y coordinates (placing the object roughly in the middle of the room). At this point the programming logic for the collision event with the `obj_leftgoal` object should look like the example shown in Figure 4.26.

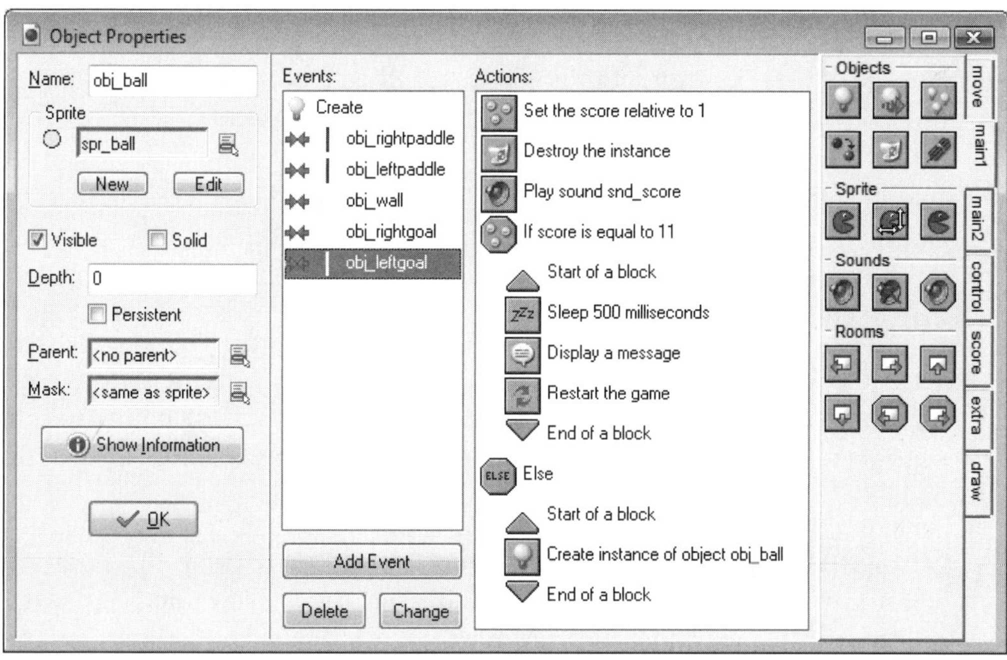


**Figure 4.26**
The programming logic used to control what happens with collisions between the ball and the left goal.

**Trick**

Game Maker provides built-in actions for keeping track of player scores in single-player games. However, it does not provide equivalent actions for keeping track of a second player's score. One quick and easy way around this limitation is to use Game Maker's lives actions to keep track of the second player's score. You will learn more about how to work with both score and lives actions in Chapter 7.

15. All that remains is to add a collision event with the `obj_rightgoal` object. The program logic used by this event is almost identical to that used by the `obj_leftgoal` object. The only difference being that lives actions are used in place of score actions. To save time in setting up this event, right-click on the `obj_leftgoal` event and select Duplicate Event from the context menu that appears. Game Maker will prompt you to specify the type of event you want to work with. Click on the Collision button and then select `obj_rightgoal`. Now all you have to do is replace the event's Set Score action with the Set Lives action, which you will find on the Score tab, and assign a Set Lives action a value of 1 and enable its Relative option. Lastly, you need to replace the event's Test Score action with the Test Lives action and assign that action a value of 11.

The right and left paddles must move in response to keyboard input. Specifically the right paddle must move up when Player 2 presses the up arrow key and down when Player 2 presses the down arrow key. It must stop moving when the player releases both of these keys and it must also react when it bumps into the upper or lower wall.

### Adding programming logic to the `obj_rightpaddle` object

1. Double-click on the `obj_rightpaddle` object in the resource folder tree, click on the Add Event button, select the Collision Event button, and then select the `obj_wall` object.

2. Select the Reverse Vertical action and drag and drop it onto the actions area. Leave the default selection of Self and click OK on the actions configuration window to close it. This will deflect the ball backward when hit by the right paddle.

3. Click on the Add Event button and when prompted click on the Event Selector window's Keyboard button and select the `<no key>` option. Next, drag and drop an instance of the Moved Fixed action to the actions area and then select the center button in the Directions area. This will halt the movement of the paddle.

4. Click on the Add Event button and when prompted click on the Event Selector window's Keyboard button and select the `<Up>` option. Next, drag and drop an instance of the Speed Vertical action to the actions area and then enter **-6** as the value assigned to vert. speed. This will move Player 2's paddle in a downward direction when the down arrow key is pressed.

5. Click on the Add Event button and when prompted click on the Event Selector window's Keyboard button and select the <Down> option. Next, drag and drop an instance of the Speed Vertical action to the actions area and then enter **6** as the value assigned to vert. speed. This will move Player 2's paddle in an upward direction when the up arrow key is pressed.

### Adding programming logic to the `obj_leftpaddle` object

1. Double-click on the `obj_leftpaddle` object in the resource folder tree, click on the Add Event button, select the Collision Event button, and then select the `obj_wall` object.

2. Select the Reverse Vertical action and drag and drop it onto the actions area. Leave the default selection of Self and click OK on the actions configuration window to close it. This will deflect the ball backward when hit by the right paddle.

3. Click on the Add Event button and when prompted click on the Event Selector window's Keyboard button and select the `<no key>` option. Next, drag and drop an instance of the Moved Fixed action to the actions area and then select the center button in the Directions area. This will halt the movement of the paddle.

4. Click on the Add Event button and when prompted click on the Event Selector window's Keyboard button and select the `<Shift>` option. Next, drag and drop an instance of the Speed Vertical action to the actions area and then enter **-6** as the value assigned to vert. speed. This will move Player 2's paddle in a downward direction when the left Shift key is pressed.

5. Click on the Add Event button and when prompted click on the Event Selector window's Keyboard button and select the `<Ctrl>` option. Next, drag and drop an instance of the Speed Vertical action to the actions area and then enter **6** as the value assigned to vert. speed. This will move Player 1's paddle in an upward direction when the left Control key is pressed.

The controller object, as already stated, gets things started by creating the first instance of the ball and initializing player scores. It must also specify the font and color used to draw player scores on the screen and draw both players' initial scores.

**Adding programming logic to the `obj_controller` object**

1. Double-click on the `obj_controller` object in the resource folder tree, click on the Add Event button, select the Other Event button, and then select the Room Start event.
2. The next step is to select the Score tab and add an instance of both the Set Score and Set Lives actions. By default, both of these actions will default to an initial value of 0 so no changes are required.
3. By default, Game Maker displays player score as a caption in the game window's titlebar. You will need to disable this feature for this game by dragging and dropping the Score Caption action from the Score tab to the actions area and then assigning a value of Don't Show for the Show Score, Show Lives, and Show Health fields, as shown in Figure 4.27.
4. Select the main1 tab and add an instance of the Create Instance action to the actions area. When prompted, assign as its object the `obj_ball` object and assign 384 and 284 as the initial X and Y coordinates for this new instance of the object.

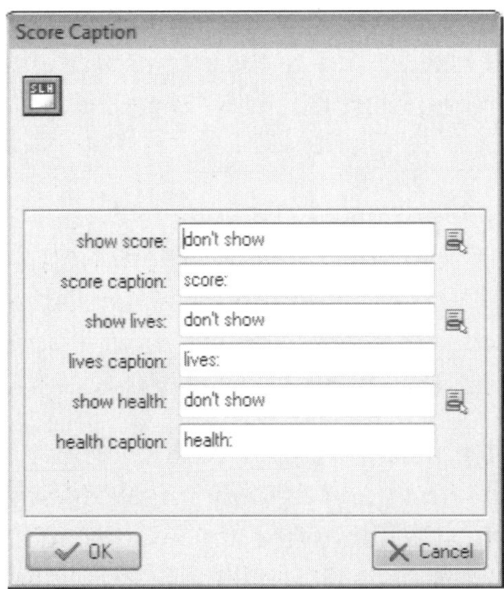


**Figure 4.27**
Disabling the display of score, lives, and health information.

5. Click on the Add Event button and then add the Draw event to the `obj_controller` object. Once added, click on the Draw tab and add the Set Font action, specifying the `font_text` font when prompted.
6. Next, add an instance of the Set Color action and select a color of yellow when prompted by clicking on the context menu located on the Set Color window and selecting the color from the color palette that is displayed.
7. Finally, click on the Draw tab and drag and drop two instances of the Draw Text action onto the actions area. Configure the first instance by entering **`'Player 1: ' + string(lives)`** in its text field and **50** and **25** as its X and Y coordinates. Likewise, configure the second instance by entering **`'Player 2: ' + string(score)`** in its text field and **630** and **25** as its X and Y coordinates.

**Hint**

The statement that you were instructed to key into the text fields of the Draw Text action window are examples of expressions created using the GML scripting language. Each of these expressions is ultimately resolved into a text string that dynamically reports a player's current score. You will learn all about GML in Chapters 9 through 11.

## Step 7—Creating a Room

The last step in the creation of the Super Pong game is to add a room in which game play will occur. To do so, click on Resources > Create Room. The Room Properties window appears. By default, Game Maker sizes new rooms at 640 × 480 pixels. This is not a lot of space for a game like Super Pong. To remedy this situation, click on the Settings tab and change the room's width to 800 and its height to 594. Also, add a caption of Super Pong to the Caption for the Room field. Next, click on the Backgrounds tab and then change the background color of the room to black by clicking on the Color field. This opens a window displaying a color palette. Select black as the background color and click on OK to close the Color window. You are now ready to begin populating the room with the objects needed to facilitate game play. The instructions for completing this final task are outlined next.

1. Click on the Objects tab and then click on the context menu in the middle of the tab pane to display a list of the game's objects. Select `obj_wall` and then, using repeated instances of this object, fill the entire upper and lower rows of the window with this object. You should end up with two solid walls, one along the top of the room and another along the bottom of the room.

2. Next, click on the context menu again and this time select the `obj_leftgoal` object and then use it to fill in the entire first column of the room.
3. Repeat step two above, this time selecting the `obj_rightgoal` and filling in the entire last column in the room.
4. Next, click on the context menu and select the `obj_rightpaddle` object and then add a single instance of it to the room in the center of the second to last far right column.
5. Repeat step 4, this time adding the `obj_leftpaddle`, placing it in the center of the second column on the left-hand side of the room.
6. Lastly, click on the context menu and select the `obj_controller` object and then add a single instance of it to the room. The object is invisible and can be placed anywhere you want within the room.

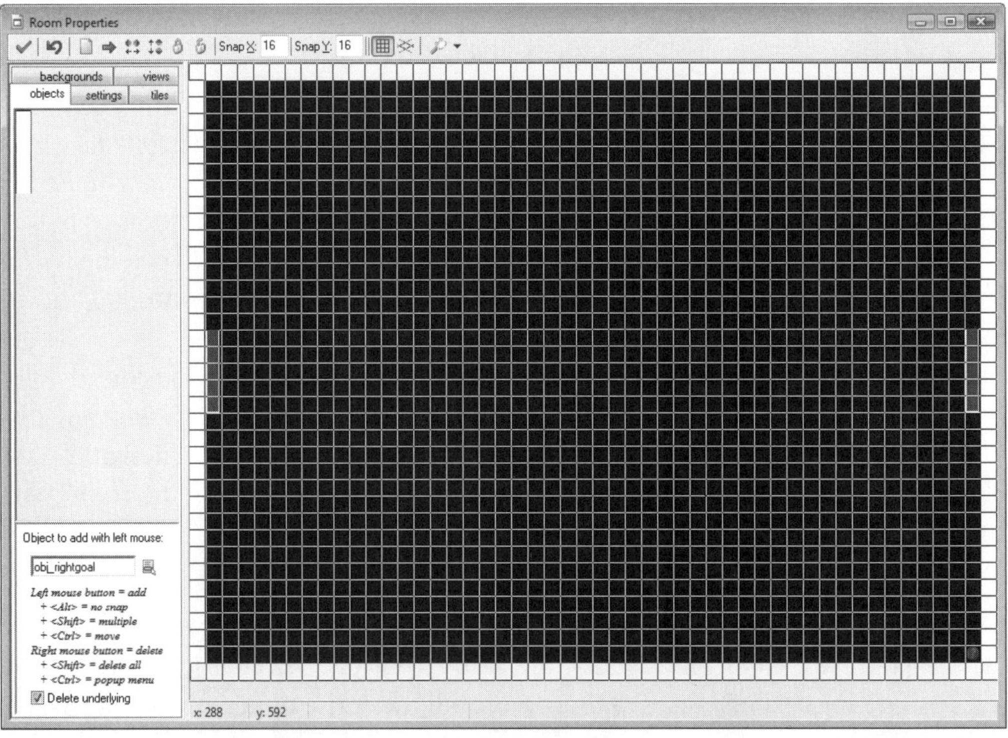


**Figure 4.28**
Adding a room and populating it with objects is the final step in the development of the game.

**Trap**

If you forget to add the special control object to a room, that object will not be able to initiate, manage, or terminate any activities within the room.

Once you are done working on the room, it should look like the examples shown in Figure 4.28.

Assuming that you followed along carefully with the instructions that have been presented and that you have not accidently skipped any steps, your copy of the Super Pong game should be ready for testing. Give it a go and see how well it works!

## Summary

This chapter rounded out your understanding of the different types of resources required to create basic computer games. You learned more about how to work with sprites and how to configure their properties. You also learned more about sounds and how they are used to generate audio effects and background music. This chapter also provided a detailed overview of backgrounds, including how to work with tile sets. Lastly, this chapter provided a detailed review of rooms and explained their importance and usage in games. Finally, you learned how to create the Super Pong game.

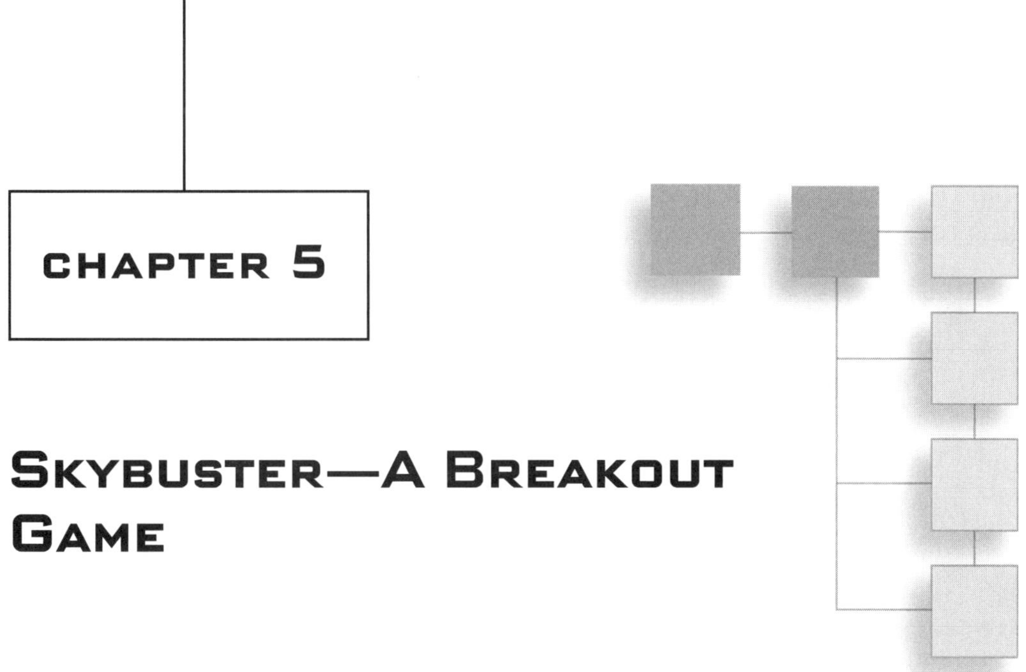


# Skybuster—A Breakout Game

Up to this point in the book, you have learned a lot about Game Maker's features and capabilities. You have also learned how to navigate Game Maker's IDE and how to work with the basic building blocks that make up Game Maker games. You've even created both a demo and your first game. Now that you have a good understanding of the mechanics involved in creating games, this chapter takes a step back and focuses on the principles of good game design. By applying this information, you will be able to create better and more challenging games.

An overview of the major topics covered in this chapter includes:

- An examination of the importance of setting goals for game play and rewarding players when they accomplish those goals
- A review of different ways in which developers can provide players with a feeling of control
- An examination of different options that you can use to ensure game play remains challenging throughout the game

## Focusing on Good Game Design

The first step in creating a new computer game is to come up with a good and unique idea. Typically, this involves the creation of an innovative character and story line or a formula for the development of a challenging and exciting playing experience. In addition to these primary ingredients, all good computer games also consist of the following features.

- Visually appealing graphics that help bring a sense of realism and excitement
- Quality sound effects and background music that are seamlessly integrated into the game and help establish a sense of realism and excitement
- A good design backed by clear understanding of the goal of the game

In professional games, the creation of visually stunning graphics for use as sprites and backgrounds is performed by professional graphic artists with years of education, training, and experience. Likewise, realistic sound effects and mood setting background music are developed by professional sound effect specialists and musicians.

**Hint**

Exploration of graphic design and audio development is well outside the scope of this book. You can learn more about these topics from other books and from colleges and universities with game development, multimedia, and music programs.

Instead of trying to teach you graphic design and audio engineering skills, this chapter's focus is on teaching you the basic principles of good game design. Once you understand the qualities that make games fun and appealing, you can worry about the rest later. In the interim, you can take a stab at creating your own graphics and audio using free or low-cost multimedia applications or you can also look for graphic and audio content on the internet, where graphic artists and audio engineers eagerly wait to show off and sell their hard work to aspiring game developers.

**Hint**

If you know someone who is a talented graphic artist or who has a musical background, you might want to consider forming a partnership with him or her. By combining your game development talent with their unique skills, you can create a win-win situation for everyone.

## Designing Your Game

Before you sit down at your computer to begin creating the world's next great computer game, you should first set aside a little time to plan the design of the game. Professional game development companies typically assemble teams of professionals who lock themselves away in rooms outlining the premise and design of their next new game, before anyone starts working on it. By taking the time to put a plan or outline on paper, you help to focus your thoughts.

Begin by writing down a sentence of two that describes the overall premise of your game. Next, write down the goal of the game. Is it for the player to go on an adventure and find a lost treasure or to race right through a series of challenging levels and to overcome an ultimate foe at the game's final level? Once you have the goal defined, develop subgoals for the game. These subgoals may be things achieved at regular intervals during game play. For example, players may have to achieve a different subgoal on each level of the game in order to advance to the next level.

Next, describe the different characters (objects) that you intend on adding to the game and list their major characteristics, features, and any sounds (special effects) they may make. You should also identify the controls that you will create for controlling these objects and specify how objects might interact with one another. If your game is going to consist of different rooms (levels), describe each one, explaining how it looks and identifying which rooms the game's different objects can be found in. Don't forget about specifying the different types of background music you want to use in each room.

Once you have completed putting together an overall design outline for your game, you need to go about creating or collecting the graphics and audio files you will need to create all of the game's sprites, backgrounds, and sounds. Once all of this is in place, you will be ready to sit down and begin work on your new game.

## Take Care When Designing Levels

One critical aspect of game development is the design of the different levels that make it up. Obviously, you need to start out by presenting easier levels first, saving more complicated levels for the end of the game. As you design your game's levels keep in mind that players who are new to your game have a lot to learn upfront. As such, it's a good idea to limit the number of controls that the player must learn in the beginning. You can always introduce new controls as the player progresses through the game.

By the time players advance through the first two to three levels of the game, they should be getting comfortable with the game and its controls. This is the point where the game's levels should be designed to be really challenging. If players really like your game, they should become fully engrossed and addicted, forgetting everything else. Players' skill levels should begin to grow rapidly. It is important that you continue to toss new challenges out to them at an appropriate rate. Throw them out too fast and players can get frustrated. Throw them out too slow and players may get bored.

Eventually, players who stick with the game will get really good at it. Their level of improvement will begin to level off. If you time things right, this should coincide with the point in the game where the player is introduced to the game's climax, hopefully making for a great finale and conclusion. If you do not time things correctly, and wait too long, players may not stick around long enough to reach the end. If you let the player reach the end of the game too soon, things may work out or players may come away feeling cheated because they were emotionally unprepared for the ending.

The best way to determine whether you are getting things right with the design of your levels is to lay them out carefully, going from simple to complex all the while introducing new features, obstacles, and rewards. Of course, you need to test each level and make sure that it feels right and that together they provide the player with a fun, fair, and well-balanced experience. But don't take your own word for it. Enlist the help of your friends and get their feedback. Make sure you ask them about each level and whether or not you got them in the correct order. Find out what they like about a given level and consider adding it in other levels. Find out what they don't like and consider reducing its occurrence or even eliminating it all together.

## Creating Challenging Games

A computer game is an interactive experience involving one or more players in pursuit of a common goal. In order to achieve this goal, multiple obstacles or challenges must be overcome. In order to be successful, your games must challenge players and keep them entertained. This is achieved by creating an interactive experience in which players at all skill levels are kept engrossed in the gaming experience.

Keeping games challenging for players with different skill levels is an important game design consideration. If you make your games easy enough for beginner players, more experienced players will quickly get bored and move on. On the other hand, if you make your games challenging enough to engross experienced players, beginners will feel overwhelmed and walk away. Designing a game to satisfy the needs of both of the groups is not always easy, but it can be done using some basic design techniques.

One way of satisfying the needs of players with different levels of skill is to design the game to operate at different levels of difficulty. For example, you might give players the options of clicking on buttons labeled Easy, Medium, and Hard located on the games intro screen. Then based on the player's selection, you could vary the speed at which things move or change the number of enemies that are generated at any one time. You might instead consider creating different levels to support easy, medium, and hard levels of play. Easy levels might be smaller, less complex, have fewer obstacles, and require fewer controls to navigate and control. Medium and hard levels might feature additional objects as well as new enemies and monsters that only more experienced players will be able to overcome.

You might also consider adding a few optional training levels to your game that are designed to acclimate new players to your game and to give players a chance to pick up the basic skills required to be successful without running the risk of initially overwhelming them. Another way of accommodating players with different levels of skills is to keep an eye on the player's score and to use that score as a trigger for unleashing new levels of challenges. This way, players who are unable to score lots of points quickly can advance slowly from challenge to challenge while advanced players capable of moving quickly between challenges can do so just as fast as they can rack up points.

Yet another way of accommodating the needs of advanced players is to create a number of optional or secret advanced levels, which players do not have to play in order to complete game but which provide experienced players with greater and more satisfying challenges.

**Trap**

In your quest to create challenging levels do not fall into the trap of thinking that challenging means complex. It is very easy to get carried away in game development by making things too difficult. One way of inadvertently doing so is by giving the player access to too many controls and make the use of those controls essential to playing the game. Most players can remember five to seven different controls at most. Any more than that and players tend to get confused and frustrated. This does not mean that you cannot add any number of extra controls to your games. Just don't make them all essential. This way players can use them if they want or they can ignore them all together and stick with a few fundamental controls.

## Creating Clear Goals and Objectives

Every game needs a goal and it is critical that the player knows from the outset what that goal is. This helps to focus the player's attention and keep his interest. However, if goals seem too overwhelming or distant, they may instead turn players off. A good way of overcoming this situation is to create smaller and easier to achieve objectives, the sum total of which lead the player ever closer to meeting the game's goal.

Just as important as setting a clear goal and objectives is keeping the player informed of how well he is progressing towards them. You can do this in a variety of ways. For starters, you can display a score that lets the player know how well he is doing. For example, in a treasure hunting game, you might provide players with the ability to view their inventory or provide a map that shows how far the players have progressed on their journey.

Many action shoot-up games involve a series of battles fought over a number of levels, culminating in a fight with the game's primary antagonist, often referred to as the *boss*. In these games the boss is a computer-controlled opponent that must be defeated as the climax in the game's final level. Along the way to reach the game's boss, players may need to defeat a number of tough mini bosses. To help the player keep track of his progress, you might display the player's score along with the current level.

Game Maker provides a high score mechanism that you can include in your games to let players know how well their final score matches up against that of other players. By keeping track of high scores, you can provide players with the inspiration needed to keep playing as they aspire to earn the much-cherished high score.

## Make Sure Player Choices Count

During game play all kinds of things are going on and players have all kinds of things to think about and respond to. For example, in a *Pac-man*-style maze game, players have to decide whether to move up, down, right, or left at any moment in the game, while taking into consideration where various rewards lie and the location and direction that protagonist ghosts are moving. For these types of games, the choices are pretty straightforward and the consequences are obvious. However, other types of games allow the player to make different types of choices.

Some games allow players to select the character that they will control during game play. These characters might be a Viking warrior, a wizard, or a troll. In order for the player's choice to have any real value, there must be consequences to their decision. This could be achieved by assigning different abilities to each character. The warrior might be fast and good with a sword. The wizard might be a lousy fighter but be able to ward off enemies or even hypnotize them with a magic wand. The troll might be quite slow but impervious to certain types of blows. By giving each character unique abilities, you make character selection meaningful.

As you work on your games, when you create a situation where the player has a choice to make, ask yourself, is the choice worth making? After all, if you give the player a choice between carrying either of two types of weapons, both of which are functionally identical, what is the point? Player choices should have meaning and consequences.

## Rewarding the Player for Deeds Well Done

An important feature of any game is the proper care and feeding of the player. One way of doing this is to provide players with rewards for good play or perhaps for no reason whatsoever. The proper and timely provision of rewards can have a big impact on keeping players happy. Happy players keep playing and will keep coming back for more. Unhappy players give up and move on, which is the last thing any developer wants.

Rewards are important because they provide players with a sense of satisfaction and achievement for deeds well done. For example, when players accomplish certain tasks, you can reward them with bonus points. You can also reward players with extra lives or extra time to perform tasks that must be accomplished within specific time frames. There are other ways to provide players with rewards. One easy way is to display a message acknowledging when particular tasks are accomplished. A more involved approach might be to display a clever animated sequence at the conclusion of a level. In addition to letting players know they did well, you could use this as an opportunity to help make transitions between different levels and to instruct players on what their next objective is.

Rather than just assigning rewards for performing tasks, you can add objects at various locations within the game that players can collect as rewards. For example, you might strew a collection of medical kits around a room that when collected help to repair player health. Likewise, you might strategically place various objects that when collected give the player new or temporary abilities, like invisibility, invulnerability, or extra powerful ammunition.

Be consistent with any new capabilities you provide players and don't get carried away too early in the game. This is a common mistake. It is important that as you introduce new features that you do so in a reasonable and equitable fashion. This means not giving the player access to every possible ability under the sun in the first or second level, but instead handing them out evenly throughout the course of the game. Otherwise, what do players have to look forward to? You might want to consider giving the player access to objects that provide different abilities on different levels. This can really keep things interesting and help to keep players on their toes. Also, do not give players an ability early on that they will love and then deny players that ability in later levels.

When it comes to rewards, remember two rules. First be generous but not too generous. A healthy dose of well-earned points can be a big motivator. On the other hand, loading up the player with a ridiculous number of points every time a small or menial task is performed quickly loses any motivating appeal. The second rule of rewards is to occasionally hand them out for no reason at all. Not only is this a nice surprise but it also motivates players by giving them hope that no matter how desperate a situation may be, there is always a chance that some random reward may be around the corner.

## Always Include the Expected

Another important part of game design is to make sure, unless you have a special reason for not doing so, that you provide players with all of the common features and controls that they expect. An example of something that players have come to expect from most computer games is to be able to create and reload save points. This is especially important in adventure-style games that can take hours or days to complete, as the player will get very upset if he realizes that he has to start all over from the beginning of the game or from the beginning of a level when his character dies. Game Maker helps you do this by providing `Save Game` and `Load Game` actions.

Players also expect to be able to keep track of their character's health and to be able to tell at a glance how many lives they have left. You can provide this using Game Maker's health and lives mechanisms. It is equally important that players be able to keep an eye on their score. To help you do this, Game Maker provides access to a number of score actions.

To make all of this information visible without interfering with game play or crowding up the display of the game screen, you can display an information plan at the top, bottom, or side of the screen. Players also expect to be able to take credit for their achievements in games where they earn a score. To satisfy this requirement, you can take advantage of Game Maker's `Show Highscore` action.

When considering what types of features are essential to your games, shop around and take a look at what your competition is up to. Is there a common set of features? If so, you should probably make sure your games provide the same features.

## It's Time to Break Some Blocks

All right, now it is time to begin work on the development of this chapter's application project, the Skybuster game. Skybuster is inspired by Atari's *Breakout* game, which was one of that company's original hit games. In this single-player game, the player is given control of a paddle located at the bottom of the room and challenged with the task of trying to knock out all of the bricks located at the top of the room. The bricks come in two different colors and have different point values. The game consists of three increasingly complex levels. Players advance to the next level by clearing out all of the bricks on the current level. The player is given three lives, after which the game ends. If the player manages to advance to and clear the third level, game play continues by starting over at the first level.

Figure 5.1 shows an example of how the game will appear once you are done working on it.

In order to create this game, you will need to perform a number of steps, as outlined here:

1. Define the sprites used in the game.
2. Define sounds that will be used to generate sounds effects.
3. Configure the game's background.
4. Add a room to the game and populate it with objects.
5. Define objects used to control game play and develop their program logic.

## Step 1—Defining the Game's Sprites

The first step in creating Skybuster is to add the sprites needed to represent the game's ball, walls, paddles, and red and green bricks. If you have not already done so, start Game Maker, or if it is already started, click on File > New to create a new application. Use the steps outlined below to add the game's first sprite.

1. Click on Resources > Create Sprite and then type `spr_ball` as the name for the game's first sprite.

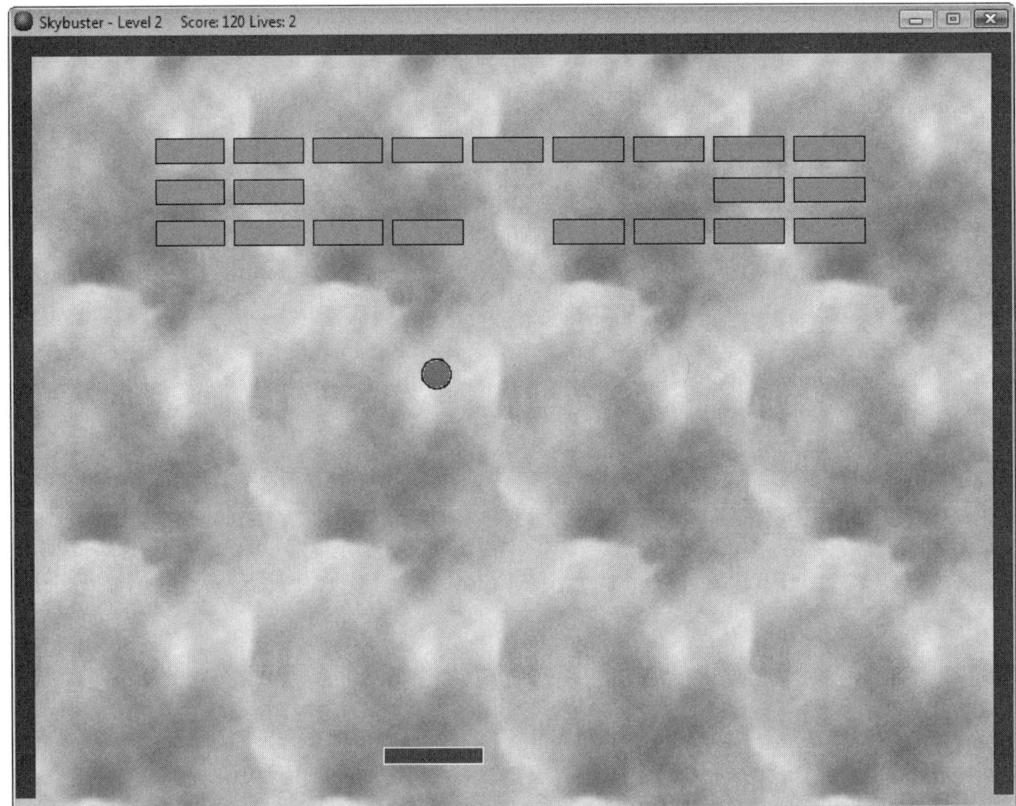


**Figure 5.1**
An example of the Skybuster game in action.

2. The graphic files you will need to create the game's sprites are available for download on this book's companion website (www.courseptr.com/downloads). Click on the Load Sprite button and navigate to the location where you saved the files, and select the `ball.gif` file and then click on Open.

3. Click on OK to close the Sprite Properties window.

Using the same set of steps outlined above, create a new sprite named `spr_paddle` assigning it the `paddle.gif` file, a sprite named `spr_goal` assigning it the `goal.gif` file, a sprite named `spr_miss`, assigning it the `miss.gif` file, and a sprite named `spr_wall`, assigning it the `wall.gif` file. Unlike all of the other graphic files, the `wall.gif` file does not have a transparent background, so disable the `spr_wall` sprite's Transparent setting. Next add another sprite named `spr_redbrick` and assign it the `redbrick.gif` file and a sprite named `spr_greenbrick`, assigning it the `greenbrick.gif` file.

**Hint**

If you have not already done so, save your game and continue to save the game as you complete each of the remaining development steps.

## Step 2—Creating Sounds

The next step in the development of the Skybuster game is to add the sounds needed to play the game's sound effects. This game will need three sounds, one for when the ball collides with the wall or a paddle, one for when the player misses the ball, and one for when the ball collides with the bricks. You will use audio files that come with Game Maker when creating these sounds. By default, these files are located in C:\Program Files\Game Maker7\Sounds.

The following procedure outlines the steps required to create the first sound.

1. Click on Resources > Create Sound. The Sound Properties window appears.
2. Assign a name of `snd_collision` to the sound and then click on the Load Sound button, navigate to the C:\Program Files\Game Maker7\Sounds folder, select the `Beep1.wav file`, and then click on Open.
3. Click on OK to close the Sprite Properties window.

Using the steps outlined above, create a new sound named `snd_miss`, assigning it the `zap.wav` file and then create another sound, naming it `snd_hitbrick`, and assign it the `beep5.wav` file.

## Step 3—Setting the Mood with a Good Background

Now it's time to define a background for the game. The steps required to add the game's background are outlined here:

1. Click on Resources > Create Background. The Background Properties window appears.
2. Enter **`bck_sky`** into the Name file.
3. The graphic file you will need to create the background is supplied with Game Maker and by default is located in the C:\Program Files\Game Maker7\Backgrounds folder. Click on the Load Background button, navigate to the Backgrounds folder, select the `sky.gif` file, and then click on Open.
4. Click on OK to close the Background Properties window.

## Step 4—Creating Rooms to Play In

The next step in the development of Skybuster is to add three rooms in which the game is played. The game consists of three levels, so three rooms will be needed. To create the first room, click on Resources > Create Room. The Room Properties window appears. Name the room `room_level1` and increase the size of the room by clicking on the Settings tab and changing the room's width to 800 and its height to 594. Also, add a caption of **`Skybuster - Level 1`** to the Caption for the Room field. Next, click on the Backgrounds tab and clear the Draw Background Color setting and then select `bck_sky` as the room background. At this point, this room contains all of the base features needed by every room in the game, so to make things easy, click on OK to close the room you just started creating and then right-click on it and select Duplicate from the list of options that appears. Game Maker creates an exact duplicate of the room. Repeat this step one more time to add a third room to the game. Right-click on the first duplication and select the option to rename it, assigning it a name of `room_level2`. Repeat this process with the second duplicate room, naming it `room_level3`.

You are now ready to begin populating each of the rooms with the objects needed to facilitate game play. Begin by opening `room_level 1` and selecting its Object tab. Next, select the `obj_wall` object and then draw repeated instances of it around the left, right, and top edges of the room, as shown in Figure 5.2. Then add 10 instances of the `obj_redbrick` object across the upper portion of the room. Next, select the `obj_miss` object and use it to draw a line across the bottom of the room. Finally, add an instance of the `obj_paddle` object just above the bottom center of the room and add an instance of the `obj_controller` object to the room anywhere you want.

Once you have finished working on this room, click on the green check button located on the Room Properties toolbar to save and close the room. Using the same steps outlined above, open `room_level2` and then configure it so that it contains three rows of green bricks laid out as shown in Figure 5.3.

When done, close this room and open `room_level3`, configuring it as shown in Figure 5.4.

When done, close this room and proceed to the next section where you will add and then configure the objects needed to bring the game to life.

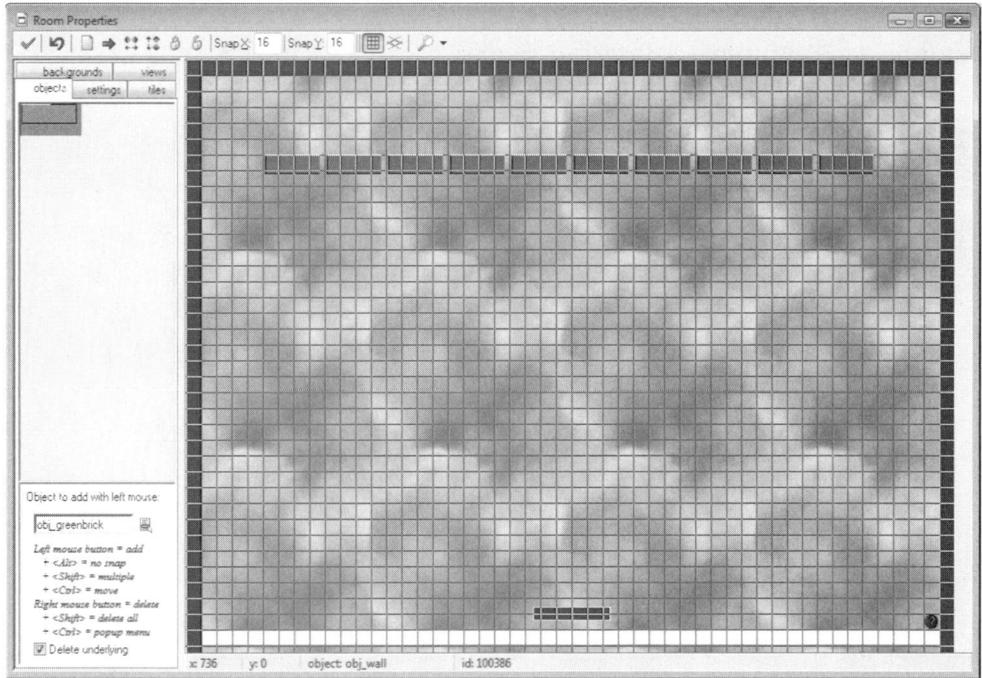


**Figure 5.2**
The first level contains a single row of red bricks.

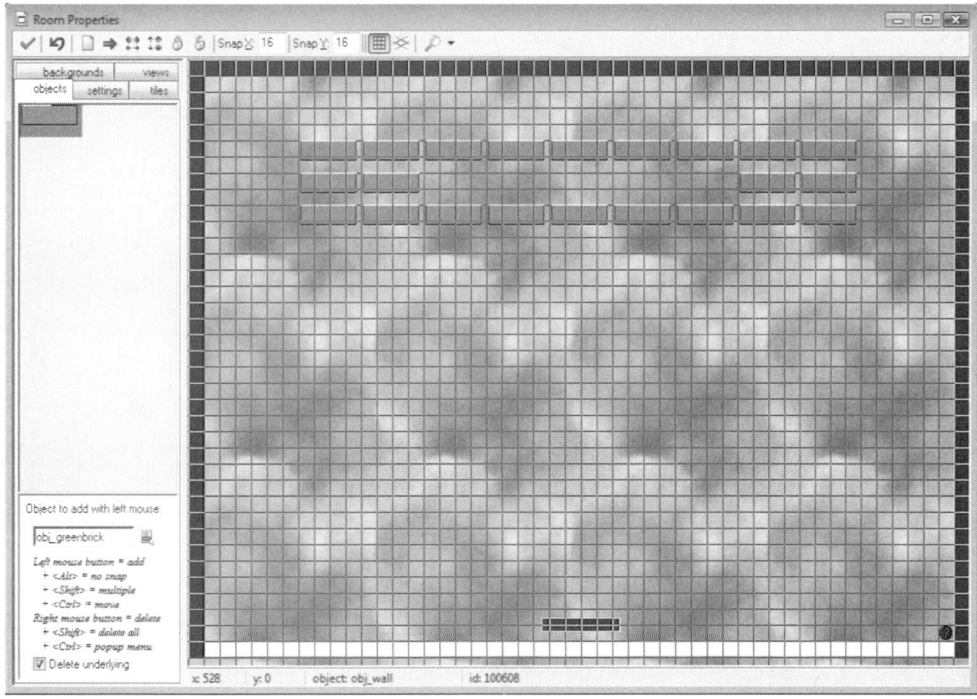


**Figure 5.3**
The second level contains three rows of green bricks.

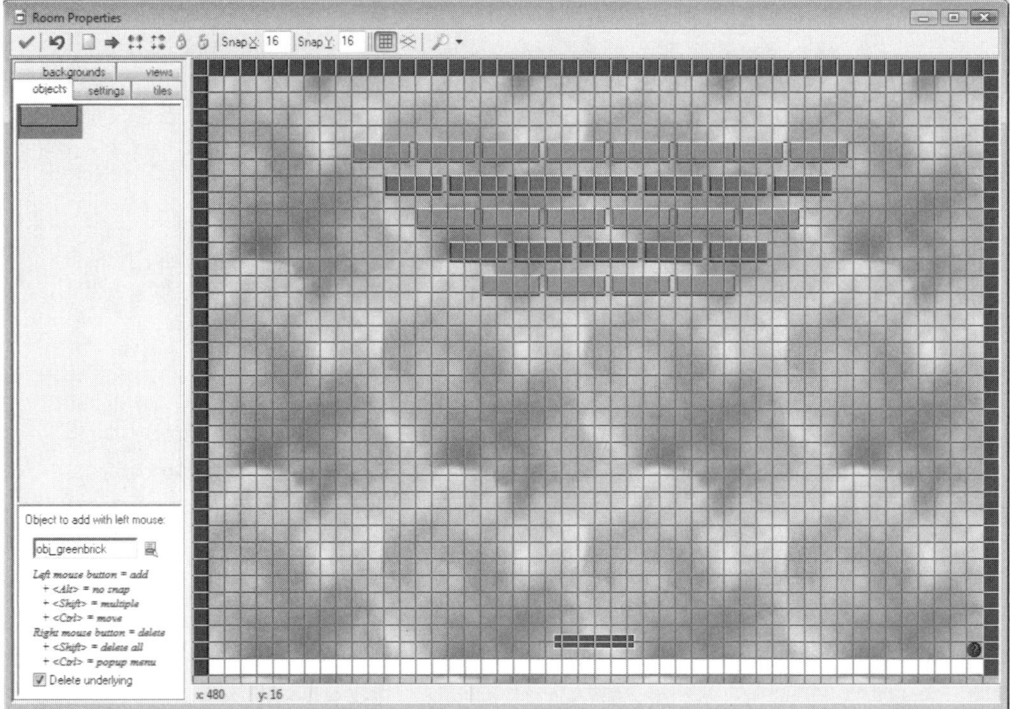


**Figure 5.4**
The third level contains five rows of red and green bricks.

## Step 5—Defining and Programming Objects

Skybuster is made up of a number of different objects, some of which are visible and some of which are not visible. The visible objects include the ball, paddles, walls, and color bricks. The invisible objects include the `obj_miss` object that will be placed at the bottom of the screen and used to determine when the player has failed to deflect the bouncing ball back into play. An invisible controller object will also be used to initiate the start of game and start of room actions as well as to track the number of bricks left in the room and manage the process of switching between rooms when all of the bricks have been knocked out. The controller object will also track player lives and determine when game play should end.

Let's begin by defining all of the objects that will be visible to the players, starting with the ball object, moving on to the paddle objects, followed by the wall object and then the red and green bricks.

### Creating the ball object

1. Click on Resources > Create Object. The Object Properties window appears.

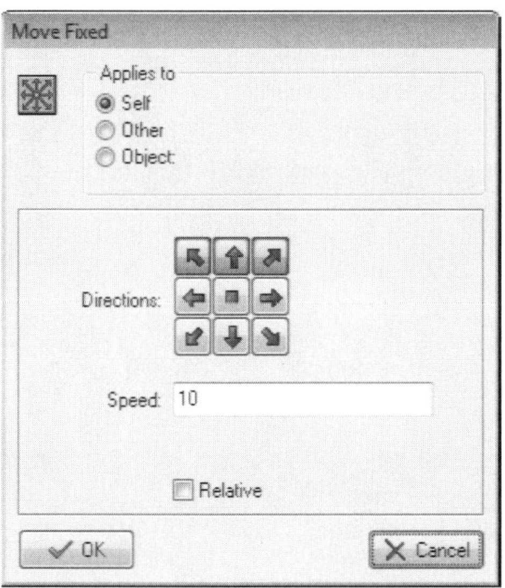


**Figure 5.5**
Specifying one of three randomly selected directions of the ball to initially move towards.

2. Type **obj_ball** in the Name field.
3. Click on the context menu icon located at the end of the Sprite text field and select `spr_ball` from the list of all the sprites that appear.
4. Add a `Create` event to the object and then click on the main2 tab and drag and drop an instance of the `Sleep` action to the actions list, entering **2000** into the Milliseconds field when prompted. Next, select the Move tab and add the `Move Fixed` action. When prompted, select all three of the buttons on the first row in the Directions area and then enter **10** into the Speed field, as shown in Figure 5.5. This will launch the ball in one of three predictable directions at the beginning of the game.
5. Add a collision event for the `obj_wall` object, select the Move tab, and add the `Bounce` action to the actions area. No configuration of this action is needed, so you can click on OK to close the Bounce window. This will make the ball bounce off all three of the game's walls. Next, select the main1 tab and add the `Play Sound` action, specifying `snd_collision` as the sound to be used as shown in Figure 5.6. Click on OK to close the Play Sound window.

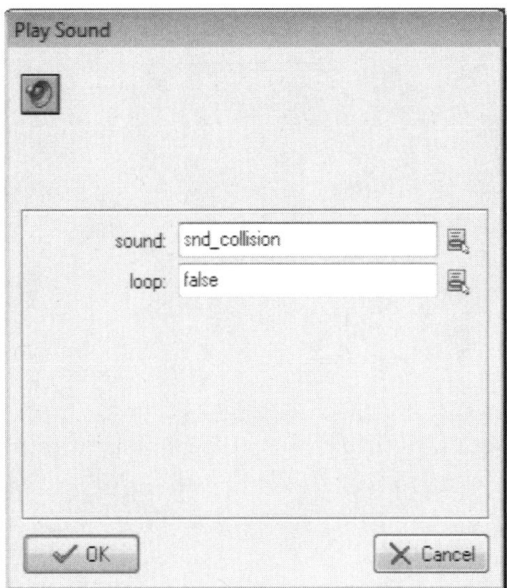


**Figure 5.6**
Configuring a sound to be played whenever the ball collides with a wall.

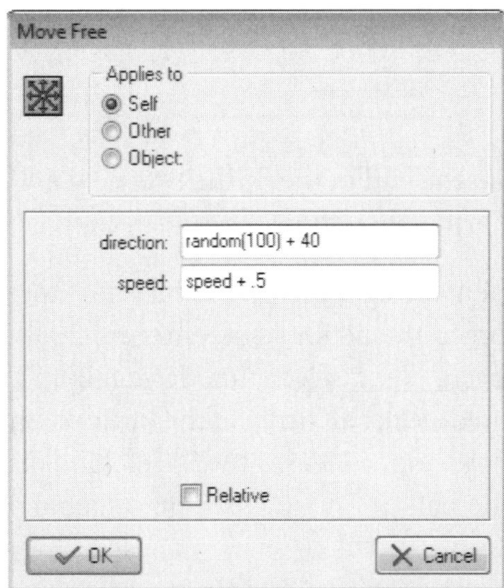


**Figure 5.7**
Configuring the ball object to move in a range of random directions at an ever increasing pace.

6. Add a collision event for the `obj_paddle` object and then select the Move tab and add the `Move Free` action to the actions area. When prompted, type **`Random(100) + 40`** in the Move Free window's Direction field and **`speed + .5`** in the Speed field, as shown in Figure 5.7.

**Hint**

The entries that you made in the Move Free window require some additional explanation. In both cases, you entered expressions whose values are calculated dynamically as the game is running. The first expression uses a built-in GML function called `random()`. This function generates a random number between 0 and a number specified inside its parentheses (e.g., 100). A value of 40 is then added to this number. The end result is a number in the range of 40 to 140. Game Maker supports the use of angles. The maximum angle you can have is 360 degrees. In Game Maker, 0 degrees points directly to the right, 90 degrees points straight up, 180 degrees point directly left, and 270 degrees points straight down.

By specifying a randomly generated number in the range of 40 to 140, you provide a wide range of possible directions that the ball may randomly travel after being deflected by the paddle. Using the `Move Free` actions in place of the `Move Fixed` action makes the game a lot more unpredictable and fun because instead of limiting the upward movement of the ball in one of three predictable directions, you instead provide for up to 100 unique angles, as demonstrated in Figure 5.9.

The second expression that you entered altered the speed at which the ball travels by increasing the number of pixels at which the ball moved–.5 every time the ball collides with the paddle. As a result, the longer the player keeps the ball in play, the faster it moves and the more challenging the game becomes. Game Maker provides access to a collection of built-in variables of which speed is one. A *variable* is a named value stored in memory. Every time Game Maker gets ready to move the ball, it checks the value of its assigned speed. You will learn more about variables, expressions, and GML programming later in Chapters 9 through 11.

7. Next, select the main1 tab and add the `Play Sound` action, specifying `snd_collision` as the sound to be used. Click on OK to close the Play Sound window.
8. Add a collision event for the `obj_miss` object and then select the Score tab and add the `Set Lives` action to the actions area. When prompted, enter **-1** into the New Lives field and click on OK to close the Set Lives window. This removes 1 from the number of lives the player has when the ball is allowed to drop off the bottom of the screen.
9. Click on the main1 tab and then add the `Destroy Instance` action. Leave the default setting of `Self` enabled and click on OK to close the Destroy Instance window.
10. Add an instance of the `Play Sound` action to the bottom of the actions area and configure it to play the `snd_miss` sound.
11. Add an instance of the `Create Instance` action and create a new instance of the `obj_ball` object at coordinates 384, 284 as shown in Figure 5.10.

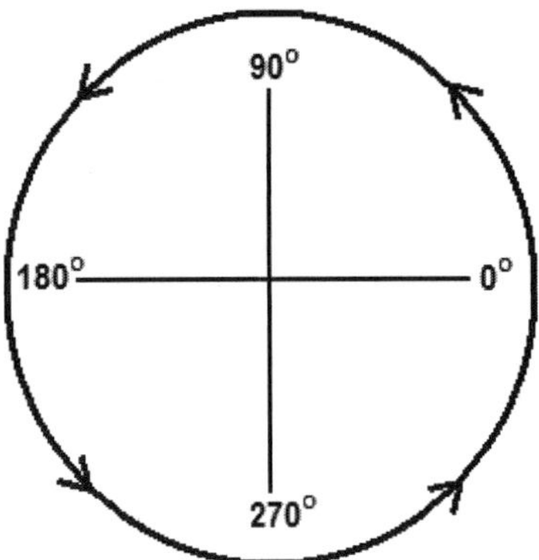


**Figure 5.8**
A depiction of how Game Maker views angles.

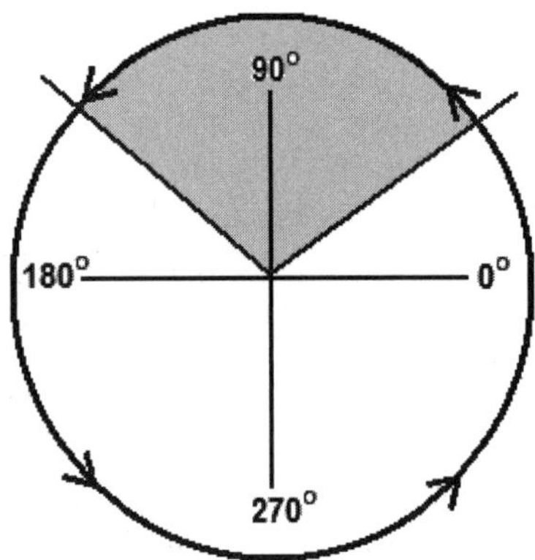


**Figure 5.9**
A depiction of the range of angles toward which the ball may bounce.

12. Add a collision event for the `obj_redbrick` object, select the Move tab, and add the `Bounce` action to the actions area. Leave the default settings in place and click on OK to close the Bounce window.

13. Repeat the last step, this time for the `obj_greenbrick` object.

14. Click on OK to close the Object Properties window.

### Creating the paddle object

1. Click on Resources > Create Object. The Object Properties window appears.

2. Type **`obj_paddle`** in the Name field.

3. Click on the context menu icon located at the end of the Sprite text field and select `spr_paddle` from the list of all the sprites that appear.

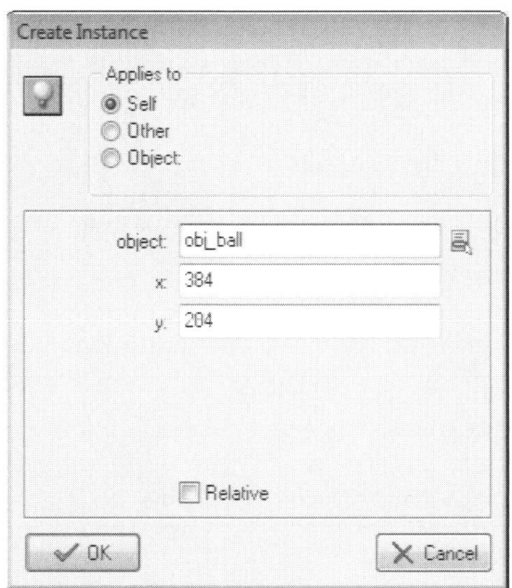


**Figure 5.10**
Configuring the ball to bounce away in the opposite direction when it hits a red block.

4. Add a collision event to the object for the `obj_wall` object, click on the Move tab, and drag and drop an instance of the `Reverse Vertical` action to the actions area. Click on the OK button to close the Vertical Reversal window.

5. Click on the Add Event button and then add a `<noKey>` keyboard event to the object.

6. Select the Move tab and then add the `Move Fixed` action to the actions area. Select the center button in the Direction area to halt the movement of the ball.

7. Add a `<Left>` keyboard to the actions area and then drag and drop an instance of the `Speed Horizontal` action. Type **-7** into the Hor. Speed field to instruct Game Maker to move the paddle 7 pixels towards the left when the left arrow key is being pressed.

8. Repeat the previous set, this time for the `<Right>` keyboard event, and assign a value of **7** to the Hor. Speed field (moving the paddle towards the right when the right arrow key is pressed).

### Creating the wall object

1. Click on Resources > Create Object. The Object Properties window appears.

2. Type **`obj_wall`** in the Name field and then enable its `Solid` property.

### Creating the red brick object

1. Click on Resources > Create Object. The Object Properties window appears.
2. Type **obj_redbrick** in the Name field and then enable its `Solid` property.
3. Click on the context menu icon located at the end of the Sprite text field and select `spr_redbrick` from the list of all the sprites that appear.
4. Add a collision event for the `obj_ball` object and then click on the main1 tab and add an instance of the `Destroy Instance` action to the actions area. Click on OK to close the Destroy Instance window.
5. Add an instance of the `Play Sound` action and configure it to play the `snd_hitbrick` sound.
6. Lastly, select the Score tab and add the `Set Score` action to the bottom of the actions area. Enter a value of **10** in the New Score field and enable the Relative setting. Click on OK to close the Set Score window.

### Creating the green brick object

1. Click on Resources > Create Object. The Object Properties window appears.
2. Type **obj_greenbrick** in the Name field and then enable its `Solid` property.
3. Click on the context menu icon located at the end of the Sprite text field and select `spr_greenbrick` from the list of all the sprites that appear.
4. Add a collision event for the `obj_ball` object and then click on the main1 tab and add an instance of the `Destroy Instance` action to the actions area. Click on OK to close the Destroy Instance window.
5. Add an instance of the `Play Sound` action and configure it to play the `snd_hitbrick` sound.
6. Lastly, select the Score tab and add the `Set Score` action to the bottom of the actions area. Enter a value of **20** in the New Score file and enable the Relative setting. Click on OK to close the Set Score window.

Now let's define the game's two invisible objects. The first of these two objects is the special controller object. The `obj_controller` object will set the number of lives available to the player to 3 at the beginning of the game. It will also set the player's score to 0 and create an initial instance of the obj_ball object to start off game play. In addition, the obj_controller object will continuously execute at every step of the game, checking to see if all of the bricks have been knocked out of the room, and if this is the case, it destroys the ball object and either moves to the next higher level (room) or if the third level has just been cleared, moves the game back to the first level (room) and then creates a new instance of the ball to initiate play. The obj_controller object also checks to see if the player has any lives left, and if he does not, it displays a message declaring the game over and then restarts the game. The obj_miss object, on the other hand, does not have any events of associated actions. All that you have to do when creating it is to make it invisible.

### Creating the controller object

1. Click on Resources > Create Object. The Object Properties window appears.
2. Type **obj_controller** in the Name field and then disable its Visible property.
3. Click on the Control tab and then add the Test Instance Count action to the actions area. Select obj_redbrick as the object to be tracked and 0 as the number of instances and leave Equal to as the operation to be performed. When configured as shown in Figure 5.11, the action will only execute when all of the red-colored bricks have been removed from the room.

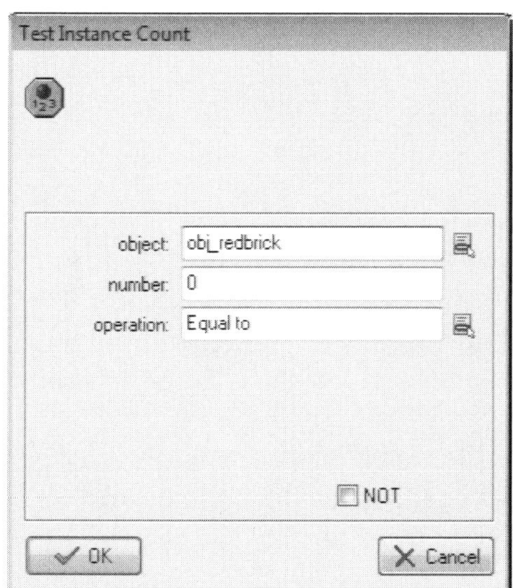


**Figure 5.11**
Configuring the conditional execution of other actions based on specific criteria.

4. Add a Start Block action followed by a Destroy Instance action (set to obj_ball) and then a Sleep action (set to 1000 milliseconds).
5. Next add a Check Next action (set to <no effect>). This will load the next room defined in the game.

**Trick**

Game Maker provides access to more than 20 (optional) special room transition effects. These effects include such things as Blend and Fade in and out when switching between rooms.

6. Add a Create Instance action and configure its target object as obj_ball, assigning coordinates of 384 and 284.
7. Add an End Block action to the end of the actions area followed by an Else action and then a Start Block.
8. Add a Different Room action (set to Room_level1) followed by the Create Instance action (set to obj_ball with coordinates of 384 and 284).
9. Next, add three consecutive End Block actions to the end of the actions area. As you add these actions, take note of how Game Maker automatically aligns them with previous Start Blocks to form logical groupings of code statements, each execution of the actions embedded within each matching set of Start Block, and End Blocks executed only when the preceding conditional actions evaluate as true.
10. Next, add a Test Lives action (set to equal to 0) followed by a final Start Block and End Block.
11. Embed a Display Message action (set to Game over. Click on OK to play again.) followed by a Sleep action (set to 500 milliseconds) and the Restart Game action within the final Start Block and End Block. At this point, the programming logic for the obj_controller object's Step event should looks like the example shown in Figure 5.12.
12. Click on the Add Event button to display the Event Selector window. Click on the Other button and then select the Game Start event from the list of events that are displayed. Add a Set Lives action (set to 3) to the Game Start event.

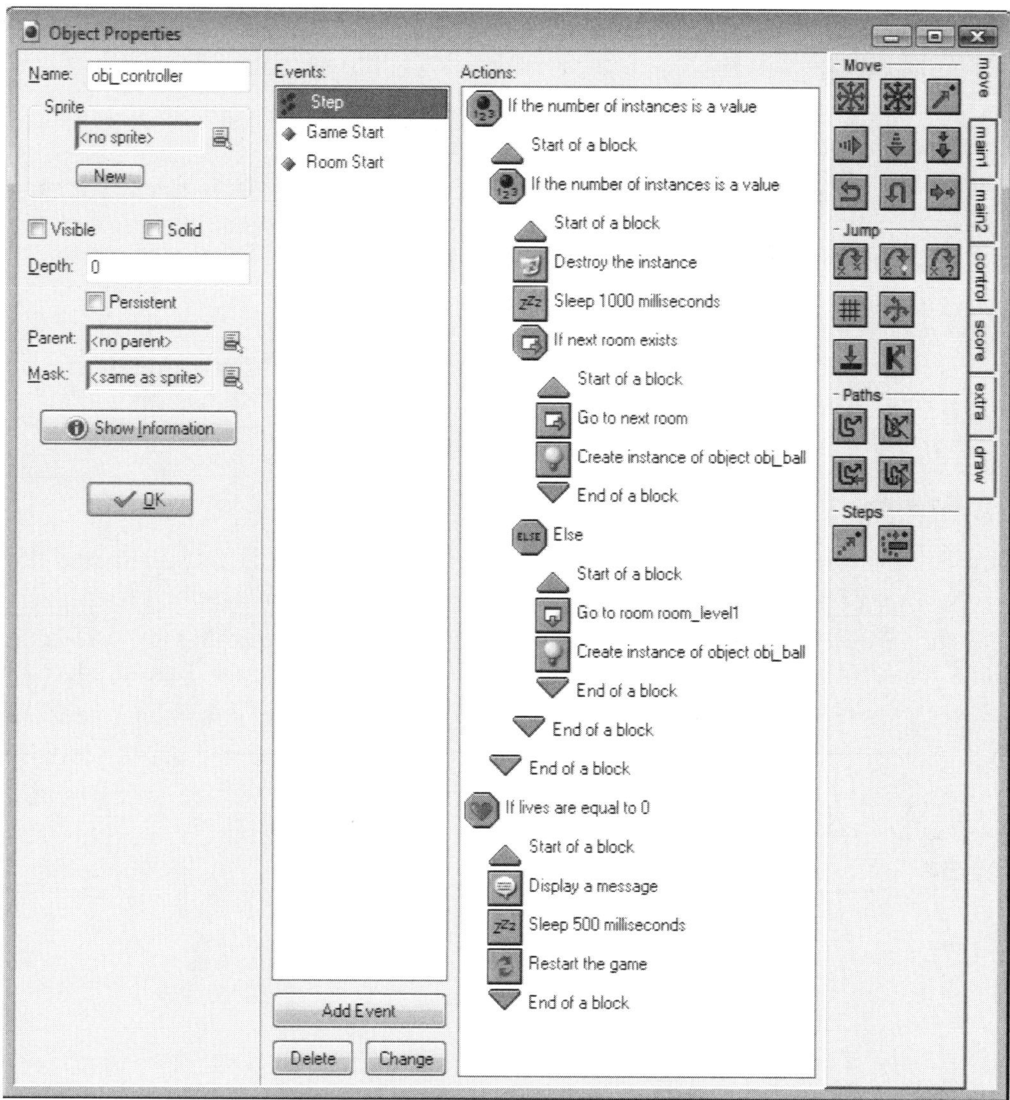


**Figure 5.12**
A review of the action icons that make the `obj_controller` object's `Step` event.

13. Click on the Add Event button to display the Event Selector window. Click on the Other button and then select the `Room Start` event from the list of events that are displayed.

14. Add a `Set Score` action (set to 0) followed by a `Score Caption` action (disabling the display of health).

15. Lastly, add a `Create Instance` action to the actions area and set its target object to `obj_ball`.

**Creating the `obj_miss` object**

1. Click on Resources > Create Object. The Object Properties window appears.
2. Type **`obj_miss`** in the Name field and then disable its `Visible` property.

That's everything! Assuming that you followed along carefully with all of the instructions that have been provided, your copy of the Skybuster game should be ready to go.

## Summary

This chapter's focus was on the principles of good game design. It explained the importance of providing your games with clear goals and the need to give players rewards. This chapter also provided you with a review of different ways in which you can ensure that players get a feeling of being in control during game play. In addition, this chapter also discussed the importance of doing your best to ensure that players of all skills levels are consistently challenged during game play. By applying the information you learned in this chapter, you will be able to build better and more challenging games.

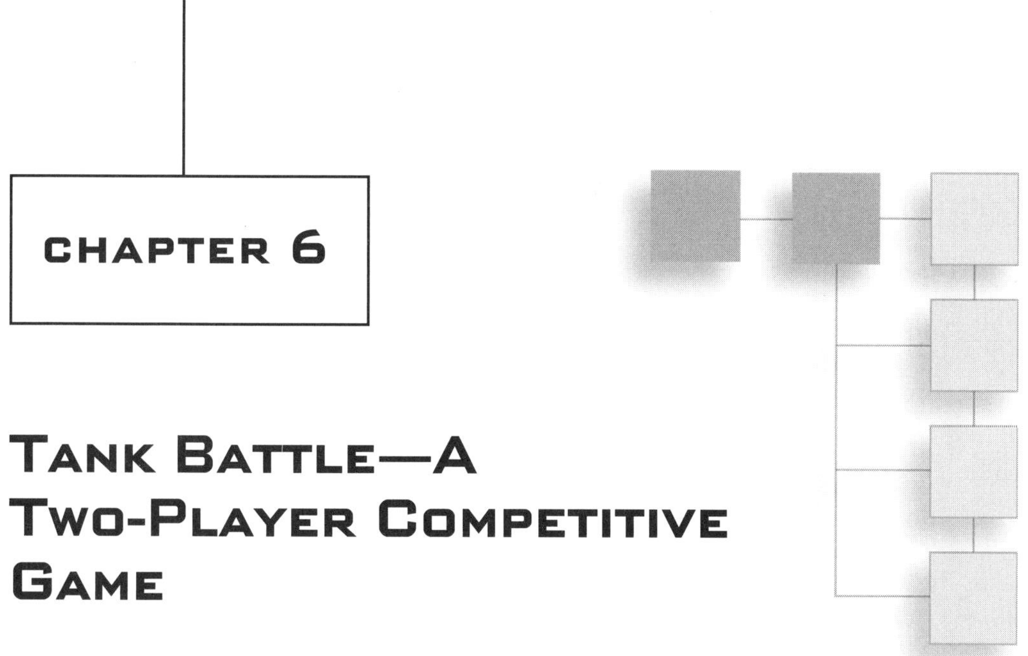

CHAPTER 6

# Tank Battle—A Two-Player Competitive Game

So far, you have learned how to work with the Game Maker IDE and to work with and configure different types of game resources. You have even created a couple of games. These games, though complete, only scratch the surface of Game Maker's capabilities. In this chapter, you will learn how to add a host of new features to your games, giving players access to game saves and game cheats. In addition, you will learn how to create your next game.

An overview of the topics covered in this chapter includes learning how to:

- Display your own custom splash screen at game startup
- Hide Game Maker's default progress bar and substitute your own
- Run games in full-screen mode
- Save and load games
- Create standalone versions of your game
- Add custom icons to your games

## Adding a Few Bells and Whistles to Your Games

Game Maker provides all of the tools you need to create truly professional-looking games. This not only includes built-in support for common game play features like motion, collision detection, sprite animation, lives, score, and health but it also includes built-in support for doing things like:

- Disabling the Escape key
- Adding game cheats
- Displaying a custom splash screen
- Hiding or replacing the Game Maker progress bar
- Running games in full-screen mode
- Adding an option to save games
- Providing the ability to load saved games
- Creating a standalone version of your game
- Adding custom icons to your games

As this chapter will show you, once you know how, it is easy to work with all of the special features outlined above. Many of these features are provided via Game Maker's Global Game Settings. Some, however, require that you use specific types of actions in order to make them work.

## Disabling the Escape Key

By default, all games created with Game Maker are set up to end when the Escape key is pressed. This behavior is fine for many types of games. However, for some games, especially more complex ones, you may want to disable this feature and instead configure your game to either ignore this keystroke or use it as a trigger (setting up a `Keyboard` event for the Escape key) for performing different events and actions such as the saving of the game. Alternatively, you might want to return the player back to the game's opening room instead of ending the game.

**Hint**

In Chapter 7 you will learn how to develop a structured framework for your games, providing them with snappy opening and closing screens. Modifying your game to return to its opening room when such a framework has been put into place will give your games a much more professional look and feel.

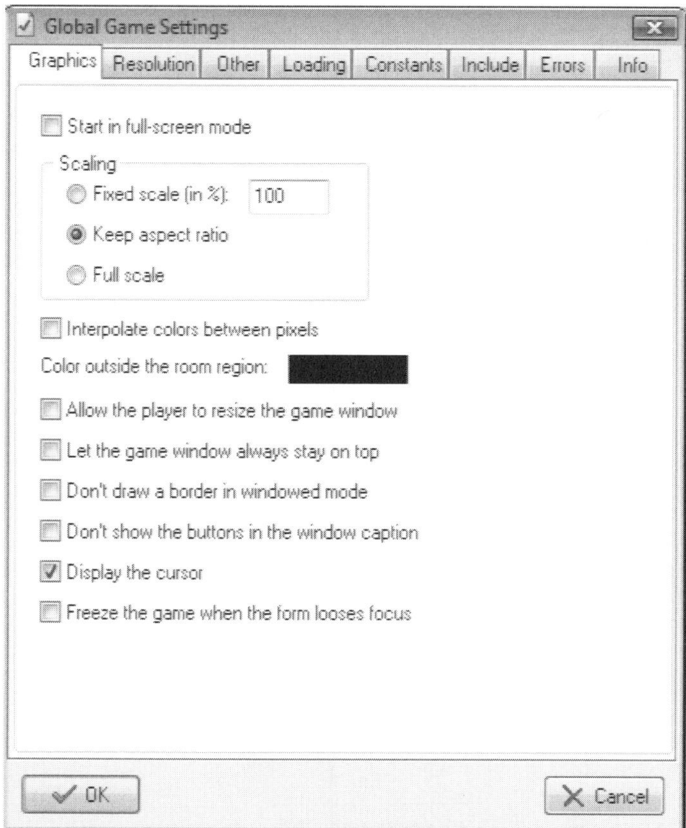


**Figure 6.1**
Game Maker's Global Game Settings exercise control over a wide range of game functionality.

Control over how Game Maker reacts to the pressing of the Escape key is configured through the Global Game Settings option located at the bottom of the resource tree folder. Double-clicking on Global Game Settings displays the Global Game Settings window shown in Figure 6.1.

To disable the Escape key, you need to click on the Other tab and then clear the Let <Esc> End the Game option (which is enabled by default), as shown in Figure 6.2.

A second option located on the Other tab determines whether the pressing of the Escape key is treated as being the same thing as if the player clicked on the game window's close button. The Treat the Close Button as <Esc> key option remains enabled unless you explicitly disable it.

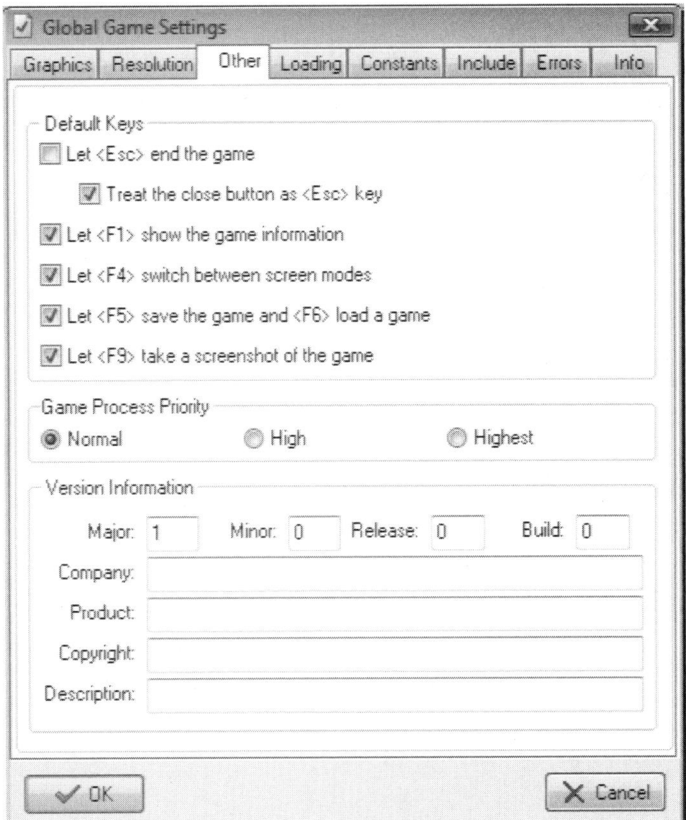


**Figure 6.2**
Default Keys settings affect the Escape key as well as a number of other special function keys.

**Trick**

> Game Maker has a `Close Button` event (located in the collection of events in the Other category on the Event Selector window) that you can add to an object in order to specify what you want to happen when the close button is clicked. Any actions associated with this event will also trigger if you disable the Escape key and configure Game Maker to treat the pressing of the Escape key as the equivalent of clicking on the close button.

## Adding Game Cheats

Many of today's computer games provide players with easy access to cheats that provide a greater degree of control over the operation of the game. Opinions on the use of cheats vary. Some people hate them, whereas others regard them as an essential part of any good game. When included, the use of cheats should be entirely optional and presented as a part of regular game play.

Cheats in console games typically involve the use of a special combination of buttons. In computer games, cheats are generally applied through the use of keystrokes. For example, you might add a `Keyboard` event to a game that executes when the U key is pressed, giving the player unlimited lives. Likewise, you might set up the H key so that when pressed it fully restores player health. Other implementation of cheats might result in the escalation of player firepower or the disablement of certain enemy features.

Cheats are easy to implement in your Game Maker games. For example, the following procedures demonstrate how to add three cheats to any multi-level game that also keeps track of player lives and health.

1. Double-click on the game's controller object to open its properties window. If the game does not have a controller object, go ahead and add one.
2. Click on the Add Event button to display the Event Selector window.
3. Click on the Key Press button and then click on the Letters category and select the letter N.
4. Select the main1 tab and drag and drop an instance of the `Next Room` action onto the actions area. This will allow the player to advance to the next room or level in the game just by pressing the N key.
5. Click on the Add Event button again, followed by the Key Press button, and then click on the Letters category. Select the letter L.
6. Select the Score tab and drag and drop an instance of the `Set Lives` action onto the actions area. Set New Lives to 1 and enable the Relative option, as shown in Figure 6.3. This will add a new life every time the player pressed the L key.
7. Click on the Add Event button again, followed by the Key Press button and then click on the Letters category. Select the letter H.
8. Select the Score tab and drag and drop an instance of the `Set Health` action onto the actions area. Set `value (0-100)` to `100` and enable the Relative option, as demonstrated in Figure 6.4. This will restore the player's health to 100 percent whenever the player presses the H key.

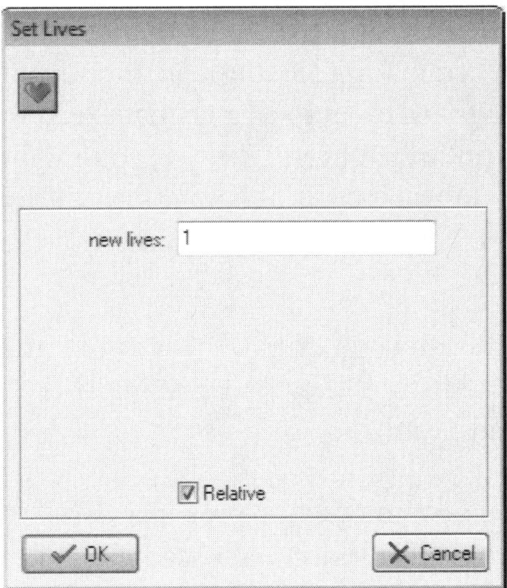


**Figure 6.3**
Creating a cheat that lets the player add new lives.

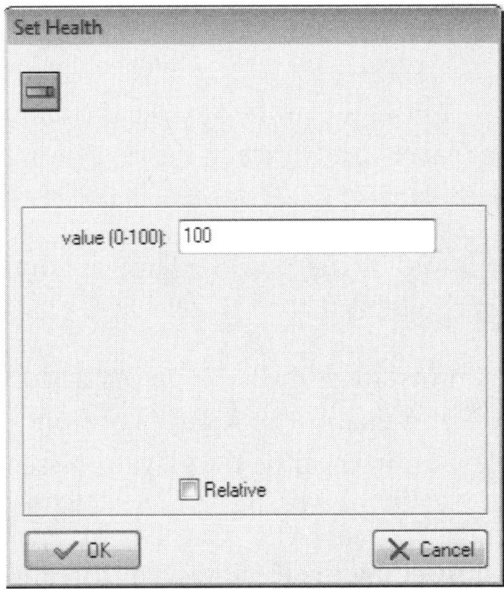


**Figure 6.4**
Creating a cheat that lets the player restore health.

## Displaying Your Own Splash Screen

Many commercial computer games and applications, especially those that may take a little time to load, display a splash screen when first started. A *splash screen*

**Figure 6.5**
Game Maker's default splash screen.

is simply a window that you can use to display any graphics and text you want. Splash screens can be used to provide the player with useful information as well as to provide something to look at while the rest of the game is busy loading.

Properly designed splash screens can add a nice finishing touch to your games. As shown in Figure 6.5, Game Maker automatically adds a default splash screen along with a progress bar to every game you create.

Game Maker allows you to replace this splash screen with one of your own making. In Game Maker a splash screen is a graphic image displayed as a special type of window. The first step in adding a splash screen to a game is to create an appropriate graphic image. Once this has been done, you can use the following procedure to configure your application to display the graphic as a splash screen.

1. Double-click on the Global Game Settings entry located at the bottom of the resource tree folder. The Global Game Settings window appears.

2. Select the Loading tab, as shown in Figure 6.6.

3. Enable the Show Your Own Image While Loading option located at the top of the window and then click on the Change Image button.

4. Using the standard Open dialog window that appears, locate and select the image file that you want to display as the game's splash screen and then click on Open. Figure 6.7 shows an example of a graphic file that might be selected.

5. Optionally, enable the Make Image Partially Transparent option and specify a value in the Make Translucent with Alpha Value field. An alpha value of 255 results in a solid splash screen. The alpha value determines the level of opacity. The smaller you set the alpha value, the more transparent the splash screen will be.

6. Click on OK to close the Global Game Settings window.

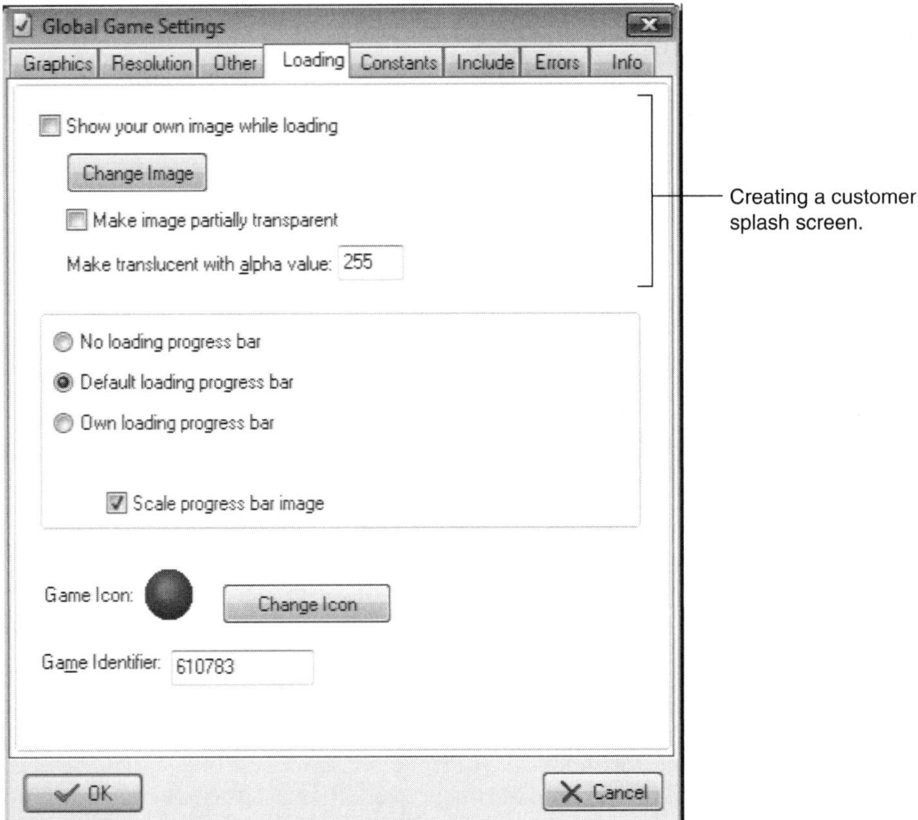


**Figure 6.6**
You can add a custom splash screen to your games.

**Figure 6.7**
An example of a graphic file that might be used to generate a splash screen.

## Modifying Game Maker's Progress Bar

As was shown in Figure 6.5, Game Maker automatically displays a progress bar at the bottom of a game's splash screen. Its purpose is to depict the progress of the loading of the game. If you want, you can customize the display of the progress bar. Doing so is easy, as outlined in the following procedure.

1. Double-click on the Global Game Settings entry located at the bottom of the resource tree folder. The Global Game Settings window appears.
2. Select the Loading tab.
3. Modify the game's splash screen as described in the previous procedure.
4. Select the Own Loading Progress Bar option. Two new buttons are then displayed on the Loading tab, labeled Back Image and Front Image, as shown in Figure 6.8.

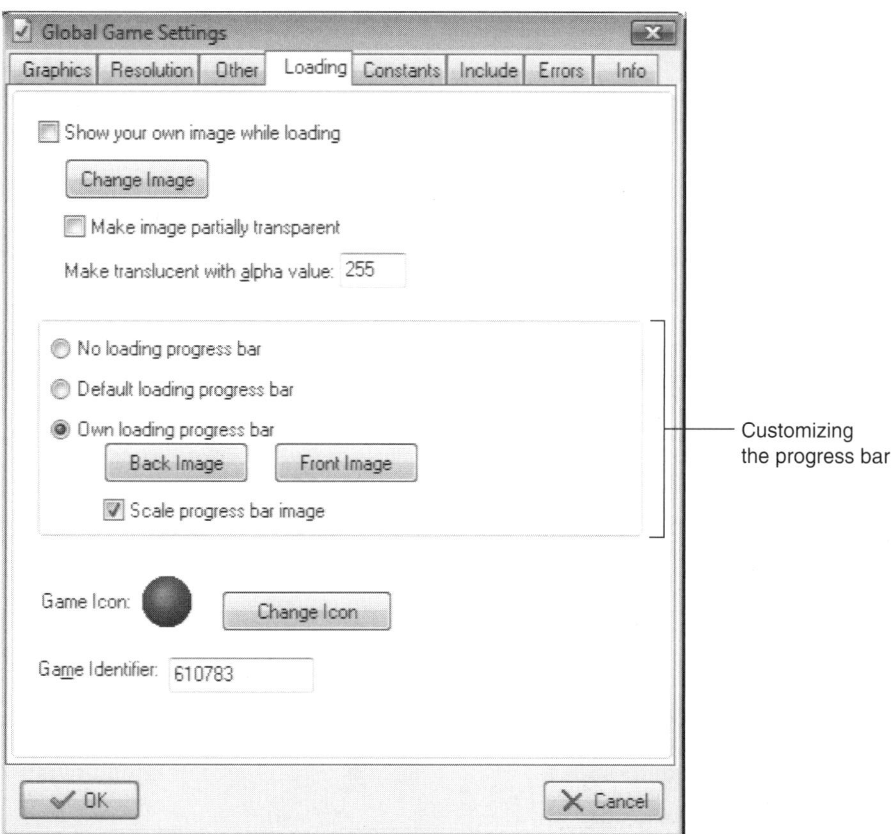


**Figure 6.8**
You can add a custom progress bar to your games.

5. Click on the Back Image button and when prompted, locate and select the image file that you want to use as a background for the progress bar.
6. Click on the Front Image button and when prompted, locate and select the image file that you want to use as a foreground for the progress bar.
7. Optionally, you can specify whether the front image must be scaled or clipped as it grows by enabling or disabling the Scale Progress Bar Image option.
8. Click on OK to close the Global Game Settings window.

Figure 6.9 shows two images that might be used as the basis for customizing the appearance of the progress bar.

Using these two images in the previous procedure would result in a custom progress bar that looks like the example shown in Figure 6.10.

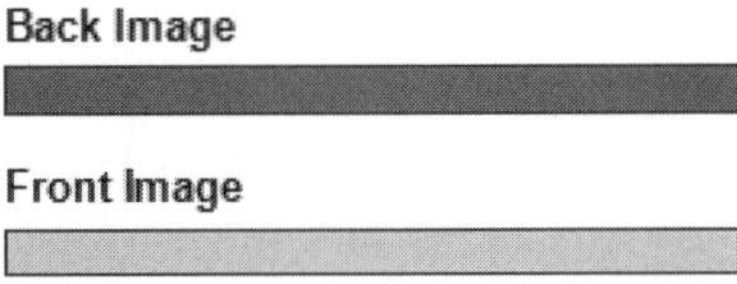


**Figure 6.9**
Graphics suitable for use when customizing a game's progress bar.

**Figure 6.10**
An example of a customized splash screen and its progress bar.

**Hint**

Make sure that the image files you use for the background and foreground images are of the same dimensions in terms of height and width.

## Running Games in Full-Screen Mode

By default, Game Maker configures all games to run within rooms that are 640 × 480 pixels. As you have already learned, you can change the size of a room by clicking on the Settings tab located on the Room Properties window and then modifying the room's Width and Height settings. If you want, you can modify your game so that it runs in full-screen mode, allowing it to fully utilize the entire computer screen. The steps required to set this up are outlined below.

1. Double-click on the Global Game Settings entry located at the bottom of the resource tree folder. The Global Game Settings window appears.
2. Make sure the Graphics tab is selected.
3. Enable the Start in Full-Screen Mode option.
4. Optionally, select one of the following three scaling settings.
   - **Fixed Scale (in %).** The room is centered in the screen and then scaled as a percentage of its actual size.
   - **Keep aspect ratio.** Fills as much of the screen as possible without distorting the game aspect ratio.
   - **Full scale.** Scales the game as required to fill the screen, even if it results in some distortion.
5. Click on OK to close the Global Game Settings window.

**Hint**

By default, if you set up your game to run in full-screen mode but it does not completely fill the entire screen, Game Maker will fill in any remaining screen area in black. If you want, you can select a different color by clicking on the color swatch located at the end of the Color Outside the Room Region setting and then selecting a different color from the Color dialog window that appears.

## Letting Players Save Game State

One feature provided by many different types of games is the ability to save the current state of the game, providing the ability for players to later restore the game back to a saved state. This is especially important in long playing games where players may be required to complete a room or level before moving on to

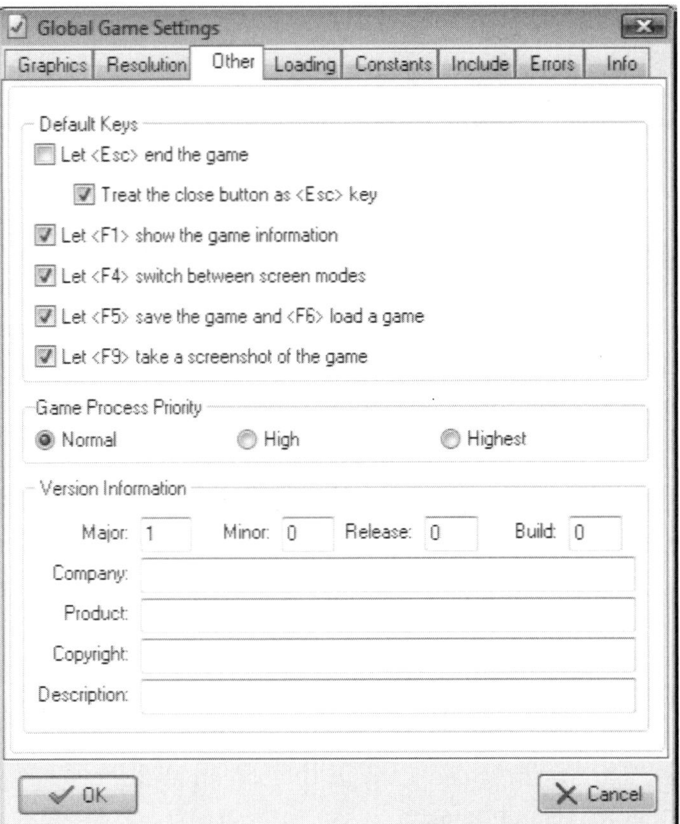


**Figure 6.11**
Configuring Game Maker's game save and game load feature.

the next room or level. By allowing players to perform a save, you enable them to resume playing from the point of the save in the event their character should meet its demise.

Game Maker makes saving game state a simple task by providing you with various options located on the Other tab in the Global Game Settings window, shown in Figure 6.11.

**Hint**

Saving and loading games only works with Game Maker Pro.

The game save and restore feature is enabled by default and is controlled by the F5 and F6 keys. If you prefer, you can disable these features or you can disable them and replace this functionality using the `Save Game` and `Load game` actions. Using the `Save Game` action, you might enable an automatic save at certain points in the game or you might instead provide the player with the ability to create a save and reload from a save using alternative keystrokes.

To disable the default save and load feature, open the Global Game Settings window and clear the Let <F5> Save the Game and <F6> Load a Game option. The following procedure demonstrates one way of replacing the default load and save option and instead uses the `Save Game` and `Load Game` actions.

1. Double-click on the Global Game Settings entry located at the bottom of the resource tree folder. The Global Game Settings window appears.
2. Select the Other tab and then disable the Let <F5> Save the Game and <F6> Load a Game option.
3. Click on OK to close the Global Game Settings window.
4. Select and open the object in your game that you want to make responsible for performing save and load actions. A good choice might be the game's special controller object (if it has one).
5. Click on the Add Event button followed by the Key Press button and then select Letters followed by the Letter S.
6. Select the main2 tab and then drag and drop the `Save Game` action onto the actions area.
7. Leave the default file name of the save in place and click on OK to close the Save Game window.
8. Click on the Add Event button followed by the Key Press button and then select Letters followed by the Letter L.
9. Select the main2 tab and then drag and drop the `Load Game` action onto the actions area.
10. Leave the default file name of the save in place and click on OK to close the Save Game window.
11. Click on OK to close the Object Properties window.

Players will now be able to save the current state of the game whenever they want by pressing the S key and can reload from that saved state by pressing the L key.

## Displaying Game Information

An important feature that should be part of every game is its instructions. There are many different ways that you can provide the player with instructions and help. For starters, you might create a room and use it to display text that tells the player everything he needs to know about the game. You might also display help and instructional information on the screen during game play. Alternatively, you can provide players with the ability to display information about the game at any time through the Game Information window, which players can access by default at any time by pressing the F1 key.

To populate the Game Information window with useful information, double-click on the Game Information entry in the resource tree folder. This will open the Game Information window shown in Figure 6.12.

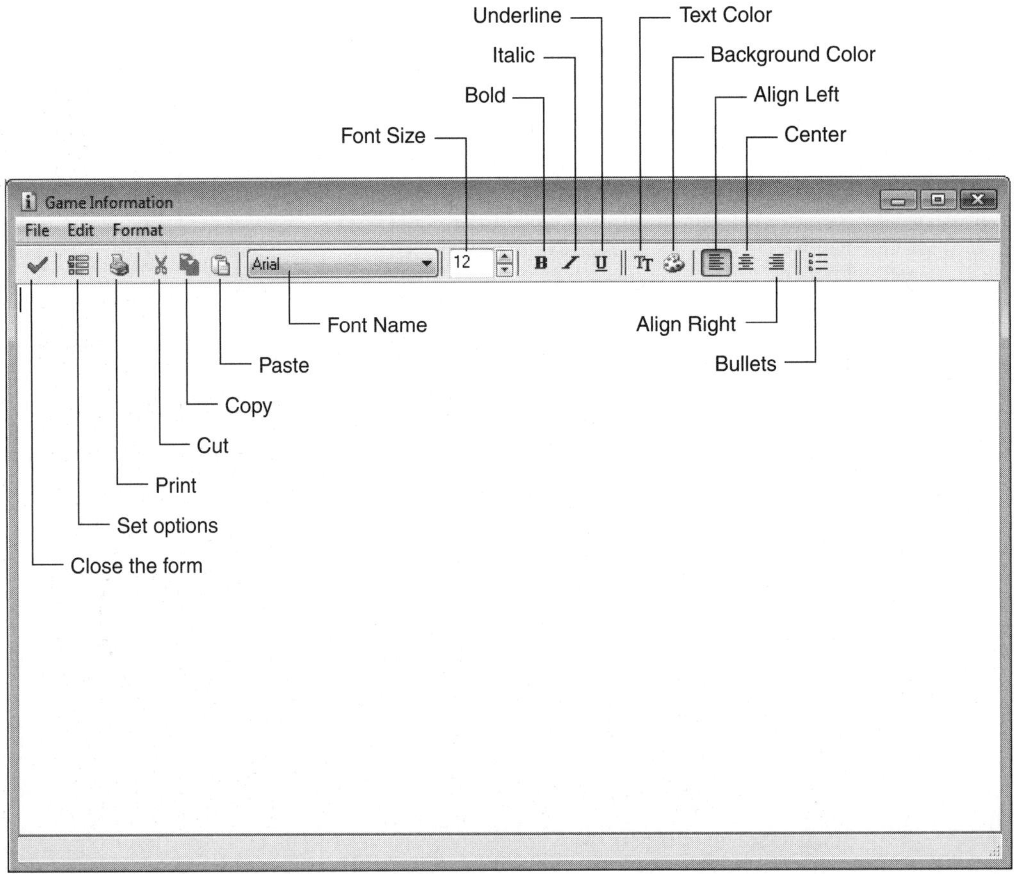


**Figure 6.12**
Key functionality is provided by the Game Information window's toolbar.

The Game Information window looks and works like a basic word processor application. You can format text using different font types, sizes, and styles. You can display text using different colors and even assign a background color. You can right align, center, or left align text. You can even display text using bullets. You can specify whether game information is displayed in the game window or in a separate window. Basic editing features are also available, including cut, paste, and copy. Anything you type can also be sent to the printer.

To enter game information all you have to do is start typing it into the window. When entering game information, be sure to tell players the goal of the game and the rules for playing it. Outline all of the controls used to play the game. You might also want to include information about yourself, including your email address or URL. Figure 6.13 shows an example of how you might use the

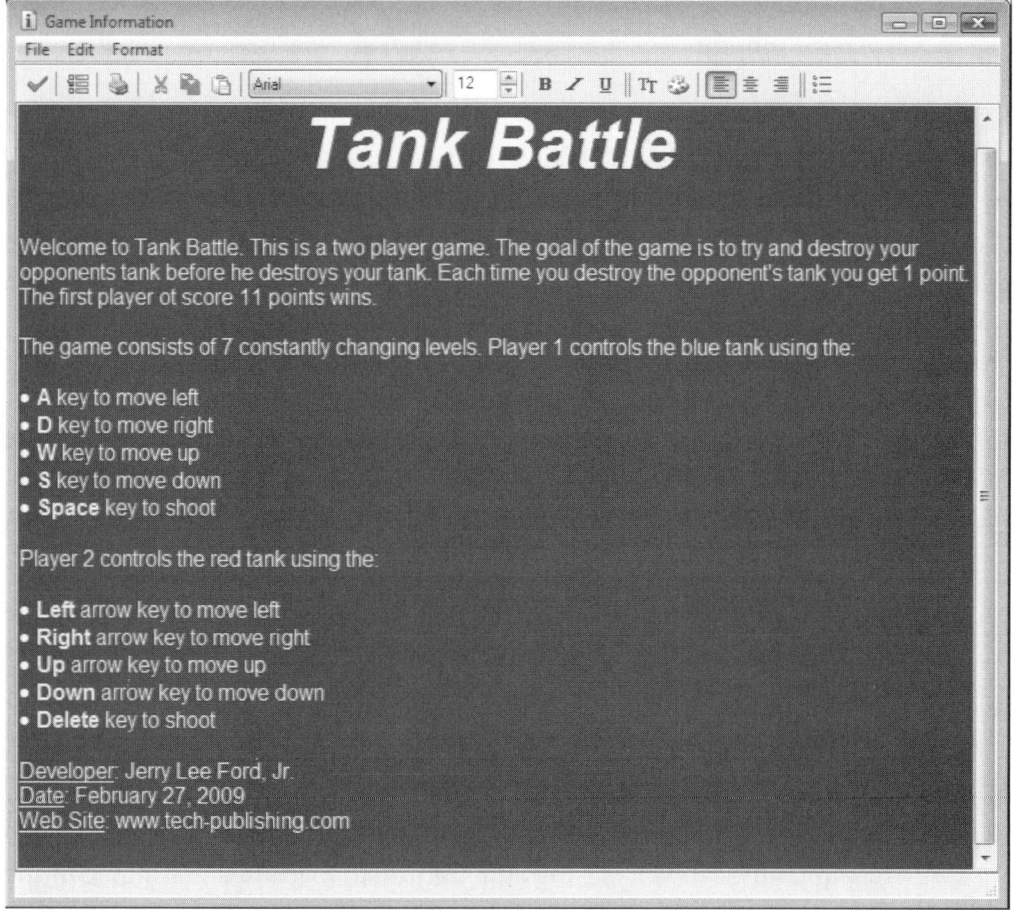


**Figure 6.13**
Configuring Game Maker to display game information in a separate window.

Game Information window to provide players with the information needed to play the game.

**Hint**

By default, Game Maker displays Game Information inside the game window. If you prefer, you can instruct Game Maker to display this information in a separate window by clicking on File > Options to open the Game Information Options window. Once opened, you can enable the Show Help in a Separate Window option, as demonstrated in Figure 6.13.

If you want, you can even specify the coordinate location where the external Game Information window is displayed on the screen and can enable or disable any of the following settings.

- Show the window border and caption
- Allow the player to resize the window
- Stay always on top
- Stop the game while showing help

## Creating Standalone Games

So far, every time you have run your Game Maker games, you have done so by clicking on the Run > Run Normally or by clicking on the green Run the Game button. When run this way, your games are compiled and executed within the confines of the Game Maker IDE. This works fine when developing games. However, to package up your game so that it can execute as a standalone application outside of Game Maker, you must create an executable version of your games. To do so, click on File > Create Executable. Game Maker responds by displaying a standard dialog window that allows you to enter a name for the executable copy of your game and specify the location where you want to save it.

Once created, you can run your game by double-clicking on its icon. To share the game with others, all you have to do is provide them with a copy of its executable file. However, before you begin widely distributing your game, you might want to assign it a custom icon as outlined in the next section.

## Adding Custom Icons to Your Games

By default, every game that you create with Game Maker is assigned a circular red icon. If you want, you can spice things up a bit by uploading a graphic icon file (ico) of your own choosing. The following procedure outlines the steps that are involved.

**Hint**

There are a number of free icon creation applications available on the internet. These applications provide everything needed to create your own icons. Game Maker only supports $32 \times 32$ icons, so make sure you properly size your icons when you create them.

1. Double-click on the Global Game Settings entry located at the bottom of the resource tree folder. The Global Game Settings window appears.
2. Select the Loading tab.
3. Click on the Change Icon button.
4. Using the standard Open dialog window that appears, locate and select your .ico file.
5. Click on OK to close the Global Game Settings window.

Figures 6.14 and 6.15 show an example of how a game's icon can be changed using this above procedure.

In addition to modifying the icon that is generated for the game, this procedure also modifies the icon image that is displayed in the game's titlebar. Figures 6.16 and 6.17 provide a before and after view of the effects that this procedure has on a game's titlebar.

**Figure 6.14**
An example of the default icon Game Maker generates for all applications.

**Figure 6.15**
An example of the game that has been assigned its own custom icon.

**Figure 6.16**
An example of the default icon displayed in every game's titlebar.

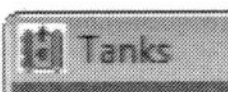


**Figure 6.17**
An example of a game window's titlebar after a custom icon has been assigned.

## Creating the Tank Battle Game

Now it is time to begin working on the creation of the Tank Battle game. In this two-player game, the players are each given a military tank, one red and one blue, and are challenged to fight out a series of battles in the desert. Players control their tanks via the keyboard. Player 1 controls the blue tank using the following keys.

- **A.** Moves the blue tank left.
- **D.** Moves the blue tank right.
- **W.** Moves the blue tank up.
- **S.** Moves the blue tank down.
- **Space.** Instructs the blue tank to shoot a bullet in the direction it is currently pointed.

Player 2 controls the red tank using the following keys.

- **Left Arrow.** Moves the red tank left.
- **Right Arrow.** Moves the red tank right.
- **Up Arrow.** Moves the red tank up.
- **Down Arrow.** Moves the red tank down.
- **Delete.** Instructs the red tank to shoot a bullet in the direction it is currently pointed.

The game consists of seven constantly changing backgrounds that place different configurations of walls in between the players to keep things challenging. Game play ends after one of the players scores 11 hits. Figure 6.18 shows an example of how the game looks when being played.

In order to create this game, you will need to perform a number of steps, as outlined here:

1. Define the game's sprites.
2. Define the game's sounds.

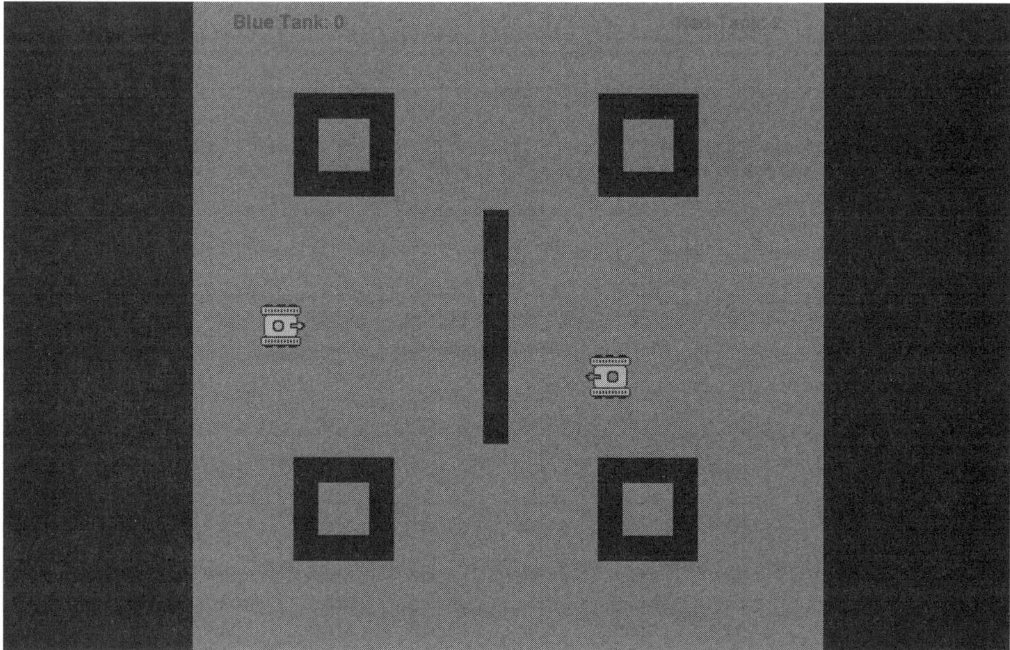


**Figure 6.18**
An example of the Tank Battle game in action.

3. Configure a background for the game.
4. Create a font.
5. Define objects that control game play and develop their program logic.
6. Add rooms to the game and populate them with objects.

## Step 1—Creating the Game's Sprites

The first step in the development of the Tank Battle game is to add the sprites needed by the game. These include two tank sprites, two bullet sprites, and two wall sprites. If you haven't done so already, start Game Maker, or if it is already started, click on File > New to create a new application. Use the steps outlined next to add the game's first sprite.

1. Click on Resources > Create Sprite. The Sprite Properties window opens. Type `spr_tank_red` as the name for the game's first sprite.
2. The graphic files you will need for the game's sprites can be downloaded from the book's companion web page (www.courseptr.com/downloads).

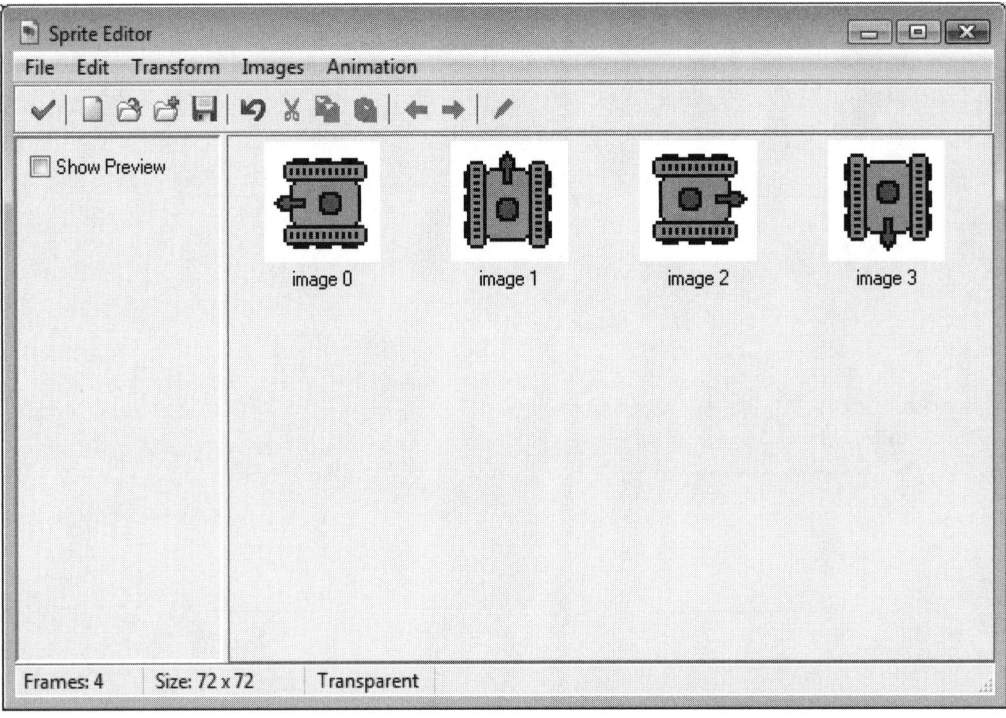


**Figure 6.19**
This sprite consists of four graphic files, each of which shows a tank facing in a different direction.

Click on the Load Sprite button, navigate to the location where you saved the files, select the `RedTankWest.bmp` file, and then click on Open.

3. Click on the Edit Sprite button and then add the following additional three graphic files to the sprite: `RedTankNorth`, `RedTankEast`, and `RedTankSouth`. When you are done, the Sprite Editor window should look like the example shown in Figure 6.19. Click on the green check mark button to close the Sprite Editor window and return to the Sprite Properties window.

**Trap**

It is essential that the four graphic files are added in the order shown in Figure 6.19. If they are not, you can rearrange them by clicking on individual images and then moving them left or right using the blue left and right arrow buttons located in the Sprite Editor's toolbar.

4. Click on the center button located in the middle column of the Sprite Properties window. Cross hairs should appear over the center of the graphic image displayed in the window, indicating the sprite's central alignment.

5. Click on OK to close the Sprite Properties window.

Using the same series of steps outlined above, create a second sprite named spr_tank_blue, assigning the following sprites–BlueTankEast, BlueTankNorth, BlueTankWest, and BlueTankSouth. Make sure that once added the four images are listed in the order listed here. Next, add a sprite named spr_red_bullet, assigning it the redBullet.gif and then center its alignment. Then create a sprite named, spr_blue_bullet, assigning it the BlueBullet.gif and then center its alignment as well.

Lastly, create a sprite named spr_invisible_wall, assigning it the Invisible-Wall.gif file and clear its Transparent setting, and then create a sprite named spr_blackwall assigning it the BlackWall.gif file and clearing its Transparent setting as well.

## Step 2—Adding Sound

The second step in the development of the Tank Battle game is to add a sound that will be played whenever a tank is blown up (hit). To set this up, you will use an audio file that comes with Game Maker. By default, you will find this file located in C:\Program Files\Game Maker7\Sounds. The following procedure outlines the steps required to add this sound to your game.

1. Click on Resources > Create Sound. The Sound Properties window appears.
2. Assign a name of snd_explosion to the sound, click on the Load Sound button, navigate to the C:\Program Files\Game Maker7\Sounds folder, select the explosion.wav file, and then click on Open.
3. Click on OK to close the Sprite Properties window.

**Hint**

You might want to consider looking for an appropriate midi file and using it to add background music to the game, giving it more of an arcade feel.

## Step 3—Adding an Appropriate Background

The next step you need to complete is the addition of a suitable background to the game, which you can do using the steps outlined here:

1. Click on Resources > Create Background. The Background Properties window appears.
2. Enter **bck_desert** into the Name file.

3. The graphic file you will need to create the background is supplied with Game Maker and by default is located in the C:\Program Files\Game Maker7\Backgrounds folder. Click on the Load Background button, navigate to the Backgrounds folder, select the `desert.jpg` file, and then click on Open.
4. Click on OK to close the Background Properties window.

## Step 4—Adding a Font

Players' scores are displayed in the top-left and top-right corners of the screen. Game Maker's default font size of 12 is not sufficient to ensure that players' scores are adequately displayed. To remedy this situation, you need to add a font to the game using the steps outlined here:

1. Click on Resources > Create Font. Game Maker will respond by displaying the Font Properties window.
2. Enter **`font_text`** into the Name file.
3. Leaving the Font type set to Arial, enter **18** as the size of the font.
4. Enable the font's Bold setting.
5. Click on OK to close the Font Properties window.

## Step 5—Creating and Programming Objects

The Tank Battle game consists of a number of different objects, both visible and invisible. Objects that are visible include the blue and red tanks, their red and blue bullets, and the black wall object. The game's invisible objects include its invisible wall and the special controller object. Let's begin by defining all of the objects used by the game.

1. Click on Resources > Create Object. The Object Properties window appears. Type **`obj_tank1`** in the Name field, click on the context menu icon located at the end of the Sprite text field, and select `spr_tank_blue` from the sprites list.
2. Click on Resources > Create Object. The Object Properties window appears. Type **`obj_tank2`** in the Name field, click on the context menu icon located at the end of the Sprite text field, and select `spr_tank_red` from the sprites list.

3. Click on Resources > Create Object. The Object Properties window appears. Type **obj_invisible_wall** in the Name field, click on the context menu icon located at the end of the Sprite text field, and select spr_invisible_wall from the sprites list. Lastly, disable the object's Visible property and enable its Solid property.

4. Click on Resources > Create Object. The Object Properties window appears. Type **obj_black_wall** in the Name field, click on the context menu icon located at the end of the Sprite text field, and select spr_black_wall from the sprites list. Lastly, enable the object's Solid property.

5. Click on Resources > Create Object. The Object Properties window appears. Type **obj_blue_bullet** in the Name field, click on the context menu icon located at the end of the Sprite text field, and select spr_blue_bullet from the sprites list.

6. Click on Resources > Create Object. The Object Properties window appears. Type **obj_red_bullet** in the Name field, click on the context menu icon located at the end of the Sprite text field, and select spr_red_bullet from the sprites list.

7. Click on Resources > Create Object. The Object Properties window appears. Type **obj_controller** in the Name field and then clear its Visible settings.

Now that all of the game's objects have been added, it is time to develop the program logic that will bring these objects to life, except, that is, for the two wall objects, which have no events or actions.

### Programming the blue tank object

1. Open the Properties window for the obj_tank1 object and then add a Create event to the object. Click on the main1 tab and drag and drop an instance of the Change Sprite action to the actions area, entering **spr_tank_blue** into the Sprite field, **0** in the Subimage field, and **0** in the Speed field, as shown in Figure 6.20. This instructs Game Maker to display the first of the sprite's four subimages (e.g., an image of the tank facing west).

2. Click on the Control tab and add the Set Variable action to the Create event, assigning a value of 0 to a variable named tank1_direction. Add a second Set Variable action, assigning a value of false to tank1_firing. This variable will be used to control when the tank is allowed to fire its gun.

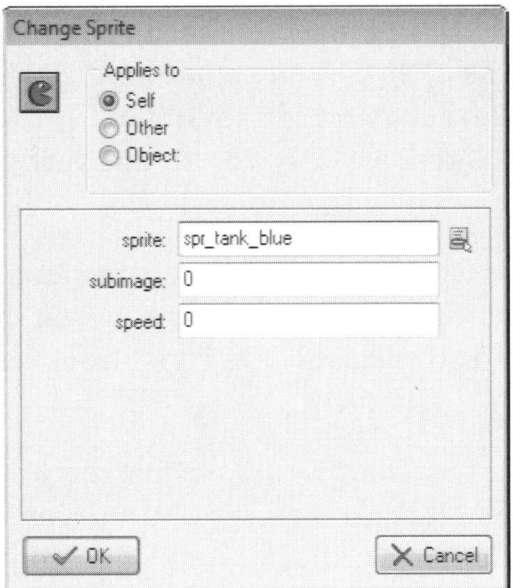


**Figure 6.20**
Instructing which subimage Gamer Maker should use when displaying an object.

3. Add a `Collision` event for the `obj_tank2` object, select the Move tab, and add the `Moved Fixed` actions to it. Select the action's center button, halting the object's movement.

4. Add a collision event for the `obj_invisible_wall` object and then add the `Moved Fixed` actions to it. Select the action's center button, halting the object's movement.

5. Add a collision event for the `obj_black_wall` object and add the `Moved Fixed` actions to it. Select the action's center button, halting the object's movement.

6. Add a keyboard event for `<no key>` and then add the `Moved Fixed` actions to it. Select the action's center button, halting the object's movement.

7. Add a keyboard event for `<Space>`, select the Control tab, and add the `Test Variable` action to the actions area, setting a variable named `tank1_firing` equal to a value of `false`, as shown in Figure 6.21.

8. Next, add a `Start Block` followed by a `Set Variable` action, setting the value of `tank1_firing` equal to `true`.

9. Click on the main1 tab and add the `Create Moving` action, setting object to `obj_blue_bullet`, speed to `10`, direction to `tank1_direction`, and then enable the Relative option as shown in Figure 6.22. Finally, add an `End Block`.

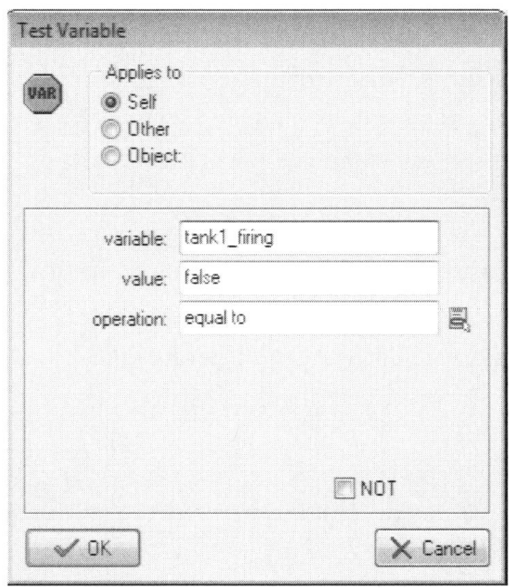


**Figure 6.21**
A tank cannot fire again until the bullet it just fired hits something.

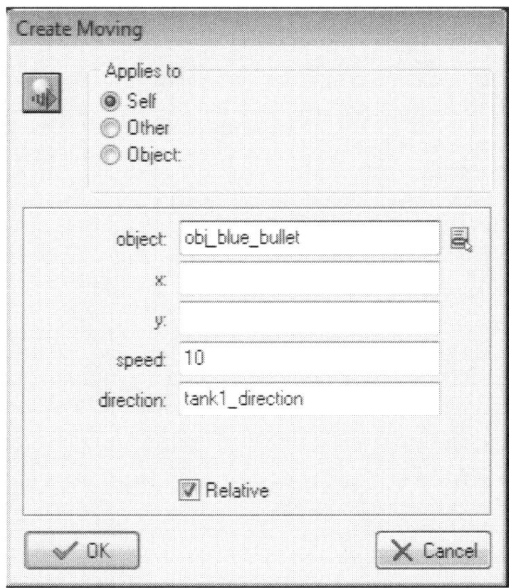


**Figure 6.22**
Creating a moving bullet in the direction the blue tank is facing when Player 1 presses the spacebar.

10. Add a keyboard event for `<A-key>` and then add the `Change Sprite` action, assigning it the `spr_tank_blue` sprite.Then set its subimage to 2. Next, add the `Set Variable` action and assign `tank1_direction` a value of 180 (e.g., left). Lastly, add the `Move Fixed` action, enabling its left arrow button and assigning it a speed of `5`.

11. Add a keyboard event for <D-key> and then add the `Change Sprite` action, assigning it the `spr_tank_blue` sprite. Then set its subimage to 0. Next, add the `Set Variable` action and assign `tank1_direction` a value of 0 (e.g., right). Lastly, add the `Move Fixed` action, enabling its right arrow button and assigning it a speed of `5`.

12. Add a keyboard event for <S-key> and then add the `Change Sprite` action, assigning it the `spr_tank_blue` sprite. Then set its subimage to 3. Next add the `Set Variable` action and assign `tank1_direction` a value of 270 (e.g., down). Lastly, add the `Move Fixed` action, enabling its down arrow button and assigning it a speed of 5.

13. Add a keyboard event for <W-key> and then add the `Change Sprite` action, assigning it the `spr_tank_blue` sprite .Then set its subimage to 1. Next, add the `Set Variable` action and assign `tank1_direction` a value of 90 (e.g., up). Lastly, add the `Move Fixed` action, enabling its up arrow button and assigning it a speed of `5`.

### Programming the red tank object

1. Open the Properties window for the `obj_tank2` object, add a `Create` event to the object, click on the main1 tab, and drag and drop an instance of the `Change Sprite` action to the actions list, entering **`spr_tank_red`** into the Sprite field, **0** in the Subimage field, and **0** in the Speed field. This instructs Game Maker to display the first of the sprite's four subimages (e.g., an image of the tank facing west).

2. Click on the Control tab and add the `Set Variable` action to the `Create` event, assigning a value of `180` to a variable named `tank2_direction`. Add a second `Set Variable` action, assigning a value of `false` to `tank2_firing`. This variable will be used to control when the tank is allowed to fire its gun.

3. Add a collision event for the `obj_tank1` object, select the Move tab, and add the `Moved Fixed` actions to it. Select the action's center button, halting the object's movement.

4. Add a collision event for the `obj_invisible_wall` object and then add the `Moved Fixed` actions to it. Select the action's center button, halting the object's movement.

5. Add a collision event for the `obj_black_wall` object and then add the `Moved Fixed` actions to it. Select the action's center button, halting the object's movement.
6. Add a keyboard event for `<no key>` and then add the `Moved Fixed` actions to it. Select the action's center button, halting the object's movement.
7. Add a keyboard event for `<Delete>` and select the Control tab, and add the `Test Variable` action to the actions area, setting a variable named `tank2_firing` equal to a value of `false`.
8. Next, add a `Start Block` followed by a `Set Variable` action, setting the value of `tank2_firing` equal to `true`.
9. Click on the main1 tab and add the `Create Moving` action, setting object to `obj_red_bullet`, speed to `10`, direction to `tank2_direction`, and then enable the Relative option. Finally, add an `End Block`.
10. Add a keyboard event for `<Left>` and then add the `Change Sprite` action, assigning it the `spr_tank_red` sprite. Then set its subimage to 0. Next, add the `Set Variable` action and assign `tank2_direction` a value of 180 (e.g., left). Lastly, add the `Move Fixed` action, enabling its left arrow button and assigning it a speed of `5`.
11. Add a keyboard event for `<Right>` and then add the `Change Sprite` action, assigning it the `spr_tank_red` sprite. Then set its subimage to 2. Next, add the `Set Variable` action and assign `tank2_direction` a value of 0 (e.g., right). Lastly, add the `Move Fixed` action, enabling its right arrow button and assigning it a speed of `5`.
12. Add a keyboard event for `<Down>` and then add the `Change Sprite` action, assigning it the `spr_tank_red` sprite. Then set its subimage to 3. Next, add the `Set Variable` action and assign `tank2_direction` a value of 270 (e.g., down). Lastly, add the `Move Fixed` action, enabling its down arrow button and assigning it a speed of `5`.
13. Add a keyboard event for `<Up>` and then add the `Change Sprite` action, assigning it the `spr_tank_red` sprite. Then, set its subimage to 1. Next, add the `Set Variable` action and assign `tank2_direction` a value of 90 (e.g., up). Lastly, add the `Move Fixed` action, enabling its up arrow button and assigning it a speed of `5`.

### Programming the blue bullet object

1. Open the Properties window for the `obj_blue_bullet` object and then add a collision event with the `obj_tank2` object.

2. Add the `Play Sound` action and set it to play the `snd_explosion`.

3. Add the `Create Effect` action and set type equal to `explosion`, size equal to `small`, where equal to `below objects`, and then enable the Relative option as shown in Figure 6.23.

**Hint**

The `Create Effect` action, available in Game Maker Pro, provides an easy means of adding special effects like explosions, fireworks, smoke, sparks, clouds, rain, snow, etc. to your games. It provides these animated effects using Game Maker's particle system.

4. Add the `Set Variable` action, setting `obj_tank1.tank1_firing` to `false` (allowing the player's tank to fire again).

5. Add the `Destroy Instance` action and set it to apply to `Self`. Add a second instance of the `Destroy Instance` action and apply it to the `obj_red_bullet`

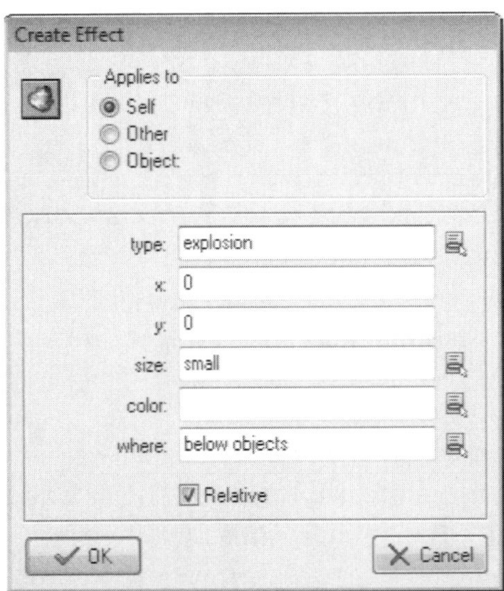


**Figure 6.23**
Adding a special explosion effect that executes when the bullet collides with the other player's tank.

object. Add a third instance of the `Destroy Instance` action and apply it to the `obj_tank2` object.

6. Add the `Set Score` action, assign a value of `1` to `new score`, and then enable the Relative option.
7. Add the `Test Score` action and set it to check to see if the player's score is equal to `11`.
8. Add the `Start Block` action, add the `Sleep` action, and enter **500** in the Milliseconds field to pause game play for half a second.
9. Add the `Restart Game` action followed by the `Display Message` action, entering **`Game over. Click on OK to play again.`** into the Message field.
10. Add the `End Block` action, followed by the `Else` action and then the `Start Block` action.
11. Add the `Create Instance` action and create a new instance of the `obj_tank2` object, setting its coordinates to 740, 330.
12. Add the `Jump to Start` action and set object to `obj_tank2`, as shown in Figure 6.24.

**Figure 6.24**
The other player's tank is moved back to its starting position.

13. Add the Check Next action followed by the Next Room action to advance the game to the next level (if present).

14. Add the Else action followed by the Different Room action, setting the new room to room_level2. This instructs the game to start over at level 2 when the last level has been completed.

15. Add the Jump to Start action and set object to obj_tank1, moving the player's tank back to its starting position.

16. Finally, wrap things up by adding the End Block action.

17. Add a collision event for the obj_invisible_wall and add the Set Variable action to it, assigning obj_tank1.tank1_firing a value of false. This allows the player to shoot again when his bullet hits the invisible wall. Next, add the Destroy Instance action and set it to Self.

18. Add a collision event for the obj_black_wall and add the Set Variable action to it, assigning obj_tank1.tank1_firing a value of false. Lastly, add the Destroy Instance action and set it to Self.

### Programming the red bullet object

1. Open the Properties window for the obj_red_bullet object and then add a collision event with the obj_tank1 object.

2. Add the Play Sound action and set it to play the snd_explosion.

3. Add the Create Effect action and set type equal to explosion, size equal to small, where equal to below objects, and then enable the Relative option.

4. Add the Set Variable action, setting obj_tank1.tank2_firing to false (allowing the player's tank to fire again).

5. Add the Destroy Instance action and set it to apply to Self. Add a second instance of the Destroy Instance action and apply it to the obj_blue_bullet object. Add a third instance of the Destroy Instance action and apply it to the obj_tank1 object.

6. Add the Set Lives action, assign a value of 1 to new lives, and then enable the Relative option.

**Hint**

Since Game Maker only provides the ability to manage a single player's score, this game uses the lives actions as a substitute for managing player 2's score.

7. Add the `Test Lives` action and set it to check if the player's score is equal to `11`.
8. Add the `Start Block` action and then add the `Sleep` action and type **500** in the Milliseconds field to pause game play for half a second.
9. Add the `Restart Game` action followed by the `Display Message` action, entering **`Game over. Click on OK to play again.`** into the Message field.
10. Add the `End Block` action, followed by the `Else` action and then the `Start Block` action.
11. Add the `Create Instance` action and create a new instance of the `obj_tank1` object, setting its coordinates to 40, 330.
12. Add the `Jump to Start` action and set object to `obj_tank1`.
13. Add the `Jump to Start` action and set object to `obj_tank2`.
14. Add the `Check Next` action followed by the `Next Room` action to advance the game to the next level (if present).
15. Add the `Else` action followed by the `Different Room` action, setting new room to `room_level2`. This instructs the game to start over at level 2 when the last level has been completed.
16. Finally, wrap things up by adding the `End Block` action.
17. Add a collision event for the `obj_invisible_wall` and add the `Set Variable` action to it, assigning `obj_tank2.tank2_firing` a value of `false`. This allows the player to shoot again when his bullet hits the invisible wall. Next, add the `Destroy Instance` action and set it to `Self`.
18. Add a collision event for the `obj_black_wall` and add the `Set Variable` action to it, assigning `obj_tank2.tank2_firing` a value of `false`. Lastly, add the `Destroy Instance` action and set it to `Self`.

**Programming the controller object**

1. Open the Properties window for the `obj_controller` object and then click on `Add Event`. This opens the Event Selector window. Click on the Other button and then select the `Game Start` event.
2. Add the `Set Score` action and assign New Score a value of 0.
3. Add the `Set Lives` action and assign New Lives a value of 0.
4. Add the `Score Caption` action and specify a value of `don't show` for the Show Score, Show Lives, and Show Health fields.
5. Add the `Draw` event to the object.
6. Click on the Draw tab and add the `Set Font` action to the actions area. Configure it to use the `font_text` font.
7. Add the `Set Color` action and set it to blue.
8. Add the `Draw Text` action and type **`'Blue Tank: ' + string(score)`** in the Text field. Set its coordinates to `50, 10` so that the first player's score will be displayed at the top left-hand side of the screen.
9. Add the `Set Color` action and set it to red.
10. Add the `Draw Text` action and type **`'Red Tank: ' + string(lives)`** in the Text field. Set its coordinates to 610, 10 so that the second player's score will be displayed at the top-right side of the screen.

## Step 6—Creating Different Levels in Which to Play

Tank Battle consists of seven different levels, which use different configurations of walls to provide the game with some variation and keep the players on their toes. The next step in the development of the Tank Battle game is to add all seven of the rooms representing these levels. To create the first room, click on Resources > Create Room. The Room Properties window appears. Name the room `room_level1` and then increase the size of the room by clicking on the Settings tab and changing the room's Width to `800` and its Height to `800`. Also, add a caption of **`Tank Battle`** to the Caption for the Room field. Next, click on the Backgrounds

**Figure 6.25**
Creating the game's first level (room `room_level1`).

tab and clear the Draw Background Color setting and then select `bck_desert` as the room's background.

Click on the Objects tab, select the `obj_invisible_wall` object, and then use the object to draw a wall around the room, enclosing all by the first three rows. Next, add a single instance of the `obj_tank1`, `obj_tank2`, and `obj_controller` to the room, placing them as shown in Figure 6.25.

At this point, the room has all of the base features needed by every room in the game. To make things as easy as possible, click on OK to close the room and then right-click on the room's entry in the resource tree folder and select Duplicate from the list of options that appears. Using this process, add a total of 6 additional levels (naming them `room_level2` through `room_level7`) to the game and then, using the `obj_black_wall` object, modify the rooms as shown in Figures 6.26 through 6.31.

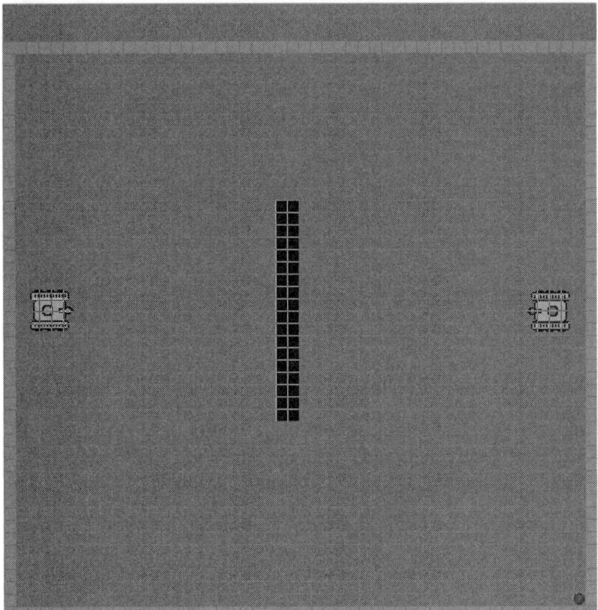

**Figure 6.26**
Designing the game's second level (room `room_level2`).

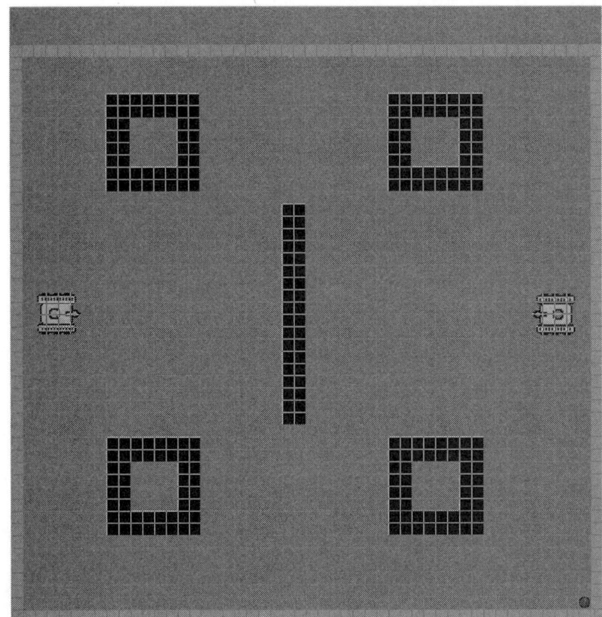

**Figure 6.27**
Designing the game's third level (room `room_level3`).

**Figure 6.28**
Designing the game's fourth level (room `room_level4`).

**Figure 6.29**
Designing the game's fifth level (room `room_level5`).

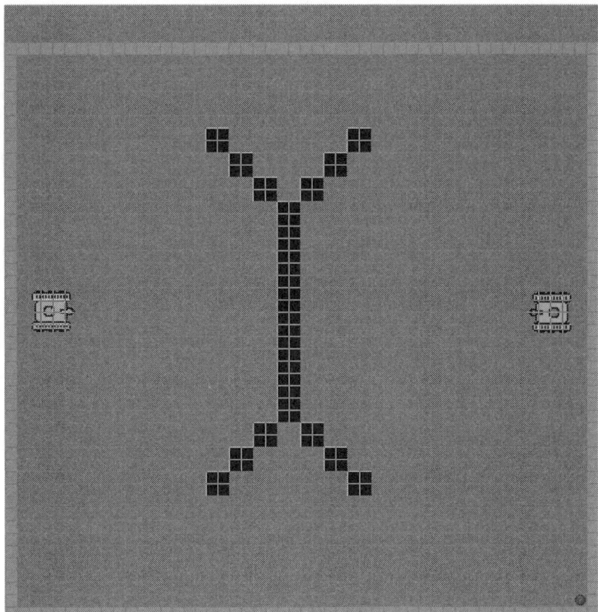

**Figure 6.30**
Designing the game's sixth level (room `room_level6`).

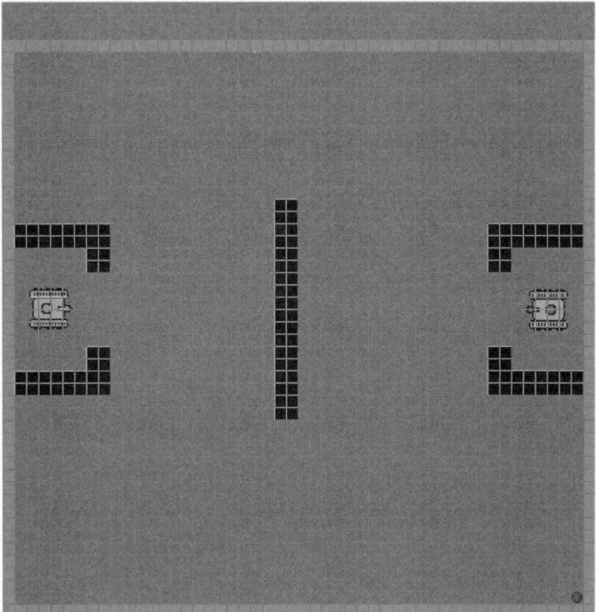

**Figure 6.31**
Designing the game's seventh level (room `room_level7`).

## Wrapping Things Up

At this point, assuming you have followed along carefully without skipping any steps, you should be ready to put your copy of the Tank Battle game through its paces. Once you have verified that everything is working like it should, let's add a few additional features to the game before calling it quits.

### *Adding Game Information*

Begin by double-clicking on the Game Information entry in the resource tree folder and then type the text outlined below into the Game Information window. Set the text to display as yellow characters on a brown background and then format it as was shown in Figure 6.13.

**Tank Battle**

**Welcome to Tank Battle. This is a two-player game. The goal of the game is to destroy your opponent's tank before he destroys your tank. Each time you destroy the opponent's tank you get 1 point. The first player to score 11 points wins.**

**The game consists of 7 constantly changing levels. Player 1 controls the blue tank using the:**

- **A key to move left**
- **D key to move right**
- **W key to move up**
- **S key to move down**
- **Space key to shoot**

**Player 2 controls the red tank using the:**

- **Left arrow key to move left**
- **Right arrow key to move right**
- **Up arrow key to move up**
- **Down arrow key to move down**
- **Delete key to shoot**

**Developer: Jerry Lee Ford, Jr.**

**Date: February 27, 2009**

**Website: www.tech-publishing.com**

### *Configuring Global Game Settings*

Let's configure the Tank Battle game to run in full-screen mode by double-clicking on the Global Game Settings entry in the resource tree folder, selecting the Graphics tab, and then enabling the Start in Full-Screen Mode option. Next, let's add a custom splash screen to the application by clicking on the Loading tab and then enabling the Show Your Own Image While Loading option. Next, click on the Change Image button and then select the `TankSplash.bmp` file, which you can download from this book's companion website.

In addition to adding a custom splash screen, let's customize the progress bar by selecting the Own Loading Progress Bar option and then using the `ProgressB.bmp` file as the back image and the `ProgressF.bmp` file as the front image. Both of these files are available on the book's companion website.

Lastly, let's assign a custom icon to the application by clicking on the Change Icon button and adding the `Tank.ico` icon to the game. When done making all of these changes, click on OK to close the Global Game Settings window.

## Summary

This chapter expanded your game development skills by showing you how to add a number of new features to your games. This included showing you how to disable the Escape key and how to add game cheats. You learned how to add a custom splash screen and to modify your game's progress bar. You also learned how to set up your game to run in full-screen mode and to work with game saves. In addition to all this, this chapter showed you how to create a standalone version of your game and demonstrated how to assign an icon of your own making to your games. On top of all this, you learned how to create the Tank Battle game.

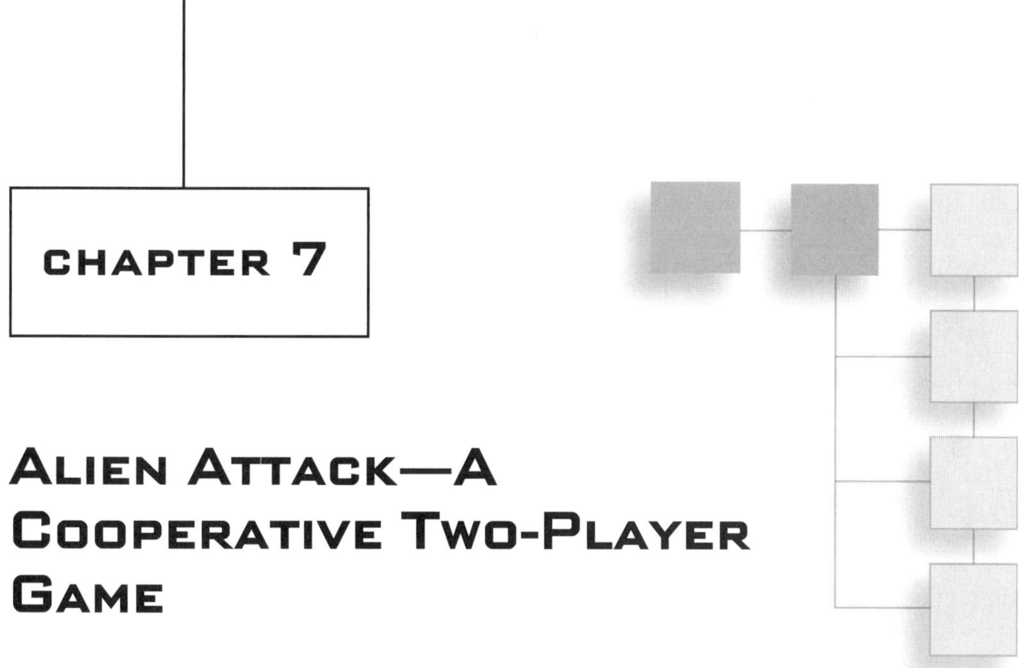


# Alien Attack—A Cooperative Two-Player Game

One feature commonly found in many computer games is a main screen, or *front end*, that presents the player with a menu of commands to start game play, access game information, display high scores, exit the game, and so on. The front end is usually redisplayed at the end of game play, allowing the player to access its options again. This chapter will show you one way in which you might set up something like this. In addition, you will learn how to create a new game, Alien Attack, which is a cooperative two-player, shoot-out game.

An overview of the major topics covered in this chapter includes:

- A review of the different steps involved in setting up a front end
- Learning how to assemble and program the logic needed to manage a game's front end
- Learning how to set up alarms and to use them to trigger the execution of actions
- Learning how to develop a back-end component for your games

## Developing Front Ends and Back Ends

So far, all of the games that you have worked on have thrown the players right into the thick of things once started. However, most games that you buy do not behave this way. Instead, they typically begin by displaying an opening menu of

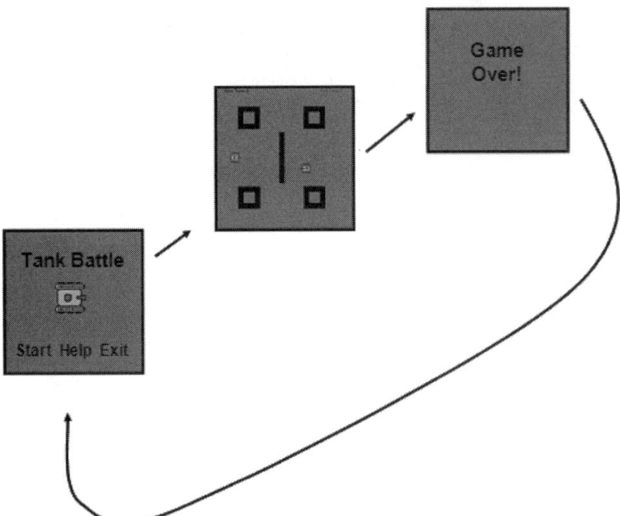


**Figure 7.1**
A well-designed game usually includes both front-end and bank-end rooms.

options, referred to by game developers as a front end, allowing players to access various game features. These features are usually accessed by clicking on buttons or text that execute various actions, like starting game play or displaying game information.

Most commercial games also include a back end that lets players know when game play has ended. Depending on how the player did, a congratulatory message may be displayed or the player may instead be encouraged to keep trying. If players accumulate points during game play, the back end may also display a high scores table. In short, a game's back end can be used to perform any actions you want to perform at the end of game play.

In Game Maker, front ends and bank ends are implemented using rooms that contain one or more objects, which in turn can be used to execute programming logic. Figure 7.1 depicts the role that front-end and back-end rooms play in relation to the rest of the game, providing it with a wrapper that manages initial and closing game activities.

## Adding a Front End to Your Games

A well-designed front end provides a nice touch to any game by presenting players with a snappy menu that gives them greater control over the execution of the game. The front end allows players to decide when to begin game play, by allowing them to click on a Play button or similar type of control. In most cases, this is highly preferable to simply throwing players into the middle of a game.

Another feature commonly found on front ends is some type of Help button, which players unfamiliar with the game can click on to learn what the game is about and how it is played. Providing access to game information in this manner is a lot more intuitive than simply expecting the players to figure out that they can press the F1 key to get game information.

Front ends also usually provide a button that allows players to close the game. Again, this is a lot more intuitive than requiring the player to have to press the Escape key. Front ends can provide players with access to all kinds of features. For example, you might want to provide access to the game's high scores table or a button that displays a room with different options that the player can use to configure or control the operation of the game. In this way, the player might be allowed to disable sound or background music or select a skill level (easy, medium, and hard).

In the sections that follow, you will learn how to create a front end that displays the name of the game and shows a graphic that provides the player with a hint pertaining to what the game is about. This front end will also contain buttons that when clicked, give the player the ability to:

- Start game play
- Display game information
- Exit the game

## Developing Background and Graphic Files

The first step in creating a front end for a game is the development of a suitable background for the front-end's room. You can often use one of the game's backgrounds for this purpose. This will help ensure a consistent look and feel between the front end and the game. You will also need to create a sprite showing the game's name. It is also usually a good idea to create a second sprite that depicts the game, perhaps showing a picture of the game in action or a picture of the game's main character.

In addition to the resources already discussed, you need to create a sprite for each command that you want to give players access to on the game's front end. You might, for example, create three sprites that resemble button controls, labeling the buttons Start, Help, and Exit. Once you have these resources at your disposal, you are ready to begin assembling your game's front end. For example, you might want to consider modifying the Skybuster game that you worked on in Chapter 5 by adding a front end to it. Figure 7.2 shows a simple graphic logo file that you could use to display the game's name.

As part of Skybuster's new front end, you might add a graphic image like the one shown in Figure 7.3.

Lastly, you'll need several sprites that can be used to create objects upon which players can click to execute commands, as demonstrated in Figure 7.4.

**Figure 7.2**
A colorful logo is an important part of any game's front end.

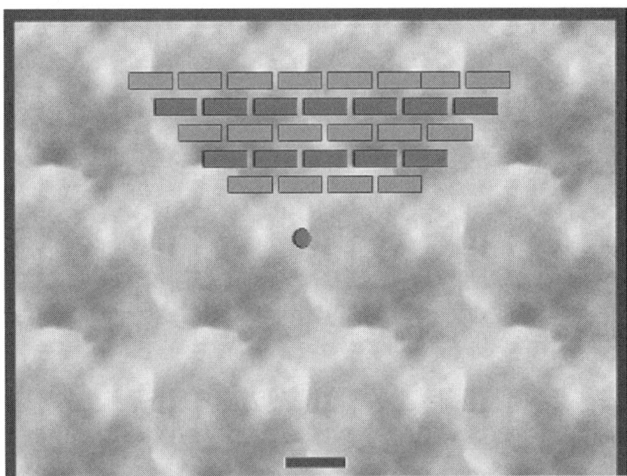

**Figure 7.3**
This graphic provides players with a preview of what is to come.

START HELP EXIT

**Figure 7.4**
Sprites to be used as the basis for creating button objects on the front end.

## Creating Front-End Button Controls

In order to be able to interact with a game's front end, you need to add a number of button-like controls to it, which you can do by creating objects consisting of the appropriate graphic sprites. For example, in creating button controls for the Skybuster game, you would create objects for all three of the sprites that represent front-end commands (e.g., Start, Help, Exit). Once created, you can add program logic to each of these three sprites so that they perform appropriate actions when players click on them.

You should also create objects for any other sprites that you have created so that you can add them to the room that you will assemble as the game's front end. Unlike the three sprites used to create button-like controls, these other sprites won't have any program logic associated with them because they are only used to spruce things up.

## Turning a Room into a Front End

Once you have a background selected for the room and have created the sprites and objects you'll need, the next step in the creation of a front end is to add a new room to the game and to make that room the game's starting room. You do this by dragging and dropping it to the beginning of the list of rooms shown in the resource tree folder. Next, assign the room an appropriate background. Again, you may simply want to use a background already used in the game for consistency. Another option is to apply an appropriate background color to the room. If you do this, make sure that the color you select is consistent with the game's overall color scheme.

Now, it is time to start adding objects to the room. For starters, add the object representing the game name followed by any graphic objects that you may have created to help set the mood. Then, add the objects that will represent the front end's button controls. For example, a front-end room for the Skybuster game might look like the example shown in Figure 7.5.

**Trap**

If your game has a special controller object, you may need to add an instance of it to the game's front end for everything to work correctly. Otherwise, depending on how you have set things up, any game initialization activities that the controller object is supposed to perform at the beginning of the game won't execute.

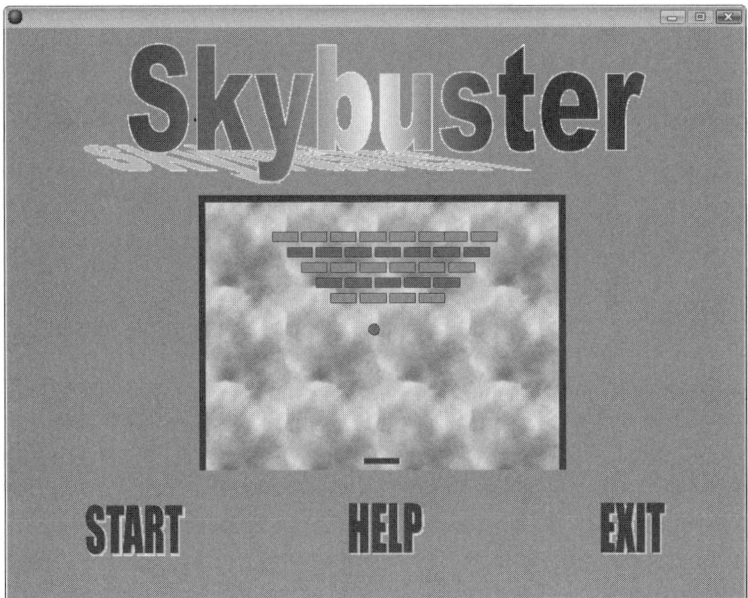


**Figure 7.5**
Using the objects that you have added to the game to lay out its front end.

## Adding Program Logic to the Front End's Controls

Once you have finished creating the game's front end, you need to add the programming logic required to turn each of the front-end's button objects into working controls. For a game with Start, Help, and Exit controls, you might accomplish this by executing the following procedures.

### Programming the Start Button

1. Double-click on the object representing the Start button.
2. Click on Add Event to open the Event Selector window.
3. Click on the Mouse button and then select the `Left Button` event.
4. Click on the main1 tab and drag and drop the `Next Room` action onto the actions area.

### Programming the Help Button

1. Double-click on the object representing the Help button.
2. Click on Add Event to open the Event Selector window.
3. Click on the Mouse button and then select the `Left Button` event.

4. Click on the main2 tab and drag and drop the `Show Info` action onto the actions area.

**Programming the Exit Button**

1. Double-click on the object representing the Exit button.
2. Click on Add Event to open the Event Selector window.
3. Click on the Mouse button and then select the `Left Button` event.
4. Click on the main2 tab and drag and drop the `End Game` action onto the actions area.

## Adding a Back End to Your Games

In addition to adding a front end to your games, you may also want to add a back end. The purpose of the back end is to let players know that game play has ended and to perform any wrap-up actions that the game may need to complete. A back end may also perform tasks like displaying the game's high score table or encouraging players to visit its developer's website.

### Creating Graphics and Associated Objects

A back end typically consists of one or more sprites that display graphic text and images along with corresponding objects. The back end is created by adding a new room to the game and then populating it with these objects. For example, Figure 7.6 shows an example of a typical back end, which is made up of a single graphic object added to a new room in the game.

### Adding the Requisite Programming Logic

Once you have added a new room to your game and populated it with whatever objects you deem necessary, drag the room to the end of the list of rooms shown in the resource folder tree. Before your work on the back end is complete, you must configure the back-end's programming logic by adding it to one of the objects that you have added to its room. The steps for doing this are outlined here:

1. Double-click on one of the objects that you added to the back-end room to open its Object Properties window.
2. Click on the Add Event button and then add a `Create` event to the object.

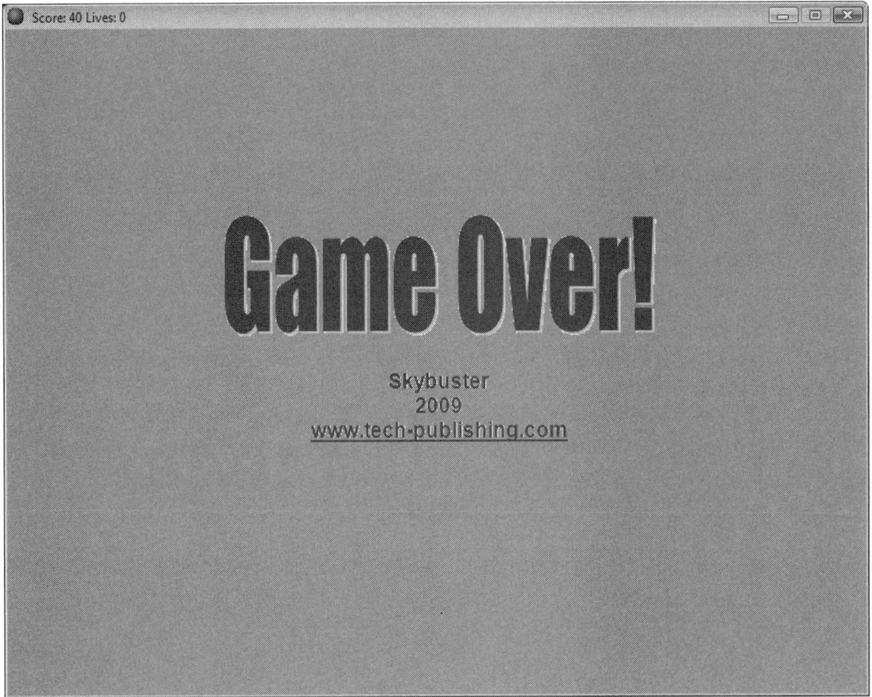


**Figure 7.6**
A simple back end made up of a single room and graphic object.

3. Select the main2 tab and then drag and drop an instance of the `Set Alarm` action to the actions area.

4. Configure the alarm to wait for 5 seconds before going off by entering a value of **150** in the Number of Steps field. Leave the In Alarm No. field set to `Alarm 0` as shown in Figure 7.7.

5. Click on the Add Event button and then add an `Alarm` event to the object, setting the event to `Alarm 0`.

**Hint**

An *alarm* is a time-triggered event. Alarms are measured in steps, where 30 steps equal one second. Every object can have up to 12 separate alarms, numbered 0 through 11. Alarms are created using the `Set Alarm` action. In order to perform actions when an alarm is triggered, you must also add an `Alarm` event to your object, setting the event number of the `Alarm` event to match that of the alarm you want to trigger it. Once added, you can assign any number of actions to an `Alarm` event.

6. Add any actions that you want to execute to the actions area for this event. Make sure that the last action you add is the `Different Room` action and set it up to load the room representing the game's front end.

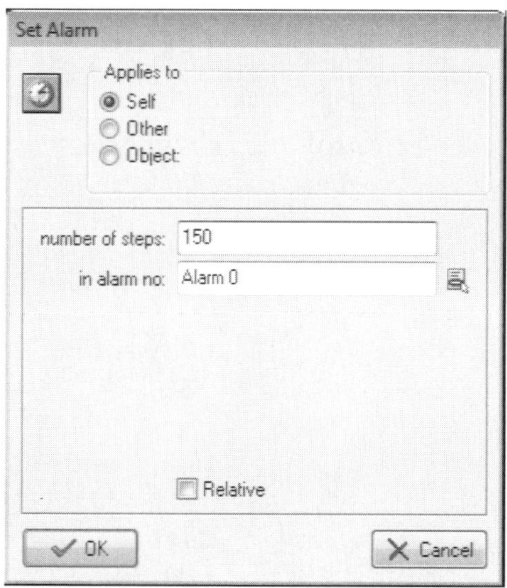


**Figure 7.7**
Setting up an alarm that will go off in 5 seconds.

## Creating the Alien Attack Game

Now it is time to turn your attention to the creation of this chapter's game project, the Alien Attack game. This game is designed as a two-player cooperative game. Alien Attack is a *scrolling shooter* game, which means that the game's background moves (scrolls) under the objects on the screen, giving the illusion that they are moving. In the case of this game it looks like the game's jets are flying across the sky.

The goal of the game is for both players to work together to shoot and destroy as many invading alien ships as possible without getting killed.

Players must fight off three different types of enemy ships. Red alien ships are the most numerous. Their mission is to try to ram into the player's jets. Blue alien ships behave like red ships, except that they sometimes fire missiles. The green ship is the alien's mother ship. Once it appears on the scene, it hovers up and down repeatedly firing its weapons until either it or one of the player's jets is destroyed.

Game play ends when one of the player's jets is destroyed or when the alien's mother ship arrives on the screen and is destroyed by the players. Player's jets are able to take multiple hits before being destroyed. Players take hits when either one of the enemy ships collides with them or when they get shot. Players are able to keep track of their individual health and their combined scores by keeping an eye on a blue status panel displayed at the bottom of the screen.

Players control their jets via the keyboard. Player 1 controls the light gray jet with the light-blue windshield using the following keyboard keys.

- **A**. Moves the jet left.
- **D**. Moves the jet right.
- **W**. Moves the jet up.
- **S**. Moves the jet down.
- **Space**. Fires the jet's guns.

Player 2 controls the dark gray jet with the yellow windshield using the following keyboard keys.

- **Left Arrow**. Moves the jet left.
- **Right Arrow**. Moves the jet right.
- **Up Arrow**. Moves the jet up.
- **Down Arrow**. Moves the jet down.
- **Enter**. Fires the jet's guns.

Players score points by shooting alien ships. No points are awarded when the player destroys an alien ship by crashing into it. Destroying a red alien ship adds 10 points to the players' combined score, and destroying a blue alien ship adds 15 points. Although players must destroy the green mother ship to win, no points are awarded for its destruction. The green alien mother ship can take 10 hits before being destroyed. If players want, they can avoid destroying the mother ship in order to rack up additional points.

Figure 7.8 shows an example of how the Alien Attack game looks when being played.

Like all of the games you have worked on up to this point in the book, you will need to perform a number of steps to develop the Alien Attack game. These steps are outlined below.

1. Add the sprites needed by the game.
2. Add the sounds used to generate sound effects.

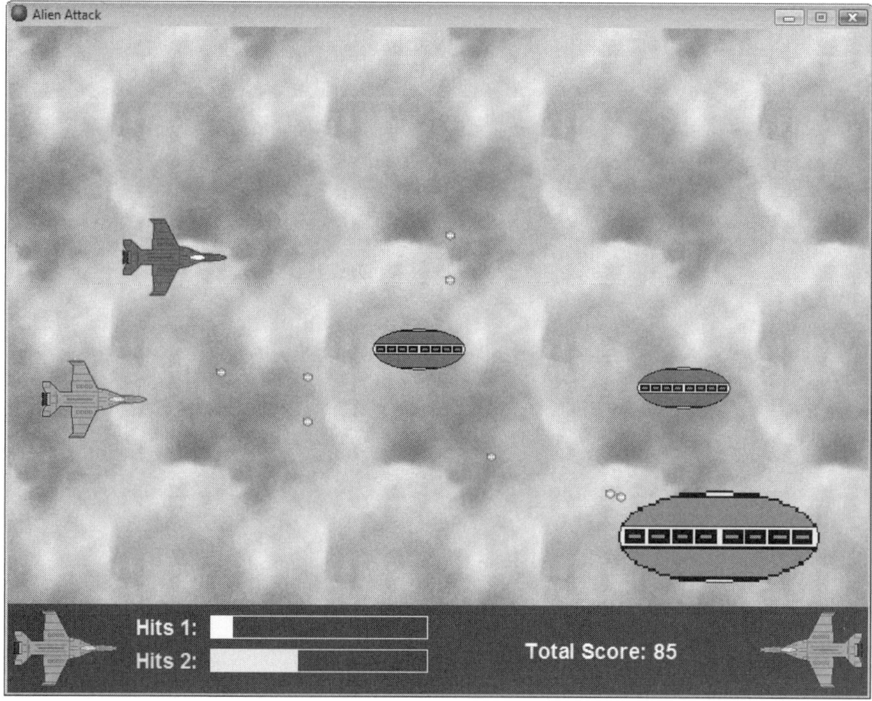


**Figure 7.8**
Alien Attack is a cooperative two-player scrolling shooter game.

3. Configure a background for the game.
4. Create the font to be used to display player health and score.
5. Create the objects needed by the game.
6. Add the rooms needed to create the game's front end, primary play area, and back end.
7. Develop the programming logic for the game's objects.

## Step 1—Adding the Game's Sprites

The first step in the creation of the Alien Attack game is to add all of the sprites that the game requires. These include two jet planes, three alien ships, a bullet, an animated explosion, and a graphic strip to be used to display a control panel for the game. If you have not done so, start Game Maker. If it is already started, click on File > New to begin a new game. Use the steps outlined below to add the sprite for the first player jet.

### Creating the Sprite for Player 1's Jet

1. Click on Resources > Create Sprite. The Sprite Properties window opens. Type **`spr_plane1`** as the name for the game's first sprite.

2. The graphic files for all of the game's sprites are available for download from the book's companion web page (www.courseptr.com/downloads). Click on the Load Sprite button, navigate to the location where you saved the files, select the `Allied1.bmp` file, and then click on Open.

3. Enable the Smooth Edges option, click on the center button to set the sprite's alignment to its center, and click on OK to close the Sprite Properties window.

### Creating the Sprite for Player 2's Jet

1. Click on Resources > Create Sprite. The Sprite Properties window opens. Type **`spr_plane2`** as the name for the game's first sprite.

2. Click on the Load Sprite button, select the `Allied2.bmp` file, and then click on Open.

3. Enable the Smooth Edges option, click on the center button to set the sprite's alignment to its center, and then click on OK to close the Sprite Properties window.

### Creating the Red Alien Ship

1. Create another sprite, assigning it a name of **`spr_alien_red`**.

2. Click on the Load Sprite button, select the `AlienRed.bmp` file, and then click on Open.

3. Click on the center button to set the sprite's alignment to its center and then click on OK to close the Sprite Properties window.

### Creating the Blue Alien Ship

1. Create another sprite, assigning it a name of **`spr_alien_blue`**.

2. Click on the Load Sprite button, select the `AlienBlue.bmp` file, and then click on Open.

3. Click on the center button to set the sprite's alignment to its center and then click on OK to close the Sprite Properties window.

### Creating the Green Alien Ship

1. Create another sprite, assigning it a name of **`spr_alien_green`**.
2. Click on the Load Sprite button, select the `AlienGreen.bmp` file, and then click on Open.
3. Click on the center button to set the sprite's alignment to its center and then click on OK to close the Sprite Properties window.

### Creating a Bullet

1. Create another sprite, assigning it a name of **`spr_bullet`**.
2. Click on the Load Sprite button, select the `Bullet.bmp` file, and then click on Open.
3. Click on the center button to set the sprite's alignment to its center and then click on OK to close the Sprite Properties window.

### Creating an Animated Explosion

1. Create another sprite, assigning it a name of **`spr_explode`**.
2. Click on the Load Sprite button, select the `Explosion.gif` file, and then click on Open.
3. Click on the center button to set the sprite's alignment to its center and then click on OK to close the Sprite Properties window.

### Creating the Control Panel

1. Create another sprite, assigning it a name of **`spr_control_panel`**.
2. Click on the Load Sprite button, select the `Panel.bmp` file, and then click on Open.
3. Clear the Transparent option and then click on OK to close the Sprite Properties window.

The Alien Attack game will also include both front-end and back-end rooms. To support the development of these rooms, you will need to add seven additional sprites to the game. The graphic files for all of the game's sprites are available for download from the book's companion web page (www.courseptr.com/downloads). Use the steps outlined below to add these sprites to the game.

1. Add a new sprite to the game, assign it a name of **spr_title**, and then assign it the `Title.bmp` file.
2. Add a new sprite to the game, assign it a name of **spr_play**, and then assign it the `Play.bmp` file.
3. Add a new sprite to the game, assign it a name of **spr_scores**, and then assign it the `Scores.bmp` file.
4. Add a new sprite to the game, assign it a name of **spr_help**, and then assign it the `Help.bmp` file.
5. Add a new sprite to the game, assign it a name of **spr_exit**, and then assign it the `Exit.bmp` file.
6. Add a new sprite to the game, assign it a name of **spr_title_graphic**, and then assign it the `Title_Graphic.bmp` file.
7. Add a new sprite to the game, assign it a name of **spr_game_over**, and then assign it the `GameOver.bmp` file.

## Step 2—Creating the Game's Sounds

The second step in the creation of the Alien Attack game is to add the sounds that the game needs to manage the playback of its sound effects. These effects include playing an explosive sound whenever one of the player's jets collides with an alien ship or missile and the playing of a second sound every time a player fires his jet's guns. To set up these two sounds, you will need to use the audio files that come with Game Maker. By default, Game Maker places these audio files in C:\Program Files\Game Maker7\Sounds.

The following procedure outlines the steps required to add and configure the game's sounds.

1. Click on Resources > Create Sound. The Sound Properties window appears.
2. Name the sound **snd_explosion** and click on the Load Sound button. Navigate to the C:\Program Files\Game Maker7\Sounds folder where

Game Maker stores the sound files that are installed with it, select the `explosition.wav` file, and then click on Open.

3. Click on OK to close the Sprite Properties window.

Using the steps outlined above, add a second sound to the game, naming it **snd_shot**, and assign it the `zap.wav` file, which you will find in the same location of that game's other sound file.

**Hint**

> To further enhance the quality of the game, consider adding an appropriate midi file to it, providing the game with some background music. The right background music can help establish an atmosphere that can make the game more engrossing and enjoyable.

## Step 3—Adding a Background to the Game

The next step in the creation of the Alien Attack game is the addition of a background to the game, which you can do using the steps outlined below.

1. Click on Resources > Create Background. The Background Properties window appears.
2. Enter **bck_sky** into the Name file.
3. The graphic file you will need to create the background is supplied with Game Maker and by default is located in the C:\Program Files\Game Maker7\Backgrounds folder. To add it, click on the Load Background button and navigate to the Backgrounds folder. Select the `sky.gif` file and then click on Open.
4. Click on OK to close the Background Properties window.

## Step 4—Creating a New Font

The game will display the health of both players using a progress bar located at the bottom of the screen. It will also display the combined total number of points earned by both players during game play. Game Maker's default font size of 12 is not large enough to adequately display this information. To remedy this situation, you need to add a Font to the game using the steps outlined below.

1. Click on Resources > Create Font. Game Maker will respond by displaying the Font Properties window.

2. Enter **font_control_panel** into the Name file.
3. Leaving the Font type set to Arial, enter **14** as the size of the font.
4. Enable the font's Bold setting and then click on OK to close the Font Properties window.

## Step 5—Creating the Game's Objects

The Alien Attack game is made up of a number of different objects. These objects include both jets, bullets for both the jets and alien ships, three alien ships, the animated explosion, and two invisible objects. The invisible objects include a special controller object and a special parent object that will be used to define certain events and actions common to the operations of both jets. Begin by defining all of the objects used by the game using the procedure outlined below.

1. Click on Resources > Create Object. The Object Properties window appears. Type **obj_allied_plane1** in the Name field, click on the context menu icon located at the end of the Sprite text field, and select spr_plane1 from the sprites list.
2. Add another object named **obj_allied_plane2**, assigning it the spr_plane2 sprite.
3. Add another object named **obj_alien_red**, assigning it the spr_alien_red sprite.
4. Add another object named **obj_alien_blue**, assigning it the spr_alien_blue sprite.
5. Add another object named **obj_alien_green**, assigning it the spr_alien_green sprite.
6. Add another object named **obj_bullet**, assigning it the spr_bullet sprite.
7. Add another object named **obj_alien_bullet**, assigning it the spr_bullet sprite.
8. Add another object named **obj_explode**, assigning it the spr_explosion sprite.

9. Add another object named **obj_controller**.
10. Add another object named **obj_plane_parent**, clearing its Visible property.

You also need to create objects for each of the seven sprites that will be used to support the creation of the game's front-end and back-end rooms. Do so by following the steps outlined here:

1. Click on Resources > Create Object. The Object Properties window appears. Type **obj_title** in the Name field, click on the context menu icon located at the end of the Sprite text field, and select spr_title from the sprites list.
2. Add another object to the game, naming it **obj_play** and assigning it the spr_play sprite.
3. Add another object to the game, naming it obj_scores and assigning it the spr_scores sprite.
4. Add another object to the game, naming it **obj_help** and assigning it the spr_help sprite.
5. Add another object to the game, naming it **obj_exit** and assigning it the spr_exit sprite.
6. Add another object to the game, naming it **obj_title_graphic** and assigning it the spr_title_graphic sprite.
7. Add another object to the game, naming it **obj_game_over** and assigning it the spr_game_over sprite.

## Step 6—Creating the Game's Rooms

The next step in the development of the Alien Attack game is to add three rooms to it. These rooms represent the game's front end, back end, and the room in which game play occurs. Instructions for creating these rooms are provided in the sections that follow.

### *Adding a Front-End Room*

To create the front-end room, click on Resources > Create Room. Click on the Settings tab and then name the room **room_front_end**. Increase the size of the

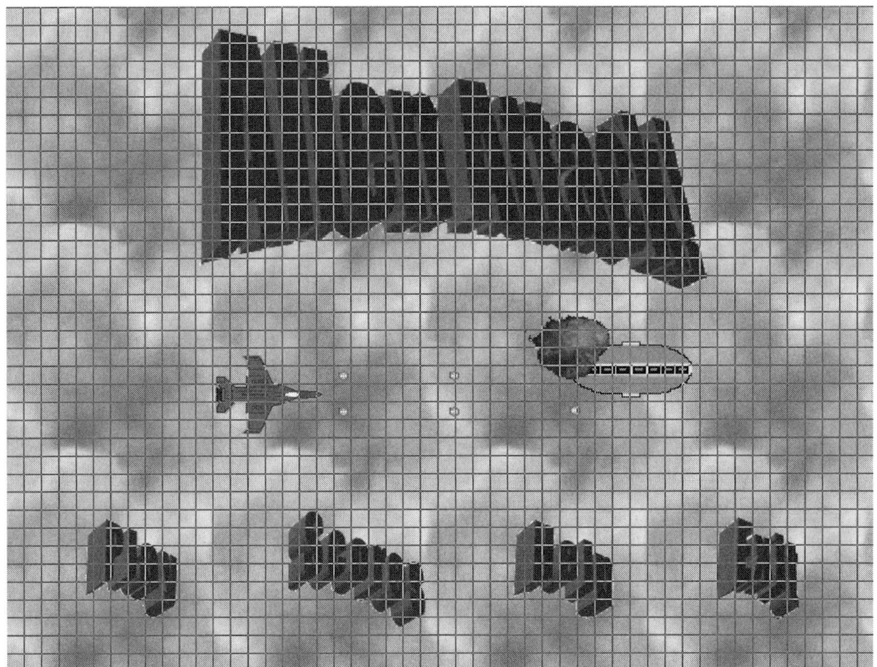

**Figure 7.9**
Designing the game's front-end room.

room by clicking on the Settings tab and changing the room's width to 800 and its height to 600, and then add a caption of **Alien Attack** to the Caption for the Room field. Next, click on the Backgrounds tab, clear the Draw Background Color setting, and then select `bck_sky` as the room's background.

To wrap up your work on the room, click on the Objects tab and then add an instance of each of the following objects to it: `obj_title`, `obj_title_graphic`, `obj_play`, `obj_scores`, `obj_help`, and `obj_exit`. Arrange these instances as shown in Figure 7.9.

### *Creating a Room in Which to Play*

Add a second room to the game, click on the Settings tab, and name the room **room_skyline**. Increase the size of the room by clicking on the Settings tab and changing the room's width to `800` and its height to `600` and add a caption of **Alien Attack** to the Caption for the Room field.

Next, click on the Backgrounds tab, clear the Draw Background Color setting, and then select `bck_sky` as the room's background. As has already been

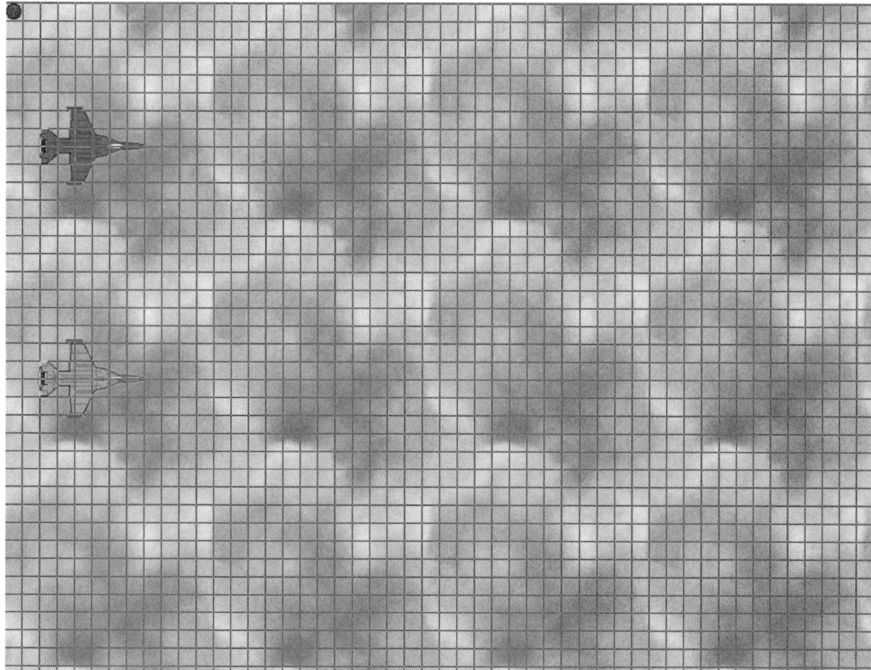

**Figure 7.10**
Creating the room in which game play will occur.

mentioned, this game will play like a scrolling shooter. Specifically, the background in this room will be scrolled horizontally from right to left to make it look like both jets are flying through the sky. In order to set up this, type a value of **-2** in the Hor. Speed field located at the bottom of the Backgrounds tab.

To finish up your work on this final room, click on the Objects tab and then add an instance of the following objects to it: `obj_allied_plane1`, `obj_allied_plane2`, and `obj_controller`. Arrange these instances as shown in Figure 7.10.

### *Adding a Back-End Room*

To create the game's back-end room, add a third room to the game, click on the Settings tab, and then name the room **`room_back_end`**. Increase the size of the room by clicking on the Settings tab, changing the room's width to `800` and its height to `600`, and add a caption of **`Alien Attack`** to the Caption for the Room field. Next, click on the Backgrounds tab, clear the Draw Background Color setting, and then select `bck_sky` as the room's background.

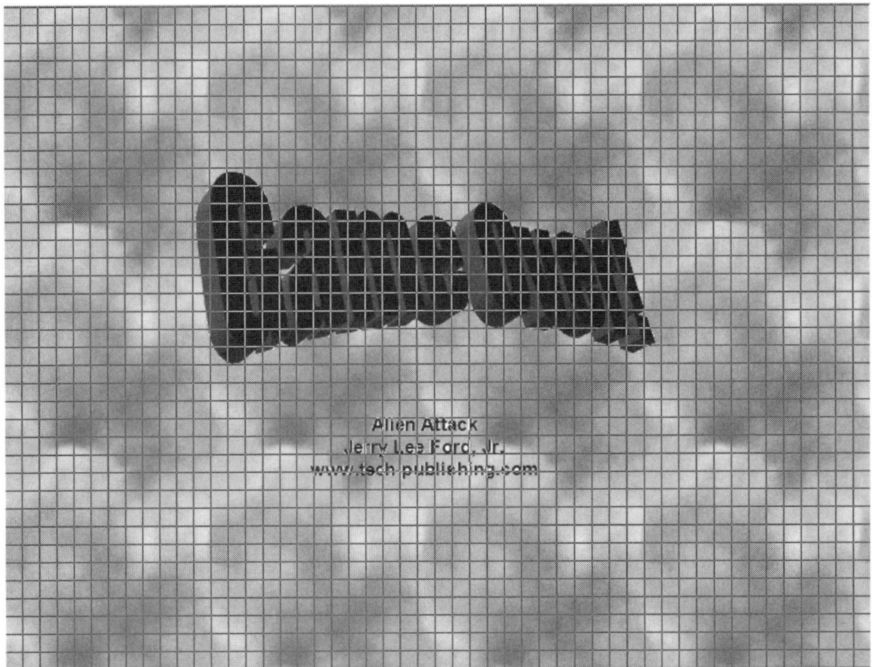


**Figure 7.11**
Designing the game's back-end room.

To wrap up your work on the room, click on the Objects tab and then add an instance of the `obj_game_over` object to it. Place this instance in the location shown in Figure 7.11.

## Step 7—Developing Object Programming Logic

All that remains in the development of the Alien Attack game is to develop the program logic required to bring the game's objects to life, as outlined in the procedures that follow.

### Creating a Parent Object for the Jets

In order to simplify the development of the jet objects, common functionality shared between those two objects will be added to a special parent object named `obj_plane_parent`. Instructions for programming this object are provided here:

1. Double-click on the `obj_plane_parent` object to open its Object Properties window.

2. Click on the Add Event button, add the Create event to the object, and then add three Set Variable actions to it. Assign a variable name of **Shoot** to the first action and give it a value of 1. Assign a variable name of **Plane1_Hits** to the second action and give it a value of 0. Assign a name of **Plane2_Hits** to the third action and give it a value of 0.

3. Add a Step event to the object and then a Set Variable action to it. Assign it a name of **Shoot** and give it a value of 1. Enable its Relative option.

### Programming Player 1's Jet

1. Double-click on the obj_allied_plane1 object to open its Object Properties window.

2. Click on the Add Event button and add a Keyboard event for the <Enter> key. Add a Test Variable action to it, configuring it to determine if the Shoot variable is larger than 0.

3. Add a Start Block, then add a pair of Create Instance actions, and set both instances to create an instance of the obj_bullet object. Assign a value of -20 to both instance's y properties and enable their Relative options.

4. Add a Play Sound action and configure it to play the snd_shot sound.

5. Add a Set Variable action and use it to assign a value of -20 to the Shoot variable.

6. Click on the Add Event button and add a Keyboard event for the <Left> key. Add a Test Variable action to it, configuring it to determine if the x variable is larger than 50. Add a Start Block action followed by the Jump to Position action and then an End Block action. Set the coordinate of the Jump to Position action to -5,0 and then enable its Relative option.

7. Click on the Add Event button and add a Keyboard event for the <Up> key. Add a Test Variable action to it, configuring it to determine if the y variable is larger than 50. Add a Start Block action followed by the Jump to Position action and then an End Block action. Set the coordinate of the Jump to Position action to 0,-5, and then enable its Relative option.

8. Click on the Add Event button and add a Keyboard event for the <Right> key. Add a Test Variable action to it, configuring it to determine if the x variable

is smaller than the expression room_width - 100. Add a Start Block action followed by the Jump to Position action and then an End Block action. Set the coordinate of the Jump to Position action to 5,0 and then enable its Relative option.

9. Click on the Add Event button and add a Keyboard event for the <Down> key. Add a Test Variable action to it, configuring it to determine if the y variable is smaller than the expression room_height - 130. Add a Start Block action followed by the Jump to Position action and then an End Block action. Set the coordinate of the Jump to Position action to 0,5 and then enable its Relative option.

### Programming Player 2's Jet

1. Double-click on the obj_allied_plane2 object to open its Object Properties window.

2. Click on the Add Event button and add a Keyboard event for the <Space> key. Add a Test Variable action to it, configuring it to determine if the Shoot variable is larger than 0.

3. Add a Start Block and add a pair of Create Instance actions. Set both instances to create an instance of the obj_bullet object. Assign a value of -20 to both instance's y properties and enable their Relative options.

4. Add a Play Sound action and configure it to play the snd_shot sound.

5. Add a Set Variable action and use it to assign a value of -20 to the Shoot variable.

6. Click on the Add Event button and add a Keyboard event for the <A> key. Add a Test Variable action to it, configuring it to determine if the x variable is larger than 50. Add a Start Block action followed by the Jump to Position action and then an End Block action. Set the coordinate of the Jump to Position action to -5,0 and then enable its Relative option.

7. Click on the Add Event button and add a Keyboard event for the <W> key. Add a Test Variable action to it, configuring it to determine if the y variable is larger than 50. Add a Start Block action followed by the Jump to Position action and then an End Block action. Set the coordinate of the Jump to Position action to 0,-5 and then enable its Relative option.

8. Click on the Add Event button and add a Keyboard event for the <D> key. Add a Test Variable action to it, configuring it to determine if the x variable is smaller than the expression room_width - 100. Add a Start Block action followed by the Jump to Position action and then an End Block action. Set the coordinate of the Jump to Position action to 5,0 and then enable its Relative option.

9. Click on the Add Event button and add a Keyboard event for the <S key. Add a Test Variable action to it, configuring it to determine if the y variable is smaller than the expression room_height - 130. Add a Start Block action followed by the Jump to Position action and then an End Block action. Set the coordinate of the Jump to Position action to 0,5 and then enable its Relative option.

### Programming the Red Alien Ship

1. Double-click on the obj_alien_red object to open its Object Properties window. Add a Create event and then add the Moved Fixed action to it. Click on the Moved Fixed window's left arrow button and assign a value of 7 to Speed.

2. Add a Collision event for the obj_allied_plane1 object and the Destroy Instance action, leaving its default setting of Self in place. Add a Create Instance action, enable its Relative option, and configure it to use the obj_explode object. Add the Set Variable action, assigning obj_controller.Plane1_Hits a value of 20. Lastly, add the Play Sound action and assign it the snd_explosion sound.

3. Repeat step 2, modifying it to handle a collision for the obj_allied_plane2 object.

4. Add a Collision event for the obj_bullet object and the Destroy Instance action, leaving its default setting of Self in place. Add another Destroy Instance action, assigning a value of obj_bullet to Other. Add a Create Instance action, enable its Relative option, and configure it to use the obj_explode object. Add the Set Score action, assign it a value of 10, and enable its Relative option. Lastly, assign the Play Sound action and assign it the snd_explosion sound.

5. Click on the Add Event button, click on the Other button, and select the Outside Room event. Add the Text Variable action, setting it to test whether

x is smaller than 0. Add a Start Block action, followed by a Destroy Instance action (set to Self) and then the End Block action.

### Programming the Blue Alien Ship

1. Double-click on the obj_alien_blue object to open its Object Properties window. Add a Create event and then add the Moved Fixed action to it. Click on the Moved Fixed window's left arrow button and assign a value of 5 to Speed.

2. Add a Step event and then click on the Control tab and add an instance of the Test Chance action. Assign a value of 80 to the Sides field. This adds a virtual 80 sides die to the game and then rolls it. Every time the die lands on 1, the action that follows is executed. Add the Create Instance action, setting object to obj_alien_bullet and enabling its Relative option.

3. Add a Collision event for the obj_allied_plan1 object and the Destroy Instance action, leaving its default setting of Self in place. Add another Destroy Instance action, assigning a value of obj_bullet to Other. Add a Create Instance action, enable its Relative option, and configure it to use the obj_explode object. Add the Set Variable action, assign a value of 20 to obj_controller.Plane1.Hits, and enable its Relative option. Lastly, assign the Play Sound action and assign it the snd_explosion sound.

4. Add a Collision event for the obj_allied_plan2 object and the Destroy Instance action, leaving its default setting of Self in place. Add a Create Instance action, enable its Relative option, and configure it to use the obj_explode object. Add the Set Variable action, assign a value of 20 to obj_controller.Plane2.Hits, enabling its Relative option. Lastly, assign the Play Sound action and assign it the snd_explosion sound.

5. Add a Collision event for the obj_bullet object and the Destroy Instance action, leaving its default setting of Self in place. Add another Destroy Instance action, assigning a value of obj_bullet to Other. Add a Create Instance action, enable its Relative option, and configure it to use the obj_explode object. Add the Set Score action, assign it a value of 15, and enable its Relative option. Lastly, assign the Play Sound action and assign it the snd_explosion sound.

6. Click on the Add Event button, click on the Other button, and select the Outside Room event. Add the Text Variable action, setting it to test whether x is smaller than 0. Add a Start Block action, followed by a Destroy Instance action (set to Self) and then the End Block action.

### Programming the Green Alien Ship

1. Double-click on the obj_alien_green object to open its Object Properties window. Add a Create event and then add the Moved Fixed action to it. Click on the Moved Fixed window's up and down arrow buttons and assign a value of 3 to Speed. This restricts the mother ship to moving only up and down on the right-hand side of the screen.

2. Add the Test Chance action. Assign a value of 20 to the Sides field, adding a virtual 20-sided die to the game and then rolling it. Every time the die lands on 1, the action that follows is executed. Add the Create Instance action, setting object to obj_alien_bullet and enabling its Relative option. This causes the mother ship to fire bullets on a fairly frequent basis.

3. Add a Collision event for the obj_bullet object and a Set Variable action, setting obj_controller.Mothership_Hits to equal 1 and enabling the Relative option. Add a Create Effect object, assigning it a Type of explosion, a Size of medium, and Where value of below objects. Lastly, enable its Relative option.

4. Add a Play Sound action to the Collision event, assign it a value of snd_explosion, and then add a Destroy Instance action, setting object to obj_bullet.

5. Next, add a Test Variable action to the Collision event and then add a Start Block action and an End Block action to it. In between the Start Block and the End Block, add a Create Instance block, setting object to obj_explode, and enabling its Relative option, followed by a Play Sound action set to snd_explosion, followed by a Destroy Instance action set to Self.

6. Add a Test Variable action to the Collision event and then add a Start Block action and an End Block action to it. In between the Start Block and the End Block, add a Sleep action (set to 2000) followed by a Different Room action, setting new room to room_back_end and transition to Fade out and in.

7. Add an Outside Room event to the object and then add the Text Variable action, setting it to test whether y is smaller than 120. Add a Start Block action, followed by a Reverse Vertical action (set to Self) and then the End Block action. Add another Text Variable action, this time setting it to test whether y is larger than 420. Add a Start Block action, followed by a Reverse Vertical action (set to Self), and then the End Block action. These actions will keep the mother ship bounding up and down within the game window.

**Programming the Jet's Bullet Object**

1. Double-click on the obj_bullet object to open its Object Properties window.

2. Add a Create event and then add the Moved Fixed action to it. Click on the Moved Fixed window's right arrow buttons and assign a value of 8 to Speed. This instructs Game Maker to shoot (move) the bullet towards the alien ships that approach from the right-hand side of the game window.

3. Add an Outside Room event to the object and then add the Destroy Instance action (set to Self). This will destroy the bullet if it exits the room.

**Programming the Alien Ship's Bullet Object**

1. Double-click on the obj_alien_bullet object to open its Object Properties window.

2. Add a Create event and then add the Moved Fixed action to it. Click on the Moved Fixed window's left arrow buttons and assign a value of 10 to Speed. This instructs Game Maker to shoot (move) the bullet towards the player's jets that approach from the left-hand side of the game window.

3. Add a Collision event for the obj_allied_plan1 object and add a Create Instance action. Enable its Relative option and configure it to use the obj_explode object. Then add a Destroy Instance action leaving its default setting of Self in place. Next, add a Set Variable action, assign a value of 10 to obj_controller.Plane1.Hits and enable its Relative option. Lastly, assign the Play Sound action and assign it the snd_explosion sound.

4. Repeat step 3, modifying it to handle a collision for the obj_allied_plane2 object.

5. Add an Outside Room event to the object and then add the Destroy Instance action (set to Self). This will destroy the bullet if it exits the room.

### Programming an Explosion Object

1. Double-click on the `obj_explode` object to open its Object Properties window.

2. Click on Add Event and then click on the Other button and select `Animation End` event.

3. Add the `Destroy Instance` action leaving its default setting of `Self` in place.

### Programming the Special Controller Object

1. Double-click on the `obj_controller` object to open its Object Properties window. Add a `Create` event and then add the `Score Caption` action to it, disabling the display of the score, lives, and health information in the game window's titlebar. Next, add three `Set Variable` actions to the event, setting `Plane1_Hits` to `0`, `Plane2_Hits` to `0`, and `Mothership_Hits` to `0`. Lastly, add the `Set Alarm` action, setting the `number of steps` to `1600` for `Alarm 0`.

2. Add an `Alarm` event for `Alarm 0` and then add a `Create Instance` action to it, creating the `obj_alien_green` object at coordinates `650,300`.

3. Add a `Step` event and then add a `Test Chance` action to it, assign a value of `60` to Sides. Add a `Create Instance` action using it to create an instance of the `obj_alien_red` object with `720` for its `x` coordinate and `random(room_height - 150)` as its `y` coordinate. This places random numbers of instances of the red alien ship at random locations along the right-hand side of the game window.

4. Add a second `Test Chance` action, assigning it a value of `300` followed by a `Create Instance` object, setting it to `alien_blue` and assigning it an `x` coordinate of `720` and a `y` coordinate of `random(room_height - 150)`. These actions create an instance of the blue alien ships, though at a slower rate than the red ships are produced.

5. Next, add a `Test Variable` action (checking to see if `obj_controller.Plane1_Hits` is larger than 200) followed by a `Start Block` action and an `End Block` action. Inside the start and end block, add the following actions:

   - `Destroy Instance`. Apply the action to `Self`.
   - `Create Instance`. Create the `obj_explode` object.

- Sleep. Set milliseconds to 2000.
- Different Room. Set new room to room_back_end and transition to Fade out and in.

6. Next, add a Test Variable action (checking to see if obj_controller.Plane2_Hits is larger than 200) followed by a Start Block action and an End Block action. Inside the start and end block, add the following actions (which are responsible for displaying and updating the status panel at the bottom of the game window):

   - Destroy Instance. Apply the action to Self.
   - Create Instance. Create the obj_explode object.
   - Sleep. Set milliseconds to 2000.
   - Different Room. Set new room to room_back_end and transition to Fade out and in.

7. Add a Draw event to the object and then add the following events to it.

   - Draw Sprite. Set sprite to spr_control_panel, x to 0, y to 520, and subimage to -1.
   - Set Font. Set Font to fnt_control_panel and align to left.
   - Set Color. Set color to the light yellow swatch.
   - Draw Text. Set text to Hits: 1, x to 120, and y to 530.
   - Draw Rectangle. Set x1 to 190, y1 to 530, x2 to 390, y2 to 550, and filled to outline.
   - Test Instance Count. Set object to obj_allied_plane1, number to 0, and operation to Larger than.
   - Start Block.
   - Draw Rectangle. Set x1 to 190, y1 to 530, x2 to 190 + Plane1_Hits, y2 to 550, and filled to filled.
   - Set Color. Set color to the light blue swatch.
   - Draw Text. Set text to Hits: 2:, x to 120, and y to 560.
   - Draw Rectangle. Set x1 to 190, y1 to 560, x2 to 390, y2 to 580, and filled to outline.
   - End Block.
   - Test Instance Count. Set object to obj_allied_plane2, number to 0, and operation to Larger than.

- Start Block.
- Draw Rectangle. Set x1 to 190, y1 to 560, x2 to 190 + Plane2_Hits, y2 to 580, and filled to filled.
- Set Color. Leave the color field empty (it will default to white).
- Draw Score. Set x to 480, y to 550, and caption to Total Score:.
- End Block.

Okay, at this point you have added all of the program logic required to animate the objects that make up the game. However, this game also has a front end and a back end so you must also define the program logic required to operate both of these components, as outlined in the following procedure.

1. Double-click on the obj_play object to open its Object Properties window and add a Left Button event for the mouse. Add a Next Room action and set its transition to Fade out and in.

2. Double-click on the obj_scores object to open its Object Properties window and add a Left Button event for the mouse. Add a Show Highscore action and set its background to bck_sky.

3. Double-click on the obj_help object to open its Object Properties window and add a Left Button event for the mouse. Add an instance of the Show Info action to the actions area.

4. Double-click on the obj_exit object to open its Object Properties window and add a Left Button event for the mouse. Add an End Game action to the actions area.

5. Double-click on the obj_game_over object to open its Object Properties window, add the Create event, and then add a Set Alarm action, setting number of steps to 120 for Alarm 0. Add an Alarm 0 event and then add the following actions to it.
   - Show Highscore. Set background to bck_sky.
   - Set Score. Set new score to 0.
   - Different Room. Set new room to room_front_end and transition to Fade out and in.

All that remains is to double-click on the Game Information entry in the resource tree folder and then to add a little text describing the game and how to play it.

Once you have done this, save your work and put the game through its paces, making sure everything works as described.

## Summary

This chapter showed you how to enhance your games through the addition of front-end and back-end screens, adding an additional element of professionalism to your games. Front-end features usually include an eye-catching background and buttons for executing commands like Start, High Scores, Help, and Exit. The front end also provides a good starting point for initiating the playback of background music and for initializing various game settings. The back end provides an appropriate place for momentarily displaying the high-scores table and performing any cleanup tasks after which it can display the game's front end. In addition to demonstrating how to set up both front ends and back ends, this chapter also showed you how to create the Alien Attack game.

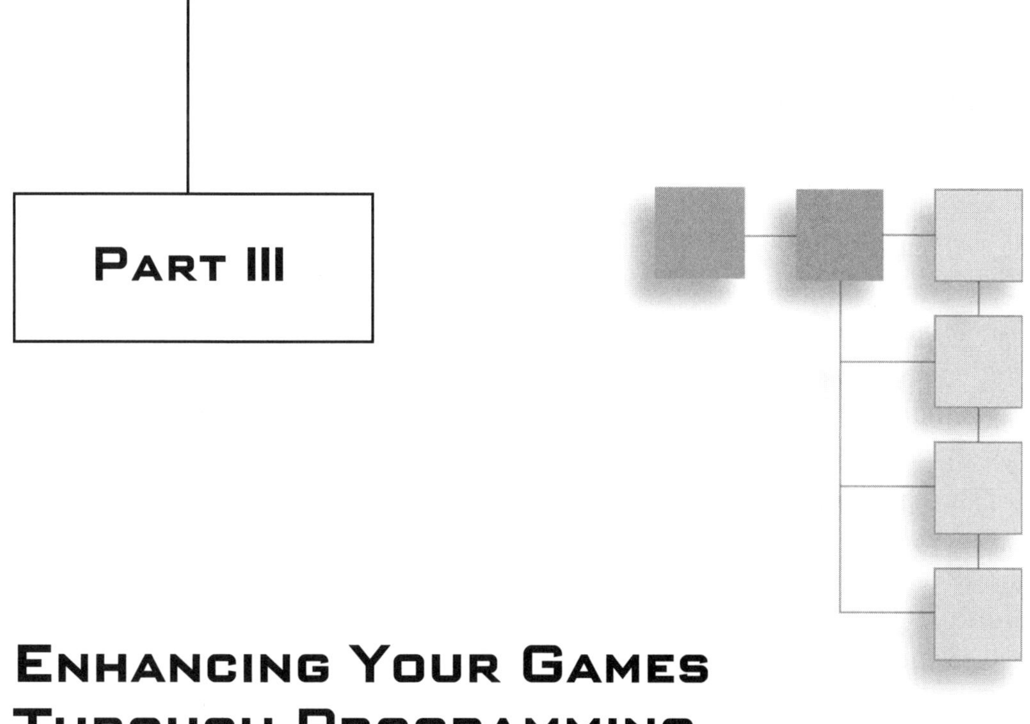

# Part III

# Enhancing Your Games Through Programming

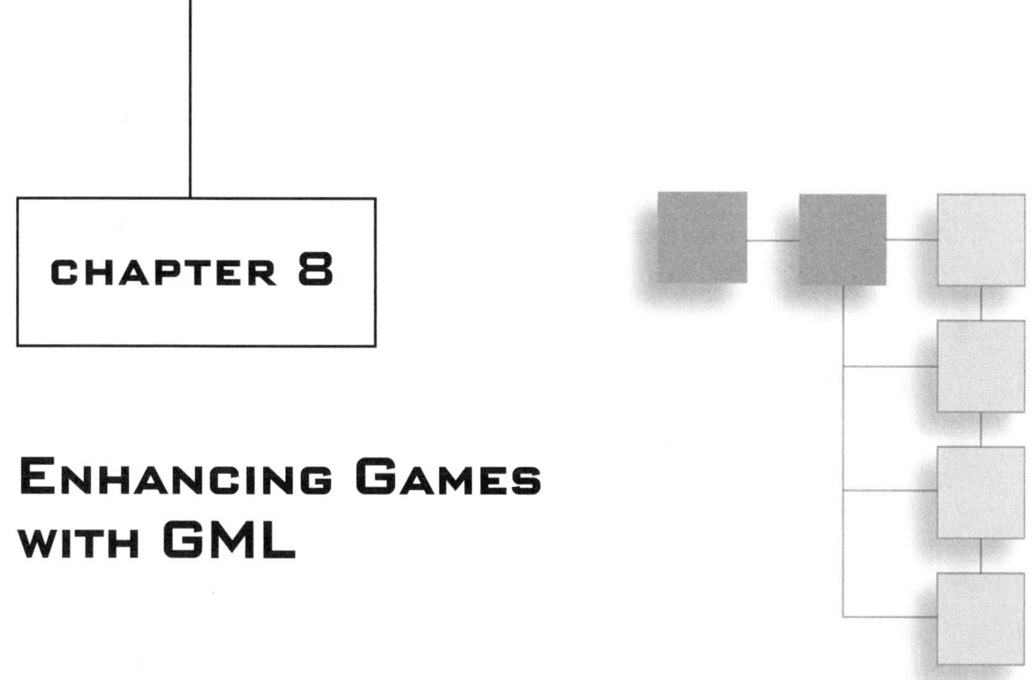

# Chapter 8

# Enhancing Games with GML

Up to this point in the book, all of the games that you have worked on have been developed using Game Maker's events and action icons. Game Maker's actions allow object instances to perform different tasks. However, with only 125 actions available, there are limits to this developmental approach. Using Game Maker's built-in programming language, GML, you get access to almost 1,000 predefined functions and variables that significantly extend Game Maker's capabilities. This allows you to develop games with additional features and greater complexity. This chapter introduces GML and its use within Game Maker.

An overview of the major topics covered in this chapter includes:

- Learning how to publish your Game Maker games on the Internet
- A basic introduction to GML and its usage
- An explanation of the different ways in which you can integrate GML into your games
- A demonstration of how to create and execute GML scripts

## Publishing Your Games

Once you have finished working on your game and are ready to share it with others, you can create a standalone executable version of your game by clicking on File > Create Executable. Once created, you can share the executable version of your game with anyone you choose. This works well if you only want to distribute your games to a small number of friends. If you have a website and want to make your game available to a wider audience, you can upload it to your web page and make it available for download. Of course, only people who know of your website and who visit it will be able to download it.

As an alternative, you can make your game immediately available to an audience over 80,000 strong by publishing it on the YoYo Games website. All you have to do is register with the YoYo Games website and then upload your game.

## Registering with YoYo Games

Registering with the YoYo Games website is free and easy. Go to http://www.yoyogames.com/user/login as shown in Figure 8.1.

**Figure 8.1**
Registering for a new account at the YoYo Games website.

To register, click on the I Don't Have a Login but I Would Like to Register for an Account option. This displays a form that you will need to fill out to complete the registration process. Once you have filled out this form, click on its Register button. The information that you supply is then validated, and if there are no errors, you are returned back to the YoYo Games login page. In addition, an email will be sent to your email account, welcoming you to YoYo Games.

Before you can use your new account to log in to the Game Maker website, you must confirm your registration. To do so, log in to your email account, locate and open the email sent by YoYo Games, and click on the embedded Click me! link. That's it; you are set up and ready to begin distributing your games.

## Publishing Your Games

Assuming that you have registered for a new account at the YoYo Games website and that you have a game that you are ready to publish, you can begin the publishing process by clicking on File > Publish Your Game. In response, Game Maker will open your default web browser and load http://www.yoyogames.com/user/login, displaying the YoYo Game's login page. Log in by entering your email address and password and then clicking on the Login button. Game Maker will display a web page showing your personal profile, which you can update if necessary.

To publish a game, click on the Share button displayed at the top of the page. This displays the Add Game Details page. Fill it out as demonstrated in Figure 8.2 and then click on the Next button.

The screen shown in Figure 8.3 appears. Click on the Select Images to Upload button. This displays a standard Select File dialog window, allowing to you select the screen prints you want to upload. You select files one at a time. An entry for each screen print that you add is displayed on the screen.

**Trick**

> Unless you disable this feature, you can generate screen prints of your game when playing it by pressing the F9 key.

Once you have specified the screen prints you want to upload, click on the Select Game File to Upload button and use the Select File dialog window that appears to locate and select the game you want to upload. When done, click on the Upload & Continue button. The files that you have specified are then uploaded. You can view the status of the upload process as it executes as demonstrated in Figure 8.4.

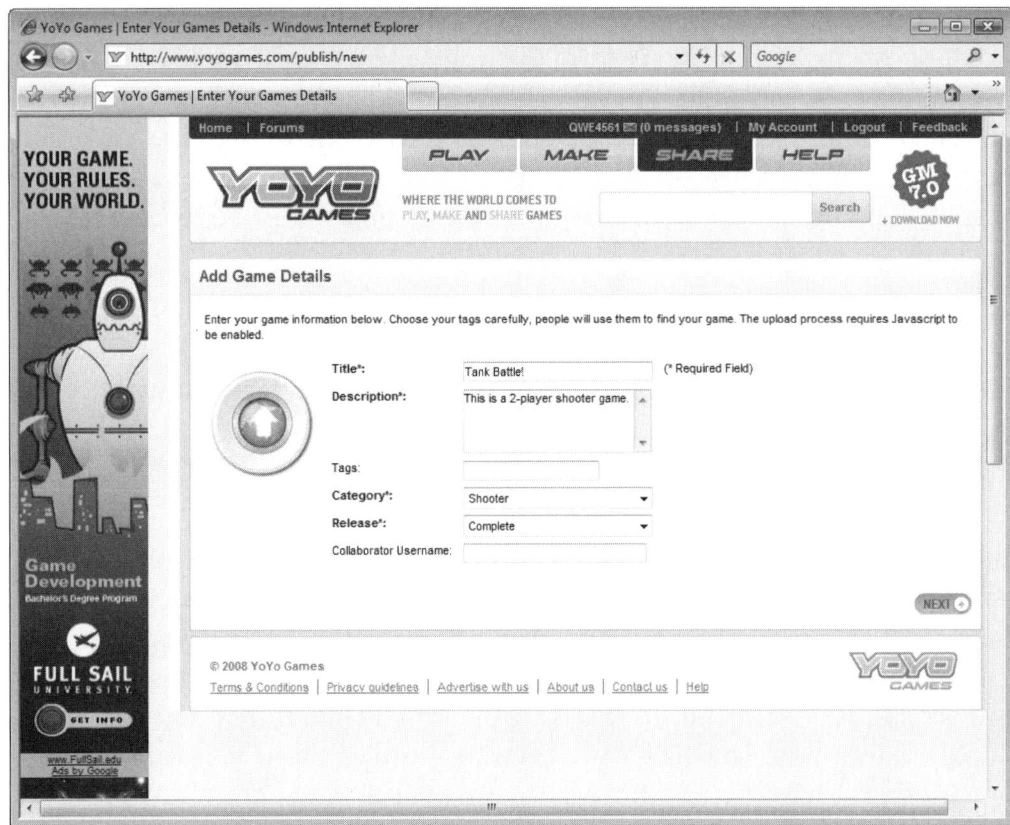


**Figure 8.2**
At a minimum, you must provide a title for any game you upload.

As soon as the upload process is complete, a screen similar to the one shown in Figure 8.5 displays.

Once uploaded, the YoYo Games website will scan your game to ensure that it does not contain any viruses and will then make it available to the Game Maker community. Once uploaded, you can manage your game by clicking on the My Account link located at the top of all YoYo Games pages. This will display your personal profile page. Any games that you have uploaded are displayed at the bottom of the page. Here you will see links that when clicked allow you to modify game details, modify game files, or delete your game.

## Introducing the Game Maker Language

*Game Maker Language* or *GML* is an interpreted programming language that you can use to substantially enhance the games you create using Game Maker. GML

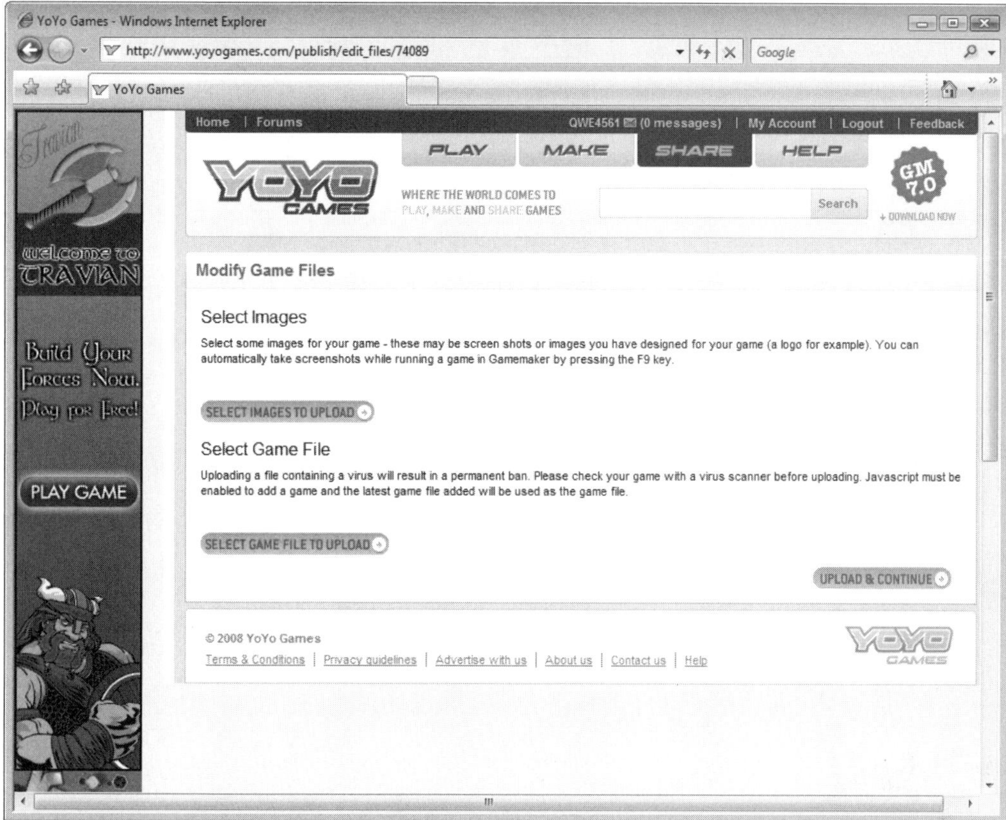


**Figure 8.3**
You are prompted to upload a few screen shots of your game and the game itself.

provides you with an alternative way of approaching game development. Using GML, you can supplement, extend, or replace Game Maker's actions. Alternatively, you can use GML as the basis for replacing action icons altogether.

**Hint**

As an *interpreted* programming language, scripts written using GML are interpreted and compiled (converted into an executable format) just before they are executed. So, every time a Game Maker application executes, every script that exists in the application must be re-interpreted before it can be executed. Interpreted programming languages are therefore slower than compiled programming languages, whose program code it compiles once at the end of the development process, allowing it to be executed repeatedly without having to be recompiled. The advantage of working with interpreted programming languages like GML is that you can quickly modify and re-execute them to see the results of your changes, whereas a compiled program must be recompiled before your changes can be tested. Fortunately, given the speed of today's modern computers, there is little noticeable difference in the performance of interpreted languages and compiled languages.

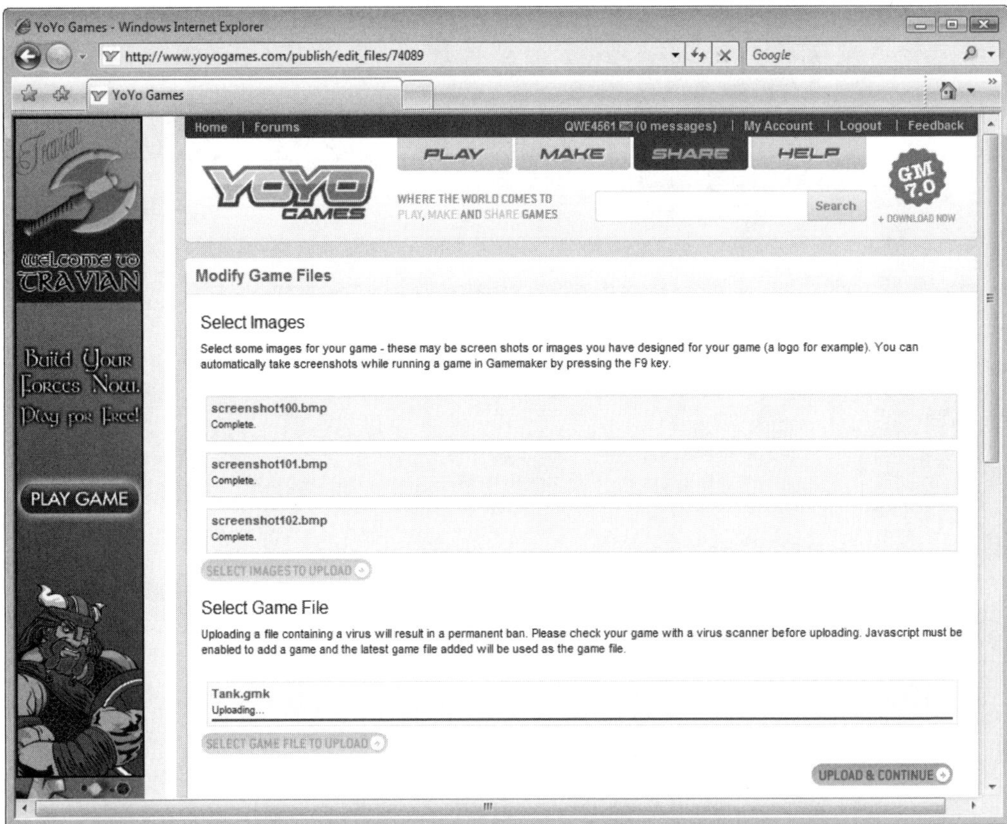


**Figure 8.4**
The game's screen prints have been uploaded and the game is being uploaded.

GML is a key component of Game Maker and is tightly integrated into every aspect of its operations. For example, every Game Maker action corresponds to a GML script or function. As such, any game that you develop using actions can also be redeveloped using GML functions. In total, GML provides access to almost 1,000 functions and predefined variables.

## Working with Game Maker's Scripts Menu

There are many different ways of working with scripts in Game Maker. One of the most obvious ways is through commands made available on the Script's menu, as shown in Figure 8.6.

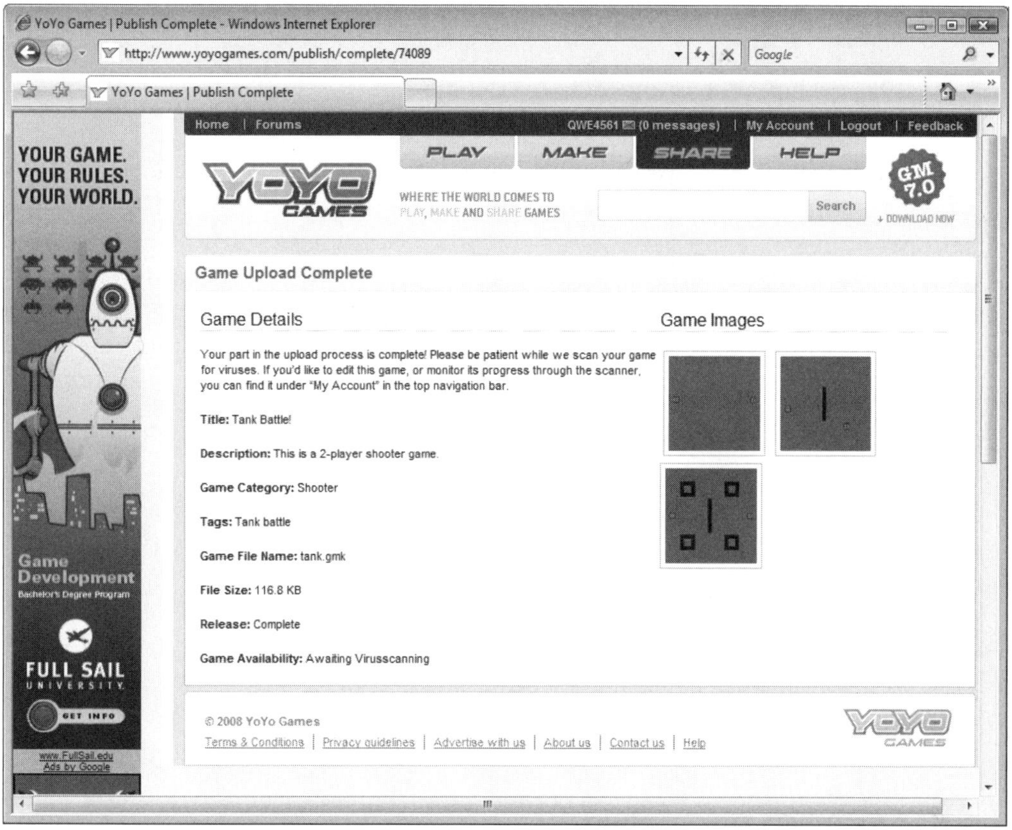

**Figure 8.5**
You can see your game's screen prints as well as a summary of the information that you provided.

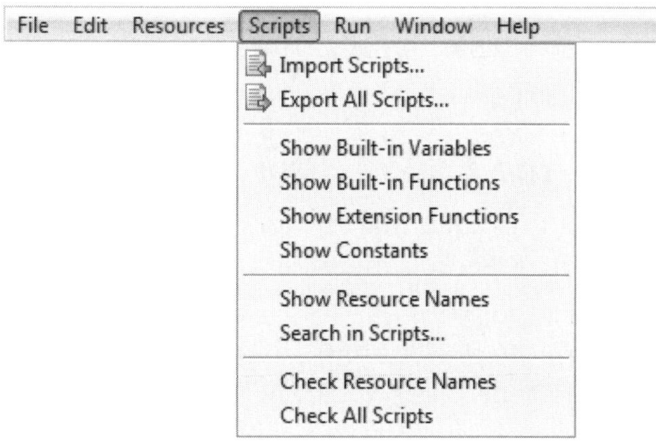


**Figure 8.6**
Game Maker's Scripts menu provides access to an assortment of script commands.

The commands that you will find on this menu are outlined below.

- **Import Scripts.** Allows you to import scripts stored in GML scripts into your application.
- **Export All Scripts/Export Selected Scripts.** Allows you to export and save all scripts or a selected script in your applications.
- **Show Built-in Variables.** Displays a list of all of the global and local variables available to your application.
- **Show Built-in Functions.** Displays a list of all of Game Maker's functions.
- **Show Extension Functions.** Displays a list of functions added to Game Maker through the installation of extension packages.
- **Show Constants.** Displays a list of all the constants available to your application.
- **Show Resource Names.** Displays a list of all of the resources that are defined in your applications (sprites, sounds, objects, etc).
- **Search in Scripts**. Allows you to search all of the scripts in your applications for a matching string.
- **Check Resource Names.** Instructs Game Maker to look for resource name conflicts within the application.
- **Check All Scripts.** Instructs Game Maker to perform a syntax check of all of the scripts in the application and to report on any errors.

## Getting Comfortable with the Code Editor

In addition to the commands located on Game Maker's toolbar, Game Maker also offers a powerful script editor. You can access this editor through the Script Properties window, as demonstrated in Figure 8.7. The script editor provides everything you need to create and edit all of the scripts that you add to your games.

**Hint**

You can also access Game Maker's script editor through the Execute Code action's window and through the Room Creation Code window, both of which are discussed a little later in this chapter.

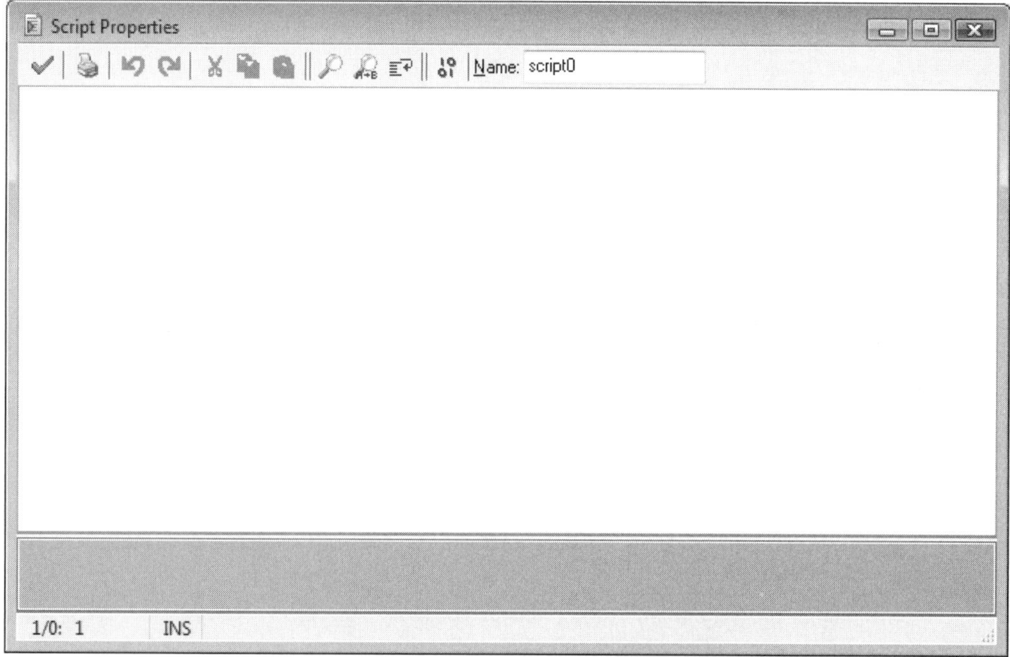


**Figure 8.7**
Game Maker's built-in code editor resides in the Script Properties window.

Scripts are created by typing GML statements into the editor's text area. As you type, you will notice that Game Maker automatically applies a color-coding scheme to the different parts of your statements that help to identify their functions and purpose. As you will learn later in this chapter, you can disable color-coding or modify its color scheme.

The script editor also assists you as you are writing code statements by monitoring what you are typing and then displaying the statement syntax for all possible matching functions at the bottom of the window, as demonstrated in Figure 8.8. This way, even if you only remember the first part of a function name, Game Maker will help you find the function you are looking for and show you its syntax.

Another feature provided includes smart tabs, in which the editor automatically indents code statements based on the indentation level of preceding statements. The script editor includes a toolbar with single-click access to all of the commands shown in Figure 8.9.

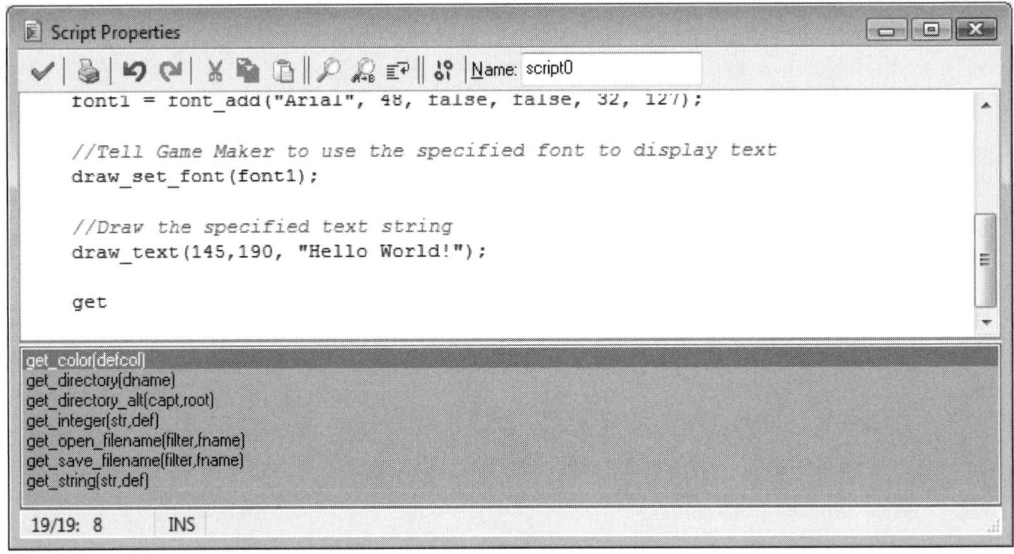


**Figure 8.8**
Game Maker monitors you as you work and offers syntactic assistance.

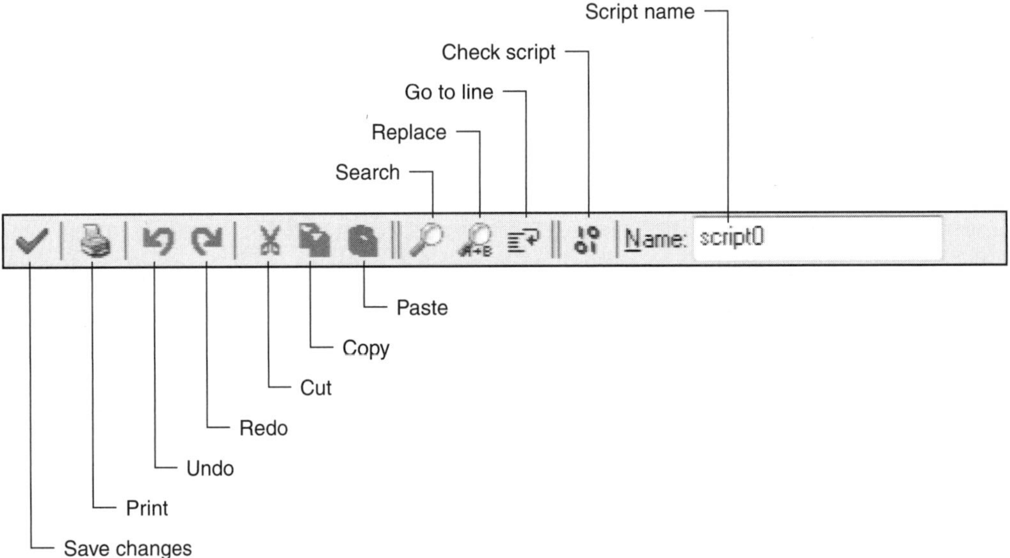


**Figure 8.9**
The Script Properties window's toolbar provides easy access to common editor commands.

## Creating Game Maker Scripts

Game Maker scripts are made up of one of more GML code statements embedded within an opening ({) bracket and a closing (}) bracket. A *statement* is a collection of GML keywords and functions that performs a specific task.

Although not strictly required, all code statements should end with a ; character, marking the end of each statement. The following example demonstrates how all of this comes together to create a script.

```
{
    statements;
    .
    .
    .
}
```

## Integrating GML into Your Games

Game Maker provides multiple integration points for GML, allowing you to use it in a number of different ways. This provides a lot of flexibility, allowing you to do anything from supplementing Game Maker's capabilities to completely eliminating the need to work with action icons at all. Different ways of using GML include:

- Creating GML scripts
- Adding GML code to events as actions
- Adding GML code to rooms
- Using GML expressions to supply actions with data

### Creating and Executing Scripts

The most obvious place you can use GML is in the development of scripts. As far as Game Maker is concerned, scripts are just another type of resource, like sprites, rooms, and sounds. To learn how to create and execute a script, start a new Game Maker application. Add a room to it and then add an object to the room. Don't worry about configuring the room or the object; you won't need to. Like other resources, you can add to your games by clicking on Resources > Create Script or by right-clicking on the Scripts folder located in the resource tree folder and clicking on the Create Script command that appears. In response, Game Maker adds a new script to your game and displays the Script Properties window as shown in Figure 8.10.

Once created, you can finish the development of the script by adding GML code statements to it. As an example of how to do this, create a new application, and

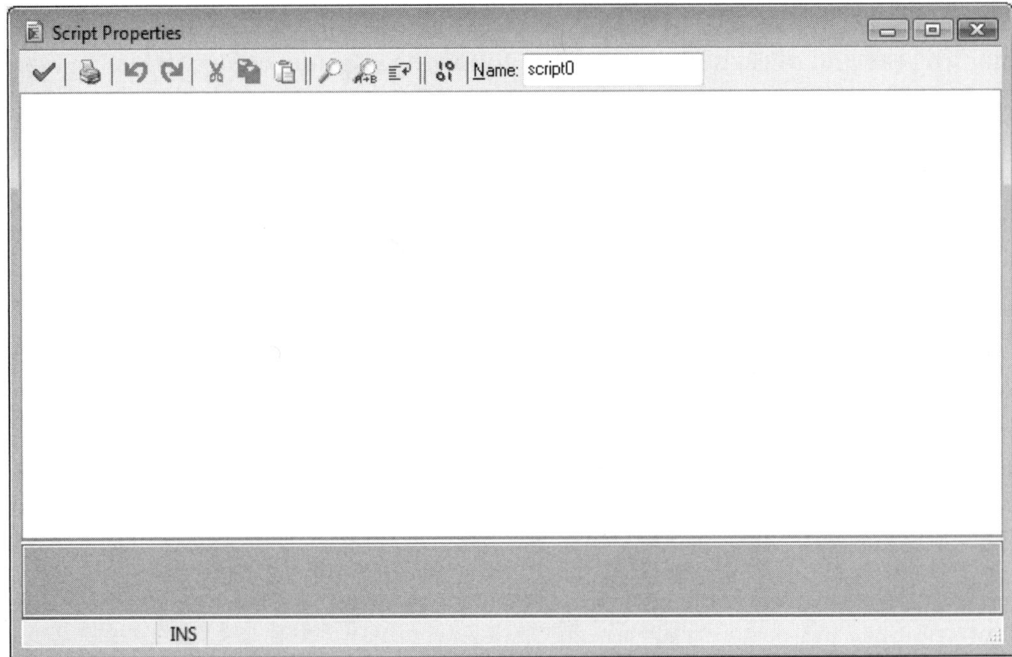


**Figure 8.10**
Adding a GML script to a Game Maker application.

then add a script to it named `scr_test`. Next, double-click on the script's name in the resource tree folder to display its Properties window and then type the following statements into it, using the Tab key as necessary to indent the statements.

```
{

    //Set the drawing color to white
    draw_set_color(c_black);

    //Draw a filled rectangle
    draw_rectangle(50,50,590,430, false);

    //Set the drawing color to black
    draw_set_color(c_yellow);

    //Add a new font
    font1 = font_add("Arial", 48, false, false, 32, 127);
```

```
    //Tell Game Maker to use the specified font to display text
    draw_set_font(font1);

    //Draw the specified text string
    draw_text(145,190, "Hello World!");

}
```

The above script begins with the { character and ends with the } character. Six code statements are embedded inside these brackets, each of which is preceded by a comment statement that describes what each statement does. You learn about GML scripting in Chapters 9 and 10, and you will get the chance to create a new game in Chapter 11 that requires GML scripting. For now, don't get too hung up on what the above statements do or how they work. Instead, keep your focus on the overall mechanics.

**Hint**

Note when you key in these code statements that Game Maker automatically applies a color-coding scheme to it, making different types of text stand out. You will learn more about Game Maker's application of color-coding, including how to modify and disable it, later in this chapter. Also, note that as you begin typing in statements, Game Maker displays syntax help at the bottom of the Script Properties window based on the input you type. You can use this information to make sure that you properly format your script statements.

Once you have added a script to a Game Maker application, you need to set up its execution. To do so, you need to select the object you added to the application and then add an event that will be used to trigger the execution of the object. In the case of this script, which draws graphic shapes and text, you will need to execute it by adding a `Draw` event. Once you have added the `Draw` event to the object, all you have to do is click on the Control tab and then drag and drop an instance of the `Execute Script` action to the actions area. Game Maker responds by displaying the Execute Script window. To configure the execution of the script, click on the context menu located at the end of the script field, and select `scr_text` from the list of scripts that is displayed, as demonstrated in Figure 8.11.

Once you have configured the object's `Draw` event to execute the script, close the Object Properties window and click on Run > Run Normally. In response, Game Maker will compile and execute the application as shown in Figure 8.12.

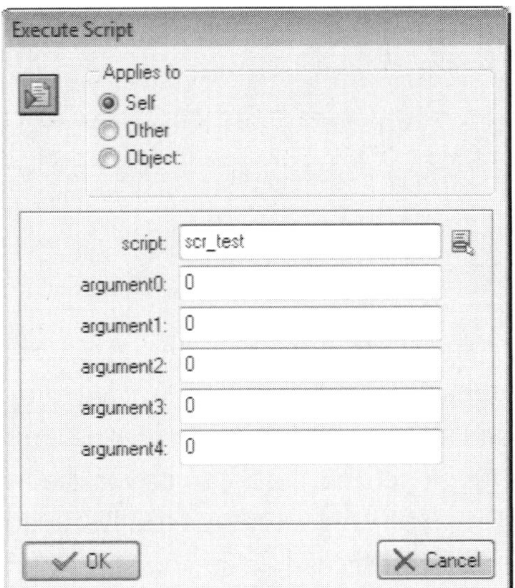


**Figure 8.11**
Configuring the execution of the GML script.

**Figure 8.12**
An example of the script in action.

**Hint**

The preceding script executed different GML functions instead of Game Maker actions. There is nothing in the preceding example that you could not have also accomplished by using Game Maker's action icons. However, there are only 125 actions, whereas there are close to 1,000 GML functions that you can call upon to do things not possible using only actions. For every action that is supported, there is a corresponding function. Often these matching functions provide enhanced control over specific types of actions.

## Adding GML Code to Events

Defining scripts as outlined in the previous sections allows you to call upon those scripts for execution at any time from any location within your game, allowing you to define the script once but reuse it in as many different places in your game as necessary. This way you don't have to redefine the same script over and over again for each event that you want to trigger it. If, on the other hand, you need to set up the execution of a set of GML statements that will only be executed in one place by one specific event, you have the option of executing the script using the `Execute Code` action.

For example, suppose you wanted to execute the following script.

```
{

    //Set the drawing color to white
    draw_set_color(c_black);

    //Draw a filled triangle
    draw_triangle(320, 20, 620, 460, 20, 460,false);

    //Set the drawing color to black
    draw_set_color(c_yellow);

    //Add a new font
    font1 = font_add("Arial", 48, false, false, 32, 127);

    //Tell Game Maker to use the specified font to display text
    draw_set_font(font1);

    //Draw the specified text string
    draw_text(210,200, "Triangle");

}
```

All you would have to do is add an `Execute Code` action to the appropriate object's `Draw` event and then add the script to it, as shown in Figure 8.13.

When executed, this script generates the results shown in Figure 8.14.

**Trick**

> One handy feature of the `Execute Code` action is that if you move the mouse pointer over an instance of that action in the actions area, Game Maker will display a popup window showing its code statements, allowing you to review its contents without having to open it.

Execute Code

Applies To: Self Other Object:

```
{

    //Set the drawing color to white
    draw_set_color(c_black);

    //Draw a filled triangle
    draw_triangle(320, 20, 620, 460, 20, 460,false);

    //Set the drawing color to black
    draw_set_color(c_yellow);

    //Add a new font
    font1 = font_add("Arial", 48, false, false, 32, 127);

    //Tell Game Maker to use the specified font to display text
    draw_set_font(font1);

    //Draw the specified text string
    draw_text(210,200, "Triangle");

}
```

19/21: 36 INS

**Figure 8.13**
Executing GML code using an `Execute Code` action.

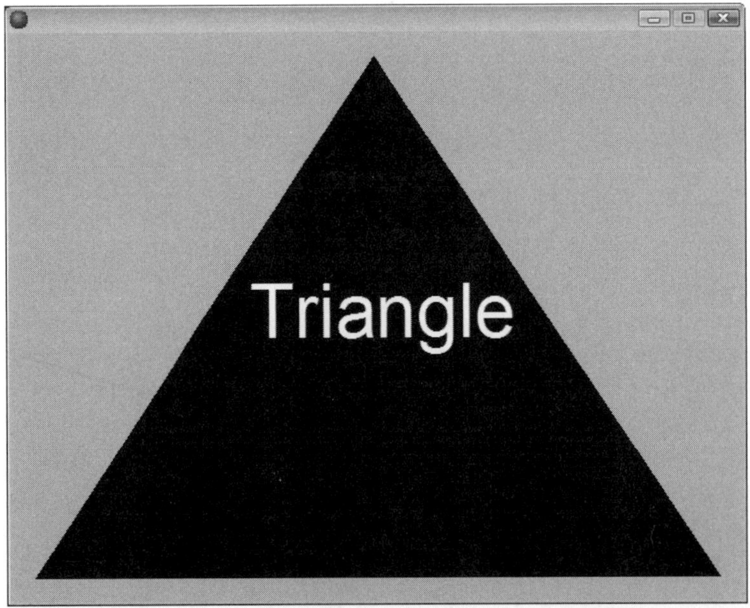


**Figure 8.14**
An example of the script executing using the `Execute Code` action.

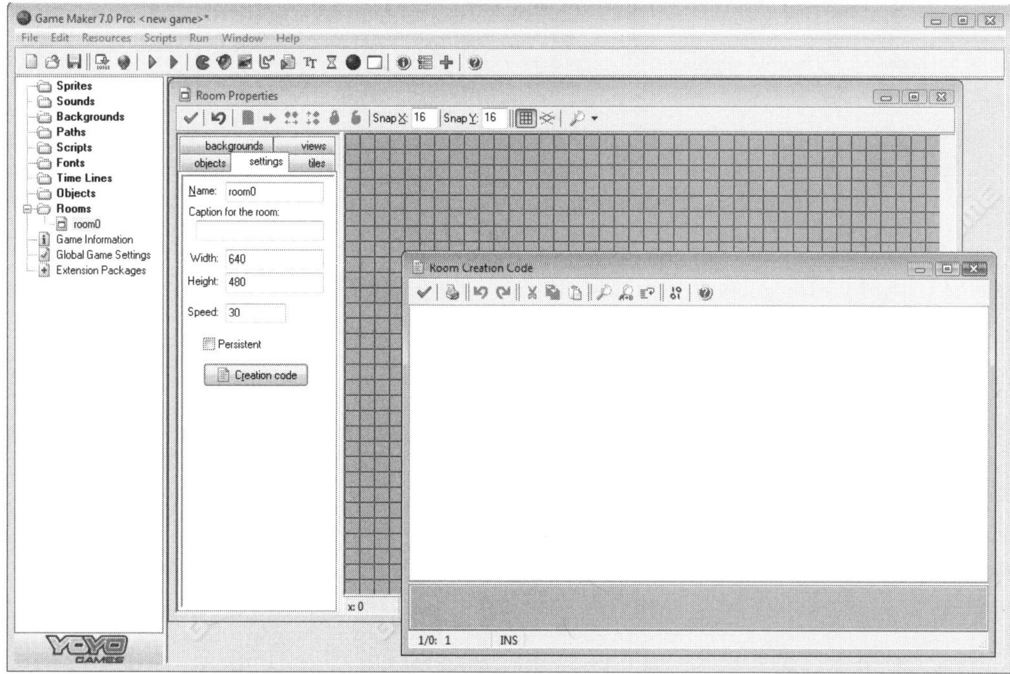


**Figure 8.15**
Assigning GML code that executes when a room is first created.

## Executing GML Code to Rooms

In addition to executing GML code as scripts or running them within `Execute Code` actions, you can also execute GML code when rooms are created. To do so, open a room and click on its Settings tab. This tab lets you change the name, caption, width, height, and speed of the room. In addition, there is a button at the bottom of the tab labeled Creation Code. When clicked, Game Maker displays the window shown in Figure 8.15.

Any GML code that you type into the Room Creation Code window is executed when the room is first created in the game (once and only once). This provides a convenient means of executing any programming logic you want. For example, you might need to initialize default values, adding randomly placed object instances to the room.

## Adding GML Expressions to Actions

One final place within Game Maker applications where you can execute GML code is by entering expressions into the text fields belonging to different Game Maker actions. An *expression* is a piece of GML code that, when executed, results in a value. You have already seen numerous examples of this in the games you

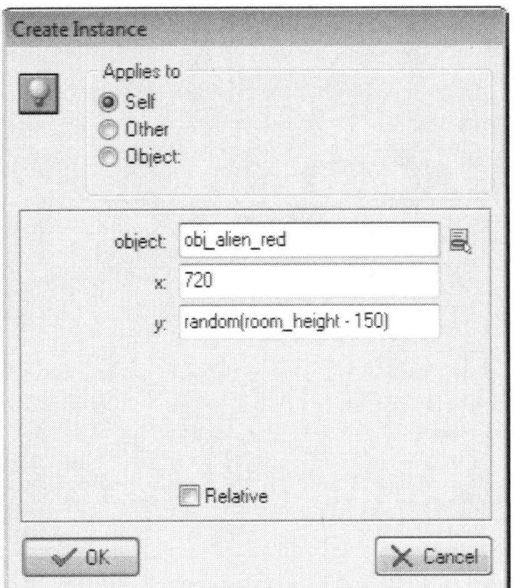


**Figure 8.16**
Using GML code to supply actions with execution data.

have worked on in previous chapters. Figure 8.16 shows another example of how to use a GML expression within an action.

In this example, a new instance of an object named `obj_alien_red` is added to the game. Each object is added on the right-hand side of the game window at an x coordinate of 720 and a randomly generated y coordinate that is calculated using the following expression.

```
random(room_height - 150)
```

Here, a built-in GML function named `random()` is used to generate a random location of the object's y coordinate. The `random()` function generates a random number between 0 and a specified value, which is passed to the function as an argument, which in this example is an expression rather than a number. The value of the expression is determined by subtracting 150 from the height of the room. The height of the room is retrieved from a built-in special variable that is automatically created by Game Maker. You will learn more about variables in Chapter 9. Once Game Maker resolves the expression to a numeric value, that value is passed to the `Random()` function providing it with the upper limit of the range from which it will generate a random number.

## Configuring Game Maker's Code Editor

Like most other aspects of Game Maker, its built-in code editor is extremely configurable. To access the code editor's configuration options, click on File >

Preferences. This opens the Preferences window. Relevant configuration options are located on two tabs, the Scripts and Code tab and the Colors tab.

## Specifying Code Editor Operations

The configuration options for the code editor are located on the Preference window's Scripts and Code tab, as shown in Figure 8.17.

The configurable code editor options include:

- **Group undo operations.** Instructs Game Maker to undo groups of previous operations.
- **Number of undo.** Specifies how many undo operations Game Maker defines as a group.
- **Automatic indentation.** Instructs Game Maker to automatically indent new statements based on the indentation of previous statements.
- **Indent amount.** Specifies how many spaces Game Maker should advance the cursor when the Tab key is pressed.
- **Smart tabs.** Instructs Game Maker to automatically indent new code statements based on the indentation of the previous statement.

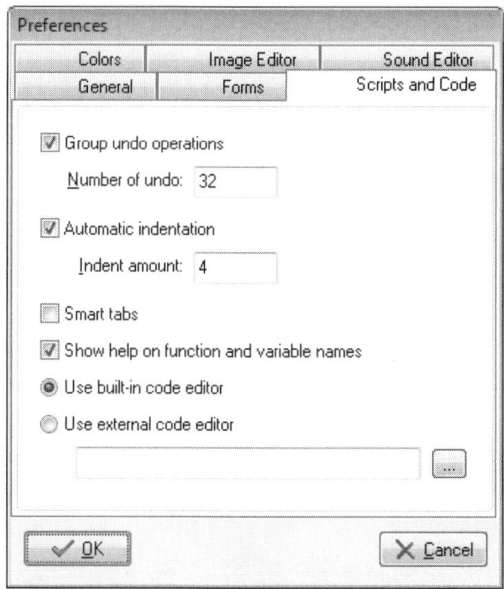


**Figure 8.17**
You can configure various code editor features from Game Maker's Preferences window.

- **Show help on function and variable names.** Displays help information for functions and variable names in your code statements.
- **Use built-in code editor.** Instructs Game Maker to use its own built-in code editor.
- **Use external code editor.** Allows you to specify an external third-party code editor in place of the Game Maker's built-in code editor.

## Modifying Code Statement Color-Coding

Game Maker automatically color-codes the text that makes up the GML code statements. To configure how Game Maker handles color-coding, click on the Preferences window's Colors tab. If you want, you can disable color-coding by clearing the Use Color-Coding option located on the Preferences window's Colors tab, as shown in Figure 8.18.

By default, Game Maker displays normal text and GML keywords in black. Comments are displayed in green, resource names (objects, rooms, sprites, sounds, backgrounds, paths, fonts, and timelines) are displayed in purple, constants are displayed in brown, local and global variables are displayed in royal blue, and functions are displayed in dark blue. To modify color-coding assignments for any of these types of resources, select the resource type from the

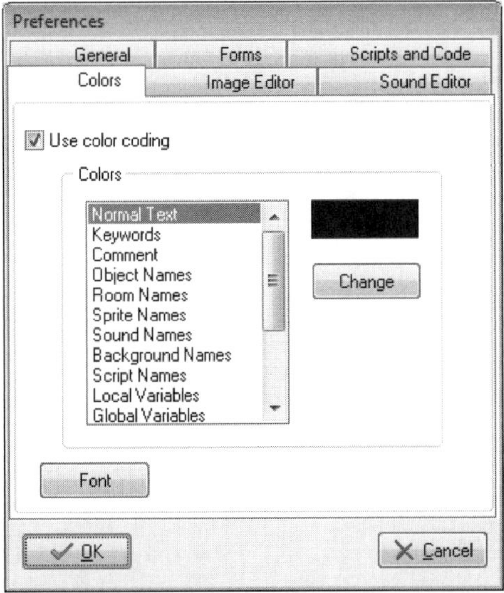


**Figure 8.18**
Game Maker allows you to modify the color-coding scheme it uses to display the different components of script statements.

resource list located on the Colors tab, then click on the Change button, and select a new color from the Colors window that appears, as shown in Figure 8.19.

In addition to configuring how Game Maker applies color-coding, you can change the font type, style, and size that Game Maker uses to display the text that makes up code statements by clicking on the Font button. This displays the Font window shown in Figure 8.20.

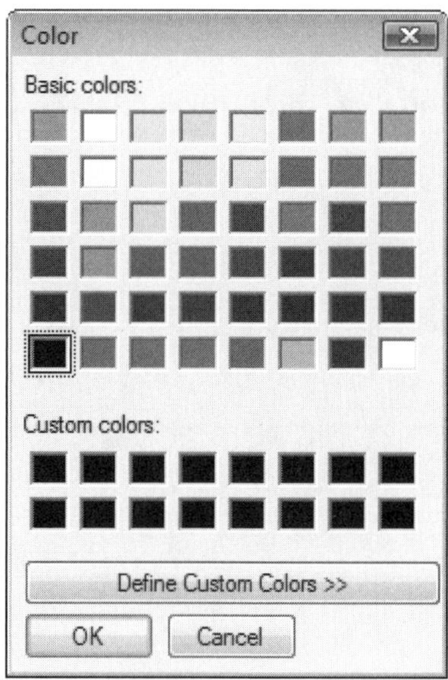


**Figure 8.19**
You can select any color displayed in the window or create a custom color.

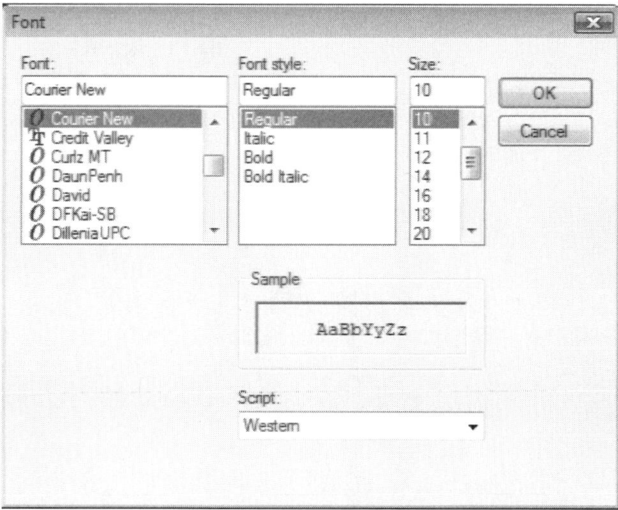


**Figure 8.20**
Modifying the font type, style, and size used to display script statements.

## Summary

This chapter began by showing you how to register for a free account at the YoYo Games website and walked you through the steps necessary to upload and publish your games at this website. This chapter also introduced you to GML and provided you with a first glimpse of how GML code looks. You learned how to work with Game Maker's Scripts menu and script editor. This chapter explained all of the different places within games where you can apply GML scripts, including scripts, action code, room code, and as expressions used to provide data to actions. You saw examples of how to create and execute scripts and to add script to `Execute Code` actions.

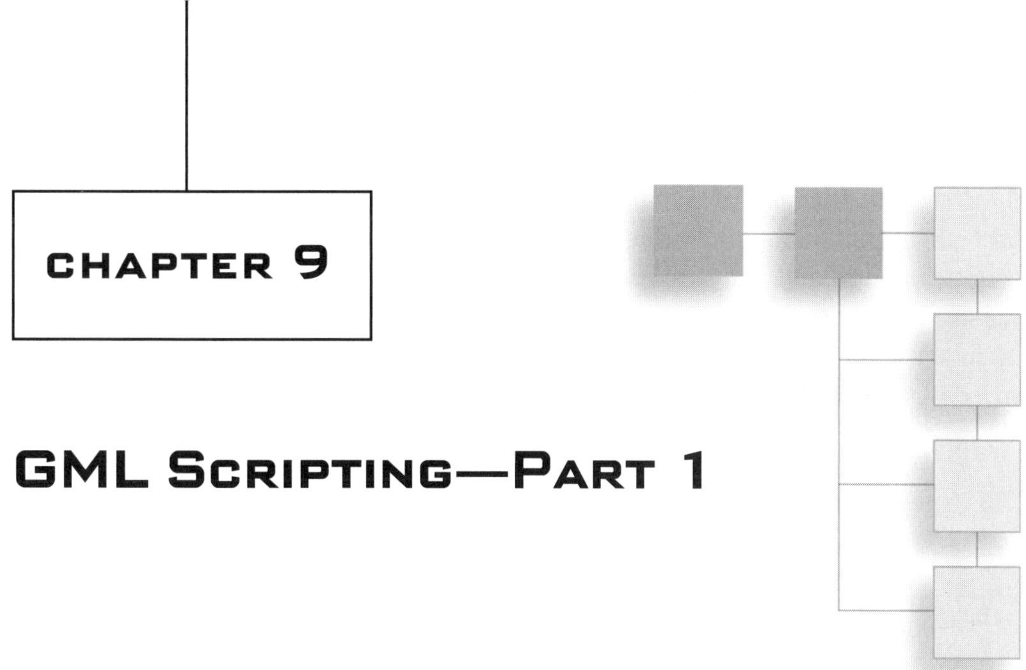

# Chapter 9

# GML Scripting—Part 1

At this point you should have a solid understanding of how to apply programming logic using Game Maker's action icons. Now, it is time to learn how to work with Game Maker's GML scripting language. GML provides greater control over program execution, allowing you to exercise detailed control over the interaction of object instances and the environment in which these objects exist. In this chapter, you will learn how to collect, process, modify, and store data within your games and to apply conditional programming logic when analyzing and processing that data. You will also learn how to work with different types of operators, allowing you to apply arithmetic and compare data.

An overview of the major topics covered in this chapter includes learning how to:

- Create and assign data using constants
- Store, access, and manipulate data stored in variables
- Store collections of data using arrays
- Apply conditional programming logic
- Work with different types of GML operators

## Working with Game Data

Like all computer applications, games developed using Game Maker need to collect, manipulate, and store data. For example, the types of data in use include the number of points, scores, number of lives, and player health. Data might also include the player's name or information about the size, location, direction, and speed of objects as they move about the screen.

Game Maker supports several different types of data, including:

- **Integer.** Any whole number, positive or negative, as well as the number 0.
- **Real.** Numbers that include decimal points.
- **String.** A set of characters embedded within single or double quotation marks.

Data may be embedded or hardcoded within code statements or it can be dynamically collected, manipulated, and stored during game play. For example, in arcade games, data is collected through interaction with the user. Data can be collected from the keyboard and mouse. Game Maker even supports the use of joysticks.

Once collected, data must be stored someplace. Game Maker lets you programmatically store individual pieces of data using variables and constants or collections of data using arrays. This data is stored in computer memory during game execution where it can be accessed and manipulated whenever it is needed.

## Embedding Data within Code Statements

All computer games require the manipulation of some type of data. This data may be collected as a result of interaction with the user or it may be stored internally within the game. Game Maker provides a number of different ways of storing data. One of the most basic ways of working with data in your applications is to embed within your code statements, as demonstrated here:

```
show_message("The value of pi is 3.14.");
```

Here, the value of the mathematic constant pi (3.14) is embedded within a string passed to a GML function named `show_message()`. A *string* is a collection of one or more characters enclosed within single or double quotation marks.

**Hint**

The `show_message()` function displays (draws) text passed to it as a string on the screen. To use this function, you must initiate its execution using a `Draw` event.

Although embedding within code statements provides an effective means of handling small amounts of static information that never changes, this approach is not satisfactory in most games, where data is constantly changing. Game Maker provides you with a number of different ways to store data within your applications, including variables, constants, and arrays.

### Working with Numbers and Strings

Game Maker supports three different types of data: integers, real numbers, and strings. Each of these types of data is handled differently. Integers and real numbers can be added, subtracted, multiplied, and divided. Strings can be concatenated together, creating a new, larger string. However, strings cannot be subtracted, multiplied, or divided. An integer is a whole number, whereas a real number has a decimal point. As previously stated, a string is created by enclosing characters within single or double quotation marks.

## Storing Data in Variables

As is the case in all programming languages, Game Maker can store and modify data within your games. One way that this is achieved is through the use of variables. A *variable* is a pointer to a location in memory where data is stored. Variables are used to store individual pieces of data.

### Creating Variables

As you define the variables used in your GML scripts, make sure you assign them descriptive names. This helps to make your code statements self-documenting and easier to understand. Game Maker variable names are case-sensitive. From Game Maker's view, a reference to a variable named `player1` is not the same thing as a reference to a variable named `Player1`. So be careful to use a consistent case when naming your variables. Variables must be uniquely named. When naming variables, you must follow the rules outlined below.

- Variable names must begin with a letter.
- Variable names can only contain upper- and lowercase letters, numbers, and underscore characters.

**Figure 9.1**
These action icons facilitate the use of variables.

- Variable names cannot contain blank spaces.
- Variable names cannot be Game Maker language keywords or the names of other defined game resources.

Game Maker does not require you to explicitly declare variables. Instead, all you have to do to create a new variable is to use it. In order to assign a value to a variable, you use the = operator, as demonstrated below.

```
name = "Alexander";
```

Here, a variable named `name` is created and assigned a string value of `Alexander`. If this variable already existed, Game Maker would simply change its value as instructed in the assignment statement.

**Hint**

When developing programming logic using Game Maker's action icons, you can also work with variables using the actions shown in Figure 9.1 to create, modify, analyze, and display variable values.

## Managing Variable Scope

Game Maker supports three types of variables, each of which has a different scope. *Scope* defines the locations within your application from which variables can be accessed. The three types of variables that Game Maker supports are outlined here:

- **Instance.** Variables accessible within the instance in which they are defined in other instances.
- **Global.** Variables accessible throughout the game.
- **Local.** Variable access is limited to the script in which they are defined.

### *Defining Instance Variables*

By default, the variables you define within your scripts have an instance scope, making them accessible to other like instances. To modify the contents of a variable in the current instance, all you have to do is reference it by name, as demonstrated here:

```
name = "Alexander";
```

Game Maker lets you access the contents of other instance variables. To do so, you use dot notation, specifying the name of the other instance, followed by a dot (period character), and then the name of the variable you want to work with, as demonstrated here:

```
x = playerOne.name;
```

Here, the value stored in a variable named `name` belonging to an object named `playerOne` is assigned to a variable named `x`.

### *Defining Global Variables*

Game Maker also supports the use of global variables, which can be accessed from any location within an application. There are two ways of working with global variables. First, you can use the `global` keyword when initially creating them, as demonstrated here:

```
global.age = 21;
```

To refer to this global variable from other locations within an application, you must use the `global` keyword, as demonstrated here:

```
global.age = 18;
```

Alternatively, rather than use the `global` keyword repeatedly throughout your scripts, you can use the `globalvar` keyword to declare a variable as global, as demonstrated here:

```
globalvar age;
age = 21;
```

Here, a global variable named `age` is defined and then assigned an initial value. If you need to, you can declare multiple variables as local using a single statement, as shown here:

```
globalvar age, name, address, phone;
```

### *Defining Local Variables*

In general, it is considered to be good programming practice to restrict variable scope as tightly as possible, as this reduces a program's memory requirements and reduces the changes of accidently modifying a variable's value. To restrict variable access to the script in which it is used, you need to declare your variables at the beginning of the script using the `var` keyword, as demonstrated here:

```
var age;
age = 21;
```

Here, a single local variable named `age` is defined and then assigned a value. If you need to, you can declare multiple variables as local using a single statement, as shown here:

```
var age, name, address, phone;
```

## Game Maker's Special Variables

As you have already seen through various action icons, Game Maker provides access to a large number of special variables that it automatically creates and maintains during program execution. These include both global and local variables. Examples of global variables are `lives`, `score`, and `health`. There are also global variables that provide information about the location and the operations of the mouse, including `mouse_x`, `mouse_y`, and `mouse_button`. Examples of Game Maker's special local variables include:

- **`x`**. The x-coordinate for a given object instance.
- **`y`**. The y-coordinate for a given object instance.
- **`direction`**. The direction (angle) an object instance is moving.
- **`speed`**. The speed (in pixels per step) that an object is moving.
- **`hspeed`**. The speed along the horizontal axis (in pixels per step) that an object is moving.
- **`vspeed`**. The speed along the vertical axis (in pixels per step) that an object is moving.
- **`solid`**. Specifies whether an object instance is solid or not.
- **`sprite_height`**. Contains the height of a sprite (in pixels).
- **`sprite_width`**. Contains the width of a sprite (in pixels).

You can retrieve and analyze the values stored in any of these variables, and in most cases, you can change their values as well, directly impacting the operations of your games as a result.

**Trick**

To view a listing of all special global and local variables created and maintained by Game Maker, click on Scripts > Show Built-in Variables.

## Working with Data That Does Not Change

Though useful, variables are not appropriate for storing data whose value does not change during game execution because variables can accidentally be modified. A better solution for storing this type of data is by using constants. A *constant* is a value whose value is known at design time and does not change when the game executes.

Game Maker automatically generates and manages a huge collection of predefined constants, whose values you can access from within your GML code in exactly the same manner as you reference variable values. An example of one such constant is `pi`, which is set to 3.14. Other examples of constants that Game Maker makes readily available to you include a range of the color constants shown below.

- `c_aqua`
- `c_black`
- `c_blue`
- `c_dkgray`
- `c_fuchsia`
- `c_gray`
- `c_green`
- `c_lime`
- `c_ltgray`
- `c_maroon`
- `c_navy`

- `c_olive`
- `c_orange`
- `c_purple`
- `c_red`
- `c_silver`
- `c_teal`
- `c_white`
- `c_yellow`

In total, Game Maker provides access to close to 300 predefined constants, offering access to keyboard, mouse, joysticks, and many other types of data.

**Trick**

To view a listing of all predefined constants created and maintained by Game Maker, click on Scripts > Show Constants.

You can create and add your own constants to your Game Maker games. For example, if you created a game that awarded the player extra lives when certain score levels were achieved, you might want to save this value in a constant. To add a constant to a Game Maker game, click on Resources > Global Game Settings. This opens the Global Game Settings window. Select its Constants tab. This window displays any constants that you choose to add to your game. For example, Figure 9.2 shows an example of three constants that have been added to the game.

Using the buttons located at the bottom of the window, you can insert, delete, append, and clear constants. You can also change the order in which the constants are defined by selecting individual constants and then clicking on the Up and Down buttons to change its location in the list. Lastly, you can click on the Sort button to sort the window's contents.

Constants offer a number of advantages. First, their values cannot be accidently changed. Second, when assigned descriptive names, constants can make your code self-documenting. Lastly, constants typically require less memory than variables, making your games more efficient.

**Figure 9.2**
You can add any number of constants to your games.

## Managing Collections of Data

As long as your applications only need to work with and manage a handful of variables at a time, you can use variables to manage the storage of all the data in your games. On the other hand, if your games require that you create and manage hundreds or thousands of values, variables alone won't get the job done. In these situations you need to use arrays. An *array* is an indexed list of data that is stored and managed as a collection. The data that you store in an array is accessed using the array's name and the index position of the data.

Game Maker lets you create one- and two-dimensional arrays. A one-dimensional array is like a list. A two-dimensional array can be thought of as being like a spreadsheet consisting of rows and columns. While Game Maker lets you create two-dimensional arrays, this chapter will focus on teaching you the basics of working with one-dimensional arrays.

## Creating Arrays

GML lets you create both one- and two-dimensional arrays. Single-dimensional arrays are created in GML by assigning them a name followed immediately by a `[` bracket and a number representing the array's index followed by a closing `]` bracket, as demonstrated below.

Like variables, you do not have to declare arrays prior to using them. The syntax that you must follow when defining an array is outlined here:

```
arrayname[indices]
```

*`arrayname`* represents the name of the array being created, *`indices`* is a comma-separated list of numeric values that specifies whether the array has one or two dimensions. The following example demonstrates how to define an array named *`animals[]`* that is capable of storing six elements.

```
animals[5]
```

All array indices in GML begin at 0, so as defined above, the `animals[]` is capable of storing six entries (0 through 5). In GML, two-dimensional arrays are created by assigning them a name followed immediately by a `[` bracket and two comma-separated numbers representing both of the array's indices, followed by a closing `]` bracket, as demonstrated here:

```
animals[4,4]
```

GML limits array index size to 32,000 and limits an array's overall storage capability to 1,000,000 entries.

## Populating Arrays with Data

Game Maker arrays are zero-based. The first element (value) in the array starts at index location 0, and the second element in the array begins at location 1. The following example demonstrates how to create an array named `names` and assign it three elements.

```
{
    names[0] = "Molly";
    names[1] = "William";
    names[2] = "Alexander";
}
```

## Retrieving Data from Arrays

Once created, you can reference any element in an array by specifying its index number, as demonstrated here:

```
{
    names[0] = "Molly";
    names[1] = "William";
    names[2] = "Alexander";

    show_message("Match!");
}
```

Here, an array made up of three elements is created, and the second element (`William`) stored in an array is retrieved and displayed. Be repeating and modifying the last statements shown above, you could modify this example to display all of the array's contents.

Rather than retrieving data an element at a time, it is usually a better idea to set up a loop to iterate through the array's contents. For example, the following script creates an array and then loops through it using a `for` loop to iterate through and display its contents. More information on loops is provided in Chapter 10.

```
{
    names[0] = "Molly";
    names[1] = "William";
    names[2] = "Alexander";

    x_coord = 50;
    y_coord = 50;

    for (i=0; i<3; i=i+1) {
        draw_text(x_coord, y_coord, names[i]);
        y_coord = y_coord + 20
    }
}
```

## Evaluating Options Using Conditional Logic

In order to create games of any level of complexity, you need the ability to analyze the data collected by your games and to conditionally execute different programming logic based on the results of that analysis. The result of any conditional

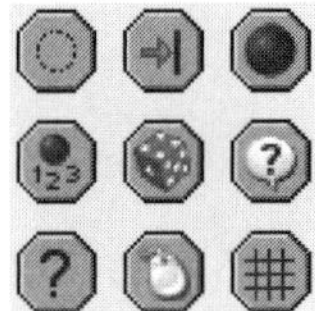

**Figure 9.3**
Any eight-sided action icon can be used to implement conditional logic.

analysis comes down to a determination as to whether the condition being tested results in a value of true or false. If the result of the analysis is true, one set of actions is taken. If the result is false, a different set of actions may be taken. Game Maker provides two programming statements that facilitate the implementation of conditional logic. The first is the `IF` statement and the second is the `SELECT` statement.

**Hint**

> Game Maker provides access to 18 action icons that facilitate various forms of conditional logic, including those shown in Figure 9.3.
>
> These actions facilitate things like analyzing collision detection and testing expressions. Action icons that perform conditional logic are easily identified; they only have eight sides.

## Introducing the if Statement

An understanding of how to work with the `if` statement, along with its corresponding `else` statement, is required to develop even the most simple scripts. Using the `if` statement, you can implement any type of conditional test. Using the optional `else` statement, you can specify what you want to happen in the event the tested conditional evaluates as false.

### *if Statement Syntax*

You use the `if` statement to evaluate an expression and then initiate an action if that expression evaluates as true. Using the `if` statement and its corresponding `else` statement, you can specify an alternate action to be performed in the event the expression evaluates as false. Using the syntax outlined below, you can set up conditional code blocks that can execute any number of code statements based on the results of that analysis.

```
if (expression) {
     statements
}
```

```
else {
   statements
}
```

Here, *expression* evaluates to a value of true or false. *statements* represents one or more code statements that will be executed. `else` is an optional keyword that tells Game Maker what to do in the event the tested condition evaluates as false.

### *Single Line if Statements*

In its simplest form, the `if` statements can be used to create a single-line statement using the syntax outlined here:

```
if (expression) statement;
```

Single-line `if` statements are well suited to situations where you do not need to perform an alternative action should the tested expression evaluate as false and where you do not have to perform more than a single action when the expression evaluates as true. As a demonstration, the following statements demonstrate the use of this version of the `if` statement in order to control the conditional display of a text statement.

```
secretNumber = round(random(2) + 1);
displayMsg = "I am thinking of a number from 1 to 3, try to guess it."

userGuess = get_string(displayMsg, "");

if (secretNumber == real(userGuess)) show_message("You guessed it!");
```

Here, a real number between 0 and 2 is generated by calling on the `random()` function and passing it a numeric argument indicating the upper range from which it is to generate its results. Next, the `round()` function is used to round the value generated by the `random()` function to the nearest integer value. A value of 1 is added to the result, resulting in a randomly generated number in the range of 1 to 3. Next, a variable named `displayMsg` is created and assigned a string.

Next a variable named `userGuess` is created and assigned a value returned to it by the `get_string()` function. The `get_string()` function displays a popup dialog. It accepts two arguments, The first argument is the message that is displayed. The second argument is the default value displayed in the popup dialog window. Passing an empty string as the second argument means that a default value is not displayed in the popup dialog window. Lastly, an `if` statement is used to compare the value assigned to `secretNumber` against a value of `userGuess`. Since `secretNumber` is an integer and `userGuess` is a string, the value assigned to `userGuess` had to be converted to a numeric value, which was done using the `real()` function.

### *if Statement Code Blocks*

In the event that you need to execute more than one statement when an `if` statement's expression evaluates as true, you need to set up an `if` statement code block using the syntax outlined below.

```
if (expression) {
   statements
}
```

**Trap**

> Note that unlike the single line version of the `if` statement, you must include the opening { and closing } characters when formulating a multi-line code block.

Using the previously outlined syntax, you can group and conditionally execute any number of code statements, as demonstrated here:

```
secretNumber = round(random(2) + 1);
displayMsg = "I am thinking of a number from 1 to 3, try to guess it."

userGuess = get_string(displayMsg, "");

if (secretNumber == real(userGuess)) {
    show_message("You guessed it!");
    sleep(3000);
    game_end();
}
```

Here, three code statements are executed in the event the user is able to guess the randomly generated secret number. The first of these three statements displays a congratulatory message. The second statement executes the `sleep()` function (equivalent to the `sleep` actions), which is used to pause script execution for three seconds. Lastly, the `game_end()` function is executed, terminating the execution of the game in which the script executes.

### *Setting Up Alternative Courses of Actions*

Using the optional `else` statement in conjunction with the `if` statement, you can specify two different sets of programming statements, one to be executed when the tested expression proves true and another to execute when the expression evaluates as false, as demonstrated here:

```
secretNumber = round(random(2) + 1);
displayMsg = "I am thinking of a number from 1 to 3, try to guess it."

userGuess = get_string(displayMsg, "");

if (secretNumber == real(userGuess)) {
    show_message("You guessed it!");
} else {
    show_message("Sorry. Your guess was wrong.");
}
```

### *Nesting if Statements within One Another*

One of the powerful features of using the `if` statement to develop conditional programming logic is that the `if` statement allows you to embed or nest it within other `if` statement code blocks. Nesting conditional code blocks within one another facilitates the development of more complex programming logic, as demonstrated here:

```
a = 5;
b = 10;
c = 20;

if (a == 5) {
    if (b == 10) {
        if (c == 20) {
            draw_text(200, 200, "Bingo!");
        }
    }
}
```

By nesting `if` statement code blocks you can create programming logic that conditionally performs one test based on the result generated by a higher-level code block. In the previous example, three `if` statement code blocks have been defined, each of which evaluates the value assigned to a different variable.

Only if all three code blocks evaluate as true is the `draw_text()` function executed.

## Comparing One Value Against a Series of Matching Values

In addition to various adaptations of the `if` statement, Game Maker allows you to implement conditional logic using the `switch` statement. This statement is designed as a substitute for using multiple `if` statement code blocks. The `switch` statement is designed for situations where you need to compare one value against a range of different values. The `switch` statement must be used in conjunction with a number of other statements, including the `case`, `break`, and `default` statements, to create a code block as outlined here:

```
switch (expression) {
    case expression:
        statement;
        .
        .
        .
        break;
    case expression:
        statement;
        .
        .
        .
        break;
    .
    .
    .
    default:
        statement;
        .
        .
        .
}
```

The `switch` statement code block begins with the `switch` statement followed by the expression to be evaluated and then a series of case blocks, each of which is designed to analyze a possible match with the expression. Each `case` block specifies its own expression that is compared to the `switch` statement's expression. The statements embedded within the first `case` statement that results in a match are executed and the rest of the statements in the switch code block are skipped. In the event that none of the case statements results in a match, the statements embedded within the default code block are executed.

Note that the `default` statement and its code block are optional. If omitted and none of the expressions belonging to the `case` statements match the expression belonging to the `switch` statement, then nothing happens. Inclusion of the `break` statements is also optional and if omitted, any `case` statement that evaluates as true will be executed.

As an example of how to set up a `switch` statement code block, consider the following example.

```
{
    userGuess = get_string("Okay, what is the game rated?", "");

    switch (userGuess) {
        case "e": draw_text(200, 200, "Yes. Of course you may."); break
        case "t": draw_text(200, 200, "Yes. I suppose you can."); break
        case "m": draw_text(200, 200, "No. Wait until you are older."); break
        case "a": draw_text(200, 200, "No. Not in my house!"); break
        default: draw_text(200, 200, "No. I need to know more about it.");
    }

    sleep(3000)
    game_end()
}
```

Here, the user is prompted to enter a video game rating (`e`, `t`, `m`, or `a`). A `switch` statement code block is then used to analyze the user's input and to compare it against a series of four case statements. A different text string is displayed based on the user's input. If the user enters something other than `e`, `t`, `m`, or `a`, the string belonging to the default statement is displayed.

## Comparing Values Using Relational Operators

So far, all of the examples that you have seen in this book have used the equality (==) operator to determine when values were equal. Game Maker supports a number of other relational operators. You can use these operators to perform comparisons based on ranges of values. Game Maker supports all of the relational operators shown in Table 9.1.

**Table 9.1** GML's Relational Operators

| Operator | Description | Example | Result |
|---|---|---|---|
| == | Equal to | 6 == 5 | False |
| != | Not equal | 6 != 5 | True |
| < | Less than | 5 < 6 | True |
| <= | Less than or equal to | 7 <= 4 | False |
| > | Greater than | 5 > 4 | True |
| >= | Greater than or equal to | 5 >= 5 | True |

## Crunching Numbers

Game Maker gives you the ability to perform addition, subtraction, multiplication, and division. The following statements demonstrate how to use the + operators to add two numbers together.

```
x = 100;
y = 50;
z = x + y;
```

When executed, z is assigned a value of 150. Table 9.2 outlines the arithmetic operators supported by Game Maker and shows examples of their use.

The last five operators listed in Table 9.2 merit additional explanation. For starters, you can use negative numbers in your expressions. Negative numbers are preceded by a - character, without any intervening space and can be used as demonstrated here:

```
x = 10
y = -5
z = x + y
```

When executed, a value of 5 is assigned to z. The remaining four operators listed in Table 9.2 combine arithmetic and assignment functionality into a single operator, providing you with the ability to modify and assign a value in a single step.

One of the best ways to understand how Game Maker performs arithmetic calculations is to work through an example like the one shown below.

```
x = 8 + 4 / 2 - 2 * -7 + 2
```

**Table 9.2** GML's Arithmetic Operators

| Operator | Description | Example | Result |
|---|---|---|---|
| + | Addition | x = 3 + 2 | 5 |
| – | Subtraction | x = 5 -- 3 | 2 |
| * | Multiplication | x = 2 * 4 | 8 |
| / | Division | x = 10 / 3 | 3.33 |
| div | Integer Division | x = 10 div 3 | 3 |
| mod | Modulo (returns remainder) | x = 10 mod 3 | 1 |
| –x | Reverses a variables sign | x = –x | –1 |
| += | Shorthand for x = x + y | x += 5 | 4 |
| –= | Shorthand for x = x – y | x –= 5 | –1 |
| *= | Shorthand for x = x * y | x *= 5 | –5 |
| /= | Shorthand for x = x / y | x /= 5 | –2.5 |

Game Maker processes this statement using the steps outlined here:

1. Working from left to right, all division and multiplication operations are performed first. Therefore, 4 is divided by 2 yielding a value of 2, and 2 is multiplied by -7 yielding a value of -14. At this point the status of the equation is as shown below.

   ```
   x = 8 + 2 - -14 + 2
   ```

2. Addition and subtraction are performed next, on a left to right basis, resulting in a final value of 26 being assigned to x.

**Hint**

If necessary, you can override Game Maker's default order of precedence by enclosing different parts of equations inside parentheses. To see how this works, take a look at the following statement.

```
x = (8 + 4) / 2 - 2 * (-7 + 2)
```

When parentheses are used, their contents are evaluated first, on a left to right basis, and then the result of the expression is processed according to GML's order of precedence. In the case of the previous statement, this results in a value of 16 instead of a value of 26.

## Commenting GML Code

In order to help make your GML code easier to understand, you should get into the habit of embedding comment statements into your scripts. Comments do not affect the performance of your games. GML supports two types of comments.

You can add comments at any location within your scripts by typing // followed by the text of your comment, as demonstrated below:

```
//Generate a random integer from 1 - 3
secretNumber = round(random(2) + 1);
```

If you want, you can also append comments to the end of your code statements, as demonstrated here:

```
secretNumber = round(random(2) + 1); //Generate a random integer from 1 - 3
```

GML also lets you add multi-line comments to your scripts placing text inside opening /* and closing */ characters, as demonstrated below.

```
/*
Display a popup dialog window that prompts the player to enter a numeric
Guess in the range of 1 to 3.
*/
```

## Summary

This chapter provided a basic understanding of how to apply programming logic using Game Maker's GML scripting language. GML allows you to execute stricter control over the execution of your games. This chapter showed you how to collect, process, modify, and store data within your games. You also learned how to apply conditional programming logic when analyzing and processing the data used by your games. You learned how to define constants and variables and to manipulate collections of data using arrays. On top of all this, you learned how to apply conditional programming logic, compare program data, and set up arithmetic operations.

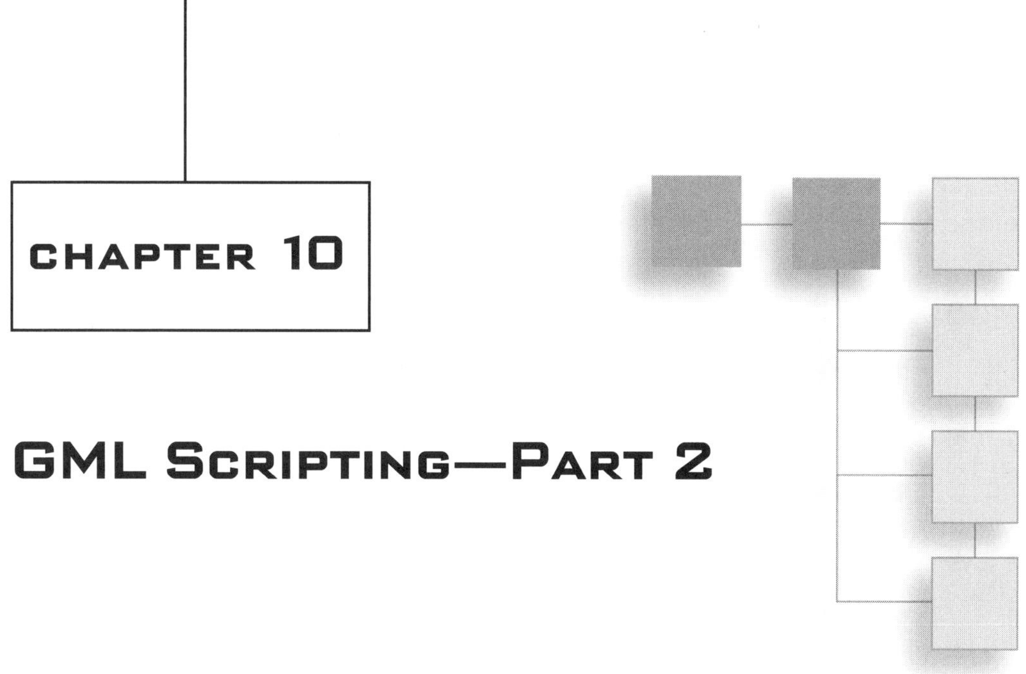

# CHAPTER 10

# GML SCRIPTING—PART 2

This is the second of two chapters dedicated to teaching you the fundamentals of GML scripting. This chapter will show you how to work with loops as a means of performing repetitive actions. You will learn how to create many different types of loops as well as how to manage and terminate their execution on different conditions. You will also learn how to create GML scripts that can process arguments and return a value as output. This will allow you to develop scripts that look and act exactly like functions, providing you with the ability to develop complex scripts and to use scripts as the basis of extending Game Maker's functionality.

An overview of the major topics covered in this chapter includes learning:

- How to set up different types of loops
- How to break out of a loop early or skip iterations
- How to develop scripts that operate like functions
- The importance of creating script libraries

## Taking Advantage of the Power of Loops

Games often require the repeated execution of programming logic. For example, in a game like *Pong*, the game must repeatedly monitor for keystrokes and then initiate actions based on which keystrokes occur (e.g., managing the movement of player paddles). Likewise, the process of managing the continuous movement of the ball as it bounces around the screen requires the repeated execution of a series of actions or programming statements (depending on whether you are working with action icons or GML statements). In programming, repetitive logic is implemented through a construction referred to as a loop.

A *loop* is a block of one or more code statements that are repeatedly executed. Loops enable the development of games that process large amounts of data. Without loops, you have to create massive applications consisting of redundant code statements. Once set up, a loop lets you repeat the execution of one or more code statements as many times as required to manage and control game play.

As a demonstration of the importance of loops and the efficiencies that they provide, look at the following example.

```
{
    draw_text(50, 50, "1");
    draw_text(50, 70, "2");
    draw_text(50, 90, "3");
    draw_text(50, 110, "4");
    draw_text(50, 130, "5");

    sleep(3000);
    game_end();

}
```

Here, five statements are used to draw the numbers 1 through 5 on the screen. The last two statements shown above pause the application's execution for three seconds and then call upon the `game_end()` function to end the application.

What if you want to count to 50, 500, or 5,000,000 instead? Clearly, using the above approach would pose some difficulties and result in a monstrous size script. A much better way of handling a challenge like this is with a loop. For example, consider the following script.

```
{
    x_coord = 50;
    y_coord = 50;

    i = 1
```

```
    do {
        draw_text(x_coord, y_coord, i);
        y_coord = y_coord + 20;
        i += 1
    } until (i > 5)

    sleep(3000);
    game_end();
}
```

Here, a `do . . . until` loop has been set up to display five numbers. Each time the loop executes, it draws the value assigned to a variable named `i` at a specified set of coordinates, as maintained in variables named `x_coord` and `y_coord`. To prevent the next iteration of the loop from writing over the previous iteration, the value assigned to `y_coord` is incremented by 20. The value assigned to `i` is incremented by 1. The loop then inspects the current value of `i` to see if it is greater than 5. If it is, the loop terminates; otherwise, it executes again. The last two statements pause the application for three seconds and then end the application.

If you compare this script to the previous script, you can see that it is a few lines larger and a little more complete. So, while it may not be the easiest way of drawing five lines on the screen, consider that all it would take to modify this script to draw 500 lines would be to change `until (i > 5)` to `until (i > 500)`.

**Hint**

> Note that in the case of both of the previous example scripts, the `draw_text()` function is used to draw text strings on the screen. This method requires that it be executed by an object's `draw` event in order for it to work.

When executed, both of these scripts produce the same output, as shown in Figure 10.1.

Game Maker allows you to set up four different types of loops, each of which is outlined below.

- **`do . . . until`**. Sets up a loop that executes until a specified expression resolves as true.
- **`repeat`**. Repeats a loop a specified number of times.
- **`for`**. Sets up a loop that executes until a specified expression evaluates as false.
- **`while`**. Sets up a loop that iterates as long as a specified expression is true.

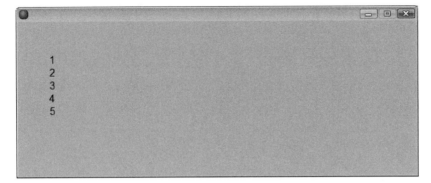

**Figure 10.1**
Loops provide a more efficient means of performing repetitive tasks.

You can often use these loops interchangeably; however, there are differences between them, making each type of loop better suited to a particular type of task.

## Setting Up a do...until Loop

Perhaps the easiest loop to set up and work with is the `do . . . until` loop. The `do...until` loop repeats the execution of a block of code statements until the value of a tested expression evaluates as being true. When you use the `do . . . until` loop, you must use a means for ending the loop's execution (e.g., for eventually turning the value of the expression that is evaluated to true). The syntax for this loop is outlined below.

```
do {
    statements
} until (expression)
```

*`statements`* represents one or more code statements that will be executed each time the loop iterates or repeats. Because the loop's expression is not checked until the end of the loop, it will always execute one time, even if the value of the tested expression starts off true. The following example demonstrates how to use a `do . . . until` loop to count to 10, drawing its output onto the screen.

```
{
    x_coord = 50;
    y_coord = 70;

    draw_text(50, 30, "Count to 100, the fast way!");
    i = 10
```

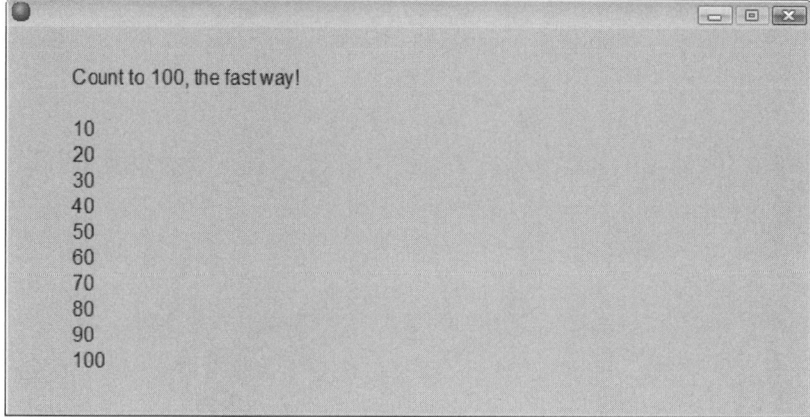


**Figure 10.2**
Using the `do . . . until` loop to count to 10.

```
    do {
        draw_text(x_coord, y_coord, i);
        y_coord = y_coord + 20;
        i = i + 10
    } until (i > 100)

    sleep(3000);
    game_end();
}
```

In this example, the loop has been set up to iterate until the value of `i` becomes greater than `100`. `i` is assigned an initial value of `10` and is incremented by 10 each time the loop iterates. As a result, the loop displays the output shown in Figure 10.2 when executed.

## Working with the repeat Loop

Another loop supported by GML is the `repeat` loop, which repeats the execution of a specified statement a set number of times. The syntax of the `repeat` loop is outlined here:

```
{
  Repeat (expression) statement;
}
```

*`statement`* represents the code statements that are executed each time the loop iterates. *`expression`* specifies the number of iterations that will occur. To develop

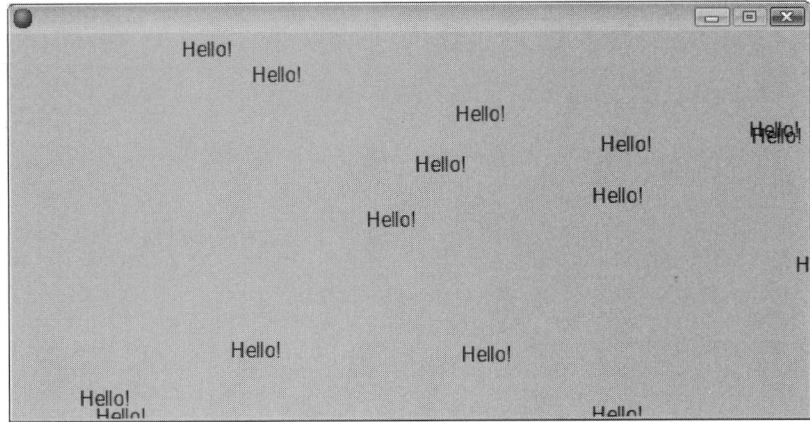


**Figure 10.3**
Using the `repeat` loop to draw 20 random text strings.

a better appreciation of how the `repeat` loop works, consider the following example.

```
{
    repeat (20) draw_text(random(640), random(400), "Hello!");
    sleep(3000);
    game_end();
}
```

Here, a `repeat` loop is used to randomly display the text string `Hello` at 20 different locations on the screen. Each instance of the word is randomly placed by using the `random()` function to randomly select both the `x` and `y` coordinates at which the word is displayed. Figure 10.3 shows an example of the output that is produced when this script is executed.

## Processing Data with the for Loop

Another type of loop supported by Game Maker is the `for` loop, which is designed to handle situations where you need to process a collection of data. Execution of the `for` loop is controlled by a counter variable, which is established by, evaluated, and updated in the `for` statement itself. The syntax for the `for` loop is outlined here.

```
for (statement1; expression; statement2] {
   statements
}
```

*statement1* represents a statement that is executed when the loop is started. *expression* is evaluated at the beginning of each iteration of the loop, allowing the loop to execute as long as it evaluates as true. *statements* represents one or more code statements that are executed if *expression* evaluates as true. Finally, *statement2* is a statement that is executed at the end of the loop's execution, after which `expression` is evaluated once again. The loop continues to iterate until `expression` evaluates as false.

To get a better understanding of how to work with the `for` loop, take a look at the following example.

```
{
    x_coord = 50;
    y_coord = 50;

    draw_text(50, 30, "Watch me count!");

    for (i = 1; i <= 10; i += 1) {
        draw_text(x_coord, y_coord, i);
        y_coord = y_coord + 20;
    }

    sleep(3000);
    game_end();
}
```

Here, a `for` loop has been set up to iterate 10 times. The first time this loop executes, the value of `i` is set to 1 and checked to see if it is less than 10. If so, the value assigned to `i` is drawn on the screen. The value of `i` is then incremented by 1, after which the loop re-evaluates its `expression` to determine if it should process again. This process continues for a total of 10 iterations, after which the value of `i` is set equal to 10, terminating the loop's execution.

The `for` loop is also well suited to processing the contents of arrays. For example, the following scripts create a small array named `names[]`, containing three elements. A `for` loop is then set up to iterate through the array, drawing a string on the screen that displays each item in the array.

```
{
    names[0] = "Molly";
    names[1] = "William";
    names[2] = "Alexander";
```

**Figure 10.4**
Using the `for` loop to process the contents of an array.

```
    x_coord = 50;
    y_coord = 50;

    for (i=0; i<3; i=i+1) {
        draw_text(x_coord, y_coord, names[i]);
        y_coord = y_coord + 20
    }
}
```

Figure 10.4 shows the output that is displayed when this script is executed.

If you need to, you can specify a negative number to make a `for` loop process in reverse order, as demonstrated here:

```
{
    x_coord = 50;
    y_coord = 50;

    draw_text(50, 30, "Begin Countdown.");

    for (i = 10; i > 0; i -= 1) {
        draw_text(x_coord, y_coord, i);
        y_coord = y_coord + 20;
    }

    draw_text(x_coord, y_coord, "Blastoff!");
    sleep(3000);
    game_end();
}
```

**Figure 10.5**
Setting up a `for` loop to run in reverse order.

When executed, this script counts down from 10 to 1, as demonstrated in Figure 10.5.

Instead of displaying a list of numbers on the screen from 1 to 10, a list of numbers from 10 to 1 is displayed. Yet another way of varying the operation of the `for` loop is to specify a value other than 1 as the loop's incremental value. For example, the following script uses an incremental value of 2 when stepping through the `for` loop.

```
{
    x_coord = 50;
    y_coord = 50;

    draw_text(50, 30, "Begin Countdown.");

    for (i = 10; i > 0; i -= 2) {
        draw_text(x_coord, y_coord, i);
        y_coord = y_coord + 20;
    }

    draw_text(x_coord, y_coord, "Blastoff!");
    sleep(3000);
    game_end();
}
```

Figure 10.6 shows the output that is displayed when this script executes.

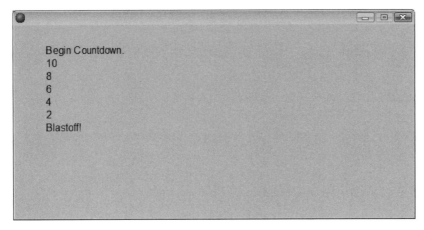

**Figure 10.6**
Skipping every other number when iterating through a `for` loop.

## Working with while Loops

The last type of loop supported by GML is the `while` loop. This loop iterates as long as its tested expression remains true. The syntax of the `while` loop is outlined below.

```
while (expression){
    statements
}
```

The value of *`expression`* is evaluated each time the loop iterates. If *`expression`* evaluates as being true, then all of the statements embedded within the loop are executed. Whereas the `do . . . until` loop evaluates its expression at the end of the loop, guaranteeing that the loop will always run at least once, the `while` loop's expression evaluates at the beginning of the loop. As a result, the loop does not run if the value of `expression` is false.

To better understand how to work with the `while` loop, take a look at this example.

```
{
    x_coord = 50;
    y_coord = 50;

    draw_text(50, 30, "Watch me count!");
    i = 1;

    while (i <= 10) {
        draw_text(x_coord, y_coord, i);
        y_coord = y_coord + 20;
```

```
        i = i + 1 ;
    }

    sleep(3000);
    game_end();
}
```

When executed, this script counts from 1 to 10, briefly pauses, and then ends the application.

## Altering Loop Execution

As your program logic grows more complex, there may be times where certain events occur that require you to prematurely halt a loop's execution. For example, you might need to use a loop to find a particular element in an array. Upon locating the element and retrieving its contents, there may be no need to process the rest of the array's content. In this situation, you would want to halt the loop's execution so that its scripts can get on with things. Likewise, there may be times during a loop's iteration when you want to skip the rest of the current iteration, while allowing the loop to continue execution. This might be the case, for example, if your loop involves statements that collect and process user data. If the user provides invalid input, you might want to toss it out by restarting the loop and prompting the user to try again.

GML supports both of these types of operations through the command outlined below.

- **break**. Halts a loop's execution, allowing its script to continue its execution.
- **next**. Stops the current iteration of the loop, allowing the next iteration to execute.

### Breaking Out of Loops Early

The `break` command can be used to cause an immediate halt in the execution of any loop without impacting the execution of the rest of the script in which it resides. An example of the use of the `break` statement is provided here:

```
{
    x_coord = 50;
    y_coord = 50;

    i = 1;
```

```
    do {

        if (i = 3) break;

        draw_text(x_coord, y_coord, i);
        y_coord = y_coord + 20;
        i += 1;

    } until (i > 5)

    sleep(3000);
    game_end();
}
```

Here a script has been set up to count from `1` to `5` using a `do . . . until` loop. However, embedded within the `do . . . until` loop is an `if` statement that executes the `break` statement when the value of `i` is equal to `3`. As a result, counting stops at 2, as demonstrated in Figure 10.7.

## Skipping a Single Iteration

Using the `continue` statement, you can halt the remainder of the current iteration of a loop, without halting the loop's execution. Instead, the loop simply brings its next iteration. To see an example of how you might use the `continue` statement, take a look at the following script.

**Figure 10.7**
Using the `break` statement to halt a loop's execution early.

```
{
    x_coord = 50;
    y_coord = 50;

    i = 1;

    do {

        if (i = 3) {
            i += 1;
            continue;
        }

        draw_text(x_coord, y_coord, i);
        y_coord = y_coord + 20;
        i += 1;

    } until (i > 5)

    sleep(3000);
    game_end();
}
```

Here a script has been set up to count from 1 to 5 using a `do . . . until` loop. However, embedded within the `do . . . until` loop is an `if` statement code block that increments the value of `i` when it becomes equal to `3` and then executes the `continue` statement. As a result, the third iteration of the loop is prematurely halted, resulting in the output shown in Figure 10.8.

**Figure 10.8**
Using the `continue` statement to skip the remainder of the current iteration's execution.

## Exiting Loops and Scripts

Depending on what the programming logic embedded within your loops does, there may be times when you find you need to terminate a loop's execution early. You have already seen how to do this with the `break` statement. As an alternative, you can also use the `exit` statement to halt a loop's execution. This statement has the following syntax.

```
exit
```

Once executed, the `exit` command immediately terminates the execution of the loop in which it is embedded. When used this way, the `exit` statement only halts the execution of the loop, allowing the script to continue its execution as demonstrated in the following example.

```
{
    x_coord = 50;
    y_coord = 50;

    i = 1;

    do {

        if (i = 3) {
            exit;
        }

        draw_text(x_coord, y_coord, i);
        y_coord = y_coord + 20;
        i += 1

    } until (i > 5)
}
```

Here, the loop halts its execution in the middle of its third iteration. If you execute the `Exit` command in a loop that is nested within another loop, only the inner loop's execution is terminated. The outer loop will continue to run. If, however, you execute the `exit` statement outside of a loop, it will halt the execution of the script in which it resides.

## Using Scripts as Functions

Functions are the most important component in your scripts. There are close to 1,000 predefined GML scripts that you can programmatically use to control and manage the execution of your games. Game Maker's predefined functions allow you to create, manage, and control game resources like objects, sounds, and sprites. GML functions have descriptive names, some accept and process arguments and some do not. Some execute and perform a task while others also return a value.

As your programming skills continue to improve, you will undoubtedly begin to develop more and more scripts. Your script's source code will grow larger and more complex. It is essential that you break down the programming logic into separate and discrete parts instead of by creating huge all-encompassing scripts. Follow the design model provided by Game Maker's action icons, where each individual action is designed to perform a single specific task.

Since GML scripts can accept and process arguments and return a result, you can use them as the basis of creating your own custom functions. As such, you can create GML scripts that extend Game Maker's built-in capabilities.

**Hint**

> Make sure that you assign descriptive names to all your scripts and that your script names are unique, following the same naming rules as those that apply to variable names.

## Passing Arguments to Scripts for Processing

As you have already seen, you can run scripts using the `Execute Code` and `Execute Script` actions. When you use the `Execute Script` action, Game Maker provides you with the ability to pass up to five arguments to the script for processing. For example, take a look at Figure 10.9. Here, a script named `scr_attackmode` is executed and passed four arguments for processing: a string, a constant, and two numbers.

By passing arguments to scripts, you give them data to process. In this way, you can create scripts whose executions vary based on the input they are passed. GML also provides the ability to call upon the execution of one script from within another script using the `script_execute()` function, which has the following syntax.

```
script_execute(scriptname, arg0, arg1, . . . , arg15)
```

Here, *`scriptname`* represents the name of the script to be executed. Scripts executed using the `script_execute()` function can be passed as many as 16 arguments for processing, as represented by *`arg0`* through *`arg15`*. The script names

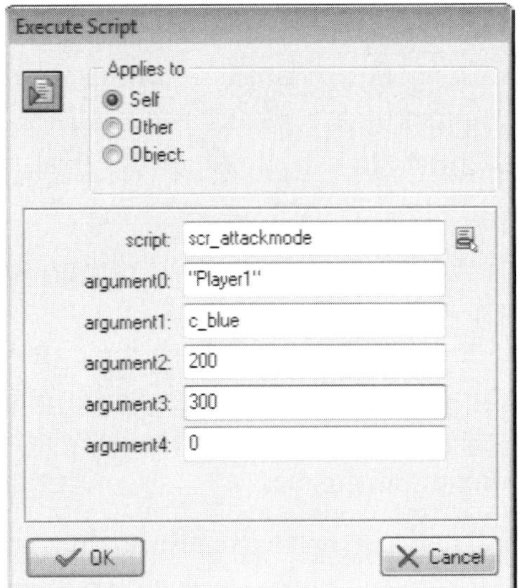


**Figure 10.9**
Executing a script named `scr_attackmode` and passing it four arguments for processing.

and any arguments being passed are separated by commas and enclosed within parentheses. The following statement demonstrates how to use the `script_execute()` function to execute a script named `scr_add` and pass it two arguments for processing.

```
script_execute(scr_add, 10, 5);
```

## Processing Argument Input

Any arguments passed to a script are made available to the script as variables named `argument0` through `argument15`. This allows you to create scripts that can alter their execution based on the arguments passed to them. For example, the following script is designed to process two numeric arguments passed to it at execution time.

```
{
    total = argument0 + argument1
    show_message(string(total));
}
```

When executed, this script adds the two arguments passed to it and then uses the `show_message()` function to display the result.

## Returning a Result from a Script

In addition to receiving and processing data passed to it as arguments, you can set up your functions to return a value back to the statement that called upon it for execution. This is accomplished using the `return` statement, which has the following syntax.

```
return expression;
```

Here, *expression* is the value to be returned by the script. As an example of how to return a value from a script, take a look at the following script.

```
{
    total = argument0 + argument1
    return total;
}
```

As you can see, this example is very similar to the example from the previous section, except that instead of adding two numbers passed to it as arguments and then displaying the result, it returns the result of that calculation back to the statement that executed it.

**Hint**

GML scripts terminate upon processing the `return` statement. Therefore, careful placement of this statement is essential. You will want to make sure that it is the last statement you want to execute within your scripts.

## Retrieving Data Returned by Scripts

In order to retrieve data returned by scripts, you need to modify the way you call upon scripts for execution. Instead of executing a script using the following syntax

```
script_execute(scriptname, arg0, arg1, . . . , arg15)
```

you need to use the syntax shown here:

```
result = script_execute(scriptname, arg0, arg1, . . . , arg15)
```

Here, *scriptname* represents the name of the script to be executed and *arg0* through *arg15* represent the arguments to be passed. For example, the following statements demonstrate how to call upon a script, pass it arguments, and store the result it returns.

```
{
    result = script_execute(scr_add, 10, 5);
    show_message(string(result));
}
```

As you can see, the value returned by the scr_add script is stored in a variable named result. This value of result is then converted to a string using the string() function and displayed using the show_message() function.

**Hint**

The show_message() function can only be used to display a string. Since the value returned by the scr_add() script and stored in result is numeric, it must first be converted into a string. Otherwise, an error occurs.

## Terminating Script Execution

All GML scripts end when their last statement is processed or when a return statement is executed. In addition, you can halt the execution of a script using the exit statement, which has the following syntax.

```
exit
```

The exit statement terminates a script's execution without returning any value back to a calling statement. The exit statement only halts the execution of the script within which it resides; it does not halt application execution. To halt application execution, you need to execute the game_end() function, as previously demonstrated in this chapter.

**Hint**

If you want to restart a game instead of ending it, you can call upon the game_restart() function.

## Building a Script Library

Over time you may find yourself generating all kinds of different scripts. You may even find yourself copying and pasting these scripts from one application to another. After a while, you might find it difficult to remember which application a given script resides in. You could have to spend a lot of time hunting it down and even give up looking for it, and as a result you will have to rewrite it. Rather than doing all of this copying and pasting and searching, consider the benefits of creating a script library (e.g., a collection of GML scripts stored on a folder somewhere on your computer).

Game Maker makes it easy to create and use such a library through its Import Scripts and Export Scripts\Export Selected Script commands, located on the Scripts menu. The key to making your script library easy to work with and manage is to make sure that when you export your scripts, you assign them descriptive names. This will make them easy to identify later on when you need to import them into new applications.

## Summary

This chapter rounded out your overview of GML scripting basics. It showed you how to work with the `do...until`, `repeat`, `for`, and `while` loops. You also learned how to break out of loops and to skip iterations of loops. This chapter explained how to create GML scripts that look and behave like functions. This included learning how to execute scripts using the `execute_script()` function as well as how to pass arguments to scripts, access those arguments from within called scripts, and to return data from scripts back to calling statements. Lastly, the chapter ended with a short discussion on the importance of creating a script library as a means of organizing your scripts and speeding up game development by importing commonly used scripts.

# Chapter 11

# Arachnid Attack!

Welcome to the final chapter of this book. This chapter rounds out your Game Maker development instruction by providing an overview of how to deal with the errors that inevitably occur when developing complex computer games and applications. This includes learning about the types of errors that you will run into and how to deal with them. The chapter will end by walking you through the development of this book's final game, Arachnid Attack! This game is designed to help tie together all of the major development and programming concepts that you have learned in this book, with specific focus on the use of both actions and scripts in developing program logic.

An overview of the major topics covered in this chapter includes:

- An examination of the different types of errors that can occur in Game Maker programs
- Advice on how to monitor program execution and track down and fix application bugs
- An overview of how to work with Game Maker's built-in debugger

## Troubleshooting Problems with Your Games

One unfortunate fact that every programmer has to come to terms with is that no matter how experienced or talented you may be, errors are going to occur within your applications. Errors, often referred to as bugs, result in unpredictable results, causing the generation of error messages, unreliable results, and potentially even causing applications to crash. As such, it is essential to understand the types of errors you will run into and that you learn a little something about how to track them down so that you can eliminate them.

The best way of dealing with errors is to try to prevent them from occurring. To do this, make sure that when you sit down to develop your games and their program code that you do so a piece at a time, testing your games as you go along. In addition, whenever possible, make liberal use of GML functions rather than trying to reinvent the wheel yourself.

When testing your applications, make sure that in addition to verifying that everything works as expected that you also test your application's susceptibility to invalid input. If your applications do not handle invalid input correctly, modify them so that they do. There are a number of additional steps that you can take to help prevent errors from occurring when your games run. These steps include:

- Commenting your code statements to make them easy to understand
- Indenting your program code to make it easier to follow
- Providing players with clear instruction on how to play the game
- Adopting a consistent and descriptive naming scheme for all game resources, variables, arrays, and scripts

## Identifying IDE Errors

Game Maker monitors everything that programmers do within its IDE, validating all programmer input to ensure that it makes syntactic sense. If a programmer attempts to enter data that does not make sense within the context of the current situation, it notifies the programmer of the error by highlighting the mistake, as demonstrated in Figure 11.1.

By flagging program errors made within the IDE, Game Maker helps make the programmer's job a lot easier, saving you the hassle of having to identify and track them down yourself.

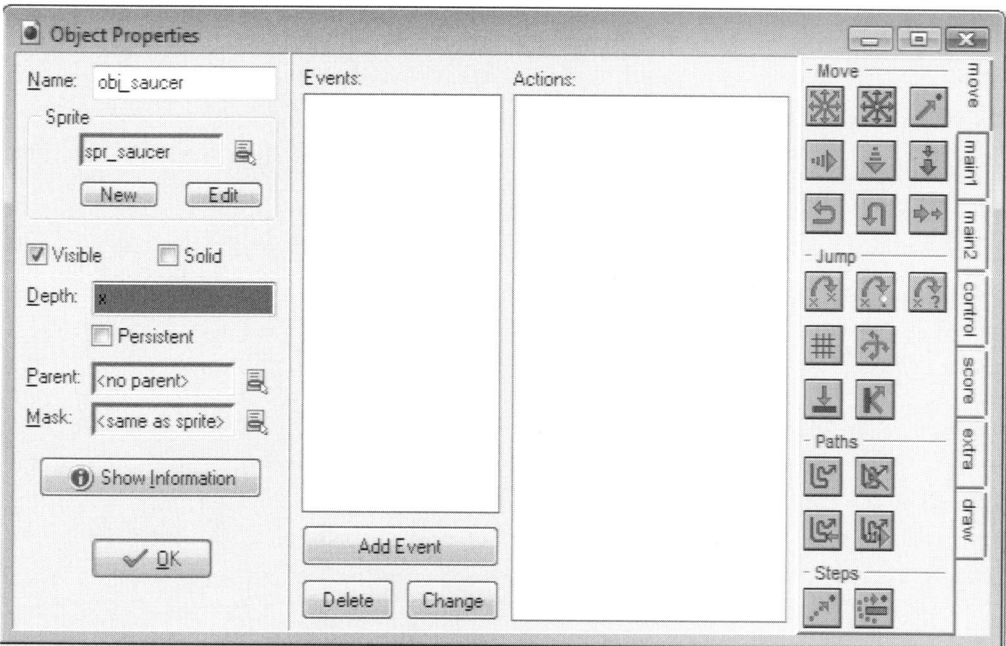


**Figure 11.1**
Game Maker has highlighted in red an error made by the programmer.

# Dealing with Different Types of Errors

Like most programming languages, Game Maker is subject to three different types of errors, as listed here:

- Syntax errors
- Logical errors
- Runtime errors

## Avoiding Syntax Errors

The most common type of error is a *syntax error*, which is an error that occurs when you fail to follow GML's syntax requirements. This can happen, for example, when you make typos when keying in code statements or when you fail to provide required arguments when calling on GML functions. Syntax errors in GML scripts prevent your games from running and result in the generation of an error message. For example, suppose you add the following statement to a GML script.

```
play_soun(snd_help);
```

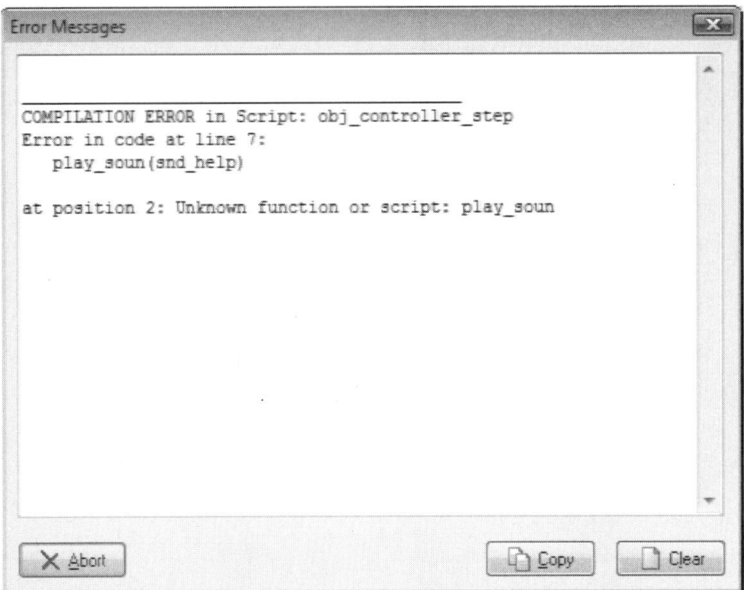
COMPILATION ERROR in Script: obj_controller_step
Error in code at line 7:
   play_soun(snd_help)

at position 2: Unknown function or script: play_soun

**Figure 11.2**
A syntax error generated because of a typo in a function name.

This statement was supposed to play a sound file. However, a typo has been made when attempting to reference the `PlaySound()` function. As a result, an error message like the one shown in Figure 11.2 is displayed if the application containing the script is executed.

Game Maker's error messages provide an explanation of the error and tell you where it was found. This error could have easily been caught prior to running the application by clicking on the Script Editor's Check the Script for Syntax Errors toolbar button. In response, Game Maker performs a syntax check of your code statement and highlights the error, as demonstrated in Figure 11.3.

## Preventing Logical Errors

Because they generate error messages, syntax errors are relatively easy to deal with. A more sinister type of error to deal with is a logical error. A *logical error* is one that occurs when you apply faulty logic when performing a task. For example, a logical error occurs if you accidentally add together two numbers that you should have multiplied or divided. As a result, your application runs and does exactly what it was told to do, yielding output that is contrary to your expectations.

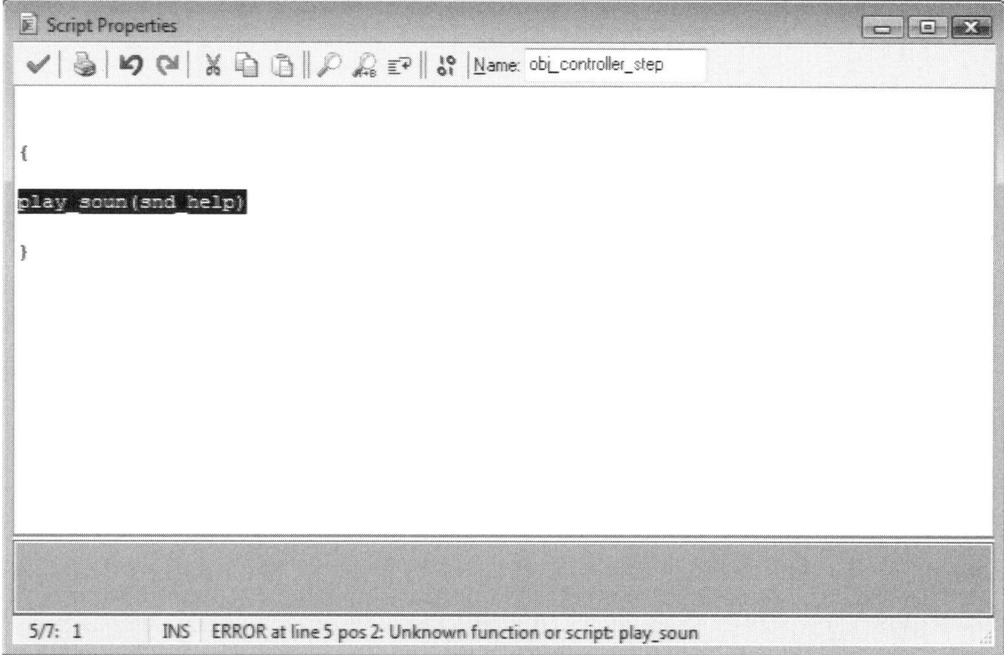


**Figure 11.3**
An example of a syntax error that has been flagged by Game Maker.

The challenge in tracking down logical errors is that they do not generate error messages. The best way of dealing with them is to prevent them in the first place, which you can do through careful planning and testing. If, despite your best efforts, you believe a logical error has made its way into a GML script within an application, you should review your script to see if you can spot the problem. If you are unable to track it down, you can try to track it down using Game Maker's built-in debugger, which is covered a little later in this chapter.

## Coping with Runtime Errors

A third type of error that you need to be on the lookout for is a runtime error. A *runtime* error is one that occurs when your application tries to perform an illegal action. One of the problems in dealing with runtime errors is that Game Maker cannot detect them when scripts are interpreting for execution. Runtime errors can occur for a number of reasons. For example, a needed file might have been deleted or the drive on which it results might crash. As a simple example of what a runtime error looks like, consider the following script.

```
{
    number = get_string("enter a number", "");
    number = real(number);
    result = 5 / number;
    show_message(string(result));
}
```

Here, a popup dialog window is displayed that prompts the user to enter a number. Since the `get_string()` function returns anything it collects as a string, the data that the user enters is converted to a real number using the `real()` function. This value is then used as the denominator in a mathematic expression, the result of which is then converted back to a string using the `string()` function and then displayed in a popup dialog using the `show_message()` function. A runtime error will occur when this script is executed whenever the user enters a non-numeric character or if the user enters a zero, because division by zero is an illegal operation.

Depending on what your application is designed to do, it may not be possible to eliminate every possible runtime error from occurring. However, careful testing and a little data validation may go a long way in helping to reduce their occurrence.

## Monitoring Game Execution

If you find yourself in a situation where you have a program with an error that you just cannot seem to track down, not all hope is lost. Game Maker provides a built-in debugger that you can use to track down the problem. A *debugger* is a program designed to execute applications in a special mode that lets you control the application's statement execution while at the same time monitoring variable values. This gives you a view as to what is happening inside your application as it executes.

To start a debug session for an application that is giving you trouble, click on Run > Run in Debug mode or click on the red Run Game in Debug Mode button located on Game Maker's toolbar. This starts your application and displays the Debug Information window shown in Figure 11.4.

**Hint**

> The Run menu provides access to commands that replicate the functionality of the debugger's toolbar.

Using the buttons located on the debugger's toolbar, you can pause the application's execution. While paused, you can display windows that show the current values of variables and keep an eye on object instances. When you are ready, you

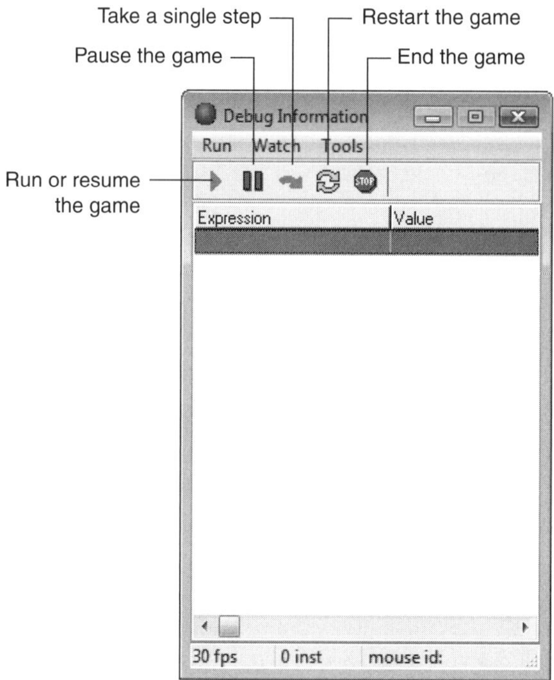


**Figure 11.4**
Game Maker's built-in debugger gives you complete control over your application's execution.

can resume execution, execute a single step, restart the application from the beginning, or halt the application's execution. By pausing your application, displaying variable values, and then stepping through its execution a step at a time, you can validate that variable values are being correctly set and that things are occurring in the order you want them to.

## Watching Expressions

The debugger's Watch menu provides access to the following commands.

- Add—Lets you enter an expression you want monitored.
- Change—Lets you change a monitored expression.
- Delete—Lets you delete a monitored expression.
- Clear—Clears out all listed expressions.
- Load—Saves the current set of expressions.
- Save—Loads a list of previously saved expressions.

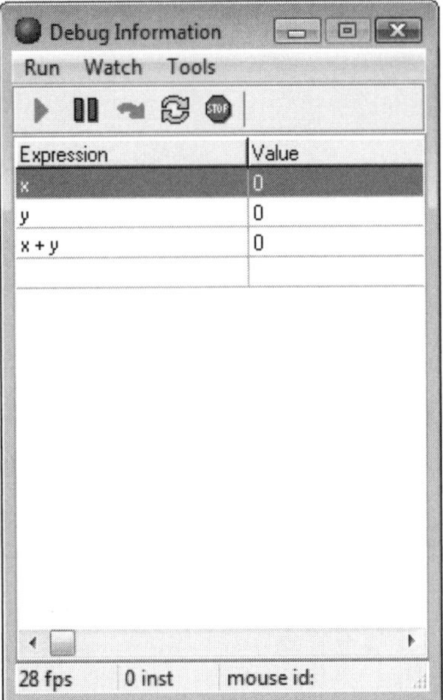


**Figure 11.5**
Monitoring expressions that you want to keep an eye on during your debug session.

Using these commands, you can enter a list of expressions whose values you want to monitor during your debug session. For example, Figure 11.5 shows how the Debugger Information window looks when monitoring three expressions.

## Monitoring Object Instance and Variable Values

One of the most important features of Game Maker's debugger is its ability to display and dynamically update both local and global variable values during the debug session. To do so, click on Tools > Show Global Variables or Tools > Show Local Variables. Figure 11.6 shows an example of what you will see when monitoring a game's global variables.

The Local Variable window displays similar data for a local variable that you want to monitor. You can monitor as many different local variables as you want at the same time. The Tools menu also provides commands that let you monitor the status of object instances.

## Executing Code Statements

If you want, you can execute a code statement during your debug session and then observe its effect on the application's execution. One reason for doing this might be to change a variable value to see what impact it has on how the

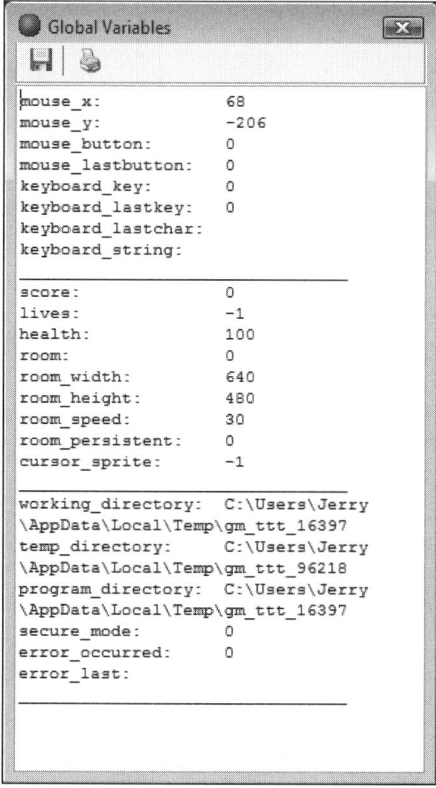


**Figure 11.6**
The data that is displayed in the Global Variables window is continuously updated, allowing you to keep an eye on how the data is being collected and managed.

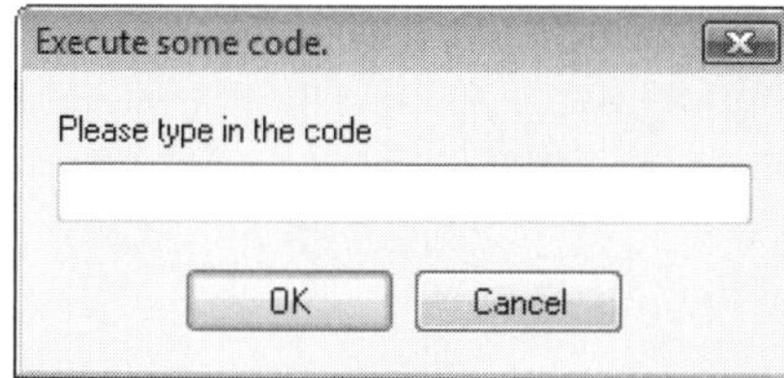


**Figure 11.7**
You can execute code statements when debugging to see how they impact your application.

application executed. To do so, click on Tools > Execute Code. This displays the popup dialog window shown in Figure 11.7.

All you have to do is enter the desired statement and click on the OK button and then monitor its effect on the application. If you want, you can also change the speed at which the application is executing, by clicking on Tools > Set Speed. This displays the popup dialog window shown in Figure 11.8.

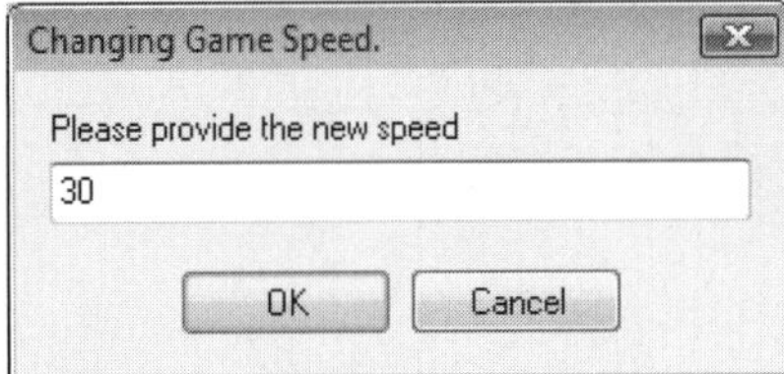


**Figure 11.8**
Changing an application's speed can slow down or speed up a debug session.

By changing an application's speed, you can temporarily slow things down so that you can more closely observe what is going on or you can even speed things up.

## Creating Arachnid Attack!

It is time to turn your attention to the development of this book's final game project, Arachnid Attack! This single-player game's goal is for the player to defend the earth from hordes of invading arachnid armies, which arrive in wave after wave. To fight off the arachnids, the player is given control over a jet fighter plane capable of shooing arachnids out of the sky. The player is given three lives (jets). Game play ends after the player's jet is shot down three times by the bugs or when they manage to overwhelm the player and descend all the way to the bottom of the screen. Player score and lives are displayed at the top of the screen throughout game play. The game keeps track of the top 10 scores and displays a high scores table at the end of the game.

The player controls the jet via the keyboard using the following keyboard keys.

- **Left Arrow.** Moves the jet left.
- **Right Arrow.** Moves the jet right.
- **Space.** Fires the jet's guns.

Players score points by shooting alien bugs. Points are awarded as follows:

- 10 points for killing an ant
- 20 points for killing a spider
- 40 points for killing a beetle
- 100 points for killing a wasp

Figure 11.9 shows an example of Arachnid Attack! in action.

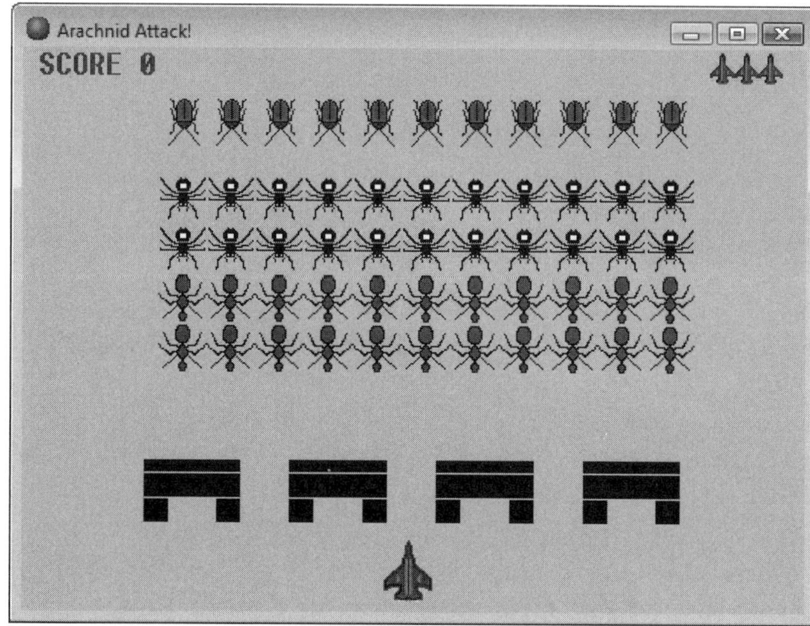


**Figure 11.9**
Arachnid Attack! is based on the classic Atari *Space Invaders* game.

The remainder of this chapter will focus on guiding you through the process of creating this game. The game's programming logic will be provided through a combination of actions and scripts. Specifically, scripts will be used to develop any programming logic that cannot otherwise be developed using fewer than 10 action icons.

## Step 1—Creating the Game's Sprites

Begin the development of the Arachnid Attack! game by adding all the sprites required by the game. Begin by starting Game Maker. If it is already started, click on File > New to begin a new game. The following procedures outline the steps required to create the game's sprites. Note that the graphic files for all of the game's sprites are available for download from the book's companion webpage (www.courseptr.com/downloads).

1. Next click on Resources > Create Sprite. The Sprite Properties window opens. Type **spr_ant** as the sprite's name and click on the Load Sprite button. Navigate to the location where you saved the game's graphic files and select the `ant.gif` file and then click on Open. Click on the center button to center the sprite's alignment.

2. Create a sprite named **spr_spider**, assign it `spider.gif`, and then center its alignment.
3. Create a sprite named **spr_beetle**, assign it `beetle.gif`, and then center its alignment.
4. Create a sprite named **spr_wasp**, assign it `wasp.gif`, and then center its alignment.
5. Create a sprite named **spr_jet**, assign it `jet.gif`, and then center its alignment.
6. Create a sprite named **spr_player_bullet**, assign it `player_bullet.gif`, and then center its alignment.
7. Create a sprite named **spr_invader_bullet**, assign it `bug_bomb.gif`, and then center its alignment.
8. Create a sprite named **spr_block** and assign it `full_block.gif`.
9. Create a sprite named **spr_half_block** and assign it `half_block.gif`.
10. Create a sprite named **spr_mini_jet** and assign it `mini_jet.gif`.

The Arachnid Attack! game will also include a front end. To support the development of this room, you will need to add five additional sprites to the game as instructed below.

1. Create a sprite named **spr_intro** and assign it `game_logo.gif`.
2. Create a sprite named **spr_start** and assign it `start.gif`.
3. Create a sprite named **spr_scores** and assign it `scores.gif`.
4. Create a sprite named **spr_help** and assign it `help.gif`.
5. Create a sprite named **spr_quit** and assign it `quit.gif`.

## Step 2—Add the Game's Sounds

The second step in the development of the Arachnid Attack! game is to add the sounds needed to provide the game's sound effects. These effects include playing an explosive sound whenever a bug or the player's jet is shot, playing a sound when the bug army advances down the screen, and playing a sound when the wasps glide across the top of the screen. Sounds are also played when shots are fired. All of the audio files you will need to create these sounds are included with Game Maker. By default, Game Maker places these audio files in C:\Program Files\Game Maker7\Sounds.

The following procedure outlines the steps required to add and configure all of the game's sounds.

1. Create the first sound by clicking on Resources > Create Sound. The Sound Properties window appears. Name the sound **`snd_bug_move`**, click on the Load Sound button, navigate to the C:\Program Files\Game Maker7\Sounds folder, assign the `click.wav` file to the file, and then click on Open. Click on OK to close the Sprite Properties window.

2. Create a new sound named **`snd_shot`** and assign it the `zap.wav` file.

3. Create a new sound named **`snd_bug_explosion`** and assign it the `gunshot2.wav` file.

4. Create a new sound named **`snd_jet_explosion`** and assign it the `explosion.wav` file.

5. Create a new sound named **`snd_wasp`** and assign it the `beep6.wav` file.

## Step 3—Creating a New Font

The game will display the player's score on the screen during game play. Game Maker's default font size of 12 is too small to adequately display the player's score. To address this situation, you must add a font to the game using the following procedure.

1. Click on Resources > Create Font. Game Maker responds by displaying the Font Properties window.

2. Assign a name of **`font_terminal`** to the font.

3. Enter **`14`** as the font's size, enable the font's `Bold` setting, and then click on OK to close the Font Properties window.

## Step 4—Creating the Game's Objects

The Arachnid Attack! game is made up of 12 objects plus an additional five objects needed for its front end. The objects include different types of bugs, the player's jet, player and bug bullets, and the wall objects that are used to build bunkers behind which the player can hide his ship. The game will use a parent object for the ant, spider, and beetle bugs, allowing behavior to be inherited and thus simplifying game development. Likewise, a parent wall object will be created. Finally, there will be a special controller object and a series of objects needed to build the front end. Instructions for creating all of these objects are provided here:

1. Click on Resources > Create Object. The Object Properties window appears. Type **obj_bug_parent** in the Name field. Click on OK to close the Object Properties window.
2. Add another object named **obj_parent_block**.
3. Add a new object named **obj_ant**, assigning it the spr_ant sprite, and setting its parent to obj_bug_parent.
4. Add a new object named **obj_spider**, assigning it the spr_spider sprite, and setting its parent to obj_bug_parent.
5. Add a new object named **obj_beetle**, assigning it the spr_beetle sprite and setting its parent to obj_bug_parent.
6. Add a new object named **obj_wasp**, assigning it the spr_wasp sprite, but do not assign it a parent.
7. Add a new object named **obj_block**, assigning it the spr_block sprite, and setting its parent to obj_parent_block.
8. Add a new object named **obj_half_block**, assigning it the spr_half_block sprite, and setting its parent to obj_parent_block.
9. Add a new object named **obj_controller**.
10. Add a new object named **obj_player**, assigning it the spr_jet sprite.
11. Add a new object named **obj_player_bullet**, assigning it the spr_player_bullet sprite.
12. Add a new object named **obj_invader_bullet**, assigning it the spr_invader_bullet sprite.
13. Add a new object named **obj_intro**, assigning it the spr_intro sprite.

14. Add a new object named **obj_start**, assigning it the spr_start sprite.
15. Add a new object named **obj_scores**, assigning it the spr_scores sprite.
16. Add a new object named **obj_help**, assigning it the spr_help sprite.
17. Add a new object named **obj_quit**, assigning it the spr_quit sprite.

## Step 5—Creating the Game's Rooms

The next step in the development of the Arachnid Attack! game is to add two rooms to it. These rooms represent the game's front end and the room that the game is played in. Instructions for creating and designing these rooms are provided in the sections that follow.

### *Adding a Room for the Game's Front End*

To create the game's front end room, click on Resources > Create Room. The Room Properties window appears. Click on the Settings tab and then name the room **room_intro**. Change the size of the room, setting width to **514** and its height to **360**, and then add a caption of **Arachnid Attack!** to the Caption for the Room field.

To finish up the development on the room, click on the Objects tab and then add an instance of each of the following objects to the room: obj_intro, obj_start, obj_scores, obj_help, and obj_quit. Arrange these instances as shown in Figure 11.10.

### *Adding a Room in which to Play the Game*

Add a second room to the game and click on the Settings tab, naming the room **room_level1**. Change the size of the room, setting width to 514 and its height to 360 and then add a caption of **Arachnid Attack!** to the Caption for the Room field. Also, modify the room's Speed stetting to 55. This will speed up the play of the game within the room to an appropriate level.

To wrap up work on this room, click on the Objects tab and then add the following object instances to it: obj_ant, obj_spider, and obj_beetle; obj_block, obj_half_block, obj_player, and obj_controller. Arrange these instances as shown in Figure 11.11.

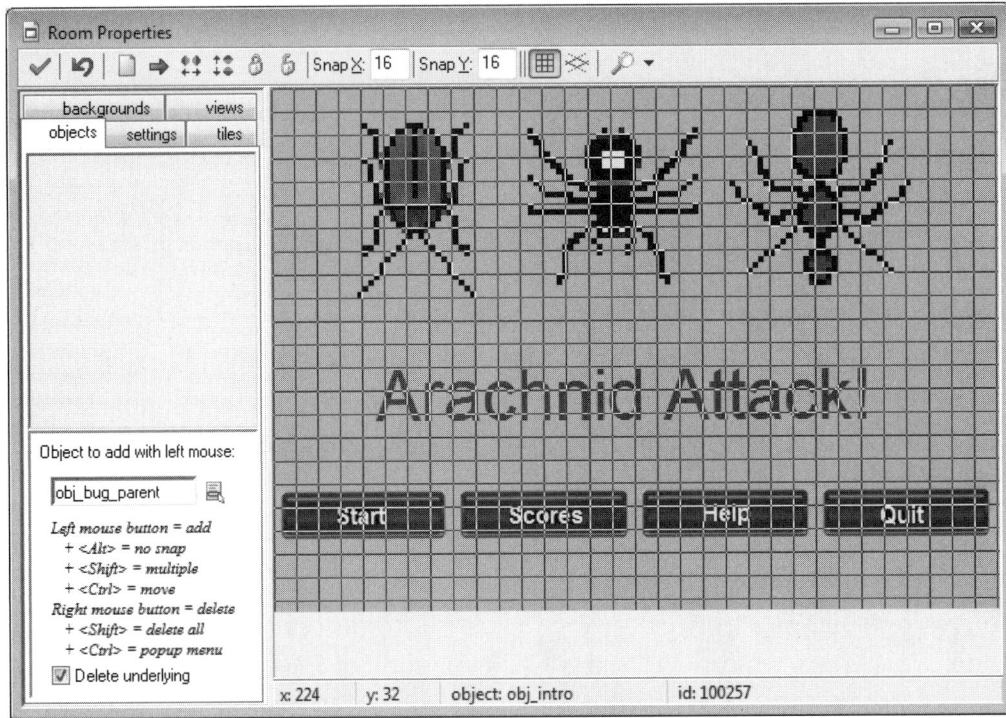


**Figure 11.10**
Completing layout and design of the game's front end room.

## Step 6—Developing Object Programming Logic

Now it is time to develop the programming logic required to bring the Arachnid Attack! game to life. As previously explained, the game's programming logic will be developed using a combination of GML scripts and action icons. Let's begin by developing the three GML scripts that will be used to do the following:

- Initialize variables for the `obj_controller` object.
- Manage the programming logic that is performed by the `obj_controller` at every step of the game.
- Control the movement of the arachnid armies.

### *Creating the Game's GML Scripts*

The first script that you need to create will be executed by the `obj_controller` object to initialize a number of variables. To create this script, click on Resources >

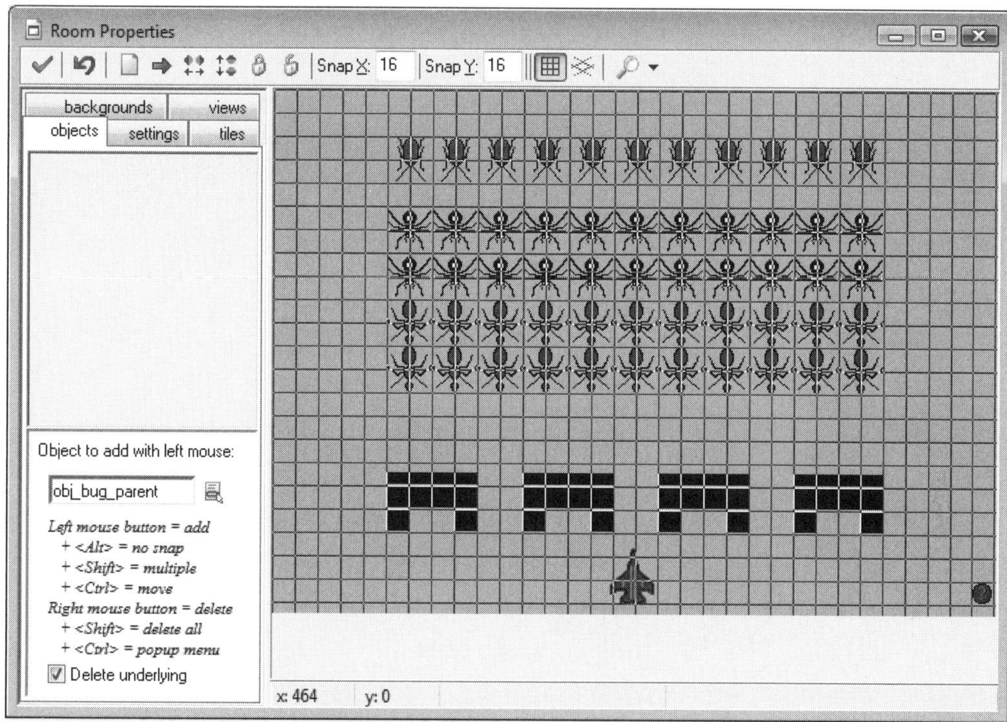


**Figure 11.11**
Creating a room that the game will be played in.

New Script. The Script Properties window appears. Assign the script a name of **scr_obj_controller_variables** and then add the following statements to it.

```
/*This script creates a number of variables for the obj_controller object*/
{
    //Used to set the bug's pace
    game_pace = 20;

    //Used to keep track of when obj_controller should do something
    counter = 0;

    //Specifies the direction the bugs are currently moving
    currentDirection = 9;

    //Specifies the direction the bugs should move (initially to the right)
    targetDirection = 9;

    //When set to true the bugs should move
    timeToMoveBugs = false;
```

```
    //When set to true the bugs should move down the screen
    moveBugsDownward = false;

    //Used to set flag indicating when the bugs have been moved downward
    downMoveComplete = false;

    //Capture the initial starting location of the player's ship
    startx = obj_player.x;

    //Capture the initial starting location of the player's ship
    starty = obj_player.y;
}
```

As you can see, there are nine assignment statements that make up the scripts, along with comments that document the purpose of each variable that is declared. When done, click on the green checkmark button located on the Script Properties toolbar to close the script.

Next, create another script named `scr_obj_controller_step` and add the following statements to it.

```
/*This script is executed by obj_controller at every step that occurs in
the game. */
{
    counter = counter + 1; //Increment the variable by 1

    //When counter equals game_pace it is time to move the bugs
    if (counter == game_pace) {
        timeToMoveBugs = true;      //Set bug movement trigger
        sound_play(snd_bug_move); //Play the sound
    }

    //See if the bugs have already been moved
    if (moveBugsDownward == true) {

        //If downcheck equals true the bugs have already been moved
        if (downMoveComplete == true) {
            moveBugsDownward = false; //No need to move bugs
            downMoveComplete = false; //Turn off variable flag
        }
    }
```

```
    //Determine if a new cycle should be started
    if (counter > game_pace) {
        counter = 0;           //Reset counter to zero to
        timeToMoveBugs = false; //Disable bug movement trigger
    }

    //See if the bugs have switched directions
    if (targetDirection != currentDirection) {
        moveBugsDownward = true; //Time to move the bugs downward
        targetDirection = currentDirection; //Update the target direction
    }
    //Check to see if the player has killed all of the bugs
    if (instance_number(obj_bug_parent) == 0) {
        room_restart() //Restart the room if all bugs are destroyed
        sound_stop(snd_wasp) //Disable sound playback
    }

    //Randomly create instances obj_wasp
    if (action_if_dice(2000) == true) {
        //Position it in the upper-left corner
        instance_create(20, 30, obj_wasp)
    }
}
```

As the embedded comments explain, the script uses a variable named `counter` to keep track of the number of steps that have occurred, and every 24 steps (e.g., when `counter == game_pace`) the `timeToMoveBugs` variable is set to `true` and the `snd_bugMove` sound is played using the GML `sound_play()` function. Since this script runs at the same time as the `scr_bug_movement` script, which you will work on next, a check is made of the value assigned to the `downMoveComplete` variable to see whether the bugs have already been moved on the screen. If this is the case, both `moveBugsDownward` and `downMoveComplete` are set to `false`. The value of `counter` is checked again to see if it has become greater than 24, in which case it is time to reset `counter` back to `0`, and `timeToMoveBugs` to `false` in order to start a new cycle.

Next, a check is made to see if the bugs have switched directions on the screen. If this is the case, they need to be moved downward, so `moveBugsDownward` is set equal to `true`, and then the bug's target direction is updated based on their current direction. A check is then made to see if the player has killed all of the bugs on the screen, in which case the room needs to be restarted. This is achieved using the GML `room_restart()` function. Also, the GML `sound_stop()` function is used to halt the playing of the `snd_wasp` sound, just in case there was an instance of the `obj_wasp` object on the screen when the round ended. Finally, the GML action_if_dice() function is used to randomly generate the creation of a new obj_wasp object. The instance of the obj_wasp object is created using the GML instance_Create() function.

**Hint**

This script made use of five built-in GML functions. These functions all have equivalent action icons as shown below.

- sound_play()---The Play Sound action
- room_restart()---The Restart Room action
- stop_sound()---The Stop Sound action
- action_if_dice()---The Test Chance action
- instance_create()---The Create Instance action

The game's final script is responsible for managing the movement of the arachnid armies on the screen. To create it, add a new script to the game, naming it **scr_bug_movement**, and then assigning the following statements.

```
/* This script controls the movement of the bugs*/
{
    //See if it is time to move the bugs
    if (obj_controller.timeToMoveBugs == true) {
        //See if the bugs should be moved to the right
        if (obj_controller.currentDirection == 9) {
            //Make sure the bugs should not be moved downward
            if (obj_controller.moveBugsDownward == false){
                x = x + 9; //Move the bugs 9 pixels to the right
                y = y + 0; //Make no changes downward
            }
        }

        //See if the bugs should be moved to the left
        if (obj_controller.currentDirection == -9) {
            //Make sure the bugs should not be moved downward
            if (obj_controller.moveBugsDownward == false){
                x = x - 9; //Move the bugs 9 pixels to the left
                y = y + 0; //Make no changes downward
            }
        }
```

```
        //See if the bugs should be moved downward
        if (obj_controller.moveBugsDownward == true) {
            x = x + 0; //Make no changes left or right
            y = y + 9; //Move the bugs downward 9 pixels
            //Mark the downward movement as complete
            obj_controller.downMoveComplete = true;
        }
    } else {
        //Make sure the bugs have not tried to move too far to the right
        if (self.x > 480) {
           obj_controller.currentDirection = -9 //Change the bugs' direction
        }
        //Make sure the bugs have not tried to move too far to the left
        if (self.x < 32) {
           obj_controller.currentDirection = 9 //Change the bugs' direction
        }
    }
}
```

As you can see, the script consists of a series of nested `if` statement code blocks, all of which are embedded within one large `if` statement code block that has an `else` block. The high level `if` statement code block manages bug movement and the lower `else` statement code block is responsible for making sure that the bugs change directions when they reach the sides of the game window.

The arachnid armies move nine pixels at a time, left or right, depending on their direction. Remember, movement occurs every 24 steps in the game. Movement left or right is controlled by adding or subtracting a value of `9` to the `x` coordinate. Likewise, movement downward is managed by adding a value of `9` to the `y` coordinate. Downward movement only occurs when the arachnid armies reach the side of the screen.

The `else` statement code block ensures that the arachnid armies do not scroll off the side of the screen by monitoring the value assigned to `self.x` and reversing direction when its value exceeds `480`. Likewise, direction is changed when the value of `self.x` becomes less than `32`.

### *Assembling the Rest of the Game's Programming Logic*

Now that you have completed the development of the game's scripts, it is time to add the programming logic that is controlled through action icons. Again, the use of action icons in this game has been restricted to tasks for which actions exist and can be completed using fewer than 10 action icons. As is the case with most Game Maker games, not all objects are going to have any action icons, either because they do not take any action or because they inherent their actions from parent objects.

### Adding Actions to the obj_bug_parent Object

In order to simplify the game's development, common functionality shared between the obj_ant, obj_spider, and obj_beetle objects will be added to a parent object named obj_bug_parent. Instructions for programming this object are provided below.

1. Double-click on the obj_bug_parent object to open its Object Properties window.

2. Add a Step event to the object.

3. Add an Execute Script action to the event and configure the action to execute the scr_bug_movement script.

### Adding Actions to the obj_beetle Object

1. Double-click on the obj_beetle object and add a Step event to the object.

2. Add a Test Chance action to the event and assign it 1500 sides.

3. Add a Start Block and an End Block to the event, then embed a Create Instance action inside these two actions, setting the Create Instance action to create the obj_invader_bullet at x coordinate 0 and y coordinate 15. Enable the action's Relative setting.

4. Add an Execute Script action to the bottom of the actions area and set it to run the scr_bug_movement script.

### Adding Actions to the obj_player Object

1. Double-click on the obj_player object.

2. Add a Create event to the object and then add a Set Variable action to the event, assigning a value of false to a new variable named gun_fired.

3. Add a Step event and assign it the following actions.

   - Test Lives—Setting it to check for a value smaller than 1.
   - Start Block

- Stop Sound—Setting it to stop playing the snd_wasp sound.
- Show Highscore
- Different Room—Setting it to go to the room_intro room.
- End Block

4. Add a collision event for the obj_ant object and then add the Set Lives action, setting new lives to 0.

5. Add a collision event for the obj_spider object and then add the Set Lives action, setting new lives to 0.

6. Add a collision event for the obj_beetle object and then add the Set Lives action, setting new lives to 0.

7. Add a <Left> keyboard event and then add the following actions to it.
   - Comment—Enter **Do not allow the player to move the ship past the left-hand side of the screen.**
   - Test Variable—Set it to test whether x is larger than 22.
   - Jump to Position—Set x to -4 and y to 0 and enable the Relative property.

8. Add a <Right> keyboard event and then add the following actions to it.
   - Comment—Enter **Do not allow the player to move the ship past the right-hand side of the screen.**
   - Test Variable—Set it to test whether x is smaller than 490.
   - Jump to Position—Set x to 4 and y to 0 and enable the Relative property.

9. Add a <Space> keyboard event and then add the following actions to it.
   - Start Block
   - Set Variable—Set gun_fired to true.
   - Create Instance—Set it to create an instance of obj_player_bullet, setting x to 0 and y to -16. Enable the action's Relative property.
   - End Block

### Adding Actions to the obj_player_bullet Object

1. Double-click on the obj_player_bullet object.

2. Add a Create event to the object and then add a Speed Vertical action to the event, assigning a value of -9 to Vert. Speed, followed by a Play Sound action set to snd_shot.

3. Add a collision event for the obj_ant object and then add the following actions to it.

   - Play Sound—Set it to play the snd_bug_explosion sound.
   - Set Score—Set New Score to 10 and enable the Relative setting.
   - Create Effect—Set type to explosion, size to small, and where to below objects, and enable the Relative setting.
   - Destroy Instance—Set Applies to to Other.
   - Destroy Instance—Set Applies to to Self.
   - Set Variable—Set Applies to to obj_player and set gun_fired to false.

4. Add a collision event for the obj_spider object and then add the following actions to it.

   - Play Sound—Set it to play the snd_bug_explosion sound.
   - Set Score—Set New Score to 20 and enable the Relative setting.
   - Create Effect—Set type to explosion, size to small, and where to below objects and enable the Relative setting.
   - Destroy Instance—Set Applies to to Other.
   - Destroy Instance—Set Applies to to Self.
   - Set Variable—Set Applies to to obj_player and set gun_fired to false.

5. Add a collision event for the obj_beetle object and then add the following actions to it.

   - Play Sound—Set it to play the snd_bug_explosion sound.
   - Set Score—Set New Score to 40 and enable the Relative setting.
   - Create Effect—Set type to explosion, size to small, and where to below objects and enable the Relative setting.
   - Destroy Instance—Set Applies to to Other.
   - Destroy Instance—Set Applies to to Self.
   - Set Variable—Set Applies to to obj_player and set gun_fired to false.

6. Add a collision event for the obj_wasp object and then add the following actions to it.

   - Play Sound—Set it to play the snd_bug_explosion sound.
   - Set Score—Set New Score to 100 and enable the Relative setting.
   - Create Effect—Set type to explosion, size to small, and where to below objects and enable the Relative setting.
   - Destroy Instance—Set Applies to to Other.
   - Destroy Instance—Set Applies to to Self.
   - Stop Sound—Set sound to snd_wasp.
   - Set Variable—Set Applies to to obj_player and set gun_fired to false.

7. Add an Outside Room event, add the Destroy Instance action (set to Self) and the Set Variable action, setting Applies to to obj_player and set gun_fired to false.

### Adding Actions to the obj_invader_bullet Object

1. Double-click on the obj_invader_bullet object.

2. Add a Create event to the object and then add a Speed Vertical action to the event, assigning a value of 5 to Vert. Speed followed by a Play Sound action set to snd_shot.

3. Add a collision event for the obj_player object and then add the following actions to it.

   - Play Sound—Set it to play the snd_jet_explosion sound.
   - Set Lives—Set New Lives to -1 and enable the Relative setting.
   - Create Effect—Set type to explosion, size to small, and where to below objects and enable the Relative setting.
   - Destroy Instance—Set Applies to to Other.
   - Destroy Instance—Set Applies to to Self.
   - Sleep—Set Milliseconds to 500.
   - Create Instance—Set object to obj_player, x to obj_controller.startx, and y to obj_controller.starty.

4. Add an Outside Room event and then add the Destroy Instance action (set to Self) .

### Adding Actions to the obj_controller Object

1. Add a Step event and then add an Execute Script action, assigning it to execute the scr_obj_controller_step script.

2. Add a Start Room event and then add an Execute Script action, assigning it to execute the scr_obj_controller_variables script followed by the Score Caption action, setting show score, show lives, and show health to don't show.

3. Add a Draw event and then add the following actions to it.

   - Set Color—Set color to black or a dark gray color.
   - Set Font—Set Font to font_terminal and align to left.
   - Draw Score—Set x to 10, y to 2, and caption to SCORE.
   - Draw Life Images—Set x to 450, y to 2, and image to spr_mini_jet.

### Adding Actions to the obj_parent_block Object

1. Add a collision event for the obj_ant object and then add the Destroy Instance action to it (set to Self).
2. Add a collision event for the obj_spider object and then add the Destroy Instance action to it (set to Self).
3. Add a collision event for the obj_beetle object and then add the Destroy Instance action to it (set to Self).
4. Add a collision event for the obj_player_bullet object and then add the Destroy Instance action to it (set to Self). Add another Destroy Instance action to it (set to Other) followed by a Set Variable action, setting Applies to to obj_player and then assigning gun_fired a value of false.
5. Add a collision event for the obj_invader_bullet object and then add the Destroy Instance action to it (set to Self). Add another Destroy Instance action to it (set to Other).

### Adding Actions to the obj_wasp Object

1. Double-click on the obj_wasp object.
2. Add a Create event to the object and then add a Move Fixed action to the event, selecting the left arrow button and setting Speed to -2. Add the Play Sound action assigning is the snd_wasp sound.
3. Add an Outside Room event and then add the Destroy Instance action (set to Self), followed by the Stop Sound action, assigning it the snd_wasp sound.

### Adding Actions to the obj_start Object

1. Double-click on the obj_start object.
2. Add a Left Button mouse event to the object and then add the following actions to it.
   - Set Score—Set New Score to 0.
   - Set Lives—Set New Lives to 3.
   - Next Room

### Adding Actions to the obj_scores Object

1. Double-click on the obj_start object.
2. Add a Left Button mouse event to the object and then add the Show Highscore action to it.

**Adding Actions to the `obj_help` Object**

1. Double-click on the `obj_start` object.
2. Add a `Left Button` mouse event to the object and then add the `Show Info` action to it.

**Adding Actions to the `obj_quit` Object**

1. Double-click on the `obj_start` object.
2. Add a `Left Button` mouse event to the object and then add the `End Game` action to it.

## Step 7—Adding Finishing Touches

You are almost done. All that remains is to add a little game information so that the player will know how the game is played and to modify the game resolution, demonstrating how Game Maker manages screen resolution settings on computers with different resolution settings. To create the game's information page, double-click on the Game Information entry in the resource tree folder, and then enter the text shown below, which describes the game and how it is played.

**Welcome to Arachnid Attack!**

**The objectives of this game are to defend the world from the onslaught of an army of arachnid invaders and to score as many points as possible in the process. Points are scored by shooting down the ants, spiders, beetles, and wasps that make up the arachnid invasion army. Killing an ant is worth 10 points. Killing a spider is worth 20 points. Killing a beetle is worth 40 points. Killing a wasp is worth 100 points.**

**Use the left and right arrow keys to control the movement of your jet fighter plane and the spacebar to shoot. You have three lives with which to play. You lose a life each time you are shot by the enemy. Game play ends when you are killed and have no more lives with which to play. Game play also ends if the arachnid horde defeats you by making its way to the bottom of the screen.**

Game Maker provides the ability to temporarily modify screen resolution on player computers and to restore the player's previous resolution setting at the end of the game. This allows you to specify and control the resolution at which your game is played. For the Arachnid Attack! game, let's adjust the resolution on the player's computer to 800x600. This will ensure that the game is played within an adequately large window at a resolution that is universally supported on all modern computers. To set this up, double-click on the Global Game Settings entry in the resource tree folder, click on the Resolution tab, and then select the 800x600 bullet entry located in the Resolution sections of the tabbed page.

At this point, your new game should be ready for testing. When testing, make sure that your computer's resolution is set to something other than 800x600 so that you can observe the manner in which the game modifies resolution.

## Summary

Congratulations on making it to the end of the book. Making it all the way to the end represents the completion of a significant commitment and has provided you with a strong foundation from which you can continue to work and learn more about Game Maker and programming in general. Before you end your journey, take a few extra minutes to look through the bonus appendices on the companion website (www.courseptr.com/downloads), including Appendix B, "What's Next?". It provides you with recommendations of links to other Game Maker and game development resources on the internet that you can visit to continue your game development and programming education.

# INDEX

## S